THE POETICS OF OLD AGE
IN GREEK EPIC, LYRIC, AND TRAGEDY

OKLAHOMA SERIES IN CLASSICAL CULTURE

Oklahoma Series in Classical Culture

Series Editor

Susan Ford Wiltshire, *Vanderbilt University*

Advisory Board

The Poetics
of Old Age in
Greek Epic, Lyric, and Tragedy

By Thomas M. Falkner

UNIVERSITY OF OKLAHOMA PRESS : NORMAN AND LONDON

Falkner, Thomas M., 1947–
    The poetics of old age in Greek epic, lyric, and tragedy / by Thomas
M. Falkner.
        p. cm.—(Oklahoma series in classical culture; v. 19)
    Includes bibliographical references and index.
    ISBN 0-8061-2775-9 (alk. paper)
    1. Greek literature—History and criticism. 2. Old age in leterature.
    3. Age in literature. I. Title. II. Series.
PA3015.043F35 1995
    880.09—dc20   95-17116
                                                                                    CIP

mls App · o 1882740 12-7-95

The Poetics of Old Age in Greek Epic, Lyric, and Tragedy is Volume 19 of the
Oklahoma Series in Classical Culture.

Book designed by Bill Cason.

The paper in this book meets the guidelines for permanence and durability
of the Committee on Production Guidelines for Book Longevity of the
Council on Library Resources.⊗

              1   2   3   4   5   6   7   8   9   10

For Renate, Annegret, and Karelisa.
οὐδὲν ἥδιον πατρὶ γέροντι θυγατρός.
—Euripides, *Suppliant Women*, 1101–2

CONTENTS

Preface and Acknowledgments

IT was ten years ago that my wife Rose, who was then writing a paper on the representation of the elderly in contemporary children's literature, asked me in passing about the treatment of old age in Greek literature. Was there anything that Greek authors had to say about this subject that might be relevant to her work? Of my answer then I remember only that it was singularly unhelpful and that I was embarassed to have never given the subject much thought. But the question stuck and has occupied me in one form or another in the years since, and the results of the inquiry are gathered in this book. To Rose I apologize for giving her a real answer long after it might have done some good, one as prolix now as it was halting then. I hope that she is pleased with the results.

This book owes much to the many institutions that provided the time, financial support, and facilities required to complete it. I owe an enormous debt of thanks to the College of Wooster, its Board of Trustees and administration, for its generous and enlightened leaves policy and for the research grants it provided in 1982–83, 1987–88, and fall 1991, during which different portions of the work were completed. In particular, I wish to acknowledge a major grant from the Henry Luce III Fund for Distinguished Scholarship, which allowed released time from teaching in spring 1990 and other support that helped to make this work a reality. I am also deeply grateful to the National Endowment for the Humanities for a Summer Seminar in 1984, spent at Dartmouth reading Homer with James Redfield, and for a Summer Stipend in 1989, spent at Cornell University. I offer my sincere thanks to the faculties and chairpersons at various departments of Classics where most of this book's writing was done: Cornell University, Dartmouth University, Princeton University, the University of California at Berkeley and at Davis, and the American School of Classical Studies at Athens. I owe these institutions a debt of gratitude for the quality of their facilities and their faculties and the opportunity to take advantage of both.

Different versions of the following sections of this volume have appeared in previous publications. Chapter 1 and the section of chapter 6 entitled "The Wrath of Alcmene: Gender, Old Age, and Vengeance in *Children of Heracles*" in *Old Age in Greek and Latin Literature,* eds. Thomas M. Falkner and Judith de Luce (The State University of New York Press, © 1989); chapter 2 in *Classical Antiquity* 8 (1989): 42–60, © 1989 by the Regents of the University of California; chapter 5 in *The Classical Journal* 86 (1990): 1–15, © 1990 by the University of Virginia; the section of chapter 6 entitled "Euripides' Stagecraft of Old Age" in *The Many Faces of Drama,* ed. K. Hartigan (University Press of America, © 1985). I would like to express my thanks to the publishers and editors of these materials for granting permission to use them here.

I am also grateful to my faculty colleagues and to friends in and out of Classics for their kindness and support over the years. Many individuals have helped to nurture the ideas in this book to completion in special ways, great and small, and of these I would thank in particular Thomas Cole, Judith de Luce, Jenny Strauss Clay, Judith Hallett, Karelisa Hartigan, Vivian Holliday, John Peradotto, James Redfield, William C. Scott, James Strickland, David Traill, and Thomas van Nortwick.

The greatest debt of all is owed to my family. They have endured massive doses of boring conversation, countless inconveniences, and at times the outright neglect that is the inevitable by-product of a project like this. It is my deepest hope that the results below will help to subtract in some way from the sum total.

Introduction

You see me here, you gods, a poor old man,
As full of grief as age, wretched in both!
                    —Shakespeare, *King Lear*

Perhaps being old is having lighted rooms
Inside your head, and people in them, acting.
People you know, yet can't quite name.
                    —Philip Larkin, "The Old Fools"

IN almost any of the standard literary anthologies, a reader can find scores of references and an array of oft-cited verse that suggest the treatment of old age in English and American poetry. While the subject has inspired poetry of both poignancy and passion, the tradition has been largely, even overwhelmingly negative. To the experience of old age, to the very prospect of its arrival, poets have typically responded in terms of dread and disgust, shame and self-consciousness, resignation and resistance. This is in part because the experience of old age is itself fractured, frought with ambiguity and uncertainty. Cole addresses what he sees as the essentially paradoxical nature of old age, one that resonates with the contradictions inherent in our being: "Aging, like illness and death, reveals the most fundamental conflict of the human condition: the tension between infinite ambitions, dreams, and desires on the one hand, and vulnerable, limited, decaying physical existence on the other—between self and body."[1] We should of course be wary of assuming that the experience of old age is so dichotomous across history and across cultures: the anxiety that attaches to old age in our own society is intimately related to the forces that have shaped our culture at large.[2] But it is true that in Western literature as a whole, old age has served as a focus for some of the elemental conflicts within human experience and the society that gives it structure. The tension between aspiration and the restrictions that time places upon it makes old age a point of intersection and a fertile ground for poets to appreciate the human condition in whatever light they wish: heroic, tragic, pathetic, ridiculous, absurd.

This is clearly the case in ancient Greek literature, which is remarkable for the pervasiveness of the theme and the consistently grim and negative character of its representation.[3] Indeed, the treatment of old age, *gêras*, is so extensive in Greek poetry as to suggest a cultural obsession. There is almost no important author preserved, even in fragmentary condition, who does not at some point touch base with the subject, and no major poet who does not reflect directly on the condition of old age and the status of the elderly. At the level of language, Greek pessimism about old age is immediately striking. In the poetic tradition, *gêras* is regularly qualified by a range of negative epithets. Homer and Hesiod describe it formulaically as "hateful," "accursed," "difficult," or "sorrowful." The elegiac poet Mimnermus, whose language is typical of much of Greek lyric, speaks of "difficult and ugly old age . . . both hateful and dishonored." The aged chorus in Euripides' *Heracles* sings of "deadly, sorrowful old age," and that in Sophocles' *Oedipus at Colonus* describes old age with a string of privatives: it is "infirm, unfriendly, loveless." For sheer negative effect, few passages can surpass that in the Homeric *Hymn to Aphrodite*, where the goddess takes leave of her mortal lover Anchises by describing old age with the most dismal epithets: "Soon the common fate of old age will cover you over, pitiless old age which comes beside every man, accursed, wearying, hated even by the gods." The pessimism at the linguistic level is matched at others: in lyric and narrative poems, which portray the suffering that old age entails; in elderly characters who are objects of scorn, pity, laughter or disregard; in images that associate old age with a host of evils, physical, social and moral. This cheerless picture, as we shall see, is not quite so uniform as it appears; there are a number of places in Greek literature where we can hear voices offering a more positive valuation of old age and which attempt to balance its liabilities against its merits. But nowhere do Greek poets sing the praises of old age, and there is none to join in Browning's invitation, "Grow old along with me! / The best is yet to be, / The last of life, for which the first was made."[4]

It would be easy to assemble a variety of passages that refer directly to old age and to comment in general on the way old age is described in Greek poetry. The more important task facing the critic is to determine the *meaning* of old age in these works, to find a path through this wealth of textual responses, to identify the poetic tradition within which they can be placed and the cultural concerns to which they correspond. The essays that follow examine the representation of old age in Greek epic, lyric, and tragedy by looking at a range of familiar texts; their purpose is to see old age as an object of interest in its own right and as a conceptual tool by which Greek poetry examines other related themes and ideas. They are based on a couple of insights that might seem obvious were they not largely ignored in discussions of Greek literature: that in the representation of age and the human life course, Greek poets found a rich and versatile language with which to talk about the social world, in ways that are revealing of the audience that they address; and that in its representation of old age and the elderly, Greek poetry developed a conceptual framework that captures certain points of conflict, tension, and ambiguity in the social order. In discussing the character and significance of these representations and the concrete ways in which they are employed, I hope to shed light on the texts and the social worlds, both historical and fictive, that are at the center of their concern.

The meaning of old age in any given text necessarily will be a product of many different factors, intrinsic and extrinsic to the text itself. The language with which a work accomplishes its rhetorical ends resonates not only within itself but also against the conventions available to a given author or dictated by genre, the social and political situation of old men and women in Greece, what the reader knows of the life history and personal experience of the author, and how the reader understands the physiology of the aging process itself. In examining the representation of old age in a work, one must try to appreciate the interplay of these various factors. Because their relative weight is so different not only from work to work but even from passage to passage, it has seemed to me that such an approach must necessarily be an exercise in *applied* criticism and look in depth and in detail at specific texts and the meanings of old age that they produce within themselves and in interrelationship with each other. The principle of selection employed in these essays is in some sense obvious, and the goal throughout is to focus on "key texts" in the poetic tradition, in particular on those works and passages that most readily come to mind in any discussion of old age. But the attempt is made to treat these texts so as to make a larger point: that discussion of a particular passage or problem necessarily requires a more comprehensive appreciation of the issue of old age for the author or genre as a whole; and that looking at these texts from the unfamiliar vantage of age affords new readings of the texts as a whole. Thus, the chapter on old age in the *Odyssey* involves extensive discussion of the *Iliad*; that on Hesiod's "Five Races" looks at age within the Hesiodic corpus as a whole. With tragedy, the chapter on *Oedipus at Colonus* also includes discussion of other relevant material on old age in Sophocles (as well as in Aeschylus and Euripides). With Euripides, where old age is such an extensive theme, I selected two plays in which age (and gender) figure most prominently and which have received relatively less discussion than others. I felt it worthwhile to preface this chapter with a discussion of old age in Euripides in general, to make clear how extensive his treatment of the subject is.

The goal in these studies is not (and I emphasize this at the beginning) to quarry the literature in an attempt to retrieve the practices or attitudes of historical Greek society, or for that matter the "views" of the authors themselves. This does not mean that a study of the literary representation of age cannot yield valuable social information, as a number of recent studies have shown.[5] Yet we must beware in the first place of pitting artistic "representations" against social "realities," as though the latter provided a bedrock of meaning against which we can measure and interpret our texts: to be sure, all of our sources are representational, whether they be discourses, institutions, material artifacts, or behaviors. The point is rather to show the importance and versatility of old age as a semiotic system; that given the extent to which concepts of age are related with other principles of organization, an understanding of the life course as it is assumed in a literary work is essential to understanding the work *itself*; that to account for conceptual worlds no less than historical ones, we need to unfold the systems of age that are embedded in the texts and the social values they assume.

The goal throughout, then, will be less that of tracing a theme through the literature than of offering new readings of the texts as a whole, vantages that come from looking at these works in a new and unfamiliar light. While the treatment is therefore selective rather than comprehensive, I attempt to establish from it a sense of the poetics of age as a whole. In speaking of such a poetics I use the expression in an enlarged sense, referring to the system of age relations that governs the texts and to the way in which critics in the humanities and social sciences use the term in the context of social interaction and performance. Here we can speak broadly of a poetics of cultural expression, as a coordinated set of practices in the context of which items of human behavior, be they word, image or action, take on social significance.[6] That categories of age provide a necessary blueprint for social relations in Greece as in other societies needs little argument. All societies conceive of life not as a continuum but as a sequence of more or less differentiated stages or grades, so that an individual's perception and experience of life are shaped by a specific cultural model of the life course. As anthropologists are quick to point out, these categories, like those of gender, class, and kinship, are not biological givens but cultural constructions and forms of communication. To occupy a given age-grade, to move from one to the next, to mediate our relations to others in terms of them—these are "events" endowed with meaning that speak uniquely to the cultural circumstances out of which they come.

Ethnographic literature has appreciated the degree to which models of the life course differ in their fundamental terms: in the number and length of the constituent stages or age grades; in the rituals and social markers between them; in their complex relation to the forms of social life: in short, how what a person is is related to age.[7] This line of inquiry requires that we establish a kind of anthropology of age in the poems. As a system of literary relations, the conventions of age provide a code, a set of structures and expectations in relation to which the various elements of the text take on significance. And here no less than the ethnographer, we must appreciate the meaning of old age not only in terms of a culture's self-professed code of behavior but also in terms of the inconsistencies between its ideals and practices, between its teachings about old age and the treatment and experience of the elderly themselves, between a deference to old age that may be merely verbal and superficial and the attitudes of the culture as they are revealed in textual performance.

The Greeks themselves understood age as a variable of parallel importance to that of gender, class, and other social factors. There is a significant passage in Plato's *Meno* in which the dialogue's name-sake attempts to explain to Socrates just what virtue (*aretê*) is:

> First of all, if it is manly virtue you are after, it is easy to see that the virtue of a man consists in managing the city's affairs capably, and so that he will help his friends and injure his foes while taking care to come to no harm himself. Or if you want a woman's virtue, that is easily described. She must be a good housewife, careful with her stores and obedient to her husband. Then there is another virtue for a child, male or female, and another for an old man, free or slave as you like; and a great many more kinds of virtue, so that no one need be at a loss to say what it is. For every act and every time of life, with reference to each separate function, there is a virtue for each one of us, and similarly, I should say, a vice.
>
> (71e–72a: tr. Guthrie)[8]

Socrates, whose goal is to establish a unified concept of *aretê* and who assumes that virtue has a single form (72c), is predictably unimpressed by the "swarm" of virtues his interlocutor presents. But Meno's response shows the extent to which the Greeks routinely understood *aretê* in a relative sense and in terms of the specifics of an individual's social situation—male or female, free or slave, young or old. As one of these variables changes, so will the content of what counts for virtue. The passage serves to remind us that when we speak of "the Greeks" and their beliefs and values, we are guilty of a certain ageism, one which they themselves invite. We tend to talk about the culture normatively as a whole from the perspective of male rather than female, of free rather than slave, and of those "of mature age" rather than young or old. One consequence of a greater attention to the subject of age is to recognize the bias with which we have been trained to look at culture in general. Interesting in this regard is the discussion of age in Aristotle's *Rhetoric* 2.12–14, which identifies three kinds of male characters according to the stages of life: youth (*neotês*), prime of life (*akmê*), and old age (*gêras*). In what is among the most lengthy and unsympathetic characterizations of old age to be found in Greek literature, old age is described as cynical, suspicious, small-minded, illiberal, cowardly, selfish, shameless, and calculating. The passage reveals the negativity of Greek attitudes toward old age, yet equally striking is the way in which Aristotle's rhetorical strategies have shaped the description. Here again prime of life is the norm against which the other ages are measured: *akmê* provides the golden mean between youth, which is rash and insolent, and old age, which is miserly and disagreeable.

A particular model of the life course thus offers not a self-contained system of classification but a window on the social and conceptual systems that circumscribe the culture. It is in this context that we should recognize the importance of age to the study of Greek literature. I would make the same argument with regard to artistic expression as to social organization: that to understand a model of the life course as it is constructed in a given text is not simply to abstract a set of terms but to take up the basic categories of its thought and organization. As Greek poetry, no less than Greek society, uses the life course as a basic expression of the social order, the study of age is interrelated with a range of other concerns in the texts; we cannot talk about the Greeks' concept of age apart from their ideas of time, person, occupation, family, gender, and so forth. We must see in the categories of age not a dry and lifeless taxonomy, a mere listing of stages, names and attributes, but a series of metaphorical relations which, because they arrange people in affective relationships with one another, are charged with tension and the potential for conflict. Because age is so basic to the ways in which we have developed our concepts of power, authority, intelligence, morality, and propriety, it provides a potent metaphor with which to describe the social world.

That the Greeks should have an interest in old age is testimony to the importance of age in any cultural system. Age was for them as for us a basic conceptual tool and a vital literary resource for exploring issues that seem to have no essential connection with age itself. Greek poetry routinely employs concepts of age for their symbolic value and assimilates the polarities of youth and old age to other conceptual structures—power and impotence, tradition and innovation, morality and corruption, foolishness and wisdom, activity and contemplation. To put it crudely, the texts either speak *about* age or, at other times, *through* age to something else, although these two aspects cannot really be separated as though metaphor were merely an instrument for getting at something else that is its true concern. Language is first and foremost revealing of who we are, in ways that are often unknown to its users and discomforting when revealed,

and it is often in the choice of its metaphors that cultures reveal
their preoccupations and their blind spots, their points of tension
and insecurity.

Given the many different forces that intersect in the production
of a text, it is to be expected that the portrayal of any theme will
appear various, inconsistent, even contradictory. Throughout my
readings I have been impressed by the range of Greek responses to
old age, by the way that they seem to eschew any monolithic or
consistent "position" on its meaning. From the opening lines of the
Iliad, these representations are shifting and ambiguous, and suf-
fused with a kind of anxiety with which our own society is familiar.
Greek literature evinces a multiplicity of meanings for old age,
meanings discovered and invented, assumed and contested, argued
and denied. That the subject should carry so high a profile in Greek
literature seems something of a paradox, in that the elderly in
Greece were as a class and as individuals at a distance from the traditional centers of power (political, legal, military). We may refer
this paradox simply to the humanism of the texts themselves,
whose interest in the final stages of life is reflected across genres in
the thematic importance of old age, in the many elderly characters
in epic and drama, and in reflections, some brief and some extended, on the nature and value of old age. Yet the Greek preoccupation
with old age is clearly not dispassionate. It reflects important
changes in the meaning and the status of old age in Greek culture,
as the polis gradually became, anthropologically speaking, less traditional in character, severing its roots in its more conservative past;
as we shall see, the representation of old age in Greek poetry can
often be measured in terms of its distance from the more positive
valuations of old age we associate with traditional societies. As
such, these texts seem clearly to reflect a society in which more traditional appreciations of old age were being called into question, as
Greek society was increasingly caught up in the whirl of historical
change. Throughout the classical period Greek literature struggled
with the collapse of traditional valuations of old age, and in the
absence of meaning revealed a need to redefine old age.

I have found in the Homeric image of "the threshold of old age"
an approach to the status of the elderly in Greek poetry that corresponds to the changing social and historical realities around them.
Like other groups in antiquity—women, slaves, resident foreign-

ers—whose marginal social and political status bedevils attempts to examine them, the elderly occupied a position that was at once in and out of the established social order. Old age seems to be literally and figuratively a gray area occupied by men and women whose participation in their culture was at the fringes rather than the center. I would suggest that it is precisely the liminality of old age that makes the subject such an attractive one for the Greeks and that accounts for the extent to which the semiotics of age are interwoven with those themes at the heart of Greek poetry: kingship, war, power, justice, society, gender, the gods, poetry itself. As figures who are at once both "us" and "other," the elderly are located in positions of convergence and ambivalence that give old age a large symbolic resonance; they offer a vantage point that can be both at once passionately interested and strategically distant.

In the metaphor of the threshold of old age, as I propose to understand it, Homer describes early and potently the problematic status of the elderly in the heroic world of the *Iliad* and their rehabilitated status in the post-heroic world of the *Odyssey*. In the course of the following centuries, Greek poetry returns again and again to old age and the marginal situation of the elderly to express its most pressing concerns. In the *Works and Days*, Hesiod relates the problems of old age to those of gender and morality, finding in old age an image of apocalypse that captures his sense of the imminent collapse of his culture. Sappho seizes upon the theme as a means of resisting a male poetic tradition that devalues old age and discards old women, while in the traditions of male poetry, from Homer and the Homeric *Hymns* to Mimnermus and Anacreon, the desexualized condition of old men provides a metaphor for their circumscribed social and political condition. Solon in his verses on the "ten ages of man" deconstructs traditional literary models of the life course in favor of a hebdomodal pattern that involves a new understanding of human nature and *aretê* based on man as the individual citizen, a political model that sees in old age a period of both continuing ability and decline. Euripides uses the suffering of old age to shape some of his most tragic situations, where the victimization of the helpless elderly by the young and powerful is meant to provoke our pity and our moral outrage; he does so with an eye to the relation between gender and old age and the kinds of role reversals that accompany old age for men and women. The treatment of old age in the classical period comes to a climax in Sophocles' *Oedipus at Colonus* in the most liminal of tragic protagonists. The aged playwright finds in this blind old exile, who stands at the threshold of the grove of the Eumenides and of death itself, an apotheosis of old age and an opportunity to respond to a literary and cultural tradition that found little value in the final stages of life. It is fitting that with such a tragic hero the curtain should fall on the playwright's life and in a real sense on tragedy itself.

A few words need to be said about the intended reader of this volume. This is a work of classical scholarship that hopes at the same time to engage and accomodate a wider audience than that of classical scholars: generalists in the humanities, students of poetry and poetics, social scientists and among these, I hope, a few gerontologists. In a time when disciplinary boundaries have become tenuous and literary studies routinely borrow critical and theoretical approaches from outside the discipline, few readers in any of these groups are likely to be put off by the somewhat eclectic methodology of this work. I have drawn extensively, though I also hope responsibly, on insights from contemporary literary theory as well as from works in the social sciences. While the general approach may be described as loosely anthropological, I have eschewed any single or monolithic theoretical school and have preferred to allow the nature of the texts under examination to suggest the approach that is suited. The readings I offer have been inspired by work from outside Classics as much as within, and it is my hope that this study will encourage others working on the subject to take advantage of critical perspectives that are available in these related areas.

Yet as a scholarly study of ancient poetry, this work provides argumentative "evidence" that draws primarily from examination of language patterns in the texts. This simply cannot be done without frequent reference to the texts in their original language. But as a work that thinks it has something to offer to non-specialists in antiquity and those without knowledge of ancient Greek, it attempts to be more readable in the following ways:

(a) All Greek in the text has been translated, either directly or in ways where the context makes clear what the word or passage in question means. (b) Most of the Greek in the text has been provided within parentheses, with the understanding that readers lacking knowledge of Greek will likely gloss over this material and gather the gist of the argument from the translations. (If a few also feel inspired to learn Greek, so much the better.) (c) A handful of Greek terms that are so basic to the argument as to be virtually untranslatable have been transliterated into their English equivalents and provided in a glossary. This will require a certain amount of page-flipping, but the terms occur so frequently that they will quickly become second nature.

The notes for each chapter, which are likely to be of most interest to specialists, are in typical scholarly form; I have not attempted to translate the Greek (and occasionally Latin) in them.

Because each of these chapters deals with a circumscribed set of authors and texts, it is my expectation that many readers will read selectively rather than cover to cover; I have therefore attempted to construct the text so that a given chapter can be appreciated and understood in itself, without reading the whole. The texts and translations employed are cited in the first note for each chapter.

Except where noted or otherwise obvious, abbreviations for ancient authors and works are as in the *Oxford Classical Dictionary*, 2nd ed. (Oxford 1970), which is readily available. Abbreviations for periodicals are according to *L'Année Philologique*, the basic bibliographical work in Classics.

THE POETICS OF OLD AGE
IN GREEK EPIC, LYRIC, AND TRAGEDY

CHAPTER 1

On the Threshold: Homeric Heroism, Old Age, and the End of the *Odyssey*

> . . . as the *Iliad* was written when his genius was at its height, he
> made the whole body of the poem lively and dramatic, but that of the
> *Odyssey* he made primarily narrative, which is characteristic of old
> age.
>
> —"Longinus," *On the Sublime*, 9.13

ANCIENT scholars and grammarians were fond of debating the chronology of the Homeric epics, but to the author of *On the Sublime* there was no question about the order of their composition: the *Iliad* was as clearly the product of inspired maturity as was the *Odyssey* that of decadent old age. "Longinus"' evaluation of the poems may be typical of the biographical and moralistic bias of ancient criticism, but it also grows out of some sound aesthetic impressions about the differences between the two poems and an intuition shared by others that the *Odyssey* was composed, if not necessarily after the *Iliad*, in response somehow to it. ("Longinus" calls it an "epilogue" to the *Iliad*.[1]) The world of the *Odyssey* is one in which the adventures in Troy have already found a place in history and song, where the only new materials from Troy are those left over (λείψανα) from the *Iliad*, and where, as Aristotle remarks, the simplicity and intensity of the *Iliad* has yielded to a story of greater narrative subtlety and ethical interest (*Poet.* 1459b). The *Odyssey* is, to use our modern expression, post-heroic, and our fascination with it derives in part from the disparity between its epic hero and a world that is scaled down enormously from the one he has left. As one study expresses the difference, the *Odyssey* takes us back to the world of the similes of the *Iliad*.[2]

The kinds of differences "Longinus" found worthy of censure are epitomized in the Laertes episode of Book 24: its fantastic narrative, its orchards and stone walls and domesticated world of farmhands and humble servants. In its representation of the aged Laertes and in the interrelation of ethos and narrative we can locate the poem's distinctive approach to character. Where the *Iliad* portrays character, as it were, in the aorist, suggesting a heroic essence in a series of dramatic confrontations, the *Odyssey* depicts character in the progressive and against the steady movement of time. The *Odyssey*, from the first line of its proem, requires us to conceive of time in terms of human life (βίος)—in its temporality and in the sequentiality of the stages that constitute it.[3] While Odysseus is in full maturity at the time of the poem, the *Odyssey* provides in its span the impression of the whole of a life: we catch a glimpse of him as an infant and newly come of age in the tale of the scar, as a somewhat younger man at Troy in the recollections of Nestor, Helen and Menelaus, and in old age and death in the prophecy of Tiresias. Unlike Achilles, whose heroism seeks to transcend time and change, we come to see Odysseus as a hero fully engaged in the world of time. Where the *Iliad* compresses the Trojan conflict into its limited time frame, the *Odyssey* provides in its compass a portrait of the hero larger than the events the poem describes.[4]

The *Odyssey* achieves a similar effect in its treatment of generations. In Telemachus, Odysseus, and Laertes, three life stages are represented synchronically and against the steady movement of time. Just as we see Telemachus in terms of his coming of age,[5] or Laertes edging precariously closer to death, we see Odysseus similarly in transition, moving toward the old age prophesied for him and away from his heroic past. One of the functions of the Laertes episode is to relate the hero's movement in time to a world that has changed along with him, and to provide an accommodation between him and a world at a distance from the heroic arena of his youth and maturity.

In what follows I will discuss the function of the episode by way of some observations about the nature of old age in Homeric society generally and in particular in relation to the end of the *Odyssey*.[6] The importance of the theme in this part of the work is underscored by the diction, where references to old age and to the elderly abound,[7] and by its elderly cast of characters: Laertes himself, the old Sicilian who tends him, the farmhand Dolius, Eupeithes the father of Antinous, Halitherses "the aged hero," and Athena herself, who takes on for one last time the guise of Mentor. I will suggest that the Homeric representation of old age is richer and more complex than has been appreciated, and that the character of Laertes is developed at two levels: (1) as a paradigm through which the poem explores what I will refer to as the problematic of old age—the nature of old age and its complications in the heroic and martial world of the *Iliad* and *Odyssey*; and (2) as a conclusion to the story of Odysseus, where the hero himself is destined to old age, a position that takes him irretrievably beyond the heroic world and locates him in one that is post-Iliadic and post-heroic. The two purposes are closely related, and the poem cannot perform the second without also performing the first—that is, Odysseus cannot survive into old age unless it is in some sense redefined and its problematic resolved.

It is obvious that I am assuming the essential unity of the *Odyssey* and of what Page and others baldly reject as the "Continuation."[8] The Alexandrians Aristophanes and Aristarchus perhaps believed that the poem ended at 23.296, but others have argued on internal evidence that the *Odyssey* cannot conclude with the reunion with Penelope, and that the *nostos* (homecoming), as we have come to understand it, must include a reunion of the hero with his father and a settlement with the families of the suitors.[9] What follows is not a defense of the episode per se but an inquiry into the question of why Homer (or, for that matter, an intelligent redactor) would end the *Odyssey* as it does. At least part of the answer lies in the tension between a hero destined to old age and the characterization of old age in heroic culture generally. A proper closure requires that both be in some sense rehabilitated.

OLD AGE IN TRADITIONAL SOCIETIES

There is no society that does not have a concept of old age and does not give it expression within its system of life stages or age-grades.[10] But while old age may be universal at the level of form, its content is culturally relative and can be constructed in fundamentally different ways. Old age is, to some extent, problematic in any society, since the long-term physiological changes that accompany it necessarily entail social changes, but the role of the elderly and societal attitudes to them differ greatly from culture to culture.

For elderly persons in many modern societies, old age initiates a process of "disengagement" from one's earlier social role and from meaningful social interaction.[11] In such cultures, especially those in which personal worth is derived from occupational work and retirement is institutionalized, the opportunities for the elderly are limited and their status is often diminished. In traditional societies, on the other hand, behavior and status are more heavily age-graded, so that the criteria by which excellence is regarded change with the nature of one's abilities and activities. As a result, the passage into old age is less a process of disengagement than of transition to a different but valued social role. Although old age precludes the elderly from certain activities, their status is determined by other factors: the political power they have accumulated, their knowledge and experience, their spiritual and moral resources.[12]

Thus in many traditional societies elderly men enjoy continued or enhanced political power and prestige. Simmon's ethnographic study of seventy-one traditional peoples surveys the power they wield in political, religious and familial contexts, and while he acknowledges that prestige of the elderly is "practically universal in all known societies," such is especially the case in societies in which the aged perform important functions.[13] He notes the frequency with which chieftainship is a prerogative of old age and the influence the elderly wield as advisers to chieftains, as members of "great councils," as "authoritative dispensers of information," and as mediators in cultural disputes.[14] Anthropologists, particularly of East African cultures, note the prominence of gerontocratic social orders, in which a man's political power and prestige increase with the ascent from one age grade to the next and peak in old age.[15] The elderly often play crucial roles in religious and ritual life as repositories of ceremonial knowledge, controlling rites of initiation and acting as mediators between supernatural forces and the community.[16] Finally, almost all traditional cultures provide roles in which the elderly serve as "wise counselors" to the community, as judges, advisers, teachers and storytellers. A quantitative study of twenty-six traditional societies establishes a connection between the esteem given the elderly and "the degree of control that the aged possess over utile information"—a kind of cost-benefit analysis of aged wise counsel.[17]

Where anthropological study of the elderly tends to measure their status in terms of their political control of a culture's traditions, and to attribute this to extrinsic or social factors, recent psychological studies of traditional and preliterate cultures relate the social roles of the elderly to intrinsic or developmental factors as well. Cross-cultural field work by Gutmann among the the Druze, Navaho, and Maya suggests that younger men "reveal motives, attitudes and images characteristic of an active, production-centered, and competitive stance," where older men "give priority to community rather than agency, to receptivity rather than productivity, and to mildness and humility rather than competition."[18] This change, from what Gutmann calls "active mastery" to "passive mastery," is reflected in the frequency with which the elders of the community function as reconcilers, arbiters, and maintainers of traditions, particularly in their heightened religious and ritual activity.[19] Among the Druze, for instance, the "passive mastery" of elderly men finds expression in the role they play as priests, or *Aqil*, prestigious mediators between the divine and the mundane and bringers of life-sustaining forces into the community. In spite of—and in some sense because of—the physical diminution old age entails, the *Aqil* acquire new power and status, as "passive affiliation with supernatural power tends to replace the control and deployment of individual strength."[20]

The underlying ideology of traditional cultures serves to sustain or enhance the position and prestige of the elderly. As such groups identify themselves in terms of their past and the hallowed traditions that sustain them, the elderly, closer by birth to the sacred past and by death to divine and ancestral sources of power, are associated with their tribal history and participate in its sacred character: Max Weber describes the elders in gerontocratic communities as those "most familiar with the sacred traditions of the group."[21] In such cultures the aging process as a whole will be perceived more in terms of enhancement and opportunity than of diminution and loss, and it is in this light that Fortes claims that where the modern world may regard the idea of aging with dread or disgust, "the idea that one might fear or resent growing up or growing old does not evidently occur in traditional preliterate, preindustrial societies."[22]

The literary configuration of old age in the Homeric poems is more complex and ambiguous than what we see in these social representations. In certain respects, Homeric society seems to correspond to traditional age-grade systems.[23] Warfare and athletic competition, along with the more practical aspects of ruling and management of the *oikos*, are primarily youthful occupations, while speaking ability and wise counsel distinguish the elderly. The community in principle treats them with respect, and there is abundant evidence of a deference to age that Roussel, speaking in the historical context, calls "the principle of seniority."[24] Nestor, whose antiquity is carefully documented (1.247–52; cf. *Od.*3.245, 15.196), offers the first response to the quarrel of Agamemnon and Achilles, enjoining them to heed his age and experience (259 ff.). Nestor recognizes Diomedes as the best speaker "among his peers," but claims preeminence by reason of his greater years (IX.53–62), and throughout the poem both gods and men lay claim to "know more" by reason of age.[25] Nowhere is the principle of seniority more explicit than at XI.783–89, where Nestor, as Patroclus' elder, counsels him to remember the advice of the elderly Menoetius and Peleus, and, as Achilles' elder, to give him good counsel. In Troy we see the elder counselors (δημογέροντες) kept by age from fighting but excellent speakers still, discussing the war and the well-being of the city (III.150 ff.).

Likewise in the Assembly of *Odyssey* 2 it is Aegyptius, "who was bent over with age and had seen things without number" (2.16: tr. Lattimore), who speaks first, just as among the Phaeacians it is Echeneus, "most advanced in age" (7.156, 11.343), who breaks the silence upon Odysseus' arrival and negotiates between king and queen. In addition, the youthful Telemachus describes a traditional deference to age in his reluctance to approach Nestor (3.24).

As a social group the elderly lay claim to such counsel as their special prerogative; the *portion of honor* (γέρας) derives etymologically from *gêras/gerôn* and originally described the prerogatives of the elderly, a connection preserved in the formula "for this is the privilege of the old men" (τὸ γὰρ γέρας ἐστὶ γερόντων).[26] When Agamemnon reminds Nestor of the weakness of old age, Nestor uses the occasion to discuss the age-graded nature of excellence:

> Son of Atreus, so would I also wish to be that
> man I was, when I cut down brilliant Ereuthalion.
> But the gods give to mortals not everything at the same time;
> if I was a young man then, now in turn is old age upon me.
> Yet even so I shall be among the riders, and command them
> with word and counsel; such is the privilege of the old men.
> The young spearmen shall do the spear-fighting, those who are born
> of a generation later than mine, who trust in their own strength.
>   (IV.318–23: tr. Lattimore)

Fighting is for the young men (κοῦρος, νεώτεροι, ὁπλότεροι) who trust in their strength (βίη). However, Nestor's own skill in word and counsel (βουλῇ καὶ μύθοισι) wins him visible privilege. Agamemnon honors him most of his advisors (II.21), recognizes him for his speaking skill, and wishes he had ten more like him (II.370–72). He gives him the place of honor at a feast for the princes (II.405), and the Greeks award him the captive Hecamede "because he was the best of all in counsel" (XI.627). Even an old servant may profit by her age, as an angry Penelope tells Eurycleia (23.24).

As wise counselors, the elderly argue not for their own advantage but for the common good, advising the leaders and charting a course through the selfish interests of the other *basileis* (kings), so that Segal speaks of Nestor as "the voice of social expectation and approval" and of his "commitment to the established order of things."[27] In Homer the elderly are the visible link between the present generation and the past and benefit from the reverence given to ancestral traditions. The shield of Achilles presents an idealized image of this tradition, where the elders, who are presiding over a court case concerning a blood feud, are seated on polished stones in a "sacred circle" (ἱερῷ ἐνὶ κύκλῳ, XVIII.504), holding in their hands the scepters that are described elsewhere in the *Iliad* as "ancestral, always imperishable" (II.46, 186).

Such in principle is the relation in Homer between the "passive mastery" of the elderly and the "active mastery" of the youth, and the basis of the privilege and prestige they are given in return. To this extent, old age in Homer can be viewed as traditional, and most scholarship has regarded old age and its exemplars in Homer's works in this spirit. Yet alongside this respect and deference stands a second valuation which is in conflict with it since it intimates a more critical and ambiguous perception of old age, suggesting an underlying disdain and even contempt for it, reflected at a number of levels. This perspective is underpinned by the poem's diction and formulaic expression, and in the negative epithets old age bears in both epics, where *gêras* is regularly described as *difficult* (χαλεπόν, VIII.103, XXIII.623, 11.196), *sorrowful* (λυγρόν, V.153, X.79, XVIII.434, XXIII.644, 24.249–50), *hateful* (στυγερόν, XIX.336), and *deadly* or *destructive* (ὀλοόν, XXIV.487). These epithets and their associations locate old age within a conceptual nexus almost uniformly negative: death, disease, wrath, grief, Ares, the Erinys, and so on. They are consistent with the negative verbs used elsewhere in conjunction with *gêras*: *wears* (τείρειν, IV.315, 24.233), *seizes* (μάρπτειν, 24.390), *oppresses* (ὀπάζειν, IV.321, VIII.103), and *holds* (ἔχειν, 11.497). That they are not unique to Homer (they are frequent in Hesiod, lyric, and the Homeric *Hymns*) and are a part of the formulaic repertoire in no way compromises their force.

While it is sometimes suggested that these expressions are in contrast with the descriptions of old age as sleek or shining (λιπαρόν),[28] the contexts reveal that the expressions are not antithetical. The "sleek old age" (which exists as a concept only in the *Odyssey*) represents a particular kind of *gêras* spent in comfort, prosperity and security, sleek as though it glistened with oil.[29] Menelaus tells Pisistratus that his father is clearly blessed by the gods, who have granted him excellent sons and allowed him "to grow old prosperously", literally "sleekly" (λιπαρῶς γηρασκέμεν: 4.210). The "sleek old age" represents an ideal completion of the heroic life, both as Nestor possesses it and as it is promised to Odysseus in conjunction with a gentle death and a prosperous people (11.134–37).

The various negative epithets, however, are used differently. There it is old age itself which is dreadful, and not the particular circumstances in which the elderly find themselves. Nestor, for instance, is said not to yield to "sorrowful old age" (γήραι λυγρῷ, X.79), and Achilles fears that Peleus has died already or is still hanging on in "hateful old age" (γήραι ... στυγερῷ, XIX.336). Nor do the elderly hesitate to apply these expressions to themselves: Nestor concedes that he can no longer compete in athletic contests and must give way to "gloomy old age" (γήραι λυγρῷ, XXIII.644). In this perspective, old age is simply wretched, so that these adjectives suggest its irreducible essence.

This negative perception is reflected in the representation of the elderly, who are often presented as objects of pity, neglect, or even scorn. Consider the precipitating event of the *Iliad*, Agamemnon's refusal to return Chryseis to her suppliant father:

> Never let me find you again, old man [γέρον], near our hollow
> ships, neither lingering now nor coming again hereafter,
> for fear your staff and the god's ribbons help you no longer.
> The girl I will not give back; sooner will old age come upon her
> in my old house, in Argos, far from her own land, going
> up and down by the loom and being in my bed as a companion.
> So go now, do not make me angry; so you will be safer."
> So he spoke, and the old man in terror obeyed him.
>
> (I.26–33: tr. Lattimore)

It is no accident that the first two occurences of vocative "old man" (γέρον) in the poem come from Agamemnon: here (as often) with a contemptuous force, and at I.286 more respectfully to Nestor. Here Agamemnon ignores Chryses' status as priest, seeing in him only a helpless old man whom he thinks he can abuse with impunity. He dishonors (ἠτίμασεν. I.11) and does not respect (αἰδεῖσθαι, I.23) him. He flaunts the sexual service his daughter will be forced to render, and in such a way as to underscore his contempt for Chryses' age: Chryseis herself will be old before he will give her up. That Agamemnon's behavior is reprehensible is clear from the human and divine reactions it provokes and is also an index of his personal character.[30] But this aberration from the "normal" canons of behavior also serves to highlight the problematical position of the elderly in a community of warriors for whom old age may be a thing of little or no account.

Framing the poem at the other end is Priam's supplication of Achilles in Book XXIV, which resumes the same theme: the confrontation between an intractable hero and a suppliant old man bearing ransom for his children. As with Chryses, it is Priam's status as old man rather than his kingship that is emphasized throughout, and commentators have observed the many verbal correspondences between the two episodes.[31] At one level, the scene functions as a reversal of the earlier scene. Not only does Achilles yield to Priam, but young and old achieve a rapproachement signaled by a return to the norms of deference to the elderly: when the two have had their fill of lamenting, Achilles rises to offer his chair to Priam, a simple gesture in honor of Priam's age, just as the providing of food and sleep indicates his status as guest.[32] The significance of these kindnesses is underscored by other moments when Achilles must struggle to control his anger at his enemy and the father of the slayer of Patroclus (560, 582–86). There is clear irony in the way the young hero even appropriates for himself the office of wise counselor, consoling Priam with the parables of the urns of Zeus and Niobe.

But unlike Chryses, Priam bases his appeal not only on his own tragic circumstances but on the pathos of age itself and on his ability to summon up images of suffering that Achilles will assimilate to his own. Earlier Priam had sought to go and beseech Achilles, hoping to appeal to him as an old man who might remind him of his father (XXII.419–21). There is even a hint of divine approval for his strategy when Hermes in disguise cautions Priam at XXIV.368–71 that he is not

young and that his attendant is old, and speaks to Priam of his own
"dear father." Priam commences his supplication in just such terms,
linking himself and Peleus as agemates on the "deadly threshold of old
age" (486–87), and reminding him of how Peleus is surely harassed by
those around him (488–89). But Priam also contrasts their situations:
while both old men must sorrow without their sons, Peleus can at
least hope to see his again (490–95). The poet suggests that Priam's
portrayal of old age has had its desired effect. Achilles is moved to pity
his "gray hair and beard" (515–16), and when Achilles compares
Priam and his father, it is in terms of the suffering he has brought on
each at the end of lives that had been prosperous: on Peleus who grows
old (γηράσκοντα, 541) without his care, and on old Priam (γέρον,
543) to whose children he has brought such sorrow.

Priam succeeds by becoming for Achilles an instance of pathetic
old age and, more specifically, of the elderly's plight in war and in situations where sons are absent or dead. The pathos of the passage is
enhanced by the theme of the *threptêria* (in Homer shortened to *threp-
tra*), that system of *gêrotrophia* whereby sons cared for their parents in
old age. This is prepared for by two earlier passages that describe fallen
warriors with allusions to the custom. The warriors, who are killed by
Aias, are, first, Simoeisius, struck down we are told in the bloom of
youth (IV.474), and, second, Hippothous, who is killed while trying to
capture the corpse of Patroclus (XVII.288ff).[33] Of each we are told that

> . . . he could not
> render again the care (θρέπτρα) of his dear parents; he was short-
>   lived (μινυνθάδιος . . . αἰών),
> beaten down beneath the spear of high-hearted Aias.
>   (IV.477–79 = XVII.301–3: tr. Lattimore)

Derived from the verb to raise or nourish (τρέφω), the *threptêria* is
represented not as filial beneficence but as a kind of repayment; hence
it is here, as elsewhere, used with the verb to give back (ἀπο-δοῦναι).
Its rendering fulfills a contract entered into by the son who has been
nurtured in youth and therefore must repay his parents when they are
in similar need of care (κομιδή). Historically, repayment of the *threptêria* was a matter of law.[34] The responsibility of the son to perform the
role of what Hesiod calls the *gêrokomos,* "caretaker in old age"
(*Th.*605), was automatic and unconditional, apart from any continu-

ing contribution the parents might have continued to make and without respect to their particular needs or circumstances. In the *Iliad* the institution provides both a link with the social world and a powerful example of Homeric reciprocity: even the raising of one's children is conceived as a transaction that extends through the life course, a giving back according to what one has received.

Achilles is himself the macrocosm of the warrior described in the two passages above. In the first book of the *Iliad* he is described as short-lived (μινυνθάδιος, I.352) and as having a short fate (αἶσα μίνυνθα, I.416). Although his final inability to render the *threptêria* to Peleus lies outside the scope of the *Iliad*, his absence and its consequences are increasingly an issue in the end of the poem. In book XIX Achilles imagines Peleus in Phthia: as dead or near death due to hateful old age and the ever imminent prospect of his death (334–37), and again, as already weeping "for bereavement of such a son, for me, who now in a strange land / make war upon the Trojans for the sake of accursed Helen" (323–25: tr. Lattimore). In Book XXIV Priam offers Achilles a troubling image of his father in which

> . . . they who dwell nearby encompass him and afflict him,
> nor is there any to defend him against the wrath, the destruction
> (XXIV.488–89: tr. Lattimore).

Priam invites Achilles to imagine Peleus in his loneliness and vulnerability, clearly hoping to stir up his guilt over his absence from Phthia. Achilles seems to contest Priam's claim that he is the more tragic father, pointing out that Peleus, unlike his suppliant, did not have many children,

> [but] a single all-untimely child he had, and I give him
> no care as he grows old (οὐδέ νυ τόν γε γηράσκοντα κομίζω), since far
>   from the land of my fathers
> I sit here in Troy, and bring nothing but sorrow to you and your
>   children.
> And you, old sir, we are told you prospered once.
> (XXIV.540–43: tr. Lattimore)

Achilles openly acknowledges the suffering he has brought to Priam and his children (cf. XXII.421–22), as well as his present and future failure as caretaker. He is short-lived, and even now gives his aging father no care. Priam's bereavement recalls to Achilles the neglect that is already his father's condition, the more serious for the family's single line of succession. Priam has enjoyed neither food nor sleep since Hector's death, but before he returns to Troy, has his needs carefully and insistently ministered to by Achilles, who provides him with meat, bread, and wine and has a fine bed made up for him. While critics have traditionally seen these kindnesses in the context of the rituals of hospitality, they also sustain the filial overtones the passage labors to establish. Achilles and Priam here assume surrogate roles in a shattered institution: Achilles in effect rendering to Priam the *threptêria* he will not provide for Peleus, Priam receiving it from the man who has taken the life of the son who should have provided it.

OF COUNSELORS AND KINGS: NESTOR AND PRIAM IN THE *ILIAD*

Nestor, as is often observed, is as conspicuous a gerontocrat as is to be found among the Achaeans, and is often held up as the model of Homeric "attitudes" toward old age. But this portrait can be read more ambiguously than is usually the case. That the superannuated hero should be present at Troy, much less participate in combat, is anomalous by Homeric standards,[35] although the incongruity is somewhat reduced by his remarkable physical and moral capacities. The cup Nestor uses easily would be difficult for any man to lift (XI.632–37). He sleeps with full armor at the ready (X.73–79), and when he awakens Diomedes, the latter complains of his boundless energy, how he assumes tasks proper to the young, and how impossible he is to deal with (X.164–67). Agamemnon commends his youthful fighting spirit (IV. 313–16). Yet Nestor's strength has its inevitable limits. When he is caught in the thick of battle before Hector's advance, Diomedes saves his life and reminds him that he is no match for the young with "hard old age" upon him (χαλεπὸν δέ σε γῆρας ὀπάζει, VIII.103), and Achilles uses a similar expression in awarding him a consolation prize after the chariot race (ἤδη γὰρ χαλεπὸν κατὰ γῆρας ἐπείγει, XXIII.623). The poet characterizes Nestor's role as passive and advisory: he alone is distinguished as the "watcher" for the Greeks,"[36] and Nestor himself defines such a role as the privilege (γέρας) of the old, recommending that combat be left to the young (IV.322–25, XXIII.643–45). But the incongruities in Nestor's representation serve to point up the ambiguities that attend old age in general. While his continuing military role is a tribute to his excellence and that of an earlier generation of heroes, it also suggests a restricted concept of *aretē:* namely, that the dispensing of wise counsel is not sufficient in itself; and that in disengaging from the arena of battle and youthful competition the elderly risk the loss of heroic status.[37]

Correspondingly, Nestor is remarkable for his frequent appeals to his own authority and the seniority of age in general, from his opening speech in which he reminds Agamemnon and Achilles that both are younger than he (I.259). In his advice to Patroclus at XI.783–90, he insists that because Patroclus is older than Achilles, the former should give good counsel to the latter, as he himself had earlier been instructed by his father Menoetius: just as in the formula he who is older "knows more," so those who are oldest presumably know most. In Book VII he tries to shame his comrades into standing up to Hector in a duel, invoking the authority of "Peleus, the aged horseman, / the great man of counsel among the Myrmidons, and their speaker (ἐσθλὸς . . . βουληφόρος ἠδ᾽ ἀγορητής)" (125–26: tr. Lattimore). And he describes for Agamemnon the elders' right to "word and counsel" as the privilege of old men (γέρας . . . γερόντων), aptly using *gerontes* in its literal rather than extended sense of "counselors" in general (on other occasions any one of the princes, regardless of age, can be described as a *gerōn,* and Achilles uses the same formula to refer to the Achaean chiefs as a whole (IX.422).[38])

Nestor's statement has a proverbial ring, recalling those traditional cultures in which the elderly have a distinctive status as counselors to the community and may truly claim this as their prerogative. That Nestor should himself do so is not accidental, nor is his own perspective disinterested. To what extent is he justified? While the *Iliad* alludes explicitly to the conventions of aged wise counsel, it also calls these traditions into question, offering both in theory and practice a series of conflicting perspectives on the relation of age and counsel. Part of the problem is that when we speak of "the wisdom of the elders" we are referring to a variety of related functions: their knowledge of the past, the beauty of their speech, the quality of their advice, their spiritual, moral, and religious resources. Nestor's rhetoric is perhaps the most clearly marked in the poem; the narrator introduces him with praise for the beauty of his speech: he is "the fairspoken . . . the lucid speaker of Pylos / from whose lips the streams of words ran sweeter than honey" (I.248–49; cf. IV.293: tr. Lattimore).

The ambiguous status of Homeric wise counselors, and the opposition between the beauty and the ineffectuality of their speech, is suggested twice early in the poem: in the contrast between the honeyed sweetness of Nestor's words (I.249–50) and his failed diplomacy, and in the portrayal of Trojan city-elders who sit with Priam and watch the battle from the Scaean gates:

> Now through old age these fought no longer, yet were they excellent
> speakers still, and clear, as cicadas who through the forest
> settle on trees, to issue their delicate voice of singing.
>
> (III.150–52: tr. Lattimore)

Though the simile grants them the beauty of their speech, it questions its efficacy: their words are like the "lily-thin voices" of cicadas, a pleasing sound but easily ignored, a gentle background noise in the summer's heat.[39] Moreover, the image of the cicada (as we shall see in the myth of Tithonus) is traditionally associated with the weakness and impotence of age.[40] This ambiguity is sustained throughout the poem. When Hector announces at VI.114–15 that he is returning to Troy, it is not to consult with the elders but to ask them and their wives to pray for the Trojans, and he later criticizes the "cowardice of the elders" (XV.721) that kept him earlier from attacking the Greek ships. The *dêmogerontes* (elders of the people) observe that the best course of action would be to return Helen and bring the war to a halt (III.159–60), and Antenor even proposes this to the Trojan assembly, but Paris overrules him and Priam acquiesces (VII.347–64).

That wisdom is the particular province of old age is only one point of view in the *Iliad* and is openly at odds with others. The Trojans find perhaps their wisest counselor in Polydamas, who is the same age as Hector even to the day (XVIII.251). On one of several occasions in which he opposes the will of Hector, he offers his account of the origins of wisdom:

> Hector, you are too intractable to listen to reason.
> Because the god has granted you the actions of warfare
> therefore you wish in counsel also to be wise beyond others.
> But you cannot choose to have all gifts given to you together.
> To one man the god has granted the actions of warfare

to one to be a dancer, to another the lyre and the singing,
and in the breast of another Zeus of the wide brows establishes
wisdom, a lordly thing, and many take profit beside him
and he saves many, but the man's own thought surpasses all others.

(XIII.726–34: tr. Lattimore)

Like Paris earlier (III.63–66), Polydamas sees one's interests and talents not as a function of age but as a gift of the gods: some have wisdom, others do not. In another passage Helenus tells Hector and Aeneas that they are the best in fighting and in thought (VI.78–79)—another reminder of the extraordinary abilities of these heroes. Among the Achaeans the elderly clearly have no monopoly on wise counsel, and the younger heroes are liberal with their advice. It is Achilles who takes the initiative in calling the Achaeans to assembly in Book I, and Odysseus, not Nestor, who salvages the collapsing assembly in Book II; revealingly, once again, the Greek Council princes are regularly called *gerontes* regardless of their age.[41]

We do better to see the proverbial wisdom of the elders not as a given but as one set of claims in contest with others. Even as Agamemnon and Achilles must defend their special portion (γέρας) and the honor inherent in it, Nestor seems to understand that the right to offer "word and counsel" is to be jealously guarded. Diomedes in particular is conspicuous among the young for the frequency and quality of his counsel. In Book IX Agamemnon shocks his counselors by advocating retreat, and when Diomedes comes close to charging him with cowardice, Nestor must openly pull rank on him:

Son of Tydeus, beyond others you are strong in battle,
and in counsel also are noblest among all men of your own age.
Not one man of all the Achaians will belittle your words nor
speak against them. Yet you have not made complete your argument,
since you are a young man still and could even be my own son
and my youngest born of all; yet still you argue in wisdom
with the Argive kings, since all you have said was spoken fairly.
But let me speak, since I can call myself older than you are,
and go through the whole matter, since there is none who can
    dishonour
the thing I say, not even powerful Agamemnon.

(IX.53–62: tr. Lattimore).[42]

In Book XIV Agamemnon makes a similar proposal and invites anyone "young or old" (XIV.108) to offer better advice. Diomedes again
rises to the occasion and offers sound counsel, balancing against his
youth—he is again identified as the youngest of the princes there
assembled—his distinguished lineage (XIV.110ff.).

Nestor's rhetoric is characterized by its lengthy digressions and its
evocation of a superheroic past of which he is the sole surviving exemplar (I.254–74, II.337–38, IV.308–9, VII.124–60, XI.631–36).[43] He
typically introduces a specimen of his counsel by digressing, sometimes at length, about his youthful exploits on the battlefield or in athletic competition, with the formula "would that I were young again, as
when . . . " (IV.318–19, VII.132–33,157, XI.670–71, XXIII.629–30).
Although this kind of reminiscing is typical of old age—in the
Odyssey, as we shall see, its latent humor is exploited—gerontologists
rightly remind us that what is often dismissed as senile garrulity can
be deeply significant. The faculty of memory is, in most societies, an
important source of prestige and respect for the elderly.[44] Gutmann's
cross-cultural work sees in the so-called nostagia of old age and reminiscing of the elderly an attempt to avoid being viewed as "other" and
to secure their well-being by recalling to others their personal history.[45] Similarly, Butler describes such behavior in terms of what he calls
the life review, an attempt in old age and in the face of approaching
death to bring back into consciousness significant past experience and
address unresolved areas of conflict.[46]

Nestor's speeches in the Iliad, as Edwards observes, "are not just
senile rambling or self-glorification, but establish the credentials of
the speaker, to show on what grounds he claims a right to be listened
to."[47] His experience provides important models for heroic behavior
and serves to bolster morale and calm tempers among the younger
warriors by placing the present in a historical context. Yet in addition
to their paradigmatic value, Nestor's digressions constitute carefully
constructed appeals for his own authority. He repeatedly grounds his
authority in his youthful achievement and the respect he used to command rather than in his age per se, implying that the latter in itself is
no guarantee of his status.[48] Nestor's digressions provide explicit arguments for his continued self-value and base his present status not on
his age but on his prior accomplishments and valor as a young warrior.
Indeed, Nestor himself nowhere claims that his wisdom is the product
of his age. There is a certain disproportion between the precocious-

ness of his past achievements and his claim to authority. At I.259ff. Nestor works himself into the story of the battle of the Lapiths and Centaurs, where he once fought along with the earlier and greater generation of heroes, men like Theseus and Perithoos. They had invited him to help, and despite his youth, they "listened to the counsels I gave and heeded my bidding."[49] At VII.153 he claims to have been the youngest of all who fought Ereuthalion, and at XI.716ff. he tells how he distinguished himself as the best of the Pylians in war before Neleus even considered him old enough to fight. Although the virtues of the heroes of the previous generations are sometimes praised by others (Agamemnon attempts to rouse Diomedes with a similar argument at IV.372ff.), only Nestor claims personally to embody the superiority of the past. Like his continuing presence on the battlefield, Nestor's reminiscences of his past glory as a warrior have a self-validating function. While they are tribute to the excellence of an earlier generation of heroes, they also suggest a concern on the part of the elderly for their status in a heroic culture and particularly in a martial situation: just as the young encroach throughout upon the elders' special privilege of wise counsel, so Nestor in turn is reluctant to disengage fully from the arena of youthful competition and so bolsters his authority by recalling his earlier glory.

Nestor's words, to be sure, are always spoken "in good order" (κατὰ μοῖραν), and his counsel is often the best (cf. I.325, IX.94). The Greeks, we are told, had awarded him the captive Hecamede "because he was the best of all in counsel" (XI.627). His tactical advice, though generally uncontroversial, is sound and sensible.[50] In Book IV he is "the old man wise in fighting from of old" (310), marshalling his troops according to old-fashioned battle tactics, advising them to stay in a group rather than break rank and fight individually; this, he says, is how the men of the past fought. Agamemnon honors him above the rest of his elders (II.21) and at one point wishes that he only had others like him (II.370–72; cf. IV.315–16).

But Nestor's success as a wise counselor is limited, and his advice is often empty, ignored, or tragically off-course. That the youthful protagonists of epic should disregard the advice of the elderly is in one sense a precondition of their own greatness, and the tragedy of an Achilles or Hector is enhanced by their rejection of advice from their comrades both older and younger. But the experience of Nestor also furthers the overall impression that elderly counsel is typically failed counsel. In Book I he does manage to keep Achilles and Agamemnon from coming to blows, but his recommendations to them are disregarded, and it is ironic that the "Evil Dream" suggesting the disastrous assembly of Book II takes the form of Nestor and is seconded by him (II.79–83). It is Nestor who suggests the failed embassy to Achilles, though the latter implies that a reconciliation really requires a personal visit from Agamemnon (IX.372–73). And of course it is Nestor who suggests to Patroclus, who has come only to seek information about the wounded Machaon, that he attempt to deceive the Trojans by doing battle in Achilles' armor (XI.793–802).[51] At several points the poem hints that others find Nestor's penchant for instruction a bother. When Nestor awakens Diomedes in the middle of the night, he calls him harsh and impossible to deal with (X.164–67). On two occasions the *Iliad* comes close to using humor at his expense. In Book XI.647–53, when Patroclus, with all deference due to the "aged sir beloved of Zeus," declines his invitation to take a chair and explains to Nestor that he must report to Achilles forthwith, Nestor responds with his longest speech in the poem (147 lines). And Nestor's futile diplomacy in Book I is echoed in the comic parody of the quarrel on Olympus that ends the book, with the officious and lame Hephaestus serving as almost a burlesque of Nestor.

In Homer the whole type of the wise counselor is honored more in the breach than in the observance. A case in point is Phoenix, who, like Nestor, serves in several capacities. He leads one of the battalions of the Myrmidons (XVI.196) and serves as referee in the games for Patroclus (XXIII.360). As ambassador to Achilles, he admittedly makes more headway than does Odysseus, managing to keep Achilles from leaving Troy forthwith, but his counsel stills falls short of its declared purpose. We will examine elsewhere the sexual significance of Phoenix's autobiography, but as Scodel has observed, the content of Phoenix's story—his sordid affair with his aged father's concubine, his flight from home, the domestic service he renders the house of Peleus—is clearly offered as a negative example for Achilles and is as much an exercise in self-abasement as a demonstration of wise counsel.[52] Phoenix succeeds largely to the extent that he reveals himself an impotent old man and a pathetic anti-hero, and illustrates for Achilles the kind of future that might result from his threats to return to Phthia.

Nestor is of course king as well as counselor, and as such provides an opportunity to study the effectiveness of old men as rulers. Among the Achaeans old age is clearly not a prerequisite for kingship, since it is only one of a number of factors that give one the authority to rule. As Donlan says of the structure of authority in the *Iliad*, "The Homeric basileus is both leader and warrior/counselor," and the position-authority on which he draws is "a complex of inheritance, remote divine sanction, age, personal wealth and numbers of followers."[53] Perhaps because the subject was obscure to the author, there is little in the Homeric world that seems fixed or automatic about the business of royal succession among Greek or Trojans. (Old age does, however, seem the occasion for the transference of domestic authority, as exemplified by Laertes, who seems earlier to have given rule of the *oikos* to Odysseus.[54]) In a number of ways the *Iliad* suggests an incongruity between old age and kingship, and by offering different configurations of age and kingship provides a kind of comparative study in political structures and of the relative strengths and weaknesses of the elderly as kings.

The majority of the Achaean kings, such as Agamemnon, Menelaus, and Odysseus, are in the period of their maturity. Nestor, who has clearly been king for a long time, is again the exception to the rule:

> In his time two generations of mortal men had perished,
> those who had grown up with him and they who had been born to
> these in sacred Pylos, and he was king in the third age.
> (I.250–52; cf. Od. 3.245: tr. Lattimore)

As the "Pylos-born king" (II.54), he is lord of sandy Pylos and eight nearby cities, and comes to Troy in command of an impressive fleet of "ninety black ships" (II.602). He is a "high-hearted king" (ὑπερθύμοιο ἄνακτος, XXIII.302), a formula that he shares with a number of heroes. The epithet is well chosen: Agamemnon compliments him for his high spirits (IV.313), and Diomedes comments on his boundless energies in service to the Greeks (X.164–67). Nestor's kingship is further tribute to his remarkable constitution, but other factors are also involved. Antilochus, who is if not his eldest the only one of his sons to come to Troy, is still considered a young man. Nestor gives him wise counsel and practical advice on the chariot race in Book XXIII, after which Antilochus apologizes to Menelaus for his intemperate behavior and youthful immaturity (587 ff.). It appears that Antilochus is not

married and is presumably not yet "ready" to assume the rule of the
oikos or of Pylos. We have something of the same situation in Phthia,
where Peleus remains king despite his age and Achilles has not yet
come to his majority. Achilles speaks of Peleus in Phthia as being dead
or near death for "hateful old age" and as being distraught at the ever
imminent prospect of his son's death (XIX.334–37). Peleus' decline is
also implicit in Thetis' complaint that she alone of the Nereids was
married to a mortal who lies in his halls "broken by mournful old age"
(XVIII.434–35) and in Zeus' lament that a team of horses that is
immortal and ageless (VII.444) should be given to him. Hence the
twofold significance of Achilles' reply to the ambassadors in *Iliad* IX
that he would prefer a long life in Phthia, married to a local princess
and delighting in the inheritance left by "aged Peleus" (400): as a snub
to Agamemnon and his offer of his daughter in marriage, and as an
indication of a genuine eagerness to return to Phthia, marry, and
assume the rule of his people.

Because Nestor ministers more often to the Achaeans at large than
to the Pylians themselves (as when he marshalls his troops at
IV.310ff.), we need to look elsewhere for a closer study of the relation
between old age and kingship. Priam has long been king of Troy and
will continue as such until he gives the rule to one of his sons, presumably Hector, and apparently over the objections of Aeneas, who har-
bors royal aspirations and openly feuds with Priam on this account.
Deiphobus once finds Aeneas

> at the uttermost edge of the battle
> standing, since he was forever angry with brilliant Priam
> because great as he was he did him no honour (τίεσκεν) among
> his people.
>
> (XIII.459–61: tr. Lattimore)

Achilles later taunts Aeneas for thinking that even killing him in battle
could affect Priam's plans.

> Aineias, why have you stood so far forth from the multitude
> against me? Does the desire in your heart drive you to combat
> in hope you will be lord of the Trojans, breakers of horses,
> and of Priam's honour (τιμῆς). And yet even if you were to kill me

Priam would not because of that rest such honor (γέρας) on your hand.
He has sons, and he himself is sound, not weakened.

(XX.177–83: tr. Lattimore)

Priam, Achilles reminds Aeneas, is still *compos mentis*, not unbalanced or flighty, and unlikely to change his plans for the succession.[55] Aeneas counters with a careful genealogy of the Trojan monarchy designed to establish his own distinguished lineage and his equal claim to the rule (XX.213–41). As with Achilles' anxieties for the honor (τιμή) of Peleus (*Od.* 11.495, 503) or Odysseus' for his own kingship (γέρας, 11.175), these remarks suggest the situation of the king in old age, who must contend with the designs of younger men.

In the *Iliad* Troy, its people, and the man who rules them are so closely identified as to be at times indistinguishable. From the opening of the poem, Troy is described by variations on the formula "the great city of king Priam,"[56] and the Trojans themselves by such phrases as "Priam and the sons of Priam," "Priam and the Trojans," "father Priam and his people" and "the race of Priam."[57] In view of Priam's remarkable prolificacy there is a kind of literalness in this identification of king and city. As father of fifty sons and twelve daughters, Priam sustains a larger presence than any of the Greeks: we are always it seems bumping into his children on and off the battlefield and being treated to a description of their lineage and connection to the palace.[58] In other mythical contexts, this kind of sexual capacity and reproductive success can be an index of heroic status, but in the *Iliad* the dimensions of Priam's progeny suggest his patriarchal status and the extent of his identification with his family, a theme underscored by the variety of references to the "house of Priam" and the complicated domestic arrangements in and around it.[59] This identification is also an important part of the poem's symbolic strategy: just as Troy in its defensive capacity is personified in Hector, whose death signifies the inevitability of its destruction (cf. XXII.410–11), so is the city's imminent demise suggested by Priam, the city's life and heart. His horrific vision of his own death in Book XXII, as we will see below, is also a glimpse into the fate of his city.

A range of heroic epithets belongs to Priam. He is on different occasions "with the goodly spear of ash" (ἐυμμελίης), "nurtured of Zeus" (διοτρεφής), "great-hearted" (μεγαλήτωρ), "wise hearted" (δαίφρων), "brilliant" (δῖος), "glorious" (ἀγακλεής), "godlike" (θεοειδής) and "great" (μέγας).[60] He is frequently described as king (βασιλεύς or ἄναξ), both simply and in combination with other epithets, and also as *gerōn*. The discrepancy between his role as old man and as king is captured linguistically in the use of these epithets, and Priam is never called both "old man" and "king" at the same time. Unlike Peleus and Nestor, each of whom commands several formulas that suggest both their sovereignty *and* their age, with Priam these functions are kept separate. Also significant is the way in which these epithets are distributed. In most of the poem, indeed until the closing books, Priam is referred to both in his royal aspect and as *gerōn*, and in ways that suggest a division and a tension between these roles. Yet in the conclusion of the poem he is identified repeatedly and almost exclusively as *gerōn*: beginning with the references at XXI.526 and XXII.25 where he makes his appeal from the wall to Hector, divesting himself entirely of his role as king and presenting himself only as father and old man; and reaching a climax in book XXIV where he is described throughout in age-related terms. In many ways the "story" of Priam in the *Iliad* changes from that of a king who is old to that of an old man who is, almost incidentally, a king. At one level this change of representation is precisely what the poem says it is going to do. Just as Priam understands that his best hope of moving Achilles to pity will be by playing up his old age and reminding him of his own father (cf. XXII.415–22), so in presenting Priam insistently from this point on as *gerōn* rather than king the poet helps to shape this perception, encouraging the reader to see Priam as he wants to be seen.

This change in the representation of Priam brings to a climax the poem's treatment of the incompatibility of his age and his kingship. This is anticipated in his first appearance in the poem, when Iris, disguised as Polites, alerts the Trojans that the Greeks are on the move:

> These were holding assembly in front of the doors of Priam
> gathered together in one place, the elders and the young men.
> (II.788–89: tr. Lattimore)

The Trojan assembly is open and orderly. Priam presides over the people from his porch, with young and old taking part in the deliberations. But in what follows his effectiveness as a ruler is implicitly questioned. While Polites observes the proprieties (he addresses his opening remarks to Priam, and gives a nod to his authority in his subsequent reference to "the great city of Priam," II.803), he says:

> Old sir, dear to you forever are words beyond number
> as once, when there was peace; but stintless war has arisen.
> (II.796–97: tr. Lattimore)

Polites teases his father for his willingness to indulge in words rather than action, implying that his style of leadership, appropriate perhaps in peacetime, is inadequate to the realities of war. When he gets to the point of his speech, he does not address Priam at all: "Hector, on you beyond all do I urge this, to do as I tell you . . . " (II.802), and informs him of the situation. Hector responds decisively by dissolving the assembly and marshalling his troops.

The same point is made in the following book in the preparations for first duel and in the *teichoscopia* (view from the wall). In order to guarantee the oath sworn over the sacrifice, Menelaus demands that the Trojans summon "the strength of Priam" (Πριάμοιο βίην, III.105), a rare form of expression connoting tradition and antiquity and used only this one time in reference to Priam. But the formula is effectively undercut when Menelaus explains that Priam's presence is required not for the authority he personally commands but for its generic function.

> Always it is, that the hearts in the younger men are frivolous,
> but when an elder man is among them, he looks behind him
> and in front, so that all comes out far better for both sides.
> (III.108–10: tr. Lattimore)

Here, as so often, Priam's rule is largely honorific and ceremonial, with the real power wielded by the younger heroes.

We noted above how the simile of the cicadas, used to describe the *dēmogerontes*, hints at their powerlessness. Priam is listed in this same scene as one of these elder counselors (III.146–48), and in the following lines gives a public demonstration of his weakness. As Helen ascends the tower, the elders, while struck by her beauty and understanding of the Greeks' and Trojans' desire to fight for her, whisper to one another that she should nonetheless be returned for the good of all. Priam, whether oblivious to their advice or ignoring it, blithely bids Helen to sit by his side and help him identify the Greek leaders. In each of his three requests for information, Priam is described as old (III.181, 191, 225), linking his age to his docile attitude to his family and to the woman who is the occasion of the war. When Idaeus arrives to tell him of the duel and request his participation in the sacrifice, Homer says of the herald that

> Standing beside the aged man he spoke words to arouse him:
> "Son of Laomedon, rise up"
> (III.249–250: tr. Lattimore)

When Priam hears of the duel, we are told that "the old man shuddered" (III.259).[61] Thus we feel the distance between his age and his impressive title. The poet characterizes Priam's age and concern for his children as running counter to his kingly functions; it comes as no surprise that he is unable to watch his "dear son" Paris and Menelaus test the fates and that he quietly returns to Troy instead (III.304–9).

Later that same day, when the Trojans hold a second assembly "before the doors of Priam," Antenor, who is repeatedly distinguished for his good counsel,[62] proposes publicly what the *dēmogerontes* had whispered among themselves: Helen and her possessions should be returned. After Paris rejects the idea out of hand and even charges that Antenor has lost his mind, Priam is given an impressive introduction:

> . . . among them rose up
> Priam, son of Dardanos, equal of the gods in counsel,
> who in kind intention towards all stood forth and addressed them.
> (VII.365–67: tr. Lattimore)

But Priam makes no mention of Antenor's proposal and acquiesces to Paris' bitter response. He directs Idaeus to report to the Greeks "the word of Alexander," neither reiterating the terms of the decision nor endorsing it as his own, asking only for a truce to bury the dead. There is perhaps something compensatory in his later behavior when "great Priam" (VII.427) orders the Trojans not to cry out in grief as they gather their dead on the plains of Troy (VII.427–28), in what seems a deliberate show of toughness toward the Trojans designed to counter his indulgence of his son.

Priam's royal authority and judgement are repeatedly compromised by his age and his devotion to his family, especially Hector, to whom he is blatantly partial (cf. XXIV.247–64). This conflict between kingly effectiveness and parental love contrasts sharply with the representation of Nestor, who does not allow his age or fatherhood to affect his activity as king or his dealings with his sons and only grudgingly curtails his activity on the battlefield. He treats Antilochus with a sternness and formality that never hints of ambivalence. And where Nestor has an unlimited supply of stories of his youthful heroism and accomplishments we get only one glimpse of Priam's past. Amazed by the size of the Greek forces, he recalls the war the Phrygians once made on the Amazons in which "I myself, a helper in war, was marshalled among them" (III.188).

One final way in which the role of the elderly in Homeric society is not clearly defined relates to the issue of religious authority. Religious authority is not a function of age per se, although the elderly in the *Iliad* are on the whole a pious lot. The poem opens with the story of Chryses, and Nestor presides over sacrifices to Poseidon and Athena, as does Priam over that before the duel in Book IV. In one of the few descriptions we get of Peleus, Nestor describes how he was occupied with the details of a sacrifice and libation to Zeus when he entrusted Achilles to Patroclus' care (XI.772–75). But in Homer, as in Greek culture generally, neither the role of seer nor priest is age-specific: these figures may be old (Tiresias) but are not necessarily so (Calchas).[63] While prayer may be a sphere of activity left to the elderly, their prayers seem no more efficacious than those of the young; appeals to the gods are based not on one's age but rather on one's history of service and sacrifice to them. While old age and prayer are associated in the references at *Iliad* VI.87, 113, 270, 287, we are told there specifically how the gods did *not* listen to the prayers of the elderly women of Troy and how unbending they were in their hatred of Troy. The varied fortunes of Homer's elderly kings and counselors are another indication of the ambiguity of old age, and are related to tensions within the heroic values that circumscribe the poem.

HOMERIC HEROISM AND THE THRESHOLD OF OLD AGE

Few formulas from the Homeric epics are as well-known and yet as unclear as those that describe "the threshold of old age." In *Iliad* XXII Priam pleads with Hector from the walls of Troy, describing the destruction Zeus will visit on him "on the threshold of old age" (ἐπὶ γήραος οὐδῷ, 60). In Book XXIV he uses the same formula (ὀλοῷ ἐπὶ γήραος οὐδῷ) when he begs Achilles to be mindful of his father who is old like him (487). In the *Odyssey*, Odysseus uses the formula when he asks Eumaeus about Laertes, whom he left behind twenty years ago "on the threshold of old age" (ἐπὶ γήραος οὐδῷ, 15.348). Theoclymenus, who traces his genealogy for Telemachus, tells of Amphiareus, who "did not come to the threshold of old age" (οὐδ' ἵκετο γήραος οὐδόν, 15.246). Penelope uses a similar phrase (γήραος οὐδὸν ἱκέσθαι, 23.212) in telling Odysseus how the gods begrudged them of the opportunity to enjoy their youth and arrive at old age together. The range of the formulas used and the various contexts in which they appear suggest that they and the metaphor they employ were not original to Homer but were a ready resource in the formulary repertoire of heroic poetry.

The precise meaning of the formulas is less certain. As has often been observed, the usage in the *Iliad* might suggest a threshold from old age to Hades, implying that one is at an advanced old age. This is clearly how Plato understands the formula in the *Republic* when Socrates uses it of Cephalus (328e). The instances in the *Odyssey*, however, appear more to refer to a threshold from the prime of life to old age, implying, therefore, early old age (as Herodotus uses it of Psammenitus at 3.14). But the formulas admit of another interpretation: that the threshold is neither to nor from old age but is old age itself, conceived as a threshold between life and death. That is, we should read the formulas as describing "the threshold (that is) old age," and understand "of old age" (γήραος) in each case as a genitive of definition, by analogy with similar expressions (μοῖρα θανάτοιο, ὀλέθρου πείρατα, and θανάτοιο τέλος).[64]

Such an interpretation has the virtue of providing a single meaning in all cases. With this formula Priam can describe himself and Peleus as situated in the period between life and death, and Odysseus can indicate that Laertes was "already old" when the Trojan war began. To "make it to old age" (γήραος οὐδόν with a form of ἱκέσθαι) can be applied to the premature death of Amphiareus and to Penelope's complaint that she and Odysseus did not have a conventional married life: old age after a youth spent together. To view old age as a threshold is in keeping with the significance of thresholds cross-culturally and their prominence in Greek culture. Far from being epic periphrasis, to describe "the threshold of old age" is to tap into its cultural significance, and that heroic poetry should describe old age as specifically liminal in character is to touch on a fundamental ambivalence in the poems. Where we might see old age as the final stage or even the culmination of a life, the heroic temper sees it as a passage away from real life and a diminution of its fullness. As a result old age is seen as a kind of transition, and is associated as much with death as with life: in the *Odyssey*, the hero wishes continued joy to Arete "until old age / comes to you, and death, which befall all human creatures" (13.59–60: tr. Lattimore), pairing life's joys with the gloomy realities that signal life's decline.

Nowhere is this perspective clearer than in the religious context of the poems, where deity is defined as "deathless and ageless for all days" (ἀθάνατος καὶ ἀγήρως ἤματα πάντα). As has been observed, the formula is not a hendiadys: the gods are deathless *and* timelessly frozen in the radiance of youth or maturity, effected by a preservative diet of nectar and ambrosia.[65] In the *Odyssey*, the force of the formula is captured in the description of Odysseus' approach to the bronze threshold of Alcinous' house (7.84), where he admires its fine metalwork and the gold and silver watchdogs that Hephaestus wrought "to be deathless and ageless for all days" (7.94). Like works of art, the gods are fixed in the fullness of their perfection, not subject to the laws of nature and corruption. Unlike the divine dogs of Alcinous, Odysseus' once-keen hunting dog Argus, whom he similarly sees as he approaches his own palace in Book 17, lies on a dungpile aging and dying. As the divine and the aesthetic realms are assimilated in their immutable perfection, the human world in its perishability stands in opposition to both.

Death, of course, represents a negation of heroic values, of the pursuit of glory (κῦδος) and of delight in the physical and social world, as given quintessential expression in Achilles' rejoinder to Odysseus that he would rather be a hired laborer on earth than king of the dead (11.488–91). Yet while the Homeric hero despises death, he recognizes it as the boundary that creates heroic possibilities. The hero chooses to make life not long but meaningful, and finds in his prowess in war and in imperishable fame (κλέος ἄφθιτον) a partial escape from death.[66] Old age becomes despised as marking the beginning of the process whereby the hero loses what he most values, and as the harbinger of death itself. In more traditional cultures the status of the

elderly is enhanced precisely because of their proximity to death and
reunion with sacred beings or ancestral shades: Gutmann suggests
that "besides intersecting with the mythic past, the aged overlap the
spirit world which they will soon enter; and as they blend with that
world they acquire its essential physiognomy and powers."[67] But the
grim afterlife that awaits the Achaean hero devalues, by association,
the aging process.

Schadewaldt observes that nowhere in Homer do the young directly lament the fact of aging or speak of it as a terrible destiny, and he
attributes this to a healthy and natural attitude to old age.[68] However,
just as with the many negative epithets applied to old age, the association of age and death results in their seeming equally dread and unwel-
come. Calypso's offer to make Odysseus "deathless and ageless for all
days" (5.136) is predicated on her assumption that he will find agelessness as well as immortality enticing. She recalls for Odysseus the
horrible destiny of Tithonus, who was granted the latter but not the
former.[69] Sarpedon reminds Glaucus in *Iliad* XII that because they
cannot live together "ageless and deathless" (323), they should fight
in the front ranks and go forth into battle "where men win honor"
(κυδιάνειραν, 325). In the flush of martial success the hero can even
experience himself as godlike and triumph over the doom of old age
and death, as when Hector wishes only that he could be "deathless and
ageless for all days" and honored like Athena and Apollo (VIII.
538–40). The Homeric hero thus aspires to escape old age in two
ways: as the ageless god he would (in Odysseus' case, could) be, or as
the warrior who transcends age, permanently by his noble death or
temporarily by the glory won in battle.

As old age is demeaned by its association with death, so it is
excluded from those opportunities whereby the hero transcends
death. While the word hero (ἥρως) in Homer may not be age-specific,
heroism clearly means youthful heroism, and as its mark is to be the
speaker of words and the doer of deeds (IX.443), the elderly can aspire
to distinction only in the first. The heroic ethos, to which the elderly
themselves subscribe, identifies the fullness of life with heroic vitality
and its public display; an individual life obtains meaning primarily
through the winning of fame and glory (φήμη, κῦδος). But the physical degeneration of old age disqualifies the elderly from the activities
that mark one as a hero and redound to one's glory. The egotistical and
competitive excellences, which are regarded more highly than the

"quiet" ones,[70] and the identification of what is "good" with youth and its activities, leave little room for the old-age values of community and continuity.

As a threshold between life and death, old age is both like and unlike each. Because of the close association of old age and death, the elderly are situated in both states. On the other hand, because they stand between the fullness of heroic existence and its antithesis in Hades, the elderly are in neither state.[71] Hence in the heroic and martial world of the *Iliad*, old age is *merely* a threshold, one that Priam describes as baneful (ὀλοῷ, XXIV.487). In this light we can make sense of the "twin fates" that drive Achilles: the one to imperishable fame (κλέος ἄφθιτον) that involves death, and the other to a homecoming and long life (αἰών . . . δηρόν, IX.413–15) without fame. To the degree that Achilles' destiny entails a choice, it implies not only an affirmation of deathless glory but a rejection of enfeebling old age.[72] Indeed, it is only with the dishonor Agamemnon does him that Achilles calls into question the value of his fame and imagines a long life, married to a local princess and delighting in the inheritance left by "aged Peleus" (IX.400). It is in the same vein that Phoenix, expressing the depth of his loyalty to Achilles, declares that he would not be left behind, "not were the god in person to promise/ he would scale away my old age and make me a young man blossoming / as I was at that time when I first left Hellas, the land of fair women" (IX.445–47: tr. Lattimore). Youth and age are antithetical values, the latter a growth to be "scraped away" (ἀποξύσας) from the smooth and perfect bloom of youth beneath. That Phoenix would prefer an old age with Achilles to the fullness of young manhood without him is a kind of reversal of Achilles' choice, rendered more profound by the contrast between Phoenix's youthful sexuality and the sexual curse called upon him by his father, Amyntor (IX.453–56), which will persist into Phoenix's own childless old age.

It is in war that the status of old age becomes most marginal. This is symbolized on the shield of Achilles: in the city in peace, the elderly sit in judgement over a murder trial (XVIII.503–8), but in the city at war the elders, along with the women and children, anxiously mount battle stations on the wall, itself a kind of threshold between city and battlefield.[73] The image of the threshold applies with particular force to Priam. His authority is nebulous and his kingship largely honorific, with the real decision-making exercised by Hector and the younger heroes. His spatial orientation is similarly liminal: his vantage is from the city wall, while on other occasions he traverses the threshold between Greeks and Trojans, escorted by Hermes psychopompos, underscoring his location between life and death.

It is from the wall that Priam pleads with Hector, rehearsing the destruction Zeus will visit on him "on the threshold of old age" (XXII.60) and on his whole household. Just as Priam will base his supplication of Achilles on an appeal for respect and pity for his old age, so this strategy is rehearsed in the appeal to Hector, which involves a careful and self-conscious manipulation of the rhetoric of old age. We are prepared for this in the immediately preceding references to "old Priam": first at XXI.526, when Priam gives directions to the gate-keepers to help the routed Trojans get inside the city (the only time Priam gives any direct battle instructions, and clearly with his own children in mind); again at XXII.25, when he is the first to see Achilles charging back to the city, his armor flaming like the baneful Dog Star.

Where Hecuba's appeal to Hector is directed entirely at the fate her son will suffer at the hands of Achilles, Priam's focuses on the misery in store for himself. He moves quicky through a number of lesser arguments: Achilles' greater strength; his other sons who have been slain or captured; the importance of Hector's own "dear life," since he alone can save the Trojan people; the glory his death will win for Achilles. Priam then appeals directly for pity for the death and the suffering Zeus will inflict on him on the threshold of old age, describing the horrors he will witness—sons slain, daughters enslaved, treasures plundered, children murdered—and concludes by describing the final indignities he will not see but will suffer nonetheless:

> And myself last of all, my dogs in front of my doorway
> will rip me raw, after some man with stroke of the sharp bronze
> spear, or with spearcast, has torn the life out of my body;
> those dogs I raised in my halls to be at my table, to guard my
> gates, who will lap my blood in the savagery of their anger
> and then lie down in my courts.
>
> (XXII.66–71: tr. Lattimore)

Priam envisions his corpse at the entrance to his palace, savaged and consumed by his own table dogs in a kind of anti-funeral, a hideous extension of the threat to make one's enemy "a feast for birds and dogs." (Earlier Priam wishes the same fate on Achilles at XXII.42–43, and his use of ὠμησταί (raw) at 67 anticipates Hecuba's description of Achilles at XXIV.207). There is a powerful irony in his use of the theme of nurture (τρέφον), refering equally to the raising of animals and of children by their parents, and with it an allusion to the *threptêria* that would not be lost on the reader. In conjuring up the image of his body mangled at the threshold of his own palace by the very dogs he himself had raised, Priam suggests the cruelty and ingratitude of Hector, who disregards the father that raised him and whose behavior threatens his very life. Priam concludes with a horrific appreciation of the aesthetics of death in battle, in which he regards himself neither as king nor even as an individual but in his generic status as old man:

> "For a young man all is decorous
> when he is cut down in battle and torn with the sharp bronze, and
>   lies there
> dead, and though dead all that shows about him is beautiful;
> but when an old man is dead and down, and the dogs mutilate
> the grey head and the parts that are secret,
> this, for all sad mortality, is the sight most pitiful."
>   So the old man spoke, and in his hands seizing the grey hairs
> tore them from his head, but could not move the spirit in Hektor.
>   (XXII.71–78: tr. Lattimore)

Extending the traditional aesthetic that locates the standard of beauty in the youthful form, Priam contrasts the "beauty" of the slain youth, where all is becoming, with the pitiful sight of a dead old man, with his gray hair and beard and genitals mutilated. Later, Homer allows Priam's distinction between the young and the old who have been slain in war a kind of eerie fulfillment in the fate of Hector's corpse, whose beauty cannot be spoiled despite Achilles' best efforts and whom Andromache in her lament over his corpse calls (stretching the word a bit) *neos* (XXIV.725).[74]

Priam's speech has been criticized as incoherent and even hysterical,[75] but it is crucial to his characterization, for it reveals how the effects of war have deprived him not only of his kingly status but also of his very humanity. Priam's reduction and redefinition of himself in this scene is finally signalled, following Hecuba's maternal plea to Hector, with the series of verbs in the dual linking the couple in their common plight as a pair of aged parents:

So these two in tears and with much supplication called out
to their dear son.
(κλαίοντε προσαυδήτην . . . λισσομένω, XXII.90–91: tr. Lattimore).

Priam's desperate words give expression to the anxieties of the elderly
in a community of warriors, and his position on the wall captures
effectively the marginal relation of the elderly to the struggle of the
younger heroes to demonstrate their own *aretê*. The image of his
corpse, unburied and unmourned on the palace threshold, suggests
not only the destiny of the defeated in war but the elderly's sense of
themselves as peripheral.

LAERTES AND THE PROBLEMATIC OF OLD AGE

In the postwar and domesticated world of the *Odyssey*, the prospect of
old age is somewhat brighter—it is only here that the concept of a
"sleek old age" (λιπαρὸν γῆρας) is raised as a possibility—but the tensions between heroism and old age are still very much present. The
suitors behave with a youthful egotism that pays little deference to the
elderly, and their hybris extends beyond the house of Odysseus to the
community at large. In the assembly of Book 2, Aegyptius, Halitherses, and Mentor all offer wise counsel, reminding the suitors of
Odysseus' kingly virtues and warning them of his return. The suitors
ridicule and ignore them, and Eurymachus openly threatens
Halitherses for taking up the part of Telemachus. Just as in the *Iliad*,
the ambivalent attitude toward old age is marked by the overtones of
vocative "old man" (γέρον) as it first appears in the poem: in
Telemachus' deferential response to Halitherses (2.40) and in Eurymachus' contemptuous address to him (2.178, 192, 201).

Common practice is to see in the suitors the violation of "correct"
behavior and an inversion of the "normal" order to be restored, as well
as a contrast with the more respectful attitude of Telemachus and his
age-mate Pisistratus. But one can see in the suitors, whom Odysseus
calls "the best of the young men in Ithaca,"[76] extensions of tendencies
rooted in the nature of heroism itself. Preisshofen characterizes the
suitors as a closed circle of youth, drawing attention to the youthfulness of even their servants (15.330) and their scornful abuse of
Odysseus in his guise as aged beggar.[77] The suitors at any rate espouse
heroic values, and their delight in feasting, song, and athletic competition are within the context of normal heroic practice.

Where the *Odyssey* differs from the *Iliad*, with regard to old age as with so much else, is in reformulating and even redefining the nature of heroism and heroic values. We see this in the *Odyssey's* Nestor, where the ambiguities in his representation are marked more purposefully than in the *Iliad*. Nestor's rhetoric in the *Odyssey* becomes not just lengthy but long-winded, with the situation bordering at moments on the humorous. Nestor treats the newly arrived Telemachus to a pair of speeches, 98 and 74 lines respectively, and is self-conscious about his wordiness: were Telemachus to listen for years to his war stories, he would sooner exhaust himself than the speaker (3.113–17). Athena-Mentor finally must cut short the conversation so they can all go to bed (3.331–36).[78] Although Telemachus' express purpose is to seek news of his father, Nestor's recollections are of inspirational value. But here in Nestor the normally complementary functions of memory and advice are separated, so that he comes to represent only the former and becomes almost a caricature of the wise counselor. His punctilious religiosity and smothering hospitality seem ostentatious, and his rhetoric of the heroic past more like garrulity and self-aggrandizement.

Nestor's continued dominance over his *oikos* may suggest, like his extended service on the battlefield, that he is reluctant to transfer his authority. He continues to rule Pylos and his extended family: sons and sons-in-law, daughters and daughters-in-law, and his "revered wife" Eurydice (3.381, 403, 451). Antilochus has died at Troy, and Pisistratus is apparently the youngest of his six surviving children, a contemporary of Telemachus (3.49), and the only one still unmarried (3.401). Nestor is remarkable for his attention to the details of hospitality and sacrifice; an enormous amount of Book 3 is spent describing his planning, supervision and participation in the sacrifices for Poseidon and Athena. The poem also pays special attention to the character of his rule:

> Then Nestor the Gerenian horseman rose up from his bed,
> and went outside and took his place upon the polished stones
> which were there in place for him in front of the towering doorway,
> white stones, with a shine on them that glistened. On these before him
> Neleus, a counselor like the gods, had held his sessions,
> but he had been beaten down by his doom and gone down to Hades'

house, and now Gerenian Nestor, the Achaians' watcher,
sat there holding his staff, and his sons coming out of their chambers
gathered in a cluster about him, Echephron and Stratios,
Perseus and Aretos and Thrasymedes the godlike,
and sixth was the hero Peisistratos who came to join them.

                                                  (3.405–15: tr. Lattimore)

Nestor holds court among his own family, handing out instructions
for the sacrifice and clearly delighting in the dignity and the tradition
of the setting and its impressive architecture: the venerable patriarch
of a tidy kingdom that is a model of peacefulness, order, and prosperity. In the scene that opens the book, each of the nine cities under his
sway is represented by fifty men and each provides nine bulls for the
sacrifice to Poseidon, the largest sacrifice mentioned in Homer. At the
feast that follows, his sons are arranged around him, and around them
in turn his people. His children are models of dutifulness and obedience, having taken to heart his concern with the formalities of sacrifice and hospitality.

That Nestor should continue to rule when he has married sons
available to succeed him may suggest, like his extended military service in Troy, some reluctance to transfer power, and while there is
nothing to suggest that he is other than an effective ruler, his style of
leadership seems antiquated and almost quaint. Indeed, the poet's
representation of bourgeois Pylos, like that of Menelaus and Helen's
Sparta, seems increasingly obsolete and anachronistic, and functions
in part as a disavowal of Iliadic concepts of the heroic: here are heroes
incapable of sustaining heroic stature after Troy, whose existence
fairly well ends with their *nostos*.[79] There is a decadent quality about
the heroic opulence of both Pylos and Sparta, and while Telemachus
is in awe of both palaces, his journey to these centers of Mycenaean
heroism is in a sense unproductive. It comes as no surprise when he
indicates somewhat awkwardly to Pisistratus in Book 15 that he will
pass up on his father's hospitality in favor of a speedier return to
Ithaca.

The "sleek old age" embodied in Nestor is developed only to be
displaced by a different model. It is Ithaca that defines and exemplifies
the post-heroic world, and it is in "the aged hero Laertes," as he is
introduced to us (1.188–89), that the problematic status of old age is

most fully explored. Laertes functions in two related capacities. In the first, which we might call Iliadic, he provides an illustration of the devaluation of old age, though in terms that go beyond those of the *Iliad*; in the second, he suggests an alternate model of old age more appropriate to the post heroic nature of the poem and its hero. Homer thus finds in him both a statement of the problematic of old age as well as a poetic resolution of it, though in terms that are admittedly compressed and only suggestive rather than clear and detailed. That the *Odyssey*, like the *Iliad*, should conclude in the context of this theme is not accidental. In addition, there are a number of regards in which the material evokes aspects of the Iliadic Nestor and Priam.

In Laertes the image of the threshold is fully developed. Physically he is near death, and events have moved him closer to his end. Anticleia's death, itself caused by grief for Odysseus (11.202–3, cf.15.358), has aged Laertes beyond his years.[80] She tells Odysseus how he longs for his homecoming, with "harsh old age" upon him (11.195–96), and Eumaeus says that with his grief now compounded, Laertes hangs on but prays daily for his release (15.353–55). Telemachus' departure for the mainland has pushed the old man beyond the limit, so that he has ceased to eat, drink, and work, and is literally wasting away (16.142–45). The situation is so urgent that Eumaeus wants to send news of Telemachus' return as soon as possible. Laertes' critical condition is symbolized in the shroud Penelope weaves and unweaves, which suggests the slender thread of his life.

Laertes' liminality is also spatial.[81] He lives on the fringes of Ithaca, and we hear repeatedly, from the initial descriptions of Athena-Mentes on, of his isolation: he no longer comes to the city but suffers apart in the country on the farm of Dolius, withdrawn from the affairs of house and city (1.188–93). Laertes' self-ostracism is in one respect an expression of the marginal nature of his social status. Politically he is a kind of *rex emeritus*, powerless to affect the situation in his son's absence and in his grandson's immaturity, and his withdrawal suggests the impotence of the elderly before the younger and brash heroes. In the underworld Odysseus anxiously questions Anticleia about his father's status: do father and son still hold my rule (using the term γέρας as Achilles does at *Iliad* XX.18 of Priam's rule), or does another man hold it (11.174–76)? We get additional insight into the plight of such old kings in Achilles' interview with Odysseus, where he develops the anxieties implicit in *Iliad* XXIV.488–89:[82]

and tell me anything you have heard about stately Peleus,
whether he still keeps his position (τιμήν) among the Myrmidon
hordes, or whether in Hellas and Phthia they have diminished
his state (ἀτιμάζουσιν), because old age constrains his hands and feet,
        and I
am not the man I used to be once, when in the wide Troad
I killed the best of their people, fighting for the Argives. If only
for a little while I could come like that to the house of my father,
my force and my invincible hands would terrify such men
as use force on him and keep him away from his rightful honor (τιμῆς).
                                                    (11.494–503: tr. Lattimore)

Achilles uses the word τιμή to refer to the kingship itself (as he does at
Iliad XX.181 in taunting Aeneas about the Trojan succession) and
implies that without a youthful advocate the status of the elderly finds
little protection from the force (cf. βιόωνται, 503) of the young.
Laertes' retirement likewise suggests his helplessness and dishonor
before the violence of the suitors. When Penelope hears of the suitors'
plot against Telemachus, she frantically suggests summoning Laertes
to prevail upon the people of Ithaca to stop them. But Eurycleia counsels her "not to afflict the afflicted old man" (4.754), a comment surely
not only on his misery but on his ineffectuality.

      In Laertes' physical condition we see another expression of the
pathos of age and of the inner despair that can result. We learn from
Anticleia of the squalor of his clothes and living conditions, how he
sleeps in winter with the slaves in the ashes by the hearth and in summer on piles of leaves throughout the orchard (11.187–96). When
Odysseus first catches sight of his father he is the image of abject old
age: he is filthy, with a patchwork cloak, stitched greaves, work gloves,
and a goatskin cap. The poet indicates how Odysseus reads his appearance: as an expression of oppressive old age and the grief he suffers for
his son: he is "worn with old age, and with great sorrow in his heart"
(24.233). But Homer also implies that to some extent Laertes deliberately wallows in his grief: we are told of the servant woman's kindly
care for him (κομέεσκεν, 24.212), and how with his dress Laertes
deliberately feeds his own sorrow (24.231, cf. 11.195).[83]

      Odysseus declares to Telemachus his intention to "test"
(πειρήσομαι, 24.216) his father to see if he will recognize him in spite

of his long absence. As such, this trial will involve not only his father's powers of perception but the degree to which Odysseus himself has changed. As Penelope ironically told the beggar, Odysseus had surely aged with time and hardship and come to look like him: "for mortals grow old quickly in misfortune" (αἶψα γὰρ ἐν κακότητι βροτοὶ καταγηράσκουσιν, 19.360). Although Odysseus has heard repeatedly of his father's situation, he is so stricken by his appearance that he first hides and weeps under a pear tree. "But then" (235) he overcomes the urge to rush up and embrace his father and decides "first to question him and make trial of him in each thing" (πρῶτ᾽ ἐξερέοιτο ἕκαστά τε πειρήσαιτο, 238). He proceeds to test Laertes' recognition by asking why he chooses to live as he does.[84]

Critics have spent much ingenuity on this apparently purpose-less decision to "test with teasing words" (κερτομίοις ἐπέεσσιν πειρηθῆναι, 240),[85] and on Odysseus' assuming one more time the ruse of disguise, fictitious name and biography, and cautious inter-view: that it derives from an earlier version in which disguise was nec-essary; that it dramatically builds suspense; that we have here the "Autolycan" Odysseus with his insuppressable instinct for deception; even that Odysseus' intent is therapeutic, to prevent the shock of too sudden a recognition.[86] Although none of these proposals is entirely convincing, we can usefully distinguish the need for a recognition scene in this particular situation from what is accomplished themati-cally by the form it takes.[87] Here I would emphasize in particular the symbolic value of the orchard and Laertes' work in it.

Odysseus first upbraids his father for his condition: Laertes lavish-es the finest care (κομιδή) upon the orchard but no such care upon himself.[88]

> But I will also tell you this: do not take it as cause for
> anger. You yourself are ill cared for (οὐκ ἀγαθὴ κομιδή); together with dismal
> old age, which is yours, you are squalid and wear foul clothing upon you.
> It is not for your laziness that your lord does not take care of you (κομίζει), nor is
> your stature and beauty, as I see it, such as
> ought to belong to a slave. You look like a man who is royal.
>   (24.248–53: tr. Lattimore)

Despite his kingly demeanor, Laertes dresses like a slave. Laertes' neglect is to be seen in its social aspects and in relation to heroic culture. Although the suitors make no mention of Laertes, whose substance they consume along with that of Odysseus, the ongoing contrast between their feasting and his deprivation serves to implicate them (Laertes implies as much to Odysseus at 24.282; cf. 352). His condition also illustrates the situation of those in old age who are bereft of their children and denied the parent-support on which their well-being depends. In this light, the heroic ethic complicates the social situation, as is implicit in Odysseus' instructions to Penelope before his departure that she assume responsibility for his father, mother and son in the event that he does not return from Troy (18.266–70). As the hero risks his life in the pursuit of booty and fame, he also risks depriving his parents of the support he owes them—as we have seen, the two references to this institution in Homer describe slain warriors who could not properly repay their parents. Homer highlights the problem by giving us a family with a single line of descent (cf. 16.117–21), making the situation of the elderly even more precarious. Laertes' self-imposed servility and premature assumption of this condition graphically suggest the destiny of those who lack a *gērokomos*.

Odysseus' references to the theme of caretaking show that he understands the kind of life that is owed to his father and his own responsibilites in this regard, and in what follows he provides a virtual inventory of the *threptēria*. Laertes looks like

> such a one as who, after he has bathed and eaten,
> should sleep on a soft bed; for such is the right of the elders (ἡ γὰρ
> δίκη ἐστὶ γερόντων).
>
> (24.254–55: tr. Lattimore)

Laertes' labor in the orchard may reflect his anxiety about his physical survival, about where, so to speak, his next meal is coming from. The *Odyssey* places considerable emphasis on the material condition of old age, in keeping with the post-heroic world of the poem and its frequent attention to the needs of the "belly" (γαστήρ). The language with which Odysseus describes his definition of filial care—as the right of the elders (ἡ γὰρ δίκη ἐστὶ γερόντων)—sustains this perspective. In characterizing the needs of the elderly as something to which they have a right as opposed to something they are simply given, Odysseus echoes the related formula in the *Iliad* with which Nestor claims the right to "word and counsel" as the privilege of the elders (γέρας . . . γερόντων, IV.322–23). In the domesticated world of the *Odyssey*, the elderly make no such claim; the prerogative of aged wise counsel yields to their right for proper care, concerns perhaps too mundane for heroic epic. With his return, Odysseus assumes his responsibilities as Laertes' caretaker, arranging a feast and having the Sicilian servant woman bathe and clothe him. The restorative powers of these actions are symbolized in the immediate change they work on his appearance and in Athena's enhancement of his stature (365–74). Where the *Iliad* reveals the disruption of war by fracturing this vital relationship between father and son, the *Odyssey* completes the restitution of domestic order with Odysseus' rendering the *threptêria* to his father, thus providing a series of counterimages of filial foresight and heroic responsibility. But in assuming their proper roles as provider and recipient, father and son do more than reestablish order in the *oikos*. They also call into question the values that at once thrust the elderly into dependency and make demands of the young that undermine their responsibilities

We see the same critical perspective in the way that the prolonged absence or death of the hero complicates patterns of inheritance. This situation is sketched in the *Iliad* in brief descriptions like that of Phaenops, who loses his sons to war and his estate to his kinsmen (V.152–58). In the *Odyssey* the situation is intensified by the fragile line of descent and the limbo in which Telemachus finds himself. Odysseus' absence effectively freezes the status of the estates: Telemachus cannot protect them because he has not inherited them. But this crisis involves Laertes as well, whose concern is reflected in his preoccupation with the orchard—the outward sign of the inheritance and the continuity of the *oikos*.[89] He works and sleeps among its trees and labors to keep them healthy. In the end, Odysseus identifies himself by rehearsing his childhood inheritance: thirteen pear trees, ten apple trees, forty fig trees, and fifty vines. He established his sonship once in asking for the trees as a boy, and reaffirms it here in maintaining his claim to his patrimony.[90] The proper transfer of the estate is of crucial importance to the elderly, and Laertes' anxiety over its security is another dimension of the situation in which the fathers of heroes find themselves.

But particularly important is the way Laertes responds to the deprivations of old age by returning to the orchard, as well as the agricultural subtext beneath the pathos of the scene's exterior. Where the modern tendency is to see Laertes' cultivation of the orchard as servile or menial or as a "puttering in the garden," the text makes it clear that the case is precisely the opposite, making explicit the distinction between Laertes' pathetic personal condition (which Odysseus criticizes) and the impressiveness of his labor, which his son commends. Of Laertes' farm we hear that it was beautiful, extensive, well-wrought, and that he had toiled much to found it (24.205–7; cf. 23.214, 221, 226); these are perhaps the same "far-off rich fields" that Eurycleia speaks of at 4.757. It seems likely that not long after planting the orchard Laertes showed it to his young son and gave him various trees to call his own. Odysseus begins his "trial" of Laertes with a tribute:

> Old sir, there is in you no lack of expertness in tending
> your orchard; everything is well cared for (κομιδή), and there is
>   never
> a plant, neither fig tree nor yet grapevine nor olive
> nor pear tree nor leek bed uncared for (κομιδῆς) in your garden.
>   (24.244–47: tr. Lattimore)

Odysseus recognizes the achievement that the orchard represents, and commends his father for the care he has lavished on it. The significance of the orchard as a token (σῆμα) of recognition thus lies not only in its physical content but in Odysseus' reaffirmation of shared experience and interest. He appreciates the orchard for the labor it represents and identifies himself by recalling not only his holdings but their quality, noting of the vines that "each of them bore regularly, for there were/ grapes at every stage upon them, whenever the seasons/ of Zeus came down from the sky upon them, to make them heavy" (342–44: tr. Lattimore).

The orchard of Laertes resonates richly in comparison and contrast with the lush orchards of Alcinous (7.112–25). There too in four acres grow trees of pear, pomegranate, apple, fig, olive, and vine, but without any reference to the toil it took to plant them or the labor that sustains them. The orchard of Alcinous is always in bloom, nourished throughout the year by the gentle west wind. Like the "immortal and ageless" dogs of precious metal that guard his palace (7.94), these trees escape the vicissitudes of human existence, as pear ages (γηράσκει) on pear, apple on apple (7.120). The trees Laertes tends produce seasonally, however, and he has assimilated his life to theirs, sleeping indoors in winter and among them in summer. Both orchards stand as images of perfection: Laertes' won by human labor and the other the gift of the gods.

There is within the heroic line of Laertes a rich agricultural tradition, one characterized specifically as an alternative to heroic warfare.[91] It is represented in the legend in which Odysseus, to avoid conscription for the Trojan war, feigns madness with a demonstration of agricultural ineptitude, plowing his fields with yoke of horse and ox. Odysseus' behavior makes particular sense if it is seen as prompted not by a prophecy of future hardships (as Hyginus suggests) but by a preference for farming over battle and booty.[92] In the *Odyssey* the theme is explicit in the hero's challenge to Eurymachus to match him in any of three contests: mowing hay, plowing with oxen, or combat with spear and shield.[93] It is reflected in the recognition scene with Penelope in Odysseus' reference to the olive tree, a symbol of agricultural stability and of the rootedness of the line of Odysseus in the earth itself.

Throughout the poem Odysseus shows a keen eye for agricultural detail. He appraises the agricultural potential of the island of the Cyclopes (9.131–35) and stops to admire the orchards of Alcinous. He describes his relationship with his men with an agricultural metaphor (10.410–14) and is himself so described (5.488–91). He encourages Eumaeus to estimate his real worth by describing his present condition as the stubble left by good corn (14.211–15). It is no accident that when Odysseus likens Penelope's fame to that of a good king, he says that by the king's leadership "the black earth yields him/ barley and wheat, his trees are heavy with fruit, his sheepflocks/ continue to bear young, the sea gives him fish" (19.111–13: tr. Lattimore).[94] When Athena describes to him the virtues of Ithaca, she does so in terms of its agricultural abundance (13.244–47). Indeed, this entire *oikos* is characterized by unusually close relations with its farmers and herders: the *Odyssey* describes with uncommon detail the farms of Eumaeus, the extent of Odysseus' holdings (14.95–104), and even the volume of dung with which his servants manured his τέμενος (17.297–99). We shall see below the extension of this theme in Odysseus' inland journey.

Laertes' retreat to the agricultural interests in which he raised his son represents neither escapism nor self-abasement. Closer to the truth is the interpretation Cicero suggests in the *De Senectute*, where Cato describes the rewards to be found by the elderly in agriculture, declaring them superior to those of warfare and athletics (58). Clearly recalling the description of Laertes at the moment when Odysseus came upon him spading a plant (λιστρεύοντα φυτόν, 227; cf. φυτὸν ἀμφελάχαινε, 242), Cicero sees in the situation an illustration of the "advantages of fertilization" (*utilitate . . . stercorandi*) and the therapeutic value of farming: "but Homer . . . presents Laertes as easing his grief for his son by tending his field and fertilizing it with manure [*stercorantem*]" (54). Although Laertes is not specifically said to be manuring his farm when Odysseus finds him, Cicero suggests through the reference to dung (*stercus*) the regenerative nature of the soil.[95] Cicero appreciates the cyclical nature of farming, and suggests that Laertes finds an outlet for his grief in the pattern of birth, growth, and decay.

A comparison with the *Iliad* in this regard is instructive. There we read repeatedly of the dung (κόπρος) in which Priam grovels in his grief for Hector (XXII.414; XXIV.164, 640), and again of the dung (ὄνθος) in which Aias slips during the footrace (XXIII.773–81). Where in the *Iliad* this material suggests filth, disgrace, and failure, in the *Odyssey* it is associated with its agricultural and regenerative uses. Odysseus notes the dung heaped up in the cave of the Cyclops (9.329–30), and his dog Argus lies on the mounds of dung (κόπρῳ, 17.297, 306) used to manure (κοπρήσοντες, 299) Odysseus' fields. Kirk aptly suggests a parallel between the neglect Argus suffers from the servant women and the neglect of Laertes, who lacks his protector.[96] But a difference is also established between the animal world, which must dumbly wait and accept such suffering, and the human consciousness, which can transform its pain into knowledge and even life. Hence when Laertes receives the "news" of Odysseus' death, and pours the dark soil over his gray hair (24.316–17), his disfigurement, unlike Priam's, is with the very earth that he tills.

The Laertes episode draws our attention to this alternative to heroic warfare which, while less public and competitive, is no less impressive and ennobling.[97] In his immersion in the orchard, Laertes finds an occupation which is, while in one sense passive, also productive and spiritual. In the primary rituals of planting and tending he reasserts the connection between human life and the rhythms of nature. Work with the soil locates a person closer to it and engenders a literal humility: when Odysseus comes upon Laertes, he is working "with face bent down" (24.242). As cultivator, Laertes becomes a mediator between the divine and the human worlds, and the instrument by which the gods, "the bestowers of blessings" (8.325), express themselves in the fruitful and life-sustaining earth. The "passive mastery" displayed by Laertes in his tending of the orchard suggests the virtues characteristic of many traditional cultures in which the elderly continue to contribute to the community: in the ethnographic survey noted above, Simmons concludes that it is in cultures of farmers and herders that opportunities for the elderly are greatest, and documents their enhanced condition in agricultural environments in virtually every category.[98]

Like his son, Laertes is experienced with both ploughshare and sword, is at once warrior and farmer, destroyer and nurturer, a distributor of wealth and a producer of it. Alongside the references to Laertes' agricultural achievements is that to his shield, a symbol of his youthful heroism, now hidden in the palace armory:

> . . . the ancient shield (σάκος εὐρὺ γέρον), all fouled with mildew,
> of the hero Laertes, which he had carried when he was a young man.
> It had been lying there, and the stitches were gone on the handstraps
> (22.184–86: tr. Lattimore).

The description of Laertes' shield as old (γέρον)—the only time in Homer that adjective is used of a thing rather than a person—associates it with its owner's former glories and recalls perhaps the shield of Nestor, whose glory reaches the heavens (VII.192–93). Like the dusty shield, which does not get to participate in the slaughter of the suitors, Laertes' heroic abilities are hidden from sight.

After Laertes' bath, "Athena / standing close beside the shepherd of the people magnified / his limbs" (368–69; tr. Lattimore). By using the same formula that had earlier been applied to Odysseus at 18.69–70, where the verb "make to grow" (ἀλδαίνω) again suggests not literal rejuvenation but restoration and enhancement, the poet suggests in this description the heroic potential Laertes retains. Laertes' heroic aspirations are reflected in his wish that he had been present to help in the slaughter of the suitors, "as I was when I ruled the Cephallenians and took Nericus" (376–82: tr. Lattimore), and then fulfilled in the skirmish with the fathers of the suitors, which is sketched throughout in terms of the conventional *aristeia*. Both sides of the battle arm themselves according to an Iliadic formula (24.467 = 500 = XV.383). Athena takes human form, stands by Laertes' side, and breathes might (μένος) into him (516–20). He prays to her, brandishes his spear, and drives it through Eupeithes' helmet (521–24). His death is described with the formula used six times in the *Iliad* (525). The scene is throughout in Iliadic terms and the point of the passage is clear: in spite of his age Laertes retains heroic ability.

The Laertes episode as a whole serves to locate in him a bridge between conventional heroism and the broader values of post-heroic Ithaca. By combining in Laertes both agricultural and heroic achievement, the poem effects a kind of reconciliation between differing sets of values, between the world that Odysseus leaves behind and that which he enters. In Laertes' hour of martial glory and in his deep relationship with the earth and its fruits, heroism is redefined more broadly and the "sleek old age" is enhanced by a model more appropriate to the post-heroic world the poem ushers in.

ODYSSEUS ÔMOGERÔN

The hero of the *Odyssey* represents not the youth of an Achilles but maturity; he is one of the heroes in what we would call "middle age" and closer in generation to Agamemnon. In *Iliad* XIX he counsels Achilles, impatient to return to battle after the death of Patroclus, reminding him that he is older and "knows more" (219). In Book XXIII Antilochus, after losing the footrace to both Ajax and Odysseus, complains good-naturedly that the gods are now honoring the "older men" (788). Odysseus, he observes, is "of the earlier generation of older men," in a "raw" or early old age (ὠμογέροντα),[99] but still a formidable runner, second only to Achilles (XXIII.790–92). Antilochus' comment is not without its edge. Odysseus' victory is credited to divine interference, yet even with such help he could not defeat Achilles, who now in the games—as earlier by his ships—sits above and beyond the struggles in time and space before him. The *Odyssey*, not surprisingly, characterizes Odysseus' vigor otherwise. In the Phaeacian games, when Laodamas wonders about the stranger's athletic abilities, he observes that Odysseus clearly does not lack "the strength of youth" (ἥβης, 8.137–38).

While age figures deeply in the dynamic between the two heroes, the difference is not so much of age per se as of their larger relationship to time. In applying the *hapax legomenon* of "in early old age" (ὠμογέρων) to Odysseus, the *Iliad* prefigures Odysseus as hero-in-process and suggests the particular nature of his temporality. Odysseus' goal is not only the winning of glory but the winning of home; his heroism is revealed not in death but in survival and in his polytropic ability to adapt himself to different worlds and changing circumstances. Where the Achillean hero reveals a disdain for old age and seems at times to transcend the temporality of existence, the *Odyssey* presents a hero embedded in the world of time for whom the prospect of old age, as we shall see, is an attractive one. In presenting a hero whose story transgresses the temporal boundaries of the poem, the poem's form suggests the fullness of the hero's temporality.

The *Odyssey* declares the superiority of its temporal perspective by arranging a concession speech from Achilles. Nagy and others have observed how implicit in Odysseus' interview with Achilles in the underworld is the latter's admission that he would in retrospect trade fame for a homecoming (11.488–91) or, to put it differently, that he would be willing to trade the kind of fame he sought (which required death) for the kind that Odysseus has won by means of trickery (cf. 9.19–20).[100] In making this claim Achilles, as one who had himself once foresaken "long life" (IX.415), implicitly acknowledges the value of long life as it will ultimately be won by Odysseus. One cannot but wonder if the terms on which Achilles would now be willing to live ("to serve as a serf, a day-laborer for another," 11.489) are significant not only as a statement of class—he would accept the quality of life Odysseus will assume in disguise—but as a recognition of agricultural as well as more conventional heroic values.

Odysseus' ultimate survival is prophesied by Tiresias, but complicated by the inland journey that is demanded of him. On the completion of this, the hero's future is secured: a "sleek old age," a prosperous people, a gentle death away from the sea.[101]

> Death will come to you from the sea, in
> some altogether unwarlike way, and it will end you
> in the ebbing time of a sleek old age. Your people
> about you will be prosperous.

θάνατος δέ τοι ἐξ ἁλὸς αὐτῷ
ἀβληχρὸς μάλα τοῖος ἐλεύσεται, ὅς κέ σε πέφνῃ
γήρᾳ ὕπο λιπαρῷ ἀρημένον· ἀμφὶ δὲ λαοὶ
ὄλβιοι ἔσσονται.
(11.134–37; cf. 23.281–84: tr. Lattimore, with changes)[102]

The kind of old age Tiresias foretells is the literal fulfillment of Odysseus' hopes and prayers. In Book 19, Eurycleia apostrophizes her ill-fated (though present) master, complaining that no one had ever sacrificed so abundantly to Zeus that he might reach a "sleek old age" and raise his excellent son (19.365–68). The idea is foreshadowed ironically in Book 1 when Telemachus doubts his paternity and wishes instead he were the son of "some fortunate man, whom old age overtook among his possessions" (217–18). Odysseus' anticipation of long life is shared by his whole household—even Eumaeus imagines the happiness that would have been his had his master grown old at home (14.67)—and when the hero declines Calypso's offer to make him "deathless and ageless," he also accepts old age, setting him off from the Achillean hero for whom such a prospect is a matter of indifference.

The theme of the hero's old age comes into prominence at the end of the poem, only lines before its Alexandrian ending. At the moment of her recognition, Penelope complains to Odysseus of how the gods begrudged them the opportunity to enjoy their youth together and "come to the threshold of old age" (23.212). Odysseus and Penelope weep and embrace each other for hours, as Athena delays the dawn, and he finally mentions to her the "immeasurable suffering" (23.249) Tiresias has prophesied. The hero is clearly preoccupied with the suffering in store for him, as if only now appreciating the weight of the prophecy he had received without comment or complaint, and not wishing to dampen Penelope's joy, only reluctantly tells her of the inland journey and the destiny revealed by Tiresias. In her last words in the poem, Penelope consoles Odysseus and helps him work through the prophecy by emphasizing its second half and the happiness it foretells: if indeed the gods are bringing to pass a "better old age" (γῆρας . . . ἄρειον), one that will be better than the years of hardship that preceded it (almost a gloss upon λιπαρὸν γῆρας)—then clearly there is hope for an escape from the troubles that he still must face (23.286–87).

That Tiresias' words point beyond the poem to Odysseus' old age and death is determined not by a history that exists for the hero outside the poem in cult or in the epic cycle, but by the kind of hero Homer constructs and the nature of his relation to time. The *Odyssey* eschews the comfortable closure of its folktale prototype in favor of a narrative whose trajectory is outside the poem's time frame.[103] To the extent that the "real" closure of the narrative will coincide with the fulfillment of desire, such closure here is both secured and postponed. This hero will not only live into old age, but what happiness he is to have will be in old age.

While the shining old age of Odysseus is outside the poem's narrative boundaries, we catch a glimpse of it in the suggestive treatment of Laertes, which effects a certain closure on the stories of both father and son. This reading is suggested by the fact that in his pathetic condition Laertes resembles only one other character in the poem—Odysseus himself—who as a beggar is humbled in class and in age. Athena dresses him in rags, makes him bald, and gives him the wrinkled skin of an aged old man (παλαιοῦ . . . γέροντος, 13.432), and in his disguise Odysseus is referred to frequently (and sometimes simply) as *gerôn*.[104] The condition of the aged resembles that of beggars in their neglect and helplessness (as in the formula πτωχῷ λευγαλέῳ ἐναλίγκιον ἠδὲ γέροντι, 16.273 = 17.202 = 24.157) and it is significant that as aged beggar Odysseus takes up his position on the threshold to the palace (17.339, 413, 466; 18.17, 33; 20.258). Odysseus experiences heroic society's two-fold degradation of poverty and old age, concepts Penelope links in her ironic remark to the beggar that one ages prematurely in misfortune (19.360).

The poet links Laertes and Odysseus in a number of ways. Laertes' bath by the Sicilian maidservant recalls the bath Eurynome gives Odysseus before his recognition by Penelope. Athena's enhancement of Laertes employs the same formula used when Odysseus is about to box with Irus and the bystanders marvel at his build (18.69–70 = 24.268-69). The two share the title "shepherd of the people" (ποιμὴν λαῶν, 18.70, 20.106, 24.368). In his brief *aristeia*, Laertes becomes the protégé of Athena, who stands by him in human form as she has so often his son. The routing of their opponents is a reprise of the slaying of the suitors, with Laertes killing Eupeithes, the father of Antinous, with his first spear, as Odysseus had felled the son with his first arrow.

The settling of the quarrel with the suitors' families marks the end of not only the present hostilities but in effect the Trojan cycle of legend. In the Laertes episode we have a fusion of the warrior and the farmer, which redefines the "sleek old age" and links the heroic and post-heroic worlds. The agricultural tradition in the house of Laertes makes it particularly qualified to survive in such a world, and has produced in Odysseus a hero who can be rehabilitated for it: one whose experience has been with his orchards and his herdsmen, who is as ready to compete with the plow as the sword and who has experienced firsthand the vicissitudes of old age. The inland journey represents Odysseus' passage into such a world. His movement away from the sea represents an end to his wanderings and heroic adventures, just as the sacrifice he will render to Poseidon suggests the extension of his cult into new territory and the hero's appeasement of his heretofore implacable enemy. But Tiresias provides in the "clear sign" (σῆμα . . . ἀριφραδές, 11.126) another dimension of the transitional nature of Odysseus' journey:

> When, as you walk, some other wayfarer happens to meet you,
> and says you carry a winnow-fan (ἀθηρηλοιγόν) on your bright shoulder,
> then you must plant your well-shaped oar in the ground, and render
> ceremonious sacrifice to the lord Poseidon
>
> (11.127–28: tr. Lattimore).

Critics have observed that the motif of the mistaken oar is central to the prophecy, but have not appreciated its particular verbal content and unique application to Odysseus.[105] With this *hapax legomenon* from the agricultural world—ἀθηρηλοιγός, "destroyer of wheat chaff"—the chance passerby will signal not only that Odysseus has left the arena of his *nostos* but the character of what will take its place. The clarity of the sign resides both in its obscurity and its familiarity, not only in the coincidence of the traveler saying it but also in Odysseus understanding it, so that it is as much a clue about the hero as to him. That the oar, symbol of the hero's adventures, should be transformed into a winnowing fan and planted into the earth, like the olive tree of his bed or the trees of Laertes' orchard, symbolizes Odysseus' resumption of his agricultural interests. As in the earlier recognition scenes the signs of olive tree and orchard identified the hero to others, so here the prophecy of Tiresias presents a sequel in which the hero will recognize himself. The perception of his oar as a winnowing fan signals the role transition from hero to farmer and to the sleek old age he has been promised: an unheroic death away from the sea amid the prosperity of his people. The inland journey thus becomes a final farewell to the heroic age and a passage to the peaceable kingdom.

The Laertes episode functions as the thematic and structural counterpart to the *Telemachia*.[106] Each develops a figure in transition: Telemachus in his passage into manhood and the heroic world, and Laertes—as exemplary of old age as a whole—in his passage away from conventional heroic norms. But in the *Laertia*, if we can call it that, the poet more insistently calls into question the heroic and martial perspective, by revealing the devaluation of old age it entails and by providing a model of old age both inside and outside the conventional heroic world. In this portrait of the hero as an old man, the poet provides a paradigm that applies to Odysseus as well, for whom the prospect of old age is of particular concern. If there is some unevenness in the sequence, we can appreciate the poet's difficulty in balancing his traditional materials and the untraditional ends to which he puts them. "Longinus" likened the poet of the *Odyssey* to the setting sun, which retains its grandeur without its intensity. But what he (and others since) ascribed to a decline in the poet's powers[107] is better understood as a change in the epic world itself: it is not Homer who has changed but the world he describes. Where "Longinus" was right was in recognizing that the genius shines through regardless: "I am speaking of old age," he tells us, "but nonetheless the old age of a Homer."

Slouching Towards Boeotia: Age and Age-Grading in the Hesiodic Myth of the Five Races

> . . . myth has the task of giving an historical intention a natural justi-
> fication, and making contingency appear eternal.
> —Roland Barthes, *Mythologies*

THE single most sustained discussion in Greek epic of the relation of old age to the life course as a whole is to be found in what might seem an unlikely place: Hesiod's "myth of the five races" (*WD*106–201).[1] Scholarly discussion of the sequence has focused primarily on its structure and on the relation between the text as we have it and the tradition in which which the poet worked. There is no need to rehearse here in detail the various accounts—most prominently those of Walcot, West, and Vernant—which have identified the structure, coherence, and history of the text in such different ways.[2] If one truth has emerged from these closely argued treatments of the text, it is that we will do well to speak not of *the* structure of the sequence but of a number of structures that coexist, peacefully or otherwise, with each other, and that to some extent the artistry of the sequence is a product of the various directions in which the text is pulled.

An appreciation of the function of age in the sequence serves not so much to argue against other structurings of the text as to call attention to a dimension of its structure that has not been appreciated, one that serves to complicate and enrich the text and account for some of its problematic aspects. The myth of the five races employs concepts of age as a system of description and evaluation, and the manipulation of these concepts reflects the way in which Hesiodic thought and Boeotian society, in so far as Hesiod represents it, construct age. The characterization of the five races involves a distinctive appreciation of the human life course and a culturally defined view of the nature and significance of its age-grades. The following argument involves three parts: first, a description of the Hesiodic model of the life course as a schema that informs the sequence and that is consistent with other principles of organization in the *Works and Days*; then an appreciation of the relative value of the various life stages as these are implicit in Hesiod's work as a whole; and finally a detailed examination of how this model works to define the movement of the sequence and the interrelationship of the races, with particular attention to the implications of its representation of old age.

Several commentators have observed a relationship among the various references to old age in the sequence,[3] from the Golden race which did not know wretched old age (οὐδέ τι δειλὸν/γῆρας ἐπῆν, 113–14), to the Iron race whose demise will be imminent "in the time when children, as they are born, grow gray on the temples" (εὖτ' ἂν γεινόμενοι πολιοκρόταφοι τελέθωσιν, 181: tr. Lattimore), and have related this to Hesiod's grim perspective on his own times. Yet the attention to old age is just one aspect of a larger pattern in which aspects of age help give shape to the sequence. The Golden race, like other "prelapsarian" visions, provides an image of perfection that is culturally produced and that, as we shall see, is itself age-specific in its terms.[4] The following four races, which explore a series of less than ideal social orders, do so in terms that image the human life course, with the progress of the races suggesting respectively the four basic and successive life stages: childhood, youth, maturity, and old age (with of course significant differences between the Hesiodic and our sense of these terms). In this schema, with the four expressions of social imperfection corresponding to the stages of individual human life, Hesiod provides us with a curious model in which, in contradistinction to the biological dictum, it is phylogeny that recapitulates ontogeny, that is, the history of the race (or more properly *races*, since for Hesiod each is a distinct race or γένος) resumes that of the individual. Hesiod marks the correspondences in a variety of ways, but it will be clear at once that in respect to the conceptualization of the human life course, neither of the last two races is in any sense "anomalous" or forced: each rather is essential to a complete sequence.

As a cognitive and a symbolic system that gives order to social reality, age concepts, like those of gender and kinship, frequently serve as material symbols of abstract qualities and values—strength and weakness, wisdom and foolishness, autonomy and dependence, and so forth—and are easily extended to phenomena that have no essential

relation to age. Apart from its general importance as a system of differentiation, there are other factors that make this model particularly
suitable for Hesiod's purposes, particularly its representation of time.
A life-course model, while it is temporal, is not chronological or historical, for the stages of human life are distinguished not only by their
ranking but also by their quality: youth does not simply come before
maturity, but is of a different order of experience.[5] The life-span model
represents a sense of time that is primarily cyclic (consider our concept of a "life cycle"), and as early as in Homer's simile of the leaves (*Il.*
6.146–49), we find conceptions of the individual human life by analogy with the vegetal cycle. As such, a life-course model is consistent
with the other natural models of time available to the mythological
and poetic tradition: the circle of the seasons, the movement of the
planets, the patterns of birth, growth, and decay in the animal or veg-
etable world. Like these, the human life course naturalizes cultural
markers of time by assimilating them to physical processes. As such, it
is the proper model in such a poem as the *Works and Days*, which is
informed by Hesiod's attunement to the life of the farmer and his relation to the natural environment.

As categories of age also necessarily involve not only description
but evaluation, Hesiod's use of a life-course model is also prompted by
its moral possibilities and particularly its ability to represent the ambiguity and depravity of his own time (his personal experience of which
provides the occasion for the poem). In this respect the life-course
model functions differently from a strictly degenerative one. In the latter, what is prior is superior to what follows, as suggested—at least
superficially—by the decreasing value of the four metals. But in the
life-course model the nature and the relative merits of the races are
also derived from the cultural perception of the various age-grades,
and the value assigned each race is determined by how the culture
may be expected to perceive the corresponding period of life and how
the poet in turn shapes that perception. The myth of the five races naturalizes the cultural organization and evaluation of biological life, in
keeping with a poem that accomodates the patterns of social life to
those of the natural world, so that both are ὡραῖα and ἐν καιρῷ, where
and when they "belong."

Although the character of the age-grades as Hesiod employs them
will become clearer as we work through the sequence, we may comment first on their organization and expression elsewhere in Hesiod.

The Greeks, indeed, never developed a single uniform conception of the age-grades, whether in their number or names or qualities, with the result that Greek thought reveals considerable variety in the language of its age classifications.[6] Moreover, chronology per se plays only a small role in Hesiod's understanding of the life-stages, and references to chronological age are approximations to be understood in relation to other more significant principles of division.[7] As a result the structure of the age system must be inferred not only from the linguistic categories Hesiod provides, but also from the distinctions embedded in his discussion of social life.

Since Hesiod's poem is addressed to the agricultural and economic realities of Boeotian life, the construction of the life course he offers finds its corollary in the requirements of that life and is structured in accordance with changing social roles, skills, and responsibilities. The conceptualization of the male life course Hesiod presents in the *Works and Days*, one that is frequently employed in Greek thought and reflected elsewhere in the Hesiodic corpus, effectively distinguishes four age-grades.[8] That of the child (*pais*) describes male life until the arrival of sexual maturity, and in Hesiod as elsewhere in Greek thought, childhood is conceived of primarily as propaideutic to manhood in general.[9] The boundary between the stage of the child and manhood will be signalled biologically by the achievement of puberty or "youth" (*hêbê*),[10] but the passage will also coincide with changes in one's relationship to the *oikos* and incorporation into the labor force that sustains it; Finley does well to note that in the economies of peasants and craftsmen, childhood ends for all intents and purposes with the assumption of work or apprenticeship, perhaps several years earlier than puberty.[11] Such an order seems particularly likely in the context of Boeotian agricultural life and the need to engage the full energies of the *oikos* (cf. WD 379–80).

Within the age grade of manhood in general Hesiod suggests a distinction between young manhood (the *neos* or *neôteros* or *kouroteros anêr*) and the mature man, although here as elsewhere in Greek thought the distinction is marked somewhat informally and with some linguistic confusion: there is no term for "maturity" as a stage of life that corresponds to our own, and *anêr* does not in and of itself signify an older as opposed to a younger man.[12] The stage of the *neos* clearly begins with the "measure of youth" (ἥβης μέτρον, WD132),[13] but the passage from young manhood to maturity will be marked not by any clear biological differentiation but by various social markers: marriage and the begetting of children, and the assumption of authority over the *oikos*. Hesiod says that a man is ripe (ὥριος) for marriage at about age thirty (695–97), and in a generational pattern of thirty years the father's transferral of authority to son (when it has not already taken place) might occur at about age sixty. In the absence of any institutionalized concept of retirement, such a transfer of authority, accompanied necessarily by some diminution in one's productive capacities, will provide a functional marker of the passage from the stage of the mature *anêr* to that of the *gerôn*, one which roughly coincides with other chronologically based markers of old age in Greek historical contexts: in Athens age thirty made a man eligible for the *Boulê*, and his fifty-ninth birthday marked the end of his liability for military duty; a Spartan male lived in military quarters until age thirty, at which point he took up residence with his family and was eligible to become an ephor, and at sixty ended his military service and became eligible for election to the *Gerousia*.[14]

Even at a greater level of abstraction, the organization of male life as Hesiod understands it shares a number of significant features with traditional models of the life course. In the latter, the passage to manhood and arrival of puberty are regularly marked by elaborate *rites de passage,* which have some limited parallels in Greek culture.[15] Equally important is the distinction between the categories of junior and senior manhood in Hesiod's two grades of the man, in many cultures a distinction so strongly marked that the term "elders" or its equivalent functions as a comprehensive category for males who have achieved the higher grade.[16] The passage into the elder grade involves the assumption of greater political power and marital and domestic responsibilities (as opposed to mere sexual activity). In such "gerontocratic" cultures distinctive rites of initiation mark off this class as different from and superior to those before it.[17]

Although more weakly marked than in traditional cultures, Hesiod's distinction between the youth and the man who bears responsibility for farm and family maintains some of these features. As the poet correlates the nonmetallic race of Heroes, which is the best of the imperfect human worlds, to the period of senior manhood or "maturity," he gives expression to an ethics that places special value upon it. Indeed, the poem as a whole is located within the perspective of the adult male—the world of Hesiod, Perses, and the Boeotian landowners to whom the poet offers his wise counsel. Maturity is consistently regarded as the most valued stage of masculine life and the standard by which others are to be judged, and is often defined precisely in opposition to youth and old age. A man should marry at about age thirty, presumably because he then has the wisdom to select the right kind of wife (cf. 698–701) and the economic and emotional stability to assume the rule of the *oikos*. The distinction between the two stages is reflected in Hesiod's discussion of animal husbandry:

> Get yourself two oxen,
> males, nine years old, for their strength will be undiminished
> and they in full maturity, at their best to work with,
> for such a pair will not fight as they drive the furrow, and shatter
> the plow, thus leaving all the work done gone for nothing.
> And have a forty-year-old man, still young enough, to follow
> the plow (give him a full four-piece loaf to eat, eight ounces);
> such a man will keep his mind on his work, and drive a straight
> furrow, not always looking about for company, but keep
> his thoughts on business. A younger man will be no improvement
> for scattering the seeds and not piling them on top of each other.
> A younger man keeps looking for excitement with other young people.
>
> (436–47: tr. Lattimore)

The farmer should plough with nine-year-old oxen that have attained the "measure of youth" ((ἥβης μέτρον)) and whose physical strength is unspent. But in tilling his fields he should employ a man of "about forty," who can keep his hand and his mind on the plow.[18] Where the value of domestic animals is highest in their youth and physical prime, male excellence is characterized by discretion and restraint as much as sheer strength. The younger man (νεώτερος, κουρότερος ἀνήρ) is physically able to drive the plough, but lacks the self-control required to compete in an agricultural environment of limited resources. In the Hesiodic perspective only the period of maturity is credited with any real excellences, so that we can speak of Hesiod's concept of virtue as being age-graded primarily in a negative sense. The high value that Hesiod places upon maturity reflects the realities of Boeotian peasant society, standing in contrast to both the heroic idealization of the young warrior in epic and the obsession with youthful eroticism in aristocratic lyric.

In juxtaposing the Heroic race to those of Bronze and Iron, Hesiod establishes it not as a downward step in a steady degradation but as a high point between races of relatively less value. In comparison with maturity, Hesiod's perspective on old age is more complex and ambiguous. As elsewhere in the epic tradition, divinity is defined negatively as being "deathless and ageless for all days."[19] Hesiod uses that formula (ἀθάνατος καὶ ἀγήραος ἤματα πάντα) and others like it to describe the gods and those mortals on whom immortality is conferred.[20] As vitality and power are embodied in the ageless gods, so the process of aging is linked with degeneration, death, and the generally grim prospect of the Greek afterlife. The epithets applied to old age are uniformly negative—gêras is wretched (δειλόν), destructive (ὀλοόν), and baneful (οὐλόμενον),[21] although these epithets are also routine in Homer and in the Homeric Hymns. Ironically, we find the most positive representation of old age in the god Nereus, eldest offspring of Pontus, whom Hesiod describes as unlying and truthful (ἀψευδέα καὶ ἀληθέα, Th. 233). He is called gerôn, he says,

> because he is trustworthy and gentle,
>   and never forgetful
> of what is right, but the thoughts
>   of his mind are mild and righteous.
>   (Th. 235–36: tr. Lattimore).

While the comments seem to suggest an association between age and wisdom,[22] this is not reflected elsewhere, and nowhere in the human world does Hesiod credit old age with any of the excellences—wisdom, counsel, eloquence, civic-mindedness, justice, experience— that at least partially redeem old age in Homer and in other literary contexts. In fragment 321 Hesiod succinctly age-grades the male excellences: "Deeds are for the young, counsel for those in the middle, and prayers for the old" (ἔργα νέων, βουλαὶ δὲ μέσων, εὐχαὶ δὲ γερόντων). The young do, the mature advise, and the old pray, with the function of wise counsel, honored at least in principle in Homer and other appraisals of old age, appropriated to those in "middle-age"; the prerogative of the elderly becomes that of prayer, with the recognition of their spiritual potency perhaps offset by the suggestion of their helplessness, a frequent theme in Hesiod.[23]

Hesiod sees in old age an intersection of both natural and cultural evil, locating Old Age and its siblings among the offspring of Night, who bore Nemesis

> . . . and afterward cheating Deception
>   and loving Affection
> and then malignant Old Age (Γῆρας τ᾽ οὐλόμενην)
>   and overbearing Discord.
>
> (Th. 223–25: tr. Lattimore)

Old Age resembles those in its immediate conceptual neighborhood— deceit, passionate affection, and strife—in that each is an occasion of evil, a vehicle by which mortals come to harm in their social relationships and which leaves them open to abuse, ridicule or defeat.[24] Ultimately descended from primal Void (Chaos), Old Age is of a lineage characterized by its sterility, abstractedness, and predominantly negative function in the human cosmos, a necessary though despicable aspect of human nature.

Later in the *Theogony* Hesiod develops the vulnerability of old age by relating it to another cultural problematic—woman—and therewith the danger of attempting to avoid the punishment Zeus established for the sins of Prometheus.[25] Hesiod says that the man who chooses not to marry:

> . . . must come then
>   to a mournful old age (ὀλοὸν . . . γῆρας)
> bereft of one to look after it (γηροκόμοιο),
>   and in need of livelihood
> lives on, and when he dies
>   the widow inheritors divide up
> what he has.
>
> (604–7: tr. Lattimore).

If a man does not marry, he fares better in the short run because he does not have to care for a woman, who is viewed by Hesiod as an unproductive drain on the *oikos*. But in old age he fares worse because he has no son to serve as *gêrokomos* and render the *threptêria* that are his due. He lives in fear that at his death his kinsmen will divide up his possessions and his *oikos* will die along with him. Woman is viewed ambiguously since, although she is an evil (κακόν), she is necessary in preventing a greater evil, that of a childless old age. In the *Works and Days*, the connection between these two kinds of evil is brought home in the vignette of the "bad wife," the perfect leech (δειπνολόχης, 704), who can "burn" her husband without fire and drive him to "raw" old age, that is, age him prematurely (εὕει ἄτερ δαλοῖο καὶ ὠμῷ γήραι δῶκεν, 705).[26] Woman, the cultural equivalent of fire, consumes a man's substance and hastens the onset of the natural evil of old age. As in the earliest reference to old age in the poem, which suggests that mortals age quickly in misfortune (αἶψα γὰρ ἐν κακότητι βροτοὶ καταγηράσκουσιν, 93 = *Od.* 19.360), this reference suggests the coincidence of cultural and moral evil: man's natural demise is accelerated amid misfortunes of his own making.

The Hesiodic construction of old age is rooted in the social and economic situation of archaic Boeotia.[27] In an economy that is land-scarce and based on subsistence farming, poorer landowners must jealously guard such patrimony as they have. Hence the emphasis throughout the poem on self-reliance, frugality, and maximizing limited resources, and its inculcation of the virtues of aggressive individualism and competition. Such farmers must, moreover, find some guarantee for their well-being in old age when, as consumers and not producers, they become liablilities to the *oikos* (like the women they condemn for their laziness).[28] Economic survival requires caution and careful planning at every stage: one should marry at the right age and a woman of the right age (*WD* 695–99), and sustain the minimum number of children necessary to ensure the survival of the household, ideally an only son (μουνογενὴς . . . πάις),[29] although more sons might also result in greater productivity (376, 379–80). Marriage and children represent a long-term investment, a system of social security that a man "pays into" in maturity by supporting his wife who will bear the children who will support him in old age when the system "pays back." Raising additional sons is costlier in the short run but will increase one's security and perhaps one's reimbursement in old age (γηραιὸς δὲ θάνοι ἕτερον παῖδ' ἐγκαταλείπων,*WD* 378).[30] However, the system is throughout fraught with danger. One might have only daughters (a further drain on the *oikos*) or one's sons might die before one's old age or even fail to render the filial support that is due. Given the preoccupation of the head of the household with the survival of the *oikos* and himself in old age, we can appreciate the particular vulnerability of elderly Boeotian men (not to mention the women) and the cultural anxiety about old age in general.

Let us now consider the way in which the races themselves are age-graded. The five races are described in terms of both the human condition and man's social relations. The Golden race, set in the paradisiacal reign of Cronus, is free from hard work and sorrow, for the earth freely profers her gifts. The culture is defined not in terms of work but of pleasure: "they took their delight at feasts far from all evils" (115), an image that suggests not so much self-gratification as it does the civilized refinements of the banquet. "Wretched old age," from which they are free (οὐδέ τι δειλὸν / γῆρας ἐπῆν, 113–14), is presented primarily as a natural evil. They remain "ever the same in their feet and hands" (114), that is, free from disfiguring old age,[31] suggesting that (if we are to understand this race as having been "born" at all) the aging process has been arrested in the period of maturity and short of the onset of physical old age. The absence of old age serves to compensate for the presence of death, which they meet not after a long and painful old age but "overcome as if by sleep" (θνῆσκον δ' ὥσθ' ὕπνῳ δεδμημένοι, 116).

Members of the Golden race are clearly pictured as adults, like the gods they resemble (ὥστε θεοί 112, φίλοι μακάρεσσι θεοῖσιν 120),[32] and while there is death—for the Greeks an irreducible of the human condition—there are no allusions to any other period of life, whether childhood or old age, to sully the idyllic picture. Human perfection, to the Greek mind, is conceived not in terms of childhood but of maturity and its delight in the pleasures of the physical and social world. It is free from the hardships against which the mature male and head of the household must struggle; hence the description is achieved largely in terms of negatives and privatives that dissociate the race from such realities as sorrow (κῆδος), toil (πόνος), grief (ὀιζύς), evil (κακόν), and ill-will (φθόνος). To the extent that such perfection is defined in terms of maturity, the other periods of life—explicitly old age—are devalued in the schema, and the relative perfection of the Heroic race is anticipated.

By identifying a second race of a different metal as much worse (πολὺ χειρότερον) than the preceding (and it is only at this point that the reader recognizes that the sequence will involve a number of races), and as unlike the one before it both physically and intellectually (φυήν, νόημα, 129), the poet differentiates the races of Gold and Silver. Moreover, by locating it under the regime of Zeus rather than Cronus,[33] and by introducing women and implicitly the complications of gender and sexuality, he effects further contrasts with the Golden race, suggesting the move to a different model.

A correspondence between the Silver race and childhood is strongly marked in depicting the race as one of children:

> A child was a child for a hundred years,
>   looked after and playing
> by his gracious mother, kept at home,
>   a complete booby.
> (ἀλλ᾽ ἑκατὸν μὲν παῖς ἔτεα παρὰ μητέρι κεδνῇ
> ἐτρέφετ᾽ ἀτάλλων, μέγα νήπιος, ᾧ ἐνὶ οἴκῳ, 130–31: tr. Lattimore)

The Silver race is one of protracted childhood and utter dependency. From the perspective of maturity, childhood is useless immaturity, with no positive value of its own. Hence for Hesiod the *pais* here is νήπιος both in the literal sense of "childish" and in its derivative sense of foolish and unproductive (as Hesiod in his own right often uses the word to abuse Perses).[34] Hesiod's concerns are economic as well as ethical; the "hundred years" through which these children are nurtured (ἐτρέφετο) is not the blissful prolongation of an idyllic childhood but a drain upon the family's resources—until these members can contribute their labor to the household. Hesiod sees these children as fatuous and unproductive, locating them together with the women (παρὰ μητέρι κεδνῇ) in the *oikos*.

The Silver race actually follows the children's progress just beyond the arrival of young manhood—

> But when it came time for them to grow and and gain full measure
> (ἀλλ᾽ ὅτ᾽ ἄρ᾽ ἡβήσαι τε καὶ ἥβης μέτρον ἵκοιτο, 132: tr. Lattimore)

—and thus points up the developmental nature of the model. With the arrival of *hêbê* their end is as abrupt as their childhood is long: they refuse to serve (θεραπεύειν, 135) the gods and offer them sacrifice as is right (θέμις, 137), so that the folly and self-centeredness of childhood carry over into their young manhood. The end they meet in reciprocal violence is a function not of childhood per se but of the flicker of young manhood that these "fools" (νήπιοι) experience but cannot control. In showing the dire consequences upon manhood of prolonged childhood, Hesiod characterizes the inferiority of childhood by exaggerating its deficiencies, and achieves a typical mythological justification of the normal span of childhood as neither too long nor too short but "just right."[35]

With the Silver race's coming into *hêbê*, Hesiod has already intimated the succession of young manhood upon childhood; the reciprocal violence that characterizes the demise of the Silver agers—

they were not able to keep away from reckless crime against each other
(ὕβριν γὰρ ἀτάσθαλον οὐκ ἐδύναντο / ἀλλήλων ἀπέχειν, 134–35: tr. Lattimore)

—clearly anticipates the internecine warfare of the Bronze race. By associating the internal violence that concludes the adolescence of the Silver race with the fratricide that dooms the Bronze race, the poet underscores the problematical nature of young manhood in general and its inherent potential for violence. In contrast with the Silver race, the race of Bronze makes no reference to childhood or old age, this race instead being sprung from the Meliai or ash-tree nymphs (ἐκ Μελιᾶν, 145; cf. *Th*.187).[36] Hesiod may be combining two associations: that in which nymphs and other benificent female deities are regarded as nurses (κουροτρόφοι) who protect and sometimes nuture boys in the wild until they reach physical maturity,[37] and the association of ash-trees with the manufacturing of spears, which is particularly appropriate to the destiny of these *kouroi*. The asexual nature of their origins, and the lack of any reference to women or reproduction in the description (in contrast with the descriptions of the mothers of the Silver Race and Helen in the Heroic), are doubly significant: first, as befitting a race of men who are themselves, by reason of their age grade and immaturity, not yet seasonable (ὥριοι) for marriage; second, as related to the frequent characterization of young manhood in puberty rituals and elsewhere as involving a rejection of the maternal ties of youth and their effeminizing influence.[38]

The Bronze race (γένος . . . χάλκειον) is described as different from—though not necessarily inferior to—the Silver (οὐκ ἀργυρέῳ οὐδὲν ὁμοῖον, 144).[39] As noted above, Hesiod distinguishes the young man from the adult not so much by his activities per se as by the degree of maturity and responsibility with which he executes them. The poet expresses this by associating both the Bronze and the Heroic races with a common activity, warfare, but by conceiving of it in two very different ways. The Bronze race is characterized by its love of warfare and its *hybris* (οἷσιν Ἄρηος / ἔργ' ἔμελε στονόεντα καὶ ὕβριες, 145–46), and in both these attributions there is a significant link to the period of early manhood.[40] Already in Homer the *kouros* signifies the young and vigorous warrior as opposed to the commanders and counselors;[41] thus the *Iliad* epitomizes in Achilles the powerful and terrifying warrior and repeatedly distinguishes the impulsiveness of the younger warriors from the maturity of the older ones.[42] Indeed, Nagy has argued that the description of the Bronze race may suggest Achilles in particular: the birth of the men from ash-trees (145) and Achilles' ashen spear with bronze tip; their violence (βίη, 148) and the hero's capacity for savage violence; the final residence of both in Hades.[43] As we shall we in chapter 5, Solon's elegiacs on the "ten ages" likewise characterize the fourth hebdomad from age 22 to 28 as that in which a man is at the peak of his physical strength, the index of his *aretê* or military prowess (19.7–8). And in archaic and classical Athens the achievement of manhood was identified with the time at which a young man became a warrior, as reflected in his admission to his phratry at the feast of the Apaturia and in the assumption of military activities by the ephebe.[44] Hesiod describes the Bronze race as frightening and mighty (δεινόν τε καὶ ὄβριμον, 145), a race of warriors of enormous physical strength (μεγάλη δὲ βίη καὶ χεῖρες ἄαπτοι / ἐξ ὤμων ἐπέφυκεν ἐπὶ στιβαροῖσι μέλεσσι, 148–49), the latter phrase suggesting their youthful nature.

Yet Hesiod condemns this race's indiscriminate indulgence in warfare and its expression of manhood in destructive violence,[45] characterizing their obsessive warfare as *hybris* and showing the consequences of such anti-social violence to be mutual destruction. Aristotle similarly characterizes *neotês* as the period in which *hybris* is most unrestrained: it is passionate, covetous of victory and excessive in all regards, its wrongdoing the result not of baseness (κακουργία) but of *hybris*.[46] The single-mindedness (ἀδάμαντος . . . κρατερόφρονα θυμόν, 147) of the Bronze race is reflected in the negative and exclusive terms in which they are described: they eat no bread, have no names in life or death (νώνυμνοι, 154), use no metals but bronze, and do nothing but engage in warfare.

With the Bronze race Hesiod translates the immaturity of young manhood onto the grid of martial achievement and characterizes it in terms of a warrior culture manqué. With the race of Heroes (ἀνδρῶν ἡρώων, 159), Hesiod suggests the superiority of the mature male, Aristotle's *akmê* (*Rhet.*2.14), by showing the members' success in the same category, thus establishing it as the best race relative to the last four.[47] The sequence thus underscores the high evaluation of maturity by representing it twice: first as Gold and placed at the head of the list, then as Heroes where both their non-metallic nature and the moral terms in which they are described mark them with distinction. This race is "more just and better" (δικαιότερον καὶ ἄρειον, 158) than Bronze; it is the only race not charged with *hybris* (cf. 134, 146, 191) and recognized as respecting justice (δίκη), implying that in maturity one's self-restraint and moral faculties are sufficiently developed to resist resolving conflict by violence rather than by law.[48] More importantly, in the references to Helen and Oedipus, Thebes and Troy, and the cycles of epic these different generations involve, the poet characterizes the reproductive success of the race, thereby locating them in the context of marriage, family, and the prerogatives of mature domestic life.

In a certain sense, the division of warriors into "junior" and "senior" grades (the anthropological parallels to which we have noted) is implicit in the epic tradition, in which Homeric warriors are age-graded, with an older tier (e.g., Agamemnon, Odysseus, Patroclus) distinguished from (and often at odds with) such younger and more impulsive warriors as Achilles and Diomedes.[49] This division is reinforced at the sexual level: the elder warriors are normally married, while the sexuality of the younger is limited to concubines.[50] At the tactical level, the younger warriors are often teamed with older experienced ones—Achilles with Patroclus, Diomedes with Odysseus or Nestor—on the assumption that the energies of youth will be guided by the company of someone wiser. Nestor recalls this very responsibility at *Iliad* 11.782–89 when he tells Patroclus that in not giving Achilles "solid advice," he has failed to perform his function as elder in keeping the younger warrior's greater strength (βίη) under control.

Commentators have noted the links between this race and that of Gold,[51] which we suggested above is portrayed in terms of maturity: both live "with hearts free from sorrow" (ἀκηδέα θυμὸν ἔχοντες, 112, 170); the references to Cronus' rule over the Isles of the Blessed (169) recalls his reign during the Golden race; the vegetarian abundance in the afterlife of the Heroes (172–73) recalls the spontaneous generation of the earth in the Golden race. Where the Silver, Bronze, and Iron races are characterized by varieties of *hybris*, these heroes are godlike in their maturity and excellence (θεῖον γένος, 159; ἡμίθεοι, 160). Whether or not the race of Heroes was a component of the original sequence of races, Hesiod here seizes upon the idealized treatment of man and war in the epic-heroic tradition. Far from finding it forced upon him, he finds in the non-metallic race a means to distinguish the excellence of human maturity. While the Heroic race may be "anomalous" from the perspective of a model of metals of strictly decreasing value, it functions effectively as a symbol of the preeminence of maturity.

Some of these heroes who die illustriously in battle are removed to the isles of the blessed, an afterlife distinguished from the anonymous and almost punitive destiny of the Bronze race. Unlike the warriors of Bronze, the heroes who die fighting do so not indiscriminately but purposefully—for the flocks of Oedipus or for fair-haired Helen (163–65)—and the allusions to the epic traditions of Thebes and Troy associate the Heroes not with indiscriminate warfare but with organized expeditions and civilized life in general. Where the Bronze race eats no grain, it is implicit that the race of heroes does; Zeus places them "on the all-nourishing earth" (157), and in their afterlife they enjoy the earth's superabundance: "in every year / three times over / the fruitful grainland bestows its sweet yield" (172–73). Such images associate the Heroes with the stability of agriculture and the diversity of civilized life.[52] Zeus' release of Cronus and the Titans to rule them may also suggest the special merits of this race. The nature of their final destiny after the span of manhood implies that these heroes do not advance to old age but are frozen in the fullness of their lives— there is no mention of either childhood or old age in connection with them. The race of Heroes represents the relative perfection of the mature: their courage and prowess in battle, their settled lives in cities, the renown they leave behind.

That the Iron race (γένος . . . σιδήρεον, 176) and by implication old age represent the nadir of the sequence is implicit in Hesiod's categorical assertion that he would rather have been born any time but now (174–75). The race's dismal character is underscored by its juxtaposition to the relative perfection of the blessed heroes (ὄλβιοι ἥρωες,

172). Hesiod describes the particular nature of this race by presenting us with two images of it: that of the Iron race "now" (νῦν, 176), when its evils are still compounded with some goods (179), and of a later time "when" (εὖτ' ἄν, 181) it is wholly bad, its evils brought to fulfillment and unmitigated by good. By doing so he traces the race of Iron through, as it were, its death throes and extinction, thus characterizing, as he has with the Silver and Heroic, the corresponding age grade as a span of time. In marking the deterioration of the race in two distinct phases, Hesiod allows us to see the race as a whole age in a rapid and dramatic way. As Vernant points out, the race of Iron is really double.

The correspondence between the Iron race and old age is implicit in the very selection of iron, which links the race to the physical degeneration of old age. While gray (πολιός) regularly describes the hair or beards of the elderly,[53] the epithet is also frequently applied to steel (σίδηρος).[54] Hesiod plays upon both these uses in the reference to the "gray-templed babies" whose appearance will betoken the end of this race (εὖτ' ἄν γεινόμενοι πολιοκρόταφοι τελέθωσιν, 181). In gray-templed (πολιοκρόταφοι), Hesiod combines the two senses of gray (πολιός) by implying that in the last days men at birth will be both completely old and completely iron, both physically disfigured and morally hardened, their gray temples betraying the steel-gray hearts within them. As the Iron race is a kind of old age, it adumbrates the end of the sequence as a whole; when its own destruction is imminent, its members will show signs of their senescence from the beginning.

The gray-templed babies act on the natural level as an index of the evil character of old age. The combination of grayness and youth likens these newborns to the Graiae, whom Hesiod describes as "fair-cheeked and gray from birth" (καλλιπαρήους/ ἐκ γενετῆς πολιάς, Th. 270–71). Like the other offspring of Phorkys and Ceto, the Graiae are monsters, hybrids possessed at once of beauty and ugliness, youth and old age, and like the "gray-templed babies" (πολιοκρόταφοι), gray from birth. In the monstrous, we find the confounding of categories that are otherwise separate in nature, and this kind of confusion on the natural level has as its corollary the inversion of social categories that follows in the description: the behavior that normally distinguishes the treatment of friend from enemy, kin from non-kin, guest from non-guest, and so forth, becomes similarly confounded. The gray-templed babies thus become a distinctive *monstrum* that will herald the imminent demise of the race.

In describing his society as the senescence of the race, the poet suggests an age that is morally at its nadir, exhausted and on the very verge of collapse. Where each of the preceding races had—whether by reason of virtue or hybris—avoided dread old age, for the Iron race everything is old. Apart from suggesting its physical resemblance to old age, the poet thematically links the Iron race and old age in his description of the race's *hybris*. Unlike the Silver and Bronze races, where play and warfare correspond to the actual pastimes of childhood and young manhood, Hesiod does not imply that the elderly themselves act insolently and abusively but associates the race with old age by featuring acts of hybris in which the elderly are victimized.[55] Children will dishonor (ἀτιμήσουσι, 185) their aged parents, "carping and criticizing them with rough words" (μέμψονται δ' ἄρα τοὺς χαλεποῖς βάζοντες ἔπεσσι, 186), and will deny them the *threptêria* (188) on which their survival depends. The treatment of the elderly reveals the character of this race and the kind of behavior that will warrant its destruction. Mistreatment of the elderly is to the Iron race what fratricidal warfare is to the Bronze and protracted childhood is to the Silver—evidence of its brand of moral depravity and the occasion of its doom.

The moral repulsiveness of these acts is signalled by expressions of outrage at their perpetrators: they are "pitiless, and heedless of the gods' vengeance" (σχέτλιοι, οὐδὲ θεῶν ὄπιν εἰδότες, 187), "men whose justice is in their fists" (χειροδίκαι, 189).[56] The poet's words anticipate his outrage later in the poem when he presents this kind of insolence as the climax of a catalogue of injustices, of a man

> [who] speaks roughly with intemperate words
>   to his failing
> father who stands upon the hateful doorstep
>   of old age;
> with all these Zeus in person is angry,
>   and in the end
> he makes them pay a bitter price
>   for their unrighteous dealings.
> (ὅς τε γονῆα γέροντα κακῷ ἐπὶ γήραος οὐδῷ
> νεικείῃ χαλεποῖσι καθαπτόμενος ἐπέεσσι·

τῷ δ' ἦ τοι Ζεὺς αὐτὸς ἀγαίεται, ἐς δὲ τελευτὴν
ἔργων ἀντ' ἀδίκων χαλεπὴν ἐπέθηκεν ἀμοιβήν, 331–34: tr. Lattimore)

These crimes merit Zeus' special anger, who appropriately makes harsh reprisal for harsh words (χαλεποῖσι . . . χαλεπήν). As Zeus works here at the individual level, so with the Iron race he will apply collectively a fitting recompense for such crimes: those who mistreat the elderly shall themselves grow old prematurely. Unlike the Bronze race, which killed itself off in violence, Zeus himself will take the lead in destroying this race (180).

Particularly striking is the way in which Hesiod in his description of the Iron race interrelates the natural evil of old age and the social evils that will accompany it. In 185 we are told that these Iron-agers will dishonor their parents "as they grow old quickly" (αἶψα . . . γηράσκοντας), suggesting that the natural process of aging is hastened when it is accompanied by insolence rather than respect (as also implied at 93). The poet's observation that the moral environment influences a man's natural decline intensifies the allusion to the "gray-templed babies" by depicting a society so corrupt that even the newborn are tainted by it and so evil that its senescent effects are conspicuous from birth. As Yeats, in the "shape with lion body and the head of a man" slouching towards Bethlelem, found in the monstrous an image that marked the end of one age (and not coincidentally the beginning of a second cycle of human culture) and that expressed his own pessimism for modern civilization, so Hesiod finds in these gray-templed babies a succinct and a horrific image of the eschata, in which only the negative aspects of old age are represented and in which the deepest anxieties about it are realized. Here the elderly, who are socially vulnerable and whose economic survival is always precarious, suffer the loss of their livelihood and their dignity at the hands of their own children.

On a literary level, Hesiod's sequence provides an early parallel to the familiar "exercise"—from Solon's ten ages of man to Shakespeare's seven—in which the human life span is segmented, characterized, and its excellences age-graded. In portraying the varieties of moral and social life in the categories of age, Hesiod suggests in schematic and elegant form the conceptual mechanisms by which his culture organizes experience: the assimilation of human activity to the natural order, its cyclical and seasonal character, a sense of time in relation to human life (βίος), and life itself as an orderly unfolding of different capacities and incapacities. In such a life-course model, the races are welded together in a structure that respects their discrete nature and the striking differences in their value in the context of a unified whole, and that derives not from the demands of tradition or from an empty formalism but from the realities of life as they are experienced and perceived. We are struck by the conspicuous features of his model: its relative lack of appreciation of childhood, its recognition of the excellence of maturity or middle age over and against the immaturity of young manhood as reiterated in the representation of the races of Gold and the Heroes, and its portrayal of old age largely in terms of degeneration and vulnerability. As such, Hesiod's development of such a model is testimony not just to his creative abilities but to a cultural predisposition to view life in these terms, and in the absence of the kind of direct data we would like to have, it provides some precious indirect evidence about the social realities and attitudes of archaic Boeotia.

Erotic Dismembering, Poetic Remembering: Sappho on Love, the Lyre, and the Life Course

This is the use of memory:
For liberation—not less of love but expanding
Of love beyond desire and so liberation
From the future as well as the past.
— T. S. Eliot, *The Four Quartets*

A common motif, the *Lebenstreppe,* which has its origins in Renaissance art, represents life as a staircase, a series of graduated steps that rise, come to a kind of summit, and finally fall. The steps correspond to the stages of life, and on them individuals and sometimes couples are seen climbing and descending these various stages.[1] Some of the paintings feature men, others women, and a number represent men and women travelling through life together, in images meant to impress the viewer with their orderly and harmonious vision of life, marriage, and the aging process. Although it is understandably pleasant to picture men and women as moving through life in tandem, the two sexes in this respect do not, indeed cannot, represent so neat a "fit." As gerontologists have insisted, differences in biology and in the social construction of gender make it impossible for any single model of the life course to accomodate both male and female.[2] Across cultures and historical periods, age-grades for men and women are incommensurate in duration, interrelation, and social significance, and models like the *Lebenstreppe* work more often by imposing the male model on the female rather than by recognizing the differences between the genders. Like Shakespeare's famous verses on the seven ages of man—

All the world's a stage,
And all the men and women merely players.
They have their exits and their entrances,

And one man in his time plays many parts,
His acts being seven ages.
(*As You Like It*, 2.7.140–43)

—these images at first appear to offer a model that can accommodate men and women but turn out to be dominated by male experience alone.[3]

The Greeks, despite the variety of their various terms and systems of age classification, distinguished only in a broad way four life stages for men and women.[4] For men these are the child (*pais*); the young adult (*neos* or *kouros*) who has achieved physical maturity (*hêbê*); the mature man at *akmê* or prime of life (without a distinctive term); and the elderly man (*gerôn* or *presbys*). For the woman, the stages are again the *pais* or child; the young woman (*korê*) sexually of age but not married (as virgin, or strictly speaking until the birth of her first child, she is *parthenos* or "maiden"); the mature married woman/wife (*gynê*); and the elderly woman (*graia* or *graus*).[5] Yet despite their apparent similarity the models are not commensurate but reflect fundamental differences in the conception of male and female. It is not just that men and women go through different stages at different times. It is rather that the very basis on which the life course is conceived and constructed is different. Whereas in Homer, as we have seen, the stages of a man's life reflect changes in his martial, intellectual, and social abilities, or in Hesiod are coordinated with his changing relation to the *oikos* and the labor that sustains it, the model of female aging is essentially coterminous with a woman's biological development and its social application: her stage as mother/wife is preceded by that of the not-yet-capable of motherhood *pais* and followed by that of the no-longer-capable of motherhood *graia*, with the *parthenos*, sexually of age but not yet married, a bridge into the stage of reproductive activity.[6] A woman's long period of domestic and reproductive activity is not punctuated by any social rite or marker, but is of a piece until her reproductive capacity ends. And the passage to old age and the social changes that accompany it commence with menopause, when she ceases to be useful for sexual or reproductive purposes.[7]

That the stages of a woman's life are defined largely in terms of her potential for marriage and reproduction reflects the very different meaning of *aretê* for women: as Garland puts it, her primary value as a married woman is as a "reproductive machine."[8] And because a woman's potential for marriage and reproduction is tied so much to her physical attractiveness, her beauty and desirability as a wife or sexual partner, the meaning of age is necessarily different for women than for men. Greek culture is not unique in regarding a woman's beauty and age as inversely related, but the fact that Greek males tended to prefer adolescent, often barely pubescent, women as sexual or marriage partners might have made "older" women in Greek social practice particularly likely targets for derision.[9] Whatever the social and economic origins of male preferences, the aesthetic that developed around them located older women at a considerable remove from the ideals of feminine desireability. Given the aesthetics of female beauty and the typical age differential between husband and wife or lover and beloved, any woman beyond the earliest age of marriageability, regardless of her actual age or physical appearance, was vulnerable to the charge that she was *growing* old (γηράσκεις). Instructive are the sentiments voiced by the protagonist at *Lysistrata* 591–97, who complains that war is doubly hard on unmarried women, who find their marital prospects ruined "as they grow old in their chambers" (τῶν δὲ κορῶν ἐν τοῖς θαλάμοις γηρασκουσῶν). War makes marriage a buyer's market, whatever a man's age: for while "a woman's season of opportunity is brief" (τῆς δὲ γυναικὸς μικρὸς ὁ καιρός), after a war even a man who is old and gray (πολιός) can find a sweet young bride (παῖδα κόρην).

As age makes a woman less marketable for marriage, so old age in one sense marks the end of her sexual life. To the extent that woman's sexuality was identified with her reproductive capabilities, old age concludes her greatest single responsibility, that of providing for the survival of the *oikos* by giving birth to an heir. The arrival of menopause provides a "natural" demarcation between the periods in which sexual activity is appropriate and inappropriate.[10] Just as the social identity of the younger woman (wife, prostitute, or concubine) is defined according to the nature of her sexual relationships, so the post-menopausal woman, valued neither for pleasure nor reproduction, finds her definition precisely in terms of her asexuality. In the Homeric *Hymn to Demeter*, the goddess comes to Eleusis "like to an aged women (γρηὶ παλαιγενέι) who is done with childbearing and the gifts of garland-loving Aphrodite" (101–2). As Bremmer suggests, the greater freedom of public movement that old women seem to enjoy in Greek society, reflected here in the wanderings of the goddess, should be understood as a result of their being sexually uninteresting and therefore able move about outside the household without fear for their safety.[11] Simone de Beauvoir makes a similar point in speaking of the advantage that old age brings women in traditional societies, in that it frees them from various restrictions and taboos: "After the menopause the woman is no longer a being with a sex. Her state now corresponds to that of the little girl before puberty."[12]

Despite the greater freedom they enjoy, older women in Greek culture are subject to rather clear limitations on their sexuality. As Greek men regarded female sexual activity in terms of their own enjoyment rather than of the woman who provides it, a woman's sexuality is legitimate only in so far as it is put in the service of the man who has a claim upon her.[13] Sexual initiative is a privilege restricted (among mortals, at any rate) to men and to prostitutes, and this is reflected in Greek myth in the negative exempla of assertive women who choose their own lovers—Clytemnestra, Phaedra, and Sthenoboea. For an older woman to evince an interest in sex (even where her personal situation does not preclude it) involves a double infraction of the feminine code, both in presuming a beauty that is no longer hers and in acting upon her own desires. We must understand "acting" here in its cultural sense: a woman may be perceived as sexually aggressive simply by dressing or adorning herself seductively or for that matter simply by *being* in public at all—hence the restrictions on women appearing in public throughout Greek history.[14]

Expressions of sexual interest or activity by old women are thus inherently presumptuous, unseemly, and potentially ridiculous. Because the older woman is undesirable, it is understood that her sexual activity will depend on her taking the initiative.[15] Yet precisely because her asexuality allows her greater independence and visibility, her freedom of movement can be interpreted as sexual aggressiveness and immorality. In other contexts these themes are collapsed in the image and reality of the aged prostitute, who because she is unsought must earn her keep either by becoming a madam herself or by practicing fellatio, considered the most contemptible of sexual practices.[16] The *loci* on the subject are again in Aristophanes, who exploits the limited circumstances under which an old woman might hope for erotic success. In *Ecclesiazusai* 877ff. three sex-starved old women (γράες) leap upon the young man they fancy and attempt to compel him to minister to their desires, armed with the new law that has democratized sexual rights: before a young man (νέος) can have sex with a young girl (νέας), he must first "bang an old woman" (γραῦν προκρούσῃ). In *Plutus* 959–1096 the *graus* is distraught when her young gigolo, newly enriched, reveals his long contempt for her and how it was only for money that he had given her sex. In taking the sexual initiative, these women cross the line that separates proper and improper women and behave as only prostitutes have the right, and so here are portrayed as promiscuous and repulsive old hags.

It is in this sense that we can speak of the predicament of the aged and aging woman in Greece—of the negative and detrimental effects of age on her identity in the terms in which her culture defines it: maternal, domestic, sexual, and erotic. My purpose in this chapter is to look at the poetic tradition on this theme with an eye to how its perspective is affected by the gender, or perhaps better, the gendered *order of experience*, of the author. I will begin by surveying how three male authors—Homer, Hesiod, and Archilochus—respond to the theme of women and age and will demonstrate the three quite different ways in which these poets respond to the relationship between a woman's age and value. Then I will examine the very different perspective that Sappho offers on women, love, and aging. Just as Sappho's poetry suggests that love has profoundly different meanings for men and women, it also reveals that women and men do not experience aging in the same way and provides unparalled insight into that experience from a woman's point of view. Where the male poets respond with different degrees of sensitivity and insensitivity to the situation of the aging woman, Sappho—specifically by virtue of the feminine and homoerotic world of her verse—offers an appreciation and a resolution of the aging woman's predicament that is based on nothing less than a radical reappraisal of the meaning of time and its relation to love and the life course. Recognizing the relation between these sets of distinctions will help us keep in mind that the images of aged sexuality in Greek poetry that we have studied in previous chapters, and as they are often regarded, are not universal in their force but are descriptive of male experience, concerns, and anxieties. In other words, when we speak about Greek "attitudes" toward old age, these are likely to be those of men, not women.

HOMER

The *Iliad* and *Odyssey* provide only partial glimpses of the lives of old women, yet they do so in terms that are remarkable for their sensitivity

and pathos. In Homer, not surprisingly, elderly women are described
without reference to their sexuality or physical attractivness. The *aretê*
of these women consists primarily in their maternity, which is portrayed not as a past event but as a *continuing* nurturing of their loved
ones as mothers and wives: their motherhood is portrayed more in
terms of relationships than of mere reproduction.[17] Hecuba is a case in
point. When Hector comes inside Troy in Book 6, she is introduced
with the rare epithet ἠπιόδωρος (6.251), "gentle or generous with her
gifts"; she asks him to stay with her, hoping to persuade him that a
draught of wine will restore his strength. In book 22 she beseeches her
beloved son (τέκνον ἐμόν . . . φίλον θάλος, 82, 87) to come into Troy
again, baring "the breast which eases pain" (83) and recounting her
care and devotion. It is significant that where Priam bases his appeal to
Hector on what will happen to him [Priam] if he dies, Hecuba focuses
entirely on Hector and the mistreatment she fears he will suffer in
death. After his death she assumes the role of *mater dolorosa*, leading
the women of Troy in a lament (22.430ff.) and later in a dirge, where she
claims him as "of all my sons the dearest by far to my spirit" (24.748).

So too, in her single appearance in the *Odyssey* (11.152–224),
Odysseus' "queenly mother" Anticleia is defined by her maternal concern, as she tells her son all that has happened in his absence. The poet
structures her reply so that in deferring his first question (how did you
die?) to the end, her response not only reflects the conventions of ring
composition but reveals her readiness to place her own interests last.
It was not sickness, she says, that brought her life to an end

> but, shining Odysseus, it was my longing for you, your cleverness
> and your gentle ways, that took the sweet spirit of life from me.
> (11.202–3: tr. Lattimore)

Equally striking is how protective and even maternal these two aged
heroines have become toward their husbands. Hecuba rails at Priam
when he reveals his intention to ransom Hector since she wants only
to continue their grief alone (24.201ff.). When she realizes that he will
not be turned from his plan, she insists that he at least double-check
his divine sanction by asking Zeus to send some good omen. Behind
her protests lies not only her fear for his safety but the worry that grief
and age have enfeebled the mind (φρένες, 24.201) for which he was
once so famous.[18] So too Anticleia continues to worry about Laertes

even in death, describing the toll his grief has taken on him: he lives in squalor and dresses in rags, sleeping in the ashes by the hearth or on the ground in the orchard. Yet she also sees that the two of them share a common fate: as he longs for Odysseus (ποθέων, 11.195), so too did she die out of sheer longing for him (πόθος, 202).

In their mutual love and longing for their son, Anticleia and Laertes are testimony to the Homeric ideal of like-mindedness (ὁμοφροσύνη). Striking in this regard is the frequency with which Homer represents the aging process for men and women in complementary terms. The *Odyssey*, with its narrative sweep and expansive temporality, affords a larger comparative perspective on gender and the life course. In book 15 Eumaeus describes how he and Odysseus' young sister Ctimene were raised together:

> But when we had both arrived at our lovely prime, they gave her away for marriage, in Same, and for her were given numberless gifts; but the lady gave me a mantle and tunic, excellent clothing she put upon me, and giving me sandals for my feet sent me to the estate.
>
> (15.366–70: tr. Lattimore)

The *Odyssey* often regards such life transitions as occasions for delight and celebration for men and women alike: youth (*hêbê*) is for both Eumaeus and Ctimene "much-loved" (πολυήρατον),[19] and Eumaeus' new wardrobe has its counterpart in the new bride's dowry. Although the coming of age entails different changes—for the female, marriage, for the male new responsibilities—they are nonetheless presented as complementary phases of the same growth process.[20]

The complementarity of male and female is also developed in the portrayal of Nausicaa, who epitomizes the Homeric *kourê*: she is, as Homer says, "a virgin unwedded" (παρθένος ἀδμής, 6.109, 228), though Athena reminds her that she will not be so for long (6.27, 33). In the poem's treatment of Odysseus as pseudo-suitor for her hand (a prospect that she and Alcinous entertain unabashedly—cf. 6.273–84, 7.311–15) we see the typical pattern of young maiden and mature man. Nausicaa's marital ambitions are implicitly related to those of men when she alludes demurely to the marital status of her brothers (6.62–63). More important, Homer broadens the significance of Nausicaa's prospective passage from maiden to wife by describing it in

terms that clearly recall the coming of age of Telemachus.[21] Like him,
Nausicaa is introduced as a dreamer, whom Athena in disguise must
awaken from inaction and rouse to new responsibilities. As with
Telemachus, her relationship with Odysseus becomes the occasion for
public demonstrations of eloquence, courage, intelligence, and an
enlarged sense of her own abilities. In this way Nausicaa's coming of
age mirrors Telemachus' belated and more urgent maturation, and the
development of both *kouros* and *kourē* is shown to involve not a
mechanical change of grade but the willing assumption of new skills
and obligations. Behind Nausicaa's trip to the river lies the playful
Homeric counterpart to Hesiod's disgruntled comments on the frivoli-
ty of maidens: Athena herself, as patron of domestic works, appropriately teases the maiden for her laziness (6.25), bidding her to do the
family laundry and to cultivate the reputation that will win her the
best husband. She and her young servants indulge in the bathing and
skin care that are for Hesiod a source of both fascination and misgiv-
ing. Homer uses Nausicaa's encounter with Odysseus to indicate her
remarkable prudence as well. Odysseus describes her behavior to her
parents in terms of not only her status as *kourē* but of youth in general,
talking parent-to-parent about "young people today":

> It was as you could never have hoped for a young person (νεώτερον),
>   so confronted,
> to act, for always the younger people (νεώτεροι) are careless.
>   (7.293–94: tr. Lattimore)

In using the masculine "inclusive" forms (νεώτερον and νεώτεροι),
Odysseus offers Nausicaa as an exception to the general immaturity of
youth, male or female.

The *Odyssey* is also distinctive in the way it juxtaposes male and
female in the passage of time. When Odysseus take leave of Arete, he
says:

> farewell to you, O queen, and for all time, until old age
> comes to you, and death, which befall all human creatures
>   (13.59–60: tr. Lattimore).

Odysseus locates woman's growth no less than man's in a larger pattern
of time and change. Indeed, one of the most attractive features of

Homer's portrayal of marriage are his middle-aged couples—Alcinous and Arete, Menelaus and Helen, Penelope and Odysseus—whose child-bearing and child-raising years are over yet who approach old age together. Penelope, who epitomizes the Homeric wife and mother, is appraised in terms that are feminine even as they cut across lines of gender.[22] The suitors are rivals for her *aretē* (2.206); in fact it is to her alone of women that the term *aretē* is applied. The content of her excellence is in general gauged differently from that of man. Agamemnon speaks of her virtue (σὺν μεγάλῃ ἀρετῇ. . . κλέος . . . ἀρετῆς, 24.193, 197) in the context of her prudence and loyalty. Eurymachus waxes poetic in praise of her "beauty and stature and the mind well balanced" (εἶδός τε μέγεθός τε ἰδὲ φρένας ἔνδον ἐίσας, 18.249). Penelope responds demurely, first to Eurymachus and later to the beggar, that

> all of my excellence, my beauty and figure (ἐμὴν ἀρετὴν εἶδός τε
>   δέμας τε),
> were ruined by the immortals at that time when the Argives took ship
> for Ilion, and with them went my husband Odysseus.
>   (18.251–53 = 19.124–26; cf. 18.180–81: tr. Lattimore)

While Penelope's remarks are at one level an expression of her loyalty—my beauty died when my husband left—in them we also hear a woman's response to her erotic situation. Penelope is aware of the toll twenty years have taken on her physical beauty, and Homer reminds the reader that neither she nor Odysseus is immune to the ravages of time. Odysseus introduces the theme when he compares Penelope, a mortal (βροτός) and no rival to the gods in stature and beauty (εἶδός . . . μέγεθός τ'), to Calypso, who is "deathless and ageless for all days" (5.217–18). But Penelope's aging beauty serves not to distinguish her from Odysseus but to join her to him. Odysseus declines Calypso's offer to make him "deathless and ageless" (5.136), and when Penelope later comments sadly to the aged beggar how her husband has probably come to resemble him, for "mortals grow old quickly in misfortune" (αἶψα γὰρ ἐν κακότητι βροτοὶ καταγηράσκουσι, 19.360), she must also have herself in mind. Here as in other respects the *Odyssey* is remarkable for the attention it gives—in view of the male-dominated world of the poem and of the circumstances of its composition—to woman's consciousness as something of great interest and value.[23]

In this way the reunion of Odysseus and Penelope is set in the context of an aging if not an aged couple. Athena youthens and beautifies the two of them, smoothing over for each the wrinkles of time. Penelope reflects on their destiny and their life as a whole, as a couple moving through the life course together. She laments how

> the gods granted us misery,
> in jealousy over the thought that we two, always together,
> should enjoy our youth (ἥβη), and then come to the threshold of
> old age (γήραος οὐδόν)
>
> (23.210–12; tr. Lattimore).

It is no accident that in her last speech in the poem Penelope ponders the words of Tiresias' prophecy and the "sleek old age" that Odysseus has reported to her. As mentioned above, she encourages him to take comfort in the fact that the gods are bringing to pass an old age that is better (γῆρας . . . ἄρειον, 23.286) than what has preceded it, one that clearly implies an old age they will spend together, as the poem flirts gently with the prospect of an elderly hero and heroine.

HESIOD

As in Homer, Hesiod's portrayal of women and age is in keeping with his representation of gender in general. In Hesiod a woman's progress through the life course is unrelated to that of men, reflecting his perception of women as not just different but as a separate race (γένος, Th. 590). As we have seen, the Works and Days is elaborated in the context of Boeotian agriculture and economics, and the model of the life course he employs reflects the requirements of that life. Unlike the Homeric heroes, who often exceed the norms of their respective age-grades, Hesiod's interest is in the normal progression through the life course. You are of age (ὡραῖος) to marry a wife and bring her home, says Hesiod,

> when you are about thirty, not being many years short of
> the mark, nor going much over. That age is ripe (ὥριος) for your
> marriage.
> Let your wife be full grown (ἡβώοι) for four years, and marry in
> the fifth.
> Better marry a maiden (παρθενικήν), so you can teach her good manners,

and in particular marry one who lives close by you.
Look her well over first. Don't marry what will make your
      neighbors laugh at you.

                              (WD 695–702: tr. Lattimore)

A man should take every precaution to select a wife who is good
(ἀγαθῆς) and avoid one who is bad (κακῆς), a greedy woman who will
consume him and his resources (702–5). He should marry at age thirty because he then has the intelligence to pick the right kind of wife
and educate her properly in her domestic role, the emotional stability
to rule the *oikos*, and perhaps the economic wherewithal that would
come with the retirement or death of his father. While the physical and
social achievement of *hêbê* for men entails an increase in domestic
responsibility, with marriage and his period of procreative activity
coming only later, for women it is primarily a prelude to marriage. In
the passage above, the age differential between thirty-year-old groom
and eighteen-year-old bride is striking for its ethical implications.
Where the younger man should wait until he is sufficently mature
before marrying, the criteria by which the young woman is evaluated
are reversed. Like the nine-year-old oxen that have attained the "measure of maturity" (ἥβης μέτρον) and are at the peak of their strength,
she is more marriageable precisely *for* her youth: riper for instruction
by her husband; more likely to be a virgin and to save the husband
from the risk of disgrace; more fit, at least by Greek standards, for
childbirth. For the young woman the achievement of physical maturity marks a hiatus, a time of biological ripeness during which her
reproductive and ethical development is put on hold. Indeed, it is significant that Hesiod consistently describes young women as *parthenoi*,
that is, in terms of their sexual integrity and marriagability, and almost
never with the more general *kourê*.[24]

The *parthenos* is, of course, educated in the skills that she will need
as wife and mother. Hesiod hints at this in his description of Pandora,
who is a maiden (παρθενική) and has learned skills (ἔργα) from
Athena, who taught her how to do intricate weaving (64). But this
involves a dilemma since Hesiod elsewhere imagines such *parthenoi* as
pampered creatures concerned only with their own beauty and comfort. Speaking of the bitter winter wind, he says that

it does not blow through the soft skin of a young maiden (παρθενικῆς)

> who keeps her place inside the house by her loving mother
> and is not yet initiated in the mysteries (ἔργα) of Aphrodite
> the golden, who, washing her smooth skin carefully, and annointing it
> with oil, then goes to bed, closeted in an inside chamber.
>
> (WD 519–23: tr. Lattimore)

Hesiod is not insensitive to the appeal of these maidens, beautiful but inexperienced in the ways of love (ἔργα . . . Ἀφροδίτης). The imagery recalls his description of Pandora, who has the "bewitching features of a young girl" (παρθενικῆς καλὸν εἶδος ἐπήρατον, 63) but a shameless mind and deceitful nature to boot. As often in Hesiod, the mortal (male) condition is presented as a double or triple bind. The maiden's place is inside the *oikos*, which Hesiod regards as a place of both indolence and non-productivity, though also (albeit grudgingly and only implicitly) as the occasion on which she learns the skills she will need.[25] But the works (ἔργα) of Athena also anticipate the works of Aphrodite she will learn later, which Hesiod consistently regards as a source of potential destruction for men.[26] Hence Hesiod's insistence that one marry a virgin, so one can teach her "good manners": it is only *after* marriage that she is properly educated for her role, and that is done by her husband.

Hesiod's representation of the stages of female life is in terms—sexual, reproductive, domestic—that are restrictive of her identity as a whole and that work to define her over and against the broader cultural identity of man. His view of woman's domestic *aretê* is sustained in his grudging attitude toward her role in reproduction, and is illuminated in the *Theogony* where he relates the twin problematics of age and gender. Discussing the creation of women, he makes explicit what he hints at in the *Works and Days*: woman is an economic liability and a drain upon the limited resources of the *oikos*. Women "live with mortal men, and are a great sorrow to them, and hateful poverty they will not share, but only luxury" (592–93: tr. Lattimore). They are like drones, he says, that consume the product of others' labor. But Zeus in his cunning has bound together the realities of work, women, and age:

> For whoever escaping marriage and the sorrowful things women do,
> is unwilling to marry, must come then to a mournful old age
> (ὀλοὸν . . . γῆρας)

bereft of one to look after it (γηροκόμοιο), and in need of livelihood
lives on, and when he dies the widow-inheritors (χηρωσταί)
   divide up
what he has.

(603–7: tr. Lattimore)

Hesiod's farmers must find some guarantee for their well-being in old
age when, as consumers and not producers, they (like the women they
condemn for their laziness) become liabilities to the *oikos*. Woman is a
luxury item the farmer can ill afford. But she is needed to produce a
son, a *gêrokomos* to support him in old age and sustain the *oikos* after
his death. Given the extent to which Hesiod understands woman's
excellence, such as it is, in terms of her sexual integrity and reproductive ability, it is no surprise that the *graia*—her reproductive capacity
and her sexual desireability having been exhausted—is nowhere mentioned in his work, not even as aged servant woman, a literary staple
elsewhere. After producing the requisite son to serve as *gêrokomos*, the
older woman vanishes without a trace.

ARCHILOCHUS

Archilochus' abuse of old age and aging are consistent with the traditions of invective and blame (ψόγος) within which he composed.[27] He
appears to have paid little attention to the erotic situation of old men,
reserving the brunt of his age-invective for women.[28] There is no reason to believe that this kind of invective is original with him.[29] Abuse
of the sexually aggressive hag or crone was more than likely part of the
storehouse of misogynistic material available to Hesiod and Simonides. The later forms of this kind of invective are well represented
in the *Palatine Anthology*, Horace's *Epodes*, Martial's epigrams, the
Priapea, and other collections; the tradition is sustained in the West in
the abundant lore on the insatiable sexuality of hags, crones, and
witches.[30] A useful point of reference can be found in Horace *Epodes* 8,
in which the speaker attacks a wealthy woman:

> You, foul by your long century, ask
>   what unmans my strength,
> when you've a black tooth, and old age
>   plows your brow with wrinkles,

and between your dried-out cheeks gapes filthy
  an asshole like a dyspeptic cow's?
But your chest and decaying tits arouse me,
  like mare's udders,
and your soft belly and your skinny thigh
  on top of swollen shins.
Congratulations, and may images of great men
  precede your funeral train,
nor may there be a wife who walks
  laden with rounder pearls.
And so what if Stoic booklets like to lie
  between your silk pillows?
Do unlettered cocks harden less for that?
  Or does that phallus droop less,
which you have to work on with your mouth
  to raise from its proud crotch?
                                    (trans. Richlin)[31]

In her discussion of *Epodes* 8 and 12, Richlin identifies four components of this kind of invective: emphasis on the woman's age; graphic description of her physical degeneration; reference to her sexual promiscuity or insatiability; rejection of her as a fitting sexual partner. Each of these characteristics is adumbrated in Archilochus, and it is striking the extent to which the rhetoric of old age, at least as far as women are concerned, has already coordinated the polarities of youth-age with other polarized categories of abuse: sexual experience (virgin-promiscuous), social status (free-prostitute), moral character (good-bad), marriageability (desirable-undesirable). What is remarkable about the age invective of Archilochus generally is the conventionality of the terms of its abuse: he is clearly drawing on a tradition of such abuse even as he extends it in new directions.

In one fragment Archilochus chides an old woman, either a *hetaira* or someone (Neoboule?) who is compared to one, for continuing to "perfume" herself, that is, attempting to make herself sexually attractive later in life than is appropriate:

You are too old a woman to put on such airs.
(οὐκ ἂν μύροισι γρηῦς ἐοῦσ' ἠλείφεο, 205W).

According to Plutarch, who quotes the line in his *Life of Pericles* (28.5), Pericles addressed this verse to Elpinice, Cimon's outspoken sister, when she publicly criticized him for the Athenian lives lost in his campaign against the Samians. Plutarch earlier reports another occasion on which Pericles says to Elpinice, who was pleading with him on behalf of her brother's upcoming trial, "you are too old, too old, to conduct such business" (γραῦς εἶ, γραῦς εἶ, ὡς πράγματα τηλικαῦτα πράσσειν, 10.5).³² Pericles' abuse is perhaps meant to imply both that Elpinice's nostalgia for her brother's achievements is as dated as she and that the criticism she offers in public is unwomanly and inappropriate. In comparing her to a perfumed old women, Pericles treats her behavior as a kind of public lewdness—harsh words from the statesman who located woman's virtue precisely in her ability to be inconspicuous. Pericles' comments suggest the extent to which a woman's behavior, since it involves distinctions fundamental to the social order, is always a matter of public significance—her engaging in public policy is as inappropriate as an old woman's pursuit of eros. Indeed, it is no coincidence that Elpinice was criticized on both these scores: on the one hand, she was deeply involved in the negotiation of political and even military affairs; on the other, she was charged with the grossest misconduct: posing for a painting by Polygnotus and public cohabitation with and even marriage to her brother.³³

Archilochus elsewhere focuses on *growing* old rather than old age per se, exploiting the semantic ambiguity of *gēras* as both a particular time of life and the process of decline that leads to it, and finding in the figure of Neoboule a peg on which to hang the *fis anus* (you're getting old) theme.³⁴ She is the likely target in another fragment, which reviles a woman whose beauty and sex appeal are rapidly vanishing. As in later instances of this type of invective, the poem is likely stirred by revenge, the speaker punishing a woman perhaps well-known for her beauty who has rejected him:³⁵

> No longer too does your soft skin bloom; for already it is dried
>   and furrowed, and foul old age has ahold of you
> . . . and sweet desire has leapt away from your lovely face
>   . . . for indeed you are assailed again and again
> by blasts of wintry winds, and so many times . . .

> (οὐκέ]θ' ὁμῶς θάλλεις ἀπαλὸν χρόα· κάρφετα[ι γὰρ ἤδη

ὄγμοι]ς, κακοῦ δὲ γήραος καθαιρεῖ
.....] ἀφ᾽ ἱμερτοῦ δὲ θορῶν γλυκὺς ἵμερος π[ροσώπου
.....]κεν· ἦ γὰρ πολλὰ δή σ᾽ ἐπῆιξεν
πνεύμ]ατα χειμερίων ἀνέμων, μά<λα> πολλάκις δὲ [...., 188W).

Here as often in the Western tradition the woman's body is dismembered, fragmented, and analyzed. Her being becomes the sum of the
parts that constitute her, and she in turn is praised or blamed according to their condition. Skin and complexion are of course crucial
indices of female beauty. Penelope is often praised for the fairness of
her complexion, and we have seen above how Hesiod imagines the
"tender-skinned maiden" (παρθενικῆς ἁπαλόχροος, WD 519) who is
kept safe in her house from the blasts of the wintry wind.[36] In the
Cologne epode (196a), which we will examine below, the speaker
reaches the height of sexual arousal as he touches the girl's "young
skin, the charm of her youth" (νέον ἥβης ἐπήλυσιν χρόᾳ, 49–50). In
188 the indices of "foul old age" for which the speaker assails the
woman here are clearly generic, and all have to do with the condition
of the woman's complexion—dry skin, wrinkles, loss of facial charm.
As θάλλεις (you bloom) suggests a seasonal metaphor of blossoming
flowers in spring, the imagery of 5–6 presents her face as a field dried
and cracked by the icy blasts of winter. "Sweet desire" (γλυκὺς
ἵμερος), with its Homeric associations with beauty, desire, and the goddess who is their source, becomes a measure of the distance between
the woman's former perfection and present degraded condition.[37]

The emphasis throughout the fragment is on aging as a *process*, not
as a stage with some clearly defined beginning: hence the importance
of "already" (ἤδη) in line 1, the present tenses in 1 and 2, the idea of
repetition in πολλά and πολλάκις ("again and again . . . many times").
The speaker does not call the woman old—she is clearly not in any literal sense—but charts the insidious and premature advance of evil
(κακοῦ, 2) old age upon her. From an erotic perspective, old age can be
said to commence with the first signs of the aging process. In the
Hymn to Aphrodite male old age begins with maturity, as suggested in
the first gray hairs that appear on the head of Tithonus (228–29). For a
woman *gêras* is less a stage of life than a term of abuse that can be
hurled at her at any age for the impugned loss of those qualities that
made her desirable.

Although fragment 188 does not refer to the woman's sexual

behavior, this is an essential part of the conceptual complex. Just as
the untried virgin represents the most desirable female sex object, age
easily itself becomes a metaphor for sexual experience. In one sense, a
woman loses her youth *through* sex, and wealth of sexual experience
can be said to age her and make her less desirable as a sexual partner or
marital prospect.[38] This is an important theme in the Cologne epode
(196a), which by its length and content has so enlarged our understanding of Archilochus. This lengthy fragment presents a narrative in
which the speaker describes his attempt to seduce the young "daughter of Amphimedo" (10) and sister of Neoboule, and in which he
meets with at least limited success in achieving his object. This is
clearly not the occasion to take up the many complex and baffling
questions that this fragment raises: the motive of the speaker in this
attempted seduction and of the poet in writing it, the nature of the sexual favor that the speaker alludes to in 9–16 and that he describes at
44–53. We will limit ourselves here to a consideration of how extensively the poem draws on the *fis anus* theme and the relationship
between age and sexual experience.

The speaker-seducer of the poem takes pains with the young girl
to whom he speaks to establish his own youthful condition. He clearly
includes himself in the company of the "young men" (νέουσιν
ἀνδράσιν, 9) who enjoy the varieties of sexual delight (τέρψιες . . .
πολλαί, 13–14) that Aphrodite has to offer, and if the supplement suggested by Merkelbach and West in line 11 is accepted (εὖτ' ἀν
μελανθῆ[ι μοι γένυς), he deftly manages to defer discussion of marriage until his beard "grows dark," that is, until he is older and of more
marriageable age himself.[39] The two potential objects of the speaker's
desire are contrasted in terms of their age, the younger sister of
Neoboule and the "other girl" she recommends as a surrogate (clearly
Neoboule herself); age in turn is related to other categories: beauty,
sexual experience, marriageability, morality. The remarks of both
Neoboule's sister and the speaker are highly rhetorical and provide
two different representations of her age and character. Neither account is to be taken as simply "true." Both characters are driven by the
dramatic situation and their rhetorical purpose: the speaker in his
attempt to seduce the sister by flattering her at the expense of
Neoboule's defects and to abuse Neoboule in the bargain; the sister in
her attempt to deflect the urgent desire of the man who would have
her onto another object, Neoboule.[40]

The sister's youth is established independently and through the contrast with Neoboule. She is a *parthenos* (42), and her inexperience is reflected in her attempt to evade the speaker, in the timidity of her sexual response (44–50), and in the conventional metaphors of defloration in which the conclusion of the poem is couched. The pair reclines "in the blooming flowers" (ἐν ἄνθεσιν τηλεθάεσσι, 42–43); her sexual charms are "grassy gardens" (ποηφόρους κήπους, 23–24) protected by a stone fence and gate (θριγκοῦ . . . πυλέων, 21).[41] Her youthful beauty is emphasized in the language of their lovemaking, which tells of the speaker's sight of her "young skin, the charm of her youth" (νέον ἥβης ἐπήλυσιν χρόα, 49–50), of his embracing "the whole of her beautiful body" (ἅπαν τε σῶμα καλόν ἀμφαφώμενος, 51), and stroking her golden hair (ξανθῆς ἐπιψαύων τριχός, 53) as he reaches sexual climax.

Each of the competing characterizations of Neoboule exploits the semantic ambiguities of the situation and reveals the purposes of its speaker. The sister's description of Neoboule is full of kindnesses, euphemisms, and double-entendres. She recommends to the speaker the services of a "fair and tender maiden" (καλὴ τέρεινα παρθένος, 6) of "blameless beauty" (εἶδος ἄμωμον, 7) who is still within the house (ἐν ἡμετέρου, 4).[42] In doing so she plays upon the ambiguity of the word *parthenos*: she can legitimately present Neoboule as a maiden as she is still unmarried and living at home, the preserve of *parthenoi*.[43] She proceeds to speak of her sister as a girl "who is right now very eager" (ἣ νῦν μέγ' ἱμείρει, 5) and one whom "you will make a friend to you" (τὴν δὴ σὺ ποίησαι φίλην, 8), as though in speaking of such "eagerness" and "friendliness" she meant only her sister's readiness for marriage, yet clearly understanding that the speaker will catch the sexual overtones.

The speaker replies with a representation of Neoboule that is based on a different definition of her age. After a second thinly veiled proposition (21–24), he suggests that Neoboule is not a *parthenos* (6) but a *gyne* (30; cf. 33), and proceeds to exploit the abusive potential in the polarity of these terms. He challenges the sister's description of Neoboule's beauty and manipulates her language to emphasize her loss of beauty, her unbridled and promiscuous sexuality, and her unworthiness as a sexual *or* marriage partner. I translate West's conservative restoration of the text:

But now indeed know this: let some other
　　other man marry Neoboule.
Alas—she is overripe, twice so much (?)
and the flower of her maidenhood is lost to her
　　and the grace which once was upon her . . .
　　　for she . . . not enough
. . . and the crazy woman showed the measures of her . . .
　　Let her go to hell.
　　And let it not be
that I with a wife like her become a laughing stock to my
　　neighbors.
　　I much prefer you,
for you are neither deceitful nor two-faced,
　　but she is very cunning,
　　　and makes many men her friends.

> τὸ δὴ νῦν γνῶθι. Νεοβούλη[ν
> ἄ]λλος ἀνὴρ ἐχέτω·
> αἰαῖ, πέπειρα, δὶς [τόση,
> ἄν]θος δ᾽ ἀπερρύηκε παρθενήιον
> κ]αὶ χάρις ἢ πρὶν ἐπῆν·
> κόρον γὰρ οὐκ [
> ..]ης δὲ μέτρ᾽ ἔφηνε μαινόλις γυνή.
> ἐς] κόρακας ἄπεχε·
> μὴ τοῦτ᾽ ἐφοῖτ᾽ ἀν[
> ὅ]πως ἐγὼ γυναῖκα τ[ο]ιαύτην ἔχων
> γεί]τοσι χάρμ᾽ ἔσομαι·
> πολλὸν σὲ βούλο[μαι
> σὺ] μὲν γὰρ οὔτ᾽ ἄπιστος οὔτε διπλόη,
> ἡ δ]ὲ μάλ᾽ ὀξυτέρη,
> πολλοὺς δὲ ποιεῖτα[ι φίλους

(24–38)

Without ever calling Neoboule "old," the speaker associates her with a whole condition of physical, social, and moral degradation. In contrast with the verdant images of the sister's untrammeled sexuality, Neoboule's "maidenly flower" is lost (ἄνθος δ᾽ ἀπερρύηκε παρθενήιον, 27). The conventional floral image describing of the loss of her beauty and sexual integrity is extended in the following line. Neoboule is no longer the spring flower but the fruit that is soft and not just ripe (πέπειρα, 26) but rather "twice ripe," that is, "rotten," if we accept West's restoration of the line. Fallen from the branch and disregarded, Neoboule is without the godlike charm and maidenly bloom (χάρις, 28) that once was hers.[44] This word for ripe (πέπειρα) is frequently used to describe aging men and women, where the idea of ripeness suggests a fullness of sexual experience at whatever age.[45] In *Ecclesiazusae* 895–96 the first old hag uses the word to describe herself euphemistically: she says to the young man whom she hopes to seduce that "skill (τὸ σοφόν, here certainly of lovemaking) is not to be found in young girls (ἐν νέαις) but in 'ripe ones' (ἐν πεπαίραις)."[46] But the word can also be used to describe a woman who is sexually "worn out." There is a revealing use of the word in a fragment of Anacreon, where again we see the importance of skin quality in male appreciations of female beauty. Here a woman speaking in the first person says: "Already I am becoming a wrinkled old thing, over-ripe fruit (πέπειρα), thanks to your lust" (432: tr. Campbell). The speaker here apparently attributes her premature aging to her promiscuity.[47] As in Anacreon, Archilochus implies a connection between the physical condition and the morals of Neoboule, whose sexual generosity has cost her her youthful good looks. From her fallen beauty it is only a short step to suggesting her utter depravity: her insatiable (κόρον . . . οὐκ, 29—the text is incomplete) appetite for sex and a probable reference to her lack of moderation (μέτρ' ἔφηνε, 30). Neoboule becomes a sex-mad woman (μαινόλις γυνή, 30) who makes herself available to all. Picking up on the sister's reference to "friendliness" (ποίησαι φίλην, 8), he says that yes, Neoboule is friendly to *many* men (πολλοὺς δὲ ποιεῖται φίλους, 38), in effect labelling her a prostitute.[48]

The speaker pictures himself as the husband of "this kind of a woman," "the laughing stock of my neighbors" (34), recalling Hesiod's advice to young men to be sure to marry someone who is a virgin (παρθενικήν) to avoid becoming a neighborhood joke (*WD* 701). The seducer here becomes the moralist, dutifully reciting what he has learned from his teacher, lecturing and flattering his student: *she* is terribly cunning, but *you're* not deceitful or two-faced (36–37). Archilochus, exploiting the unsavory associations of old age, is able to beat Neoboule with both ends of the stick: because Neoboule behaves scandalously, she is by implication "old"; and because she is "old," she is vulnerable to the abuse that comes with old age. Already in early lyric the aging process for a woman can imply not only a movement in time but a change in social status, from maidenhood to lascivious and even promiscuous sexuality and an implicit crossing of the boundaries between free woman and prostitute.

SAPPHO

In these poets we hear three different perspectives on the situation of the aged and aging woman. In Homer she is treated with sympathy and respect, and the aging process is described in terms that reflect the Homeric ideal of "like-mindedness" between husband and wife. Hesiod, ever begrudging of woman for her seductive power and the economic toll she takes upon the house, sees her as an evil necessary to the security of one's old age; the aged woman, this duty discharged, holds no further interest for him. Archilochus, in fragments 188 and 196a, works in traditional forms of abuse that value women for their youthful beauty and virginity only to make them ever vulnerable to the charge of growing old. All three of these models need to be appreciated as male modes of description and set alongside ways in which women themselves regard their bodies, their sexuality, and the aging process.

In an insightful comment on some of Sappho's most well-known verses, DuBois suggests that in the image of the fields in fragment 96, the poet redefines the nature of the female body, subverting traditional male language, which typically regards woman's body as a field to be plowed, with a parthenogenetic description of dew-fed fields of wild flowers:

> Now she stands out among Lydian women like the rosy fingered moon after sunset, surpassing all the stars, and its light spreads alike over the salt sea and the flowery fields; the dew is shed in beauty, and roses bloom and tender chervil and flowery melilot.
>
> (96.6–14: tr. Campbell)

Says DuBois, "Sappho seems deliberately to take up the hegemonic language of Greek culture . . . and to offer a parallel universe, one that refuses the aims of male culture."[49] Such a reading attempts to appreciate the social value of the metaphors through which the female body is represented and the different meanings they have in male and female discourse: Sappho here takes the traditional imagery of flowers and virgins and by placing it in a different context allows it to yield a more distinctively feminine meaning. This perspective helps us to see Sappho's poetry as feminine not just because it opposes women's interests and activities to men's, and not simply for the different language it sometimes uses, but for the different *order of experience* that lies behind it.[50] Yet the set of erotic assumptions that is usually brought to bear on Sappho's poetry, despite the attempts of critics to "adjust" these according to its homoerotic context and content, often reflects the androcentric biases of the Greek literary tradition and of our culture.[51] As Sappho's poetry provides the only opportunity we have in archaic poetry to study the language in which women define the meaning of their own bodies, we will do well to appreciate the access it provides, in the words of another critic, to "woman's understanding of erotic experience in a totally feminine context."[52]

The relation between eros and age is an important if neglected part of this feminine context. Although Sappho mentions old age infrequently and in language that at first seems reminiscent of the male tradition, I will suggest that her poetry provides a distinctive—I would argue distinctively *feminine*—perspective on the relationship between age and eros. The following discussion is framed in the context of these larger questions: Can we speak in the context of Sappho of distinctively different voices for men and women as regards the erotic meaning of old age, and of a different world of female experience that is behind it? And is there a relation between the female experience behind these poems and the homoerotic relations that provide its social and poetic context? I believe that the answer to both questions is yes, and that Sappho's perspective on love and old age is embedded within an erotic and a poetic world that offers a different conceptualization of the life course as a whole. This understanding differs from that of the male poets not in the definition of its constituent stages but in the determination of their interrelationship, and in the role erotic poetry can play in negotiating the distance and the tension between them. This perspective is revealed most distinctively in her emphasis on the interconnectedness of the life course and the coherence of its stages and in the role of erotic and poetic memory (μναμοσύνα) in integrating the life course.

Such a perspective is foreign to the male lyric-erotic tradition, which is focused upon the erotic "moment" of seduction-possession and emphasizes those distinctions of age that provide both the preconditions of love and the obstacles to its attainment. In this male tradition the opposing roles and activities of the active lover and the passive beloved are oriented around a single goal: the seduction by the older man of the virginal boy or girl poised at the peak of erotic perfection: the *pais* in the bloom of young manhood, the barely pubescent *parthenos*.[53] The ensuing relationships are by definition transitory and ephemeral, and the lover does not look to sustain his erotic exhilaration beyond the brief period of conquest and possession. Indeed, the love object seems to have no history before or after this moment; he or she exists only as the object of the lover's desire and possession. The transient nature of these relationships reflects the duality within the male perspective, which regards the love object as both the specific individual (capable of being seduced) and as a temporary locus for the absolute Love which is the real (and impossible) object of the lover's desire.[54]

The male tradition of erotic poetry (as we will see in the following chapter) emphasizes the discreteness of the life stages and typically laments the passage from one stage to the next for the erotic loss it entails, whether as a result of the lover's old age or the beloved's maturation. Sappho's poetry, on the other hand, compensates for the realities of time and change, and suggests that love and erotic poetry are able to reintegrate experience into a connected whole. Sappho's poetic vision finds in the very mutability and temporality of erotic experience an aesthetic affirmation of the continuity of life, from girlhood through old age. In her poetry erotic experience permeates the whole of human life, bridges the distinctions between its stages, and offers a vehicle by which humans achieve a certain kind of transcendence over time.

This kind of overarching perspective on the life course is unavailable to the gods, who experience life fully but in terms only of that one stage in which they are eternally frozen. As their experience of life and love involves no real temporal limits, Sappho's representation of the gods often recognizes the differences between the divine and human condition, whether in their incomparable beauty ("it is not easy for us to rival goddesses in loveliness of figure," 96.22–23: tr. Campbell) or their immunity to the vicissitudes of eros. In fragment 1 this difference is measured in Aphrodite, whose detachment from the vicissitudes of human love allows her to console the speaker, who is struggling to win her beloved, and who reveals her detachment and serentity in the smile on her immortal face (μειδιαίσαισ᾽ ἀθανάτῳ προσώπῳ, 14).[55] Another fragment captures this kind of distance in the vow of perpetual virginity that Artemis swears by Zeus himself:

> "By your head, I shall always be a virgin (unwed), (hunting) on the peaks of the (lonely) mountains: come, grant this for my sake." So she spoke, and the father of the blessed gods nodded his consent; and gods (and men) call her (the virgin, shooter of deer,) huntress, a great title. Love, (loosener of limbs,) never approaches her.
>
> (44A.5–11: tr. Campbell)

Artemis' distance from Eros reflects not only her disdain for sexual relations but her distance from the experience of those girls who are the object of Sappho's attention, who cannot hope to remain *parthenoi* forever. The gods know only life, not the life course, and eros is for them only a source of sensual pleasure and release from their temporary desires. Accordingly, love need not serve for them any such transcendent or integrating purpose.

It is more typically through ritual that humans escape the limitations of time and temporarily achieve the absolute experience of the gods. The integrating power of ritual is illustrated in the fragment on the wedding of Hector and Andromache (44), where eros is represented in its most public and socially sanctioned form—those rites of passage for bride and bridegroom that ensure the continuity of the community. Even as the poem carefully age-grades the different populations of the Trojan community and assigns them their respective spheres of activity, it welds them together in ritual celebration. When Idaeus brings the news that "Hector and his companions" are escorting the new bride to Troy by ship, we are told that

> nimbly his dear father leapt up, and the news went to his friends throughout the spacious city. At once the sons of Ilus yoked the mules to the smooth-running carriages, and the whole crowd of women and (tender?) ankled maidens climbed on board. Apart (drove) the daughters of Priam . . . and unmarried men yoked horses to chariots. . . . and the sweet-sounding pipe and cithara were mingled and the sound of castanets, and maidens sang clearly a holy song, and a marvelous echo reaches the sky . . . and everywhere in the streets was . . . bowls and cups . . . myrrh and cassia and frankincense were mingled. The elder

women cried out joyfully, and all the men let forth a lovely high-pitched strain, calling on Paean, the Archer skilled in the lyre, and they sang in praise of the godlike Hector and Andromache.

(44.13–19, 24–34: tr. Campbell)

The wedding ritual effects a unity at every level: in the music that blends the sounds of pipes, strings, percussives, and human voices into one "marvelous echo"; in the exotic fragrances that fill the air and the offerings that are poured out to the gods; in the activities that bind together the constituent groups of the community—young and old, men and women, married and unmarried. Here eros, even as it celebrates the passage from one life stage to the next, provides a moment in which the categories that underpin the social order are transcended. The poem ends by emphasizing the role of poetry as the medium between gods and mortals, with Apollo in his triple capacity as healer (Paean), archer, and lyre player receiving the songs that are offered him. The poem thus juxtaposes two forms of timelessness: the agelessness of the gods and the holistic experience of life available to mortals in ritual celebration. And it is specifically through the power of poetry, as the men offer such song to the gods and Sappho in turn offers it back, that humans overcome the fragmentation of the life course and in some way approximate the divine condition.

While the epithalamion for Hector and Andromache works in the context of heteroerotic relationships and the conventions of age that govern marital relationships, the communal and ritual context allows a certain transcendence of these differences. In another fragment the *persona loquens* addresses, with striking familiarity, a man who is apparently a suitor for her hand and insists that he respect the conventions of age and social role.

But if you are my friend, take the bed of a younger woman, for I will not endure being the elder one in a partnership.

(121.1–4: tr. Campbell)

Here the polar structures of lover-beloved, older-younger, and husband-wife as they are institutionalized in the larger culture seem to preclude the relationship the "friend" (φίλος) proposes. In the homoerotic lyrics, on the other hand, Sappho seems to suggest a less rigid system of age relations, one in which the role definitions of older-lover and younger-beloved do not so completely define erotic experience. This distinction is central to the understanding of fragment 1, in which Aphrodite comforts "Sappho" with the assurance that in time the girl who flees her advances will have her turn at the role of helpless lover and experience the same kind of rejection.

> If she runs away, soon shall she pursue; if she does not accept gifts, why, she shall give them instead; and if she does not love, soon she shall love even against her will.
>
> (1. 21–24: tr. Campbell)

Sappho points to a kind of reciprocity of erotic roles such that the attitude of lover and beloved are poles of experience governed not so much by age as by disposition and affection: that girl who now plays the role of the elusive beloved will soon find herself in the position of the speaker.[56] This reciprocity is also reflected in fragment 24.3–4, in which the speaker tells her beloved of how she will someday recall "these (beautiful) things which we did *in our youth* (ἐν νεότατι)." Here the relationship is described not in terms of the different "actual" ages of the lover and beloved but as a mutual affection that locates the partners together in the life course.

To the extent that we wish to identify the speaker in these poems with the poet herself, relationships with members of her *thiasos* (band) may *de facto* have assigned the roles of lover-beloved to older and younger respectively.[57] Yet at the same time it is clear that this age differential does not describe the range of erotic experience that is celebrated in Sappho. Gentili has argued, on the basis of lyric and other testimonia, for the existence of liaisons within the maiden's choruses (that is, among the *parthenoi* themselves) of an "official" character, ceremonially celebrated and of "a genuinely matrimonial type." He finds one model of this in the relationship of Agido and Hagesichora in Alcman's *partheneion* and suggests that a number of Sappho's epithalamia, assumed to describe "true" marriage ceremonies, may have been written in celebration of relationships within the *thiasos*.[58] There is, at any rate, no shortage of references in Sappho to the deep affection of these young women for one another. And there is absolutely no reason to believe that these relationships were conceived or conducted according to the conventions of age that applied in adult male relationships with girls or young boys.[59]

Apart from this restructuring of the roles of lover and beloved, Sappho's "personal" homoerotic lyrics suggest a more expansive temporality than is generally the case in male lyric. They draw repeatedly on what Winkler describes as the *process* of love as the speaker struggles with "the ebb and flow of conflicting emotions, of sorrow succeeded by joy, of apprehensiveness followed by relief, of loss turning into victory."[60] The temporality of love in these poems opposes the male linear pattern of pursuit-obstacle-capture with a more sustained dynamic and a more varied arrangement of roles and behaviors. By this I do not mean simply that such homoerotic relationships "last longer" than those in the male tradition, although this is certainly one aspect of the ideal of love in Sappho's verse, which abounds in declarations of enduring love and testimony of affections that survive physical separation.[61] In Sappho Eros is characterized by a fundamentally different kind of temporality, the entire experience of love is more fluid, fixed less on the lover's consumation of his desire than on the history and the vicissitudes of the relationship. Where in the male tradition the lover attempts to find Eros in the act of sexual possession, Sappho's poetry works to drive the experience of eros through past and present, in effect eroticizing the whole life course.

The temporality of love in this homoerotic discourse is directly related to the social situation of the *parthenoi* of whom and to whom she sings. Sappho represents the loves of these women in terms not just of their physical beauty but of their whole social predicament: *en route* to marriage, the loss of virginity, the commencement of heterosexual relations, the business of motherhood, the trauma of geographical relocation and domestic reorientation. Where love is transitory or short-lived, this is not because eros is achieved and exhausted in sexual conquest or undone by the aging of the lover or beloved, but because the obstacles that devolve from the "real-life" situations separate these women against their will. These separations and dislocations, whether actual or potential, infuse Sappho's verses with an almost tragic sense of loss—what Schadewaldt calls *Trennungsschmerz*[62]—as her life and those of the women she loves move apart from one another. Sappho compensates for these changes in the ability of memory (μναμασύνα) to sustain and extend erotic experience over time and space. Gentili remarks upon the power of memory as one of the most distinctive features of Sappho's poetry: "Memory is not simply, as in Homer, a means of evoking emotions and sensations: it reactualizes shared experiences in paradigmatic fashion and offers the assurance that the life lived together exists as an absolute *reality* beyond space and time."[63] Burnett distinguishes Sapphic memory from nostalgia and sentimentality, identifying it with the discipline in which Sappho as poet-teacher schooled her young charges: "What Sappho taught was a disciplined mental process which, by reconstructing past actions in a certain way, kept one fit for the best that the present might propose."[64]

Sapphic memory becomes a kind of erotic third term, which mediates between those poles of desire (πόθος) and possession that alone provide the structure of relations in the male tradition, and that paradoxically combines in itself both the longing of desire and the fulfillment of possession. Fragment 94 evokes a dialogue, in which the speaker bids farewell to the tearful complaints of her beloved, who describes their imminent separation in terms of the "terrible things we have suffered" (δεῖνα πεπόνθαμεν, 4). "Sappho" consoles her with the power of memory, which as Burnett observes becomes an exhortation to beauty and pleasure and is followed by an object lesson, "a demonstration of memory in action, offered fictionally to the senses of the girl, and by the poem as a whole to ours."[65]

> Go and fare well and remember (μέμναισ') me, for you know how we cared for you. If not, why then I want to remind (ὄμναισαι) you . . . and the good times we had (κάλ' ἐπάσχομεν).
>
> (94.7–11: tr. Campbell)

The poem continues with a litany of their mutual desires and pleasures which, as Stigers says, "recalls a whole range of shared experience, including but not limited to the erotic."[66] In fragment 16, in which the speaker meditates upon the meaning of "most beautiful" (κάλλιστον), the example of Helen similarly prompts a reminiscence that makes present the absent Anactoria:

> . . . (and she?) has reminded (ὀνέμναισ') me now of Anaktoria who is not here.
>
> (16.15–16: tr. Campbell)

Sapphic relationships are characterized less by their literal endurance—an ideal unavailable to these young women—than by their reformation and recapitulation in memory, which bridges the physical space between lover and beloved and overcomes the fractured temporality of life itself. In the process of recollection the various stages of life are brought into a wholeness and a new interrelationship. In one fragment the speaker recalls how

> I loved you, Atthis, once long ago (πάλαι ποτά). You seemed to me a small, graceless child.
>
> (49: tr. Campbell)

Here the poetic *mis en scene* locates Sappho's favorite Atthis and the speaker at some later and deeper moment in their relationship, reflecting on their impressions of each other even before the time of their togetherness when Atthis was still a "small, graceless child" (σμίκρα ... πάις. . . κἄχαρις) and mapping out a history of the relationship from infatuation to intimacy.[67] Another fragment suggests the dramatic ups and downs of the relationship—

> Atthis, the thought of me has grown hateful to you, and you fly off to Andromeda
>
> (131: tr. Campbell)

—allowing the reader to appreciate the relationship and its vicissitudes unfolding in time. Fragment 24, which we looked at above, speaks of a recollection perhaps set in the future, even in old age,[68] of beauty and erotic experience shared jointly "in youth."

> . . . (you will?) remember (...]εμνάσθ') . . . , for we too did these things in our . . . youth: many lovely . . .
>
> (24.2–5: tr. Campbell)

The temporality of these poems does not isolate love in the past as an irretrievable moment of desire or union but extends the experience of eros throughout the life course. Sappho's ability to sustain the reality of past experience in the present is another expression of what Winkler calls her *many-mindedness*, her ability to integrate in one poem "several personal perspectives, whose multiple relations to each other set up a field of voices and evaluations."[69]

This process of erotic recollection is ultimately identified with, and indistinguishable from, the poetic process itself—that process through which Sappho as poet and persona schools these girls and teaches them how to give form, expression, and beauty to their own recollection. Burnett explains, "They had the daily experience of hearing themselves transposed into music, and by taking her songs with them when they left, they took a poetic vision of their life along—a vision of light and motion, music and perfume, all nurturing, and nurtured by, desire. That was what they were to recall, for Sappho taught them that their present experiences of love, enhanced by song and volatilised by memory, would let them recognize beauty later on, in all of its various forms."[70] Such moments of reflection are presented as occasions for lyric composition and performance, whether the speaker/composer is "Sappho" or another woman in her *thiasos*. In fragment 22 the speaker finds in the singer's longing for her beloved an opportunity for a performance of erotic verse:

> I bid you, Abanthis, take (your lyre?) and sing (ἀ[είδην) of Gongyla, while desire (πόθος) once again flies around you
>
> (9–12: tr. Campbell)

It is precisely the power of song to give body, form, and permanence to the recollection of erotic experience, even when (as here) it is not clear whether the beloved is present to hear herself celebrated in song.

It is through such recollection that poetry "re-members" erotic experience, recalling it and refashioning it as a whole so that the present—wherever that moment is located—is newly charged with erotic significance. In fragment 27 a woman is invited to put into song her memories of her childish experience with love, appropriately, on the occasion of a wedding.

> . . . for you were once a (tender?) child (πάις) . . . come and sing this (μέλπεσθ'), all of you . . . converse . . . and grant us . . . (generous?) favors; for we are going to a wedding; and you too (know?) this well; but send the maidens away as quickly as possible; and may the gods have . . . (There is no) road to great Olympus for mortals.
>
> (27.1–13: tr. Campbell)

The final verse recognizes the distance between gods and mortals but finds some compensation in song and ritual.

In another poem Atthis is consoled with the assurance that the woman she loved remembers her for her singing:

> ... Sardis ... often turning her thoughts in this direction ... (she hon-
> ored) you as being like a goddess for all to see and took most delight in
> your song (μόλπαι). Often as she goes to and fro she remembers
> (μνάσθεισ') gentle Atthis.
>
> (96.1–5, 15–16: tr. Campbell)

Here the absent lover associates the divine beauty of Atthis with the
beauty of her song. Eros is transformed from an external force that dis-
rupts the life of the lover to an integrating force that heals the divisions
of time and space and is capable of eroticizing any moment or place.
Memory and poetry become symbolic equivalents. And just as Sappho
understands that it is through memory that experience is sustained
over time, so she sees that poetry provides a guarantee of its durability
beyond her life: "Someone, I say, will remember us in the future" (147:
tr. Campbell).[71]

It is against this background that we can finally look at the two
fragments in which old age is mentioned directly, where these themes
come together with powerful results. Poems 21 and 58, which survive
only in very fragmentary condition, have only recently been given
close critical attention.[72] In each of the two poems the speaker seems
clearly to be talking about the relationship between love and old age
and to offer the condition of her own body in evidence: indeed, each
fragment uses the same phrase (χρόα γῆρας ἤδη, 21.6 = 58.13) to discuss the onset of old age, where the emphasis on the harm old age does
to the skin suggests that area where women are traditionally most vulnerable to the charge that they are growing old.[73] Campbell renders
the scant remains of the sixteen lines of fragment 21, with a few tenta-
tive restorations, as follows:

> ... (in possession of?) ... pity ... trembling ... old age now ... (my)
> skin ... covers ... (Love?) flies pursuing (the young?) ... glorious ...
> taking (your lyre?) sing to us of the violet-robed one ... especially ...
> wanders.

The speaker openly acknowledges that her body is no longer a thing of
beauty, and ὄλοφυν in line 2, a rare expression for pity or lamentation,
may report some consolation offered to (perhaps refused by?) the
speaker for the misfortune that besets her. She refers to the symptoms

of old age in highly conventional terms: the trembling (τρομέροις, 4) of her limbs (?), and the waning of her complexion (where χρόα γῆρας ἤδη (6) clearly recall Archilochus' words of abuse in 188 (οὐκέ]θ' ὁμῶς θάλλεις ἀπαλὸν χρόα· κάρφεται γὰρ ἤδη / ὄγμοις, κακοῦ δὲ γήραος καθαιρεῖ, 1–2).[74] So too, ἀμφιβάσκει (covers) in 7 recalls the use of ἀμφι- in a number of similar descriptions of old age.[75] We are told that someone—Wilamowitz suggests Eros himself—"flies off in pursuit" ("Ερος πέταται διώκων) of some other, perhaps younger, woman.[76]

In the tatters of the third stanza we can glimpse a reconfiguration of eros and age in which this predicament finds some redress in the therapeutic power of poetic song.[77] Although old age does not enjoy the experience of love immediately or physically, it is not as in male lyric a thing of erotic irrelevance. Here old age finds access to Eros in the *shared* poetic recollection of experience and in the transformation of Eros into art. The speaker of the poem, after emphasizing her own aged condition, issues an invitation for a song. Here, as elsewhere, this recollection is to be sung by a woman (λάβοισα) to a group of women (ἄεισον ἄμμι), and its subject is to be "the violet-robed one" (τὰν ἰόκολπον)—certainly Aphrodite herself.[78] The poem thus defines itself, in the pattern we have seen repeatedly in Sappho, as a kind of prelude to a performance or exchange of erotic verse. Here, despite the absence of one kind of love, Love is made present again through the traditions of erotic song, as experience preserved in the power of memory. Poetry, in Homer the repository of cultural tradition, here becomes a storehouse of erotic experience from which love can be extended through time and space and can overcome the obstacles that it cannot in the male traditions.

These themes are more fully developed in what remains of poem 58. Campbell's emendation and translation of the poorly preserved fragment represent a poem of some twenty-six lines, the first five verses of which are entirely lost. The final two lines, preserved independently, represent the actual ending of the poem.

> . . . (fleeing?) . . . (was bitten?) . . . (you of the many names?) . . . gives success to the mouth . . . fair gifts (of the deep-busomed Muses?) . . . children . . . song-lover, (player) of clear-sounding lyres . . . old age already (withers?) all (my) skin, and (my) hair (turned white) from black . . . My knees do not carry (me) . . . (to dance) like young

fawns . . . but what could I do? . . . not possible to become (ageless?) . . . rosy-armed Dawn . . . carrying (to) the ends of the earth . . . yet (age) seized (him) . . . (immortal?) wife . . . thinks . . . might give . . . but I love delicacy . . . love has obtained for me the brightness and beauty of the sun.

(58.5–26)

The symptoms of old age as they are described in the middle of the poem are in terms that again are primarily physical and deliberately conventional. The speaker complains of her withered skin (πάντα χρόα γῆρας ἤδη,13); her hair is now gray (λεῦκαι δ᾿ ἐγένοντο τρίχες ἐκ μελαίναν, 14: Hunt's restoration of the first half of the line seems secure); her limbs are weakened and no longer carry her as they once did (γόνα δ᾿ οὐ φέροισι, 15). There is a traditional emphasis on the suddenness of the onslaught of age, captured in the ἤδη of 13 ("already now old age. . . ") and the ἐγένοντο of 14 ("my hair (has) turned white from black.")[79] These symptoms are in turn underscored in a reflection on the past: her knees are now no longer "fawn-like" (ἴσα νεβρίοισι), a traditional image of youthful vitality, the speaker perhaps thinking of those dancers in the choruses she composed.

This inventory of woes concludes with a similarly conventional attitude of acceptance ("Zurücknahme"), a plaintive "but what could I do about it?" (ἀλλὰ τί κεν ποείην; 17), in which the speaker recognizes the inevitability of the aging process. More important is the way in which the verses that precede and follow place the disfigurements of age in the larger context of love, the lyre, and the life course. The speaker refers to someone—perhaps a singer, perhaps the Muses themselves who "gives to the mouth proficiency" (θῆται στύματι πρόκοψιν, 10). She refers to "beautiful gifts" (κάλα δῶρα), to "children" (παῖδες, 11), and to the "song-loving (someone) . . . of the clear-sounding lyres" (φιλάοιδον λιγύραν χελύνναν)—all doubtless references to the delights of song and the lyre and most probably to the accomplishments of the speaker herself. Di Benedetto, restoring γεραίρετε Μοίσαν at the beginning of 11 and λάβοισαι in 12, allows us to read more fully what is clearly a typical request for a song or a number of songs from the speaker to a group of young women gathered around her: "children, honor the beautiful gifts of the deep-busomed Muses, taking up the song-loving . . . of the clear-sounding lyres."[80]

In this way poem 58 juxtaposes an account of the symptoms of old age with an invitation to song that parallels that in 21.11–13 and previews the theme of the unique culture of song that will be resumed in the poem's closing references to the concept of "delicacy" (ἀβροσύνα).

In the lines that follow the mention of old age (γῆρας,13), the speaker introduces a mythological reference (one of a relatively small number in Sappho), which again serves to measure the distance between gods and mortals.[81] In 18ff. the human condition is defined in relation to "rosy-armed Eos" (βροδόπαχυν Αὔων), who is certainly also the "immortal wife" (ἀθανάταν ἄκοιτιν) referred to in 22. There is general agreement that the speaker is using the myth of Eos and Tithonus to describe the folly of seeking eternal youth. D. Page suggests, rightly I think, that in 18 (οὐ δύνατον γένεσθαι . . .) the speaker is acknowledging the impossibility of recovering youth: "it is not possible to become . . . ."[82] This in turn sustains the tone of resignation in 17, so that the myth would appear to serve its regular function of defining old age as an irreducible of the human condition. We are told how Eos carried off her beloved Tithonus to the ends of the earth (ἔσχατα γᾶς φέροισα 20), all in vain of course, since this dream of eternal youth was to fail when her lover falls prey to old age: as Page again aptly suggests, the subject of "seized" (ἔμαρψε) in 21 is in all likelihood old age (γῆρας) itself.[83]

But Page also admits his inability to see the relation of the last two lines of the poem to what precedes.

> . . . but I love delicacy . . . love has obtained for me the brightness and beauty of the sun.
>
> (58.5–26)
>
> (ἔγω δὲ φίλημμ' ἀβροσύναν,   ]τοῦτο καί μοι
>   τὸ λά[μπρον ἔρος τὠελίω καὶ τὸ κά]λον λέ[λ]ογχε)

The lines are cited in Athenaeus 687b (the lacuna and the τοῦτο are added from the papyrus) and presented as a quotation from the *Lives* of Clearchus, where the moralistic context is clearly at odds with the spirit in Sappho. Intent to prove that elegance (ἀβρότης) should never be divorced from virtue, the philosopher offers the verses as evidence that even Sappho was loathe to separate the two (ἠδέσθη τὸ καλὸν τῆς ἀβρότητος ἀφελεῖν). According to Clearchus, Sappho proclaims that her desire to live—her "love of the sun," (ἔρος τὠελίω, which he sub-

sequently paraphrases as ἡ τοῦ ζῆν ἐπιθυμία)—involves for her both
"brightness" (τὸ λάμπρον) and "honor" (τὸ κάλον). But the moral
wedge that he would drive between the two fits neither this poem nor
Sappho generally.[84] Most critics and translators, though eschewing
the moralistic interpretation that Clearchus offers, construe as he does
the phrase ἔρος τὠελίω or "love of the sun" to be the subject of
λέλογχε, and understand Sappho to be speaking of her "love of life."[85]
In justification of this reading, they point to the long association of life
and light in Greek literature: as to live is to "see the light," so the desire
to live might be expressed as the "love of the sun."[86] On the other
hand, ἔρος τὠελίω as an expression of the desire to live has no exact
parallel, and while in some other poet this phrase might suggest a
more general delight in life, ἔρος (or perhaps Ἔρος) in Sappho is far
more likely to sustain its regular *erotic* connotations.[87] I prefer to follow Schadewaldt in taking ἔρος alone without genitive complement as
the subject of λέλογχε, and with Campbell to assign the genitive
τὠελίω to the double object τὸ λάμπρον and τὸ κάλον as describing
the brilliant beauty of the sun.[88] There can be no certainty in the matter, but Campbell's translation (which does not attempt to restore the
lacuna that ends with τοῦτο) comes closer I think to Sappho's sense:

> But I love delicacy . . . love has obtained for me the brightness and beau-
> ty of the sun.

Yet Campbell too is puzzled by the meaning of the verses and suggests that they mean simply that "love has kept me alive."[89] Clearly the
verses call for careful attention. As elsewhere in Sappho, the speaker
stresses the unique value of *her* perspective: "But *I* . . . " (ἔγω δέ).[90]
Having provided an exemplum of ill-fated loved, she declares that she
finds the object of *her* affection (φίλημμι) in "elegance" (ἀβροσύνα).
The concept of elegance serves as a central idea in Sappho's discourse,
evoking the femininity of her poetry and the delicate relationships and
softness of life that characterize her world: Preisshofen rightly suggests that no word better describes Sappho's circle and no theme is
more aptly applied to her poetry as a whole.[91] More than just dainti-
ness or fastidiousness, *elegance* connotes that cult of luxurious sensuality, splendor, and style by which the Sapphic *thiasos* distinguished
itself and fashioned an aesthetic that defined the poetry and the lives
of these women.

The question is then to find the relation of this concept to the preceding mythological exemplum and to the final sentence of the poem. I believe that the speaker is suggesting here that in elegance she has found an *alternate* form of immortality, one that can be opposed to that which Tithonus attempted but lost, and that forces a rereading of the traditional myth. Gentili comments on the significance Sappho attaches to the myth of Tithonus. In other poetic contexts Tithonus stands as a symbol of the worst misfortune imaginable, yet

> here he is only a symbol of the the irreversability of earthly time. Old age is not, even in its ugliness, a disaster without remedy—a condition of total misery in which everything loved and desired in youth must be abandoned. It is, rather, an unavoidable episode in the passage of biological time, one that has failed to destroy the essence of the reality Sappho has constructed within the circle of her friends: delight in life's splendor, and love of "the brilliant and beautiful."[92]

Sappho opposes to the negative poetic and mythological traditions of old age a vision of a more spiritual dimension of life that is impervious to age and corruption.[93]

But we need also to consider the wider implications of these verses in terms of gender. Sappho here rejects the male definition of old age as it has been represented in myth and poetry, that is, in traditional poetic interpretations of the Tithonus myth and their accounts of the horrors of old age.[94] She offers a different and more authentically feminine experience, one which is able to accept the decline of the body and the loss of physical beauty without implying her devaluation as a person or limiting the possibility of love to this single dimension. Sappho opposes to traditional negative and male interpretations of old age a distinctive female value that survives the physical degeneration of time. Love *has won* for her (with emphasis on the perfect force of λέλογχε) a brightness and beauty that continue into old age. We may further note the way that Sappho extends this perspective in the interplay between the mythological exemplum and the final lines. Sappho here associates the idea of elegance with love itself (φίλημμ' . . . ἔρος), suggesting a broader range of what is meant by sexual and sensual. Where in the male tradition old age entails the obliteration of erotic delight, the speaker here refuses to regard age and eros as mutually exclusive and introduces a different level of contrast: between an understanding of erotic experience that is literal and physical, as represented in Tithonus' failure to keep Eos, and the speaker's success in winning an alternate form of eros precisely *through* elegance—that world of poetic culture that we see "in action" in the poem's opening. This contrast is captured exquisitely in the symmetry between the speaker's experience as described here and that described in the mythic exemplum. Where the male Tithonus attempts but *fails* to achieve possession of "rosy-armed Eos," the female sun/dawn, the female speaker *succeeds* in winning for her portion the sun itself in all its incomparable brightness and beauty. And most importantly, it is love itself ($\check{\epsilon}\rho o\varsigma$, 26) that has been the agent of this successful attempt at Sappho's kind of immortality. Fragment 58 is the most striking of Sappho's attempts to reconcile love and age, and distinguishes the female and homoerotic perspective she brings to the theme. In it we can hear quite clearly a tension between female old age and the male traditions of myth and poetry, as well as a different voice that attempts to find continuity through life into old age, even within the erotic context.

Sappho provides a radical response to male perspectives on the theme of aging, which emphasize the devaluation of women and the reduction of eros to what is simply physical and present. Her poems speak directly to the Archilochean equation of woman and body, and the view that as her body ages, her value, always precarious, is further "marked down." In defining the experience of women with such sensitivity, Sappho reflects the sympathy that the *Odyssey* shows for the situation of the aging Penelope. At the same time she implicitly rejects the Homeric complementarity of the life course, which sees men and women moving together through life, in favor of one that emphasizes what is different about aging for women and what is distinctive in women's experience. In this respect, ironically, she is closer to the Hesiodic appreciation of women as a separate race or $\gamma\acute{\epsilon}\nu o\varsigma$. And where Archilochus had showed the way in which the individual male poet can use poetry to wield the charge of age like a weapon against women, Sappho finds paradoxically in poetry itself, not the blame poetry of invective but the community of shared song, a means of retaining not only dignity but also erotic experience in old age. Although we have rejected Clearchus' translation and moralistic interpretation of the final lines of fragment 58, the words with which he introduces the verses capture the main point, when he attributes them to "Sappho, who was in all truth both a woman *and* a poet" ($\gamma\upsilon\nu\grave{\eta}$ . . . $\kappa\alpha\grave{\iota}$ $\pi o\iota\tau\acute{\eta}\rho\iota\alpha$).

CHAPTER 4

Geronterotic Images: Age, Sex, and Society in Early Greek Poetry

> The sexual life of both men and women continues until the climacteric, which is a momentous change or crisis . . . when the balance between tissue waste and restitution is disordered. After this event, the individual is in the afternoon of life and is again sexless from a physical standpoint.
> —Dr. James Foster Scott, *The Sexual Instinct* (1898)

> Sexuality is not the most intractable element in power relations, but rather one of those endowed with the greatest instrumentality: useful for the greatest number of maneuvers and capable of serving as a point of support, as a linchpin, for the most varied strategies.
> —Michel Foucault, *The History of Sexuality*

THERE is an intriguing moment in Plato's *Symposium* when the tragic poet Agathon, flush with his victory at the Lenaea and the focus in a room filled with admirers, takes his turn at the competition the party has arranged for itself. It has been determined that each will make a speech in praise of Love (Eros), and Agathon begins his florid panegyric by describing the god's nature in familiar and even hackneyed terms:

> First of all . . . he is the youngest of the gods. He himself provides convincing evidence of the truth of what I say by fleeing before old age, which moves fast, as we know; at any rate it advances upon us faster than it should. It is the nature of love to hate old age, and not to come even within long range of it. His whole life is passed in the company of the young, for there is truth to the saying that like clings to like.[1]

Agathon could hardly be more explicit about the incompatibility of Eros and old age, and his celebration of youthful love assumes added significance when we consider the ages of these symposiasts: the still youthful bloom of Agathon himself, the toast of Athens for his beauty as well as his talent; the mature manhood of his current lover Pausanias, whose speech prescribes a Heavenly Love requiring that both *erastês* (lover) and *eromenos* (beloved) be of the appropriate age; the tempestuous youth of the party-crashing Alcibiades, who recounts in detail his inability to arouse in Socrates the passion he ignited in so many others; and the old age of Socrates himself who, though perhaps not technically a *gerôn* at the fictive date of the conversation (416 B.C.), left at his death the image of an amorous old man and a self-proclaimed expert on the subject of love.[2]

The vicissitudes of the aged or aging lover was to become a staple of Western tradition, from the *senex amator* of New Comedy to the oversexed protagonists of modern fiction, like Nabokov's Humbert Humbert or the lecherous romantic Florentino Arizo in Garcia Marquez's *Love in the Time of Cholera*. But by the time Plato fashioned Agathon's speech, the unhappy relationship of *eros* and *gêras* was already something of a cliché. He himself draws on it again in the *Phaedrus*, where Socrates mentions his age along with his poverty among the handicaps he suffers as a lover.[3] Agathon's guest and fellow playwright Aristophanes used the theme extensively and with great success, exploiting its comic potential in a number of plays that put the elderly in erotically suggestive situations. In *Lysistrata* 254ff. he deploys a chorus of old men and women in a farce whose meaning would be transparent even without the play's blatantly sexual context. A group of gaffers lays seige to the Acropolis, which is defended by a group of crones; the men labor to carry logs that will not light and the women douse their fire and their spirits with buckets of cold water.[4] And among the entertainments with which Agathon and company might more typically have amused themselves would be drinking-songs and poems about the erotic joys of youth and the trials of old age. In this tradition the erotic implications of old age are uniformly negative. Men lament its arrival because with it they become erotically impaired, whether by incapacity, rejection, or sheer indifference. Objects of pity or scorn to themselves and the more youthful eyes that behold them, old men are portrayed as constitutionally incapable of desire, as unable to win the objects of their desire, or as only capable of a love that is a pale imitation of the real thing: as Ovid would later declaim contemptuously, *sic senes amant*.[5]

Greek sexual practice has come under a great deal of scrutiny recently, in particular with regard to the polarities of gender, class, and the meaning of hetero- and homoerotism. Groundbreaking work in feminist, gay, and cultural studies has shown how deeply Greek sexual behavior is implicated in its particular history, institutions, and ethical values, and how questionable is the application of some of our most basic concepts—including that of sexuality itself—to ancient practices. Questions of old age and sexuality, however, have been given little consideration, and the origins, history, and significance of this pervasive theme in Greek literature have attracted little scholarly attention.[6] Perhaps this reflects a predisposition to see in the antagonism between eros and *gêras* a "natural" state of affairs, as though these images required no explanation. Yet as Roland Barthes reminds us in *Mythologies*, it is precisely in matters that appear self-evident that we are likely to find myth at work, the process of representation whereby historical event is transformed into a transparent nature that would conceal its own cultural construction. For those to whom such unflattering images seem only the necessary consequence of old age, we may draw an analogy with the related distinction between sex and gender, between the facts of biological difference and the imposition on them of a social structure of distinctive behaviors and values: biological difference may indeed be necessary for the cultural process of gendering, but it cannot sufficiently account for the complex and different concepts of gender that are built upon it. It is true that sexual appetite is diminished in old age (though here too socialization may count as much as physiology) and that old age is generally accompanied by a reduction in the volume of sexual activity.[7] Yet this is better understood as an *occasion* to characterize old age in a certain way rather than as a cause for doing so; it is also true that the elderly consume less food than the young, but we do not not endow this fact with any particular cultural significance. Yet Greek literature constructs an entire mythology elaborating the sexuality of old age in a complex of images and ideas that require a cultural explanation. We ought to be especially attuned to such factors, given the way popular interest in and perceptions of elderly sexuality have changed over the last two decades, from a virtual taboo on the subject to the daily grist of television sitcoms, talk shows, and movies, changes clearly related to the graying of America and the heightened social and political profile of the elderly.

In some respects, the Greeks' concern with the erotic status of old age is only to be expected, given the cultural importance that was attached to sexuality in general. In Greece, as in patriarchal cultures generally, expressions of sexuality are closely related to definitions of male power and authority, and male social status is clearly linked to erotic and reproductive success. The signficance of these representations takes on special importance in the polis, where concepts of sexuality are fundamental to social organization. Indeed, it might be difficult to find a culture in which what Foucault calls the "instrumentality" of sex, its availability and utility as a medium of power relations, is more striking than in the polis, where expressions of sexuality are inherently charged with social meaning. In Athens, to be sure, male power is openly defined in terms of sexual dominance, and the developing male's social role is constituted by and coordinated with his sexual activity: his entrance into public life is accompanied by sexual relationships with older men, and his passage into *hêbê* is simultaneously a transition into "adult" sexuality and socio-political power. His full manhood and citizenship are in turn demonstrated in his own sexual mentoring of young men and in the varieties of his dominance over women: his wife, *hetairai* ("companions"), and prostitutes. It is on the basis of this sexual polarity that woman is politically disenfranchised and assigned her proper social category—wife, prostitute, or concubine—according to the nature of her sexual relations with men. In the androcracy of the polis the phallus is not just the symbol but the literal instrument of social power, and in such a "phallocracy" sexuality is not just one code among many but a declared measure of power and prestige.[8]

As Greek culture coordinates social and political identity within the field of sexual activity, these in turn are regulated by the complicated system of protocols of age that surround Greek sexual practice. Greek erotics are structured around the binary relation of the male lover as pursuer or seducer and the beloved (young woman or "boy") who is pursued and flees his advances. Greek cultural practice recognized a preferred age at which a man might marry, recommending that men, at the age of about thirty, marry women typically half their age.[9] They recognized ages at which the male might be elegible to be the passive *eromenos* (beloved) in a homosexual relationship, and when he might exchange that role for that of the active *erastês*.[10] But although there were limits on the age at which he might begin certain kinds of sexual activity, there was no publicly sanctioned *upper* limit when he was required or expected to give up his role as *erastês*. And while his chances of success in such relationships would be reduced with old age, it can safely be assumed that older men continued sexual relations with their wives, *hetairai,* and prostitutes, and with young boys as long as they were able, interested, and could afford to do so. Houdijk and Vanderbroeck have surveyed the literature and find the picture to be ambivalent in the extreme: the sexuality of old men is referred to in terms ranging from lustfulness to impotence.[11] Greek sexual practice seems to regard old age for men as a gray area during which they are both inside and outside: on the one hand, eligible to continue to play the game of love; on the other, regarded with concern for their inability to do so successfully.

The absence of such an upper limit on male sexuality does not mean that that the Greeks did not distinguish the sexuality of old men from that of the younger. Indeed, the preoccupation with the subject and the overwhelmingly negative character of most of these references suggests that that they treated the sexuality of older men with particular interest and concern. Greek literature provides a repertoire of images in which the sexuality of old men is largely portrayed in terms of anxiety, failure, shame, and deficiency. In some cases the *gerôn* finds in himself the obstacles to the fulfillment of his desire; at other times his desire is frustrated by the preferences of those he would love. What follows is a discussion of the treatment of this theme in some of the central texts of the epic and lyric traditions, where the treatment of sexuality and old age was first worked out poetically and its underlying assumptions formulated. The goal is to examine these "geronterotic images" with attention to both the literary tradition they establish and the different social meanings that are embedded in them, that is, to the ways in which the literary and the cultural intersect. These literary expressions of the relationship between old age and sexuality have a unique historical value, not so much as evidence of actual Greek practices or popular attitudes—always a difficult project—as for the social and symbolic meanings they are made to carry. Indeed, we should be careful not to assume that the literature stands in a passive relationship to the larger culture, merely "reflecting" an independently existing set of cultural values and practices. These texts seem to me to be crucial for the active role they play in shaping ideas about the relation between age and sexuality.

The object here then is to examine these representations of age and sexuality with a view to how poetic discourse becomes culturally paradigmatic: how various configurations of the body, old age, and sexuality function as a semiotic field and social text; in turn, how Greek culture reads such images and endows them with social significance. Indeed, certain broad lines of development suggest how increasingly the imagery of Eros works to define sexuality within certain conventions, to isolate old age in its sexual (in)capacities, and to develop a concept of aged sexuality that ultimately describes not only a *physical* but a *social* condition, and in the conclusion I will speculate on some of the social and political meanings that these images may carry. I emphasize at the outset that the treatment is not intended to be comprehensive, either in respect to the texts or to the enormous literature they have spawned. And that in looking at the development of this theme in epic and lyric I assume, notwithstanding differences in subject and style, that lyric no less than epic is public and social poetry; that the perspectives it offers are paradigmatic rather than simply individualistic or idiosyncratic; that lyric is best understand, as Ralph Johnson reminds us, less as personal expression than as a social discourse that provides the listener with various "configurations of identity."[12] As poetry that is public and persuasive in its force, we do well to consider the social implications of these identities and the archaic fascination with the theme as a whole.

THE SEXUALITY OF HEROES:
AGE AND EROS IN THE *ILIAD* AND *ODYSSEY*

That Homer says relatively little about the sexuality of the elderly is in some sense to be expected. Homeric epic is reticent about sexual matters in general, and even clearly erotic episodes like the Deception of Zeus (*Il.*14.153ff.) and the affair of Aphrodite and Ares (*Od.* 8.266–366) are remarkably unexplicit about the physical aspects of sexuality. Yet in both the *Iliad* and *Odyssey* sexual relations between men and women are an established and natural part of human life and heroic behavior.[13] Agamemnon swears that he never had intercourse with Briseis, as is right (θέμις) for men and women (9.134, 276; cf. 19.177), and Achilles and Patroclus take to their beds women captured in raids around Troy (9.664–68). Thetis consoles Achilles in his grief by reminding him that like eating and sleeping it is good (ἀγαθόν) to lie with a woman in love (24.130–31). Sexuality is regarded primarily as simple gratification, one of the pleasures of heroic and aristocratic life, and Thetis can recommend it to her son for its therapeutic effect.

Although the *Iliad* carefully charts differences in the abilities of young and old in other respects (strength in battle, intelligence, speaking ability, emotional maturity), sexual ability and experience are nowhere age-graded, as these excellences are not required for heroic success. The younger generation of warriors is distinguished from the older by their marital and domestic status, but not with regard to sexual activity per se. The *Iliad* appreciates, even celebrates, the physical beauty of youth, and in the youthful gods and heroes of epic we see the first expressions of the aristocratic ideal of *kalokagathia*, that union of outer and inner beauty, physical and moral excellence.[14] Although beauty of form (εἶδος) without a fighting spirit can be a term of reproach, such beauty marks its owner with distinction.[15] Yet while the *Iliad* idealizes such beauty and recognizes old age as a time of physical decline, it nowhere characterizes old age as intrinsically ugly or offensive (αἰσχρόν): the contrast Priam draws between the beauty of youth slain in battle and the sight of an aged corpse is a comment not on the aged body as such but on its mutilated condition, which he describes not as ugly but as "most pitiful" (οἴκιστον, 22.76). Ugliness is associated not with age but with class. It is Thersites who was the ugliest (αἴσχιστος) man to come to Troy (*Il.* 2.216ff.): lame, hunchbacked, pointy-headed, and balding; his form is an index of his inferior status and of the antisocial (or antiheroic) character of his mind and his speech.

The *Iliad* does, however, acknowledge the physical limits that come with old age. At 23.616ff. Achilles gives Nestor an urn as a consolation prize in the games, since "difficult old age" oppresses him (ἤδη γαρ χαλεπὸν κατὰ γῆρας ἐπείγει). Looking back to his youth with nostalgia and resignation, Nestor recognizes that he must yield to "gloomy old age" (γήραι λυγρῷ):

> Yes, child: all this you said to me was true as you said it.
> My limbs are no longer steady, dear friend; not my feet, neither
> do my arms, as once they did, swing light from my shoulders.
> I wish I were young again and the strength still unshaken within me
> as once, when . . .
>
> (23.626–34: tr. Lattimore).

Yet Nestor was also awarded "lovely-haired Hecamede" (11.623, 14.6) in gratitude for his good counsel, and it seems likely that as with other heroes, she serves as his concubine as well as his domestic. This is perhaps another indication of Nestor's extraordinary physical capacities.[16] More typical, one suspects, are the Trojan elder-counselors (*dēmogerontes*), who offer hushed testimony to Helen's beauty as she climbs the Scaean gate:

> Surely there is no blame on Trojans and strong-greaved Achaians
> if for long time they suffer hardship for a women like this one.
> Terrible is the likeness of her face to immortal goddesses.
> Still, though she be such, let her go away in the ships, lest
> she be left behind, a grief to us and our children.
>
> (3.155–60: tr. Lattimore)

Like the elderly chorus of Sophocles' *Antigone*, who explains the rashness of Haemon with an ode to the power of Eros (781–800), these elders understand youth's ardent sexuality and the willingness of Greeks and Trojans to fight for Helen. The sexuality of the *dēmogerontes* is at a remove from its more competitive manifestations, and their distance from the fiery passions of youth enlarges their perspective and their concern for the good of the community. Accordingly, they recommend to one another, and later formally through Antenor, that Helen be returned. The comparison of the beauty of their delicate speech to the chirping of cicadas (3.151–52)—a metaphor whose ambiguity we have discussed above—may carry an implication of sexual decline. The reference recalls the metamorphosis of Priam's brother Tithonus into a cicada, a symbol of both advanced age and erotic failure (if indeed that version of the tale was available to the poet). In the *Works and Days* (582ff.) Hesiod associates the *tettix* with sexual weakness: in the summer season when the noisy cicada sits on a tree and pours out its song, women are the most abandoned (μαχλότατοι) and men most impotent (ἀφαυρότατοι), "for the star Seirius shrivels them, knees and heads alike, / and the skin is all dried out in the heat" (tr. Lattimore). As the cicada, which is often associated with dryness,[17] is harbinger of the desiccating summer heat that brings men to their sexual nadir, it anticipates in the Tithonus myth the time when the withering of sexual strength is not a temporary but a permanent condition.

Although the *Iliad* does not single out the sexuality of the elderly for special attention, there are several occasions on which the sexual

behavior of an "older" man becomes an issue. Because the objects of
male desire are closely associated with their "owners," sexuality in
Homer is always an area of potential conflict. A challenge to a hero's
claims upon a woman (whether his wife or captive slave) is simultaneously an attack upon his honor (τιμή), as with Paris' abduction of
Helen or more pointedly with Agamemnon's seizure of Briseis. Chryseis and Briseis are each formally declared a *geras*, a badge of their
owner's honor.[18] Although there is a tendency to view these captive
women as little more than abstract symbols, their status as sexual
objects is a crucial dimension of the conflict between Agamemnon
and Achilles: Aias' complaint that Achilles' anger is "for the sake of a
single girl" (9.637–38) is unsophisticated but not off the mark. Their
confrontation is deliberately set within the codes of age and sexuality.
In seizing the captive Briseis, Agamemnon symbolically deprives
Achilles of the category of sexual partner appropriate to his age. He in
turn rebuffs Agamemnon's offer of his daughter in marriage and discusses his marriage plans for Briseis (9.340, cf.19.297–99) and his
marital prospects in Phthia (9.393–94). In this way sexual possession
is placed in a social and competitive context, a theme underscored in
the duel of Menelaus and Paris for possession of Helen in Book 4.

These conflicts are brought home with full force in the sordid story
of Phoenix and his father Amyntor, who is twice described as *gerōn*
(9.452, 469). Phoenix rehearses the tale somewhat obscurely, where
he tells Achilles of the dishonor done his mother by Amyntor,

> my father, who hated me for the sake of a fair-haired mistress.
> For he made love to her himself, and dishonored his own wife,
> my mother; who was forever entreating me
> to lie with this mistress instead so that she would hate the old man.
> I was persuaded and I did it; and my father when he heard of it
>   straightway
> called down his curses, and invoked against me the dread furies
> that I might never have any son born of my seed to dandle
> on my knees; and the divinities, Zeus of the underworld
> and Persephone the honoured goddess, accomplished his curses.
>   (9.449–57: tr. Lattimore)

Amyntor's behavior is not remarkable in itself, and his taking of a concubine (παλλακίς) for a long-term relationship is attested to in both

literature and social practice.[19] But the practice is often looked down upon for the unhealthy domestic situation it creates. Agamemnon's fate illustrates the dangers of introducing a concubine into the *oikos* alongside a wife, and the *Odyssey* comments on the good sense Laertes showed in avoiding sexual relations with Eurycleia for fear of angering Anticleia (1.430–33). There clearly was a price to be paid in bringing such a woman into the household, and Amyntor's neglect of his wife seems to be compounded by the duration and intensity of his affair (ἀτιμάζεσκε . . . φιλέεσκεν; 9.450). His indiscretion pits his wife against his concubine, and himself against a son in the fullness of early manhood (νέον ἡβώοντα, 9.446). Phoenix's mother begs him repeatedly "to have sexual relations beforehand" (προμιγῆναι, a euphemism for rape?) with the concubine "in order that she might hate the old man" (9.451–52). Her object may well be twofold: on the one hand, to spoil her husband's relations with the concubine by "damaging" his property and making the affair quasi-incestuous; on the other, to make the concubine, whose sexual activity is presumably limited to Amyntor, unhappy by preceding her tryst with him with one with a younger and more energetic lover.

The episode matches father and son in an unnatural competition. When Amyntor realizes what has happened (from his concubine's complaints, or her cooler response?), he calls down the Erinyes that "he might never sit upon his knees a beloved son begotten by me [Phoenix]" (455–56). As has been observed, the curse is to be understood not as sterility but impotence,[20] which lends the act a kind of poetic justice: as Phoenix has struck at his father's sexuality, so Amyntor finds his revenge in the same faculty. Such an interpretation adds poignancy to Phoenix's plea that he would not abandon Achilles even if the god were to "scrape away" his old age (γῆρας ἀποξύσας, 9.446) and restore him in the fullness of youth (444–45). And Phoenix's affection for Achilles is heightened when we understand him to be declining the hypothetical restoration of not only his young manhood but his sexuality in "Hellas, the land of fair women" (καλλιγύναικα, 9.447; cf. καλλικόμοιο, 9.449).

This tale of Oedipal conflict thus yields two unfortunate and polar images of old age and sexuality: Amyntor, whose excessive interest in his concubine has destroyed his son and perhaps doomed the *oikos* to extinction; and Phoenix, whose youthful foolishness has left him an impotent and effeminized old man, a domestic in the house of Peleus.

It is often urged that Phoenix offers his autobiography to Achilles as a cautionary tale, in view of the many parallels between this story and the quarrel of Agamemnon and Achilles.[21] But the objection is sometimes raised that where Phoenix had attempted to take his father's concubine, it is Agamemnon who has taken Achilles' woman. Scodel is quite right, as we observed above, in suggesting that the story is presented as an anti-heroic exemplum, and that Achilles is to understand that in running away from the Greeks (as Phoenix had his family), he risks the irrecoverable loss of his heroic identity.[22] But Phoenix's point is also to remind Achilles that the occasion of his conflict with Agamemnon was a woman, and of the dangers of interfering in the sexual arrangements of one who is "older." In comparing the domestic tragedy in which he himself was once embroiled to the public drama of Achilles, Phoenix warns him that his conflict with Agamemnon over Briseis involves the same potentially disastrous consequences. The story of Amyntor and Phoenix, like those of Menelaus and Paris and Agamemnon and Achilles, describes a challenge by younger men to older men in their sexual relationships, placing both of them in a kind of competition for the same woman. These situations are represented not as demonstrations of erotic attractiveness or sexual ability but as the intrusions of the younger upon the personal, domestic, and proprietary rights of the older and therewith his *timê* (honor). In each case, the anger of the latter is brought down in full force.

The *Odyssey*, it has been noted, pays more attention to the aesthetics of old age than does the *Iliad*, and describes, sometimes graphically, its physical characteristics.[23] When Athena makes Odysseus unrecognizable (ἄγνωστον, 13.397), she does so by concealing his true appearance beneath the twin disfigurements of poverty and old age:

> So spoke Athena, and with her wand she tapped Odysseus,
> and withered the handsome flesh that was upon his flexible
> limbs, and ruined the brown hair on his head, and about him,
> to cover all his body, she put the skin of an ancient
> old man, and then she dimmed those eyes that had been so handsome.
> (13.429–33; cf. 13.398–401: tr. Lattimore)

Old age is described as a loss of beauty and faculties of youth: the graying of hair and beard, the shriveling of the skin, the dulling of the eyes.[24] Here again it is class as much as age that makes Odysseus so loathsome, and as in the *Iliad* old age is not described as ugly in itself. When Penelope says to the beggar that Odysseus has probably come to resemble him, she does so in terms of the hardships that have aged them both: "mortals age quickly in misfortune" (αἶψα γὰρ ἐν κακότητι βροτοὶ καταγηράσκουσι, 19.360).[25] And when Odysseus first sees his father digging in his orchard the emphasis is upon his ragged clothes and squalid appearance, not the number of his years. Indeed, he suggests that Laertes' nobility shines through his servile demeanor:

> nor is your stature and beauty (εἶδος καὶ μέγεθος), as I see it, such as ought to belong to a slave. You look like a man who is royal.
>
> (24.252–53: tr. Lattimore)

It is this inherent beauty that is restored lines later when his servant woman bathes and clothes him and Athena makes him "taller and thicker" (μείζονα . . . καὶ πάσσονα, 24.369).

As with Agamemnon and Achilles, the "rivalry" of Odysseus and the suitors for possession of Penelope involves a conflict that is both generational and sexual. The youth of the suitors, those "excellent young men" (ἄριστοι κοῦροι, 23.121) of Ithaca and the neighboring lands, is given expression in their eagerness for Penelope, the erotic dimension of which is explicit,[26] and their indiscreet relations with the maidservants. Yet like Phoenix and Achilles, the suitors discover the danger of interfering with the domestic relationships of an "older" man. Indeed, Odysseus' vigorous sexuality is a gauge of both his heroism and maturity: he gives evidence of his sexual abilities without losing his sense of what is prudent and necessary. He establishes his dominance over Circe with a display of sexual prowess, defying her power to make him "weak and unmanned" (κακὸν καὶ ἀνήνορα,10.301, 341), that is, impotent.[27] He enjoys a long relationship with Calypso but declines her offer to make him make him "deathless and ageless" (5.136; cf. 23.336), rejecting the unending sexuality of the gods for the natural cycle of human desire and fulfillment.[28]

The *Odyssey* clearly recognizes that erotic appeal is diminished with age. Calypso's offer is predicated on her assumption that he will find agelessness as well as immortality enticing and recalls the horrible destiny of Tithonus, who was granted one but not the other. Her invitation is set against the backdrop of Eos' failed attempt with Tithonus, the poet eschewing the image of dawn's rosy fingers for that of her boudoir: "Now Dawn rose from her bed, where she lay by haughty Tithonus, / carrying light to the immortal gods and to mortals" (5.1–2: tr. Lattimore). As the formula anticipates the goddess' abandonment of her aging partner and the dangers of passage from mortality to divinity, it prepares us for Odysseus' imminent departure from Calypso and his refusal to accept her invitation to be his consort. Appropriately, the terms in which Calypso negotiates with Odysseus are formulaic and exact: she offers to make him deathless and ageless for all days, careful to use the full formula by which she is herself described (5.136, 218) and which Eos carelessly neglected.

Nonetheless, in folktale fashion, the *Odyssey* ultimately disposes of the tension between age and erotic appeal by negating time and allowing Odysseus and Penelope to triumph over the reality of aging. Before they proceed to the bed the poet engages the two in a ritual of courtship, in effect reinstating them as newlyweds. Athena youthens the two and enhances their sex appeal,[29] and delays the dawn so that revitalized they may enjoy a night of talk and lovemaking. The gods are themselves the agents of youth, quite literally sharing from the largess of their own beauty and the cosmetic agents by which they retain it. Athena beautifies Odysseus at three crucial moments, two of which are erotically charged: before his supplication of Nausicaa (6.229–35), his recognition by Telemachus (16.172–77), and finally his reunion with Penelope (23.156–62). She youthens Penelope too (18.190–96), making her taller and statelier and whiter (a mark of femininity) than before, applying to her face that same "ambrosial balm" with which Aphrodite annoints herself. Such, as Odysseus explains to Telemachus, is Athena's power to make him what she will, a ragged old beggar or a young man in fine raiment (16.207–12). Yet it is significant that in each case Athena stops short of literal rejuvenation, restoring mortals not to the condition of actual youth but to a fullness of perfection in keeping with their age.

THE GRAYING OF TITHONUS: THE HOMERIC *HYMN TO APHRODITE*

In its unabashed anthropomorphism epic poetry, as Greek philosophers early complained, created the gods in man's image and endowed them with the minds, forms, and feelings of their mortal counterparts. These gods provide a set of paradigms for human existence that are consonant with Greek cultural ideals: as Nietzsche remarked famously, "thus do the gods justify the life of man—they themselves live it!"

Although these representations have their origins in literature and are shaped by their individual poetic contexts, they won so broad a cultural endorsement they became canonical in state cult and popular religion.[30] And despite the careful symmetry within the Olympic pantheon in terms of gender, marital status, occupation, and cultic function, there is no god of old age, and there is no old god. Otto finds in this the "peculiar essence" of the Greek god, who "could never be imagined save in the most radiant bloom of youth."[31] To be more precise, the residents of Olympus remain fixed in either of the two middle stages of the life course, in the radiance of youth or maturity, deathless and ageless by a preservative diet of nectar and ambrosia.[32] The exclusion of old age from the Olympian achievement has important implications for the meaning of old age. That the gods serve as the embodiment of a more perfect *aretē* and as repositories of human virtues implies that that are no excellences for which old age is prerequisite, or none worthy of being enshrined in the social order of Olympus.

The *Hymn to Aphrodite* is a crucial document in establishing the structures by which mortals are assimilated to and differentiated from the gods, and mediates the two "normative" conditions—dying/aging and deathless/ageless—with a range of other configurations of death and age: the eternal youth of Ganymede, the endless aging of Tithonus, and the nymphs who die but do not age, their old age displaced onto the trees congenital with them. The distribution of these various positions sketches out a chain of being across the spectrum of the human and divine, serves to justify the human condition and the irreducibles of mortality by identifying other possible states of being more and less attractive, and focuses attention on the meaning of death and age in the greater cosmology.[33]

Although uncertainty regarding the date of the *Hymn* makes it likely that it is influenced to some degree by parallel developments in lyric,[34] it is rightly regarded as the most Homeric of the Hymns, and in its treatment of age in general and sexuality in particular draws primarily on the epic tradition. As in Homer, *gēras* is "destructive" (ὀλοιόν, 224), "hateful" (στυγερόν, 233), "leveling" (ὁμοίιον, 244), and "accursed" (οὐλόμενον, 246), and the *Hymn* adds to these epithets "pitiless" (νηλειές, 245) and "wearying" (καματηρόν, 246).[35] As in the *Iliad*, old age is a skin or an encrustation to be "scraped away" (ξῦσαι . . . ἄπο, 224; cf. *Il.* 9.446) from the younger person beneath; as in the *Odyssey*, *hēbē* (224) carries the complimentary epithet "much loved" (πολυήρατος, 225, 274). Most important, the *Hymn* trades throughout on the description of deity as "deathless and ageless for all days," which distinguishes man from god by the twin evils of senescence and death. But here it is not only the first half of the formula but also the potential ambiguity of "for all days" (ἤματα πάντα) that is crucial. Anchises looks for his mystery guest to be his wife "for all days" (148); Tros would mourn for his lost Ganymede "for all days" (209); Tithonus will live but will age too "for all days" (221); Anchises will *not* be immortal "for all days" (240); and Aphrodite herself *will* be shamed "for all days" (248) for her affair with Anchises.

The erotic context into which these figures are introduced is far more explicit than in epic. The distinctions between the human and divine situations are achieved in the context of a shared sexual ethos and the power of "sweet longing" (γλυκὺς ἵμερος, 2, 45, 53, 143), itself a Homerism.[36] Erotic desire here serves as the common denominator between gods and men, one that evaluates the worthiness of the love object along the gradients of "class" (divine-human) and age (young-old).[37] The various participants in the poem are in a sense "rated" as erotic objects according to their combined score on both counts, ranging from the perfection of a divine and eternally young Aphrodite to the repulsiveness of a mortal and endlessly aging Tithonus. Under the compulsion of "sweet longing" the gods, no less than mortals, expose themselves to social loss and public ridicule, as this power compels them to mate with mortal men and women and even to beget or bear children by them (cf. 50–52). The potential degradation and loss of status is the source of the poem's principle irony and humor. Aphrodite had found delight and superiority in her power to humiliate her fellows gods by joining them with mortals, but she comes to regard the indescribable madness that joined her to Anchises as a source of disgrace and of the "awful grief" (αἰνὸν ... ἄχος, 198–99) that will be forever recorded in the very name of her son Αἰνείας:

> But great shame (ὄνειδος) shall be mine among the immortal gods
> to the end of all time because of you.
>
> (247–48: tr. Athanassakis)

Aphrodite's shame results not from yielding to "sweet longing" nor from the fact of her being the pursuer (the cultural prohibition against females as sexual initiators applies only to mortals—compare the behavior of Circe and Calypso) but in pursuing eros across the boundary that divides gods and mortals. Aphrodite thereby loses what had distinguished her from the other gods and is in this respect "lowered" to their status. Although her shame is offset in part by the beauty of the Trojans in general and Anchises in particular, and by the proud destiny of the child she will bear by him, the fact that Anchises is mortal, *that he will age and will die*, makes the relationship a degrading one. Aphrodite's shame is, correspondingly, Anchises' distinction, who has mated as it were "above his station": hence her harsh interdiction not to publicize the truth about the birth of their son (286–87), since his glory would be at her expense. Instead, Anchises should attribute the birth of their son Aeneas to "a nymph with a petal-soft face" (284): that is, to the deities who though long-lived are not deathless and ageless, a grade below the Olympians on the scale of perfection and desirability yet still a source of pride for Anchises.

The *Hymn* further develops the bodily aesthetic implicit in Homer, locating ideal physical beauty and sexual attractiveness in youth, whether of gods or mortals. Thus the Trojans as a race are "of all mortal men . . . always closest to the gods in looks and stature" (ἀγχίθεοι δὲ μάλιστα καταθνητῶν ἀνθρώπων / αἰεὶ . . . εἶδός τε φυήν τε, 200–1). Anchises embodies the further perfection of *hêbê*; he is described as "looking like an immortal in body" (δέμας ἀθανάτοισιν ἐοικώς, 55) and as one "with beauty from the gods" (θεῶν ἄπο κάλλος ἔχοντα, 77). His face is handsome (καλὰ πρόσωπα,183), and he is capable of inspiring an awesome longing (ἐκπάγλως . . . ἵμερος, 57) in the goddess who is the source of all desire. His sexual vitality is reflected in the urgency with which he woos his new bride. Despite his initial suspicions that his surprise guest is divine (92ff.), he will brook no delay in consumating the relationship.[38]

The opposition of youth and age is emphasized in the twin exempla that are offered as the centerpiece of the *Hymn*.[39] Aphrodite groups Anchises together with Ganymede and Tithonus, in evidence of the proposition that the Trojans have always been so beautiful as to be irresistable to the gods, and in the three Trojan males constructs three different combinations of age and mortality. Zeus abducts Ganymede for his surpassing beauty (διὰ κάλλος, 203) and makes him "deathless and ageless, like to the gods" (214). His youthful beauty and vitality are suggested in the quick-stepping (ἀρσίποδας, 211) horses Zeus offers his father Tros as recompense; there is added irony in the assignment Zeus gives Ganymede, as the nectar that he pours is the very agent of the gods' own agelessness.[40]

It is likewise the youthful beauty of Tithonus, who is "like the immortals" (219), that fires passion in the heart of Eos, and as long as he enjoys "much loved youth" he is allowed his fill of her pleasures (225–26). The Tithonus story provides a series of correlaries to that of Ganymede: youth and old age; successful and unsuccessful passages to immortality; Zeus' gift to Tros, which assuages his suffering, and his gift to Eos, which brings Tithonus only an endless grief. The antithesis of youth and age is also centered in Tithonus himself, the loss of whose youth is intolerable to Eos, and the different phases of his erotic rejection are carefully coordinated with his progress through the life course:[41]

> But when the first gray hairs began to flow down
> from his comely hair and noble chin,
> mighty Eos did refrain from his bed,
> though she kept him in her house and pampered him
> with food and ambrosia and gifts of fine clothing.
> (228–32: tr. Athanassakis)

Here it is clearly implied that the youth (πολυήρατος ἥβη, 225) of Tithonus draws to a close not with the arrival of old age but with his coming into mature manhood, the midlife of an Odysseus or Agamemnon. This is heralded by the traces of gray (πρῶται πολιαὶ . . . ἔθειραι, 228) that streak his hair and beard, just as in Homer we hear of the streaks of gray (μεσαιπόλιος) that mark the midlife of an Idomeneus (Il.13.361). Here the process of the graying of the hair becomes the prelude to the full old age and death that normally follow. We are not, to be sure, told that Tithonus has actually become ugly with the first gray hairs—indeed, Eos' frantic attempt to check the process would seem to suggest the opposite—but their appearance marks the beginning of the end of that beauty that distinguished him in the first place.

The unexpected evidence of Tithonus' less than divine status impresses upon Eos his unworthiness as a love object. At the first hint of his aging she abruptly suspends the relationship and hides him inside her halls and out of sight, guarding against the ridicule she will suffer for the lover she has chosen. There she cares for Tithonus and attempts a therapeutic treatment, including regular doses of ambrosia, which is administered in the hope of retarding or reversing the degenerative process.[42] But when this prescription fails, and with the full onslaught of old age upon him, she puts him away entirely:

> But when detested old age weighed heavy upon him
> and he could move or lift none of his limbs,
> this is the counsel that to her seemed best in her heart:
> she placed him in a chamber and shut its shining doors.
> His voice flows endlessly and there is no strength,
> such as there was before in his crooked limbs.
>
> (233–38: tr. Athanassakis)

It is important to note that however negative and contemptible is the picture of Tithonus' old age, the poet does not call him ugly for this. His aged condition is described not in terms of ugliness but of loss of strength (κῖκυς), a rare word used only once by Homer and in precisely the same formula. In the first *nekyia* the ghost of Agamemnon extended his hands and tried to touch Odysseus, but "he no longer had the strength such as there was before in his crooked limbs" (οὐδέ τι κῖκυς, / οἵη περ πάρος ἔσκεν ἐνὶ γναμπτοῖσι μέλεσσι, 11.393–94). In linking the weakness of old age to that of death, the *Hymn* remains in the Homeric tradition, which as we have seen laments old age more for its physical than its aesthetic shortcomings. Tithonus no longer has the strength he had in youth, and his appearance is implicit in the emphasis on youthful *beauty* elsewhere in the poem.

The *Hymn* represents the erotic debilitude of old age in terms of its social isolation and uselessness. As Tithonus loses the strength of his youth, he comes to be nothing more than a voice (φωνή). His voice flows even as he ages, endlessly (ῥεῖ ἄσπετος, 237), but his words, whether we understand them as an eternal lament or the idle chatter of old age, seem without communicative or persuasive force.[43] As Eos had kept Tithonus inside her house (ἐνὶ μεγάροισιν ἔχουσα, 231) at the first signs of age, so with old age fully upon him she disposes of him altogether: "she placed him in a chamber and shut its shining doors" (ἐν θαλάμῳ κατέθηκε, θύρας δ᾽ ἐπέθηκε φαεινάς, 236). This formula sustains the domestic associations it assumes elsewhere in the poem. Aphrodite had withdrawn within her "house" (the temple on

Paphos) to adorn herself seductively and "closed the shining doors" (θύρας δ' ἐπέθηκε φαεινάς, 60). She tells Anchises that she is able speak the Trojan tongue because her nurse had been from Troy and raised her "at home" (μεγάρῳ, 114). Tithonus' confinement within the house thus reflects Eos' embarrassment and also defines the proper place of old age as *inside* the *oikos*—where children are raised and women practice their seductive arts—and outside of the public eye and meaningful social commerce. With old age upon him, Eos assumes the role of a female *gērokomos*, caring for her former lover as if he were an aging father, keeping him where he will not add to her disgrace. Like Aeneas, who will be raised by nymphs apart from human contact until he is old enough to enter society, Tithonus resides in a female place outside the world of social relations.[44] Old age is thereby assimilated to womanhood and childhood and stands outside the (divine or human) boundaries of normal sexual activity.[45]

Aphrodite has no interest in an aging lover—*she* would suffer no grief (ἄχος), she protests, were Anchises able to remain physically as he is (τοιοῦτος ἐὼν εἶδός τε δέμας τε, 241) and enjoy the kind of eternal youth promised but denied Tithonus. But Aphrodite does not consider even the possibility of attempting to win such a condition for Tithonus. As Clay has recently shown, her failure to do so is based upon our understanding that immortality is only Zeus' to bestow and that Aphrodite has by now come to understand that it was he who arranged the entire affair.[46] When Aphrodite tells Tithonus that old age will "soon" (τάχα) be his lot, she speaks less *sub specie aeternitatis* than from the perspective of Eos: old age effectively begins with the first signs of aging. But the generic old age that she describes to him seems almost as horrid as the fate of Tithonus, and suggests the abyss that divides gods from mortals and the contempt with which the gods regard the aging process. Perhaps nowhere else in Greek literature do we find old age described in such catastrophic proportions:

> But now you will soon be enveloped by leveling old age,
> that pitiless companion of every man,
> baneful, wearisome, and hated even by the gods.
>
>   (244–46: tr. Athanassakis)

Aphrodite's grim view of *gēras* takes on added significance given the sexual relationship she and Anchises have enjoyed. Anchises still enjoys youth, but in a different sense he is already close to old age. Although he has enjoyed the goddess for only one day, he begs her by Zeus

> not to let me live impotent among men,
> but have mercy on me; for the man who lies
> with immortal goddesses is not left unharmed.
> (188–90: tr. Athanassakis)

One who has sexual relations with the gods cannot remain unharmed (βιοθάλμιος, "in the bloom of life") but becomes impotent, ἀμενηνός, literally without μένος, the fluid source of sexual and other energy.[47] That the *Hymn* makes no reference to Tithonus' metamorphosis into a cicada (*tettix*) is frequently explained by suggesting that this version of the tale had not yet been developed, and that Homer and Hesiod were perhaps unaware even of the old age with which Tithonus was cursed.[48] Yet in another sense the value of the *tettix* as symbol of old age is already present in that very impotence with which Tithonus is afflicted and which Anchises hopes to avoid for himself. And in linking the goddess of the morning sun to the loss of strength (κῖκυς, 237) in old age, the poem emphasizes the familiar association of the dessicating summer heat, age, and impotence that are associated with the cicada. Just as Tithonus' experience with Eos left him without the necessary strength in his limbs, Anchises fears for his virility, lest his intercourse with the goddess leave him a younger version of the impotent and superannuated Tithonus.

Anchises' tryst with Aphrodite serves as a kind of education for the young herdsman about life as a whole and the relation of its constituent stages. When Anchises is first surprised by Aphrodite, he hails her as a goddess, and in typical Homeric fashion he offers her an altar and sacrifice in exchange for personal prosperity:[49]

> And with kindly heart grant me
> to be an emminent man among the Trojans,
> to leave flourishing offspring behind me,
> and to live long and behold the light of the sun,
> prospering among the people, and so reach the threshold of old age.
> (102–6: tr. Athanassakis)

Anchises conceives of life in its wholeness and continuity, as an ordered and harmonious progression that includes public distinction, security in his descendents, and prosperity into old age. His image of life and the Homeric language in which it is couched recall the "sleek old age" and peaceful death that Tiresias prophecies to Odysseus (*Od*.11.134–37) and that Odysseus himself had prayed for (19.365–68). But when Aphrodite rouses Anchises from his sleep, revealing herself in all her frightening potency and divine otherness, she shatters this integrated conception of life and drives a wedge between "much-loved youth" and "hateful old age." The power of eros fundamentally alters one's experience of the life course, as for Tithonus it had made his progress from youth to the graying of middle age and to the fullness of age a journey into decrepitude. So too, when Anchises hopes to take his pleasure with the Phrygian girl Hermes had brought to him, the urgency of his love (91,144) suddenly occasions a change in his rhetoric; he speaks no more of long life: he will happily die right then and there once he has enjoyed her (153–54).

It is first in the *Hymn to Aphrodite* that we see that how eros ruptures the integrity of the life course, and where the kind of wholeness and continuity of life available to the gods and prayed for by epic heroes is lost. As in the Homeric tradition, the *Hymn* stops short of criticizing old age for its outward appearance, and finds in the simple fact of aging grounds for erotic rejection. Eos' relationship with Tithonus, whose experiment with eternal youth had such disastrous consequences, ended with her repudiating the old man and putting him under house confinement. Anchises is guaranteed the illustrious line of descent he had originally prayed for, but this is achieved at the price of an old age that Aphrodite has identified as erotically enfeebled and contemptible. Unlike in Homer the sexual relationships the *Hymn* describes are no longer entirely private and domestic affairs; in the very selection of an erotic partner these goddesses are subject to the approval or disapproval of their peers, whose standards though higher in degree reflect the values and principles of those mortals whom they reject.

HATEFUL TO BOYS, WORTHLESS TO WOMEN: MIMNERMUS ELEGY 1

Mimnermus' treatment of old age reflects the character of Ionian elegy in general, with its greater reliance on idea and argument than concrete sensuous imagery, its relatively impersonal nature, and the virtual invisibility of its speaker. While Mimnermus' poetry makes its claims about youth and age sometimes with passionate self-interest, at other times with philosophical detachment, it does so in terms that are abstract, generalized, and without reference to personal experience. We do, however, have a connecting thread between Mimnermus and the poetic tradition in his use of the Tithonus myth, the only occasion on which Mimnermus appeals to myth in articulating his conception of old age. He says in fragment 4 that someone, probably Zeus,

> granted Tithonus to have an evil, imperishable old age (κακὸν ἄφθιτον . . . / γῆρας), which is even more horrible than burdensome death.

We cannot be sure of the historical patterns of influence between this fragment, Sappho fragment 58, the *Hymn to Aphrodite,* and the larger mythic tradition, and it is unclear whether the reference functions simply as an exemplum or as part of a fuller narrative.[50] But the allusion is evidence of the durability and flexibility of the Tithonus myth, as though any poet who wished to talk seriously about old age had at some point to touch base with it. In it are crystalized the distinctive features of Mimnermus' perspective: his view of old age as unredeemed evil, his attention to its erotic implications, and his self-conscious reference to the epic and heroic traditions. In Homer and Hesiod the epithet ἄφθιτος (imperishable) is regularly used in connection with the imperishability of the divine world (the possessions of the gods, or their counsels) and those aspects of human life that survive the individual, like the ancestral scepter of the Achaean assembly (which is ἄφθιτον αἰεί) or the imperishable fame (κλέος ἄφθιτον) of Achilles.[51] As such, the word represents a connecting link between the gods and humans, and indicates the limited ways in which humans can enjoy something of the superabundance of the gods themselves. In applying the epithet to *gêras,* Mimnermus captures the paradoxical value of this gift.[52] Even here there is a delightful ambiguity: is the antecedent of ὅ the extraordinary old age (κακὸν ἄφθιτον . . . γῆρας) of Tithonus or simply old age in general, the γῆρας of the second line? In view of the tradition one assumes the former (indeed, in the *Hymn to Aphrodite* death is made to appear a blessing in comparison to the unending decline of Tithonus), and the similar enjambement of γῆρας at 5.3 would suggest that Mimnermus' point here is the same.[53] But that even *ordinary* old age is intrinsically worse than death is at the heart of Mimnermus' perception of age, and it is possible that this was the use to which he put the myth, here or in the larger passage to which the fragment belongs.

Although much has been said about youth and age in Mimnermus,[54] his significance goes beyond his negative "attitude" to old age and needs to be placed in a broader context. Because these elegies define themselves in opposition to the Homeric and heroic possibilities of life, and (with the possible exception of fragment 14) do not seem to offer as do Solon or Tyraetus any new political ideal to replace it, they are often viewed as simple reflections on the brevity of youth and exhortations to the individual pursuit of pleasure. For Mimnermus, however, erotic success is an issue that is deeply involved with social identity. Mimnermus' poetry involves a break with the poetic tradition that can be understood as an elaboration of two themes, each of which works to make old age an issue of social significance: first, his development of an aesthetics of the male body—the "uglification" of old age—and application to old men of aesthetic categories heretofore applied to women (as we have seen in the previous chapter); second, his linking of age to the aristocratic ideal of *kalokagathia*, that harmony of beauty and goodness, exterior form and inner character, which was testimony to the natural superiority of the aristocracy and social order it advocated. Both these themes have important erotic implications: in Mimnermus, sexual activity and inactivity, success and failure, are regarded not so much as personal but *social* and *ethical* categories, so that old age takes on a broader significance and becomes a metaphor not only for sexual but social rejection as a whole.

There is no more compelling definition of this perspective than the first elegy, a kind of anthem to youth, which makes a case for the desexualized nature of old age:

> What life is there, what joy, without golden Aphrodite?
>   May I die when I no longer care about these things:
> furtive love affairs, alluring gifts, and the bed.
>   These are youth's flowers, to be eagerly seized
> by men and women. But when once approaches painful
>   old age, which makes a man ugly and base alike,
> his heart always worn thin with cruel concerns,
>   he delights not even to look upon the rays of the sun,

> but he goes hateful to boys, and worthless to women.
> So painful a thing has God made old age.[55]

Where the Homeric literary tradition appreciates human experience as unfolding throughout the life course, and reflects this perspective in the broad distinctions it draws between childhood, youth, maturity, and old age and the passages between them, in Mimnermus the life course is effectively collapsed into two stages, *hêbê* and *gêras*. To be sure, Homer and early elegy often employ a convenient opposition between youth and age or young and old,[56] but in Mimnermus this opposition defines the structure of the life course and human experience, erotic and otherwise. While these two stages do not admit of simple chronological definition, Mimnermus' prayer in fragment 6 that he meet with a "sixty-year-old fate of death" (ἑξηκονταέτη μοῖρα . . . θανάτου) suggests how extended is his concept of *hêbê* and how radical the change of life he associates with *gêras*.[57]

In poem 1 the relation between youth and its pleasures and old age and its deprivations assumes the dialectical character of archaic thought and is presented as a binary opposition that admits of no mediation: there is no hint of the notion of aging as a process we have seen in the *Odyssey*, the *Hymn to Aphrodite*, or of the more expansive temporality we have seen in Sappho. The abupt change of subject and syntax in the middle of line 5 presents *gêras* as a rude intrusion into life, and its arrival (ἐπέλθῃ) marks a precipitous plunge into decrepitude. The antithetical character of youth and age is here assimilated to that of life and death itself. In the opening line, life (βίος) is openly equated with erotic joy (τερπνόν), and joy with erotic success: only youth (ἥβης, 4) can enjoy golden Aphrodite. Old age is painful (ὀδυνηρόν, 5; ἀργαλέον, 10), the negation of joy (οὐδ' . . . τέρπεται, 8), and is by implication a kind of death (τεθναίην 2). In this way Mimnermus reformulates the Homeric association of old age and death on an erotic basis: old age is loathsome not just because it begins the passage away from heroic life to death, but because it is *already* a kind of living death to the pleasures that are the essence of life.[58]

This linking of old age and death is implicit in fragment 2, which begins by comparing man to the leaves (ἡμεῖς δ', οἶά τε φύλλα) and which defines itself in relation to the famous simile that Glaucus offers to Diomedes at *Iliad* 6 (on which more below). But the lines that follow the simile are also to be appreciated against their Homeric background. Mimnermus says of men in the brief bloom of youth that

> . . . the black Kers stand beside,
> the one with the end of burdensome old age,
> the other with that of death. And short-lived is youth's
> harvest, only as long as the sunlight scatters on the earth.
>   (2.5–8)[59]

Griffith has noted the contrast here with the "twin Kers" (διχθαδίας κῆρας, *Il.* 9.411) of Achilles that lead him to his end: where Homer offers Achilles a choice between a long obscure life and imperishable glory, Mimnermus does not recognize the heroic possibilities of life; for him the only alternative to old age is death.[60] Furthermore, where in Homer the Ker is specifically an agent of death, and Achilles' "twin Kers" represent but two different paths to death, in Mimnermus old age is *itself* a Ker, so that age and death become twin aspects of a single doom. Indeed, as the earlier lines in the passage have already reminded the reader of Homer's Glaucus and the simile of the leaves, these verses in turn recall the speech with which Sarpedon later reminds Glaucus that because they cannot live ageless and deathless (ἀγήρω τ' ἀθανάτω τ'), they should win for themselves glory in battle (*Il.*12.310ff.). There Sarpedon too speaks of the inevitability of death in the image of "the countless Kers of death" that set upon them, and there are also several close parallels in expression between the passages in Homer and Mimnermus.[61] But where in Homer it is the Kers of death alone that stand by a man, in Mimnermus 2.5–7 the Kers of death *and* old age are his companions, even in youth. Mimnermus further associates old age and death in his insistence throughout his poetry that with the passing of youth death is to be preferred over the life that remains: in fragment 1.2 (τεθναίην, ὅτε . . .); at 2.10 (αὐτίκα δὴ τεθνάναι βέλτιον ἢ βίοτος); in his prayer for a gentle and early death in fragment 6; and as we suggested perhaps even in the Tithonus fragment (4). Mimnermus distinguishes old age and death primarily in that old age is *worse* than death, and death the lesser of two evils.[62]

Why does Mimnermus assume that golden Aphrodite is no longer the concern (μηκέτι . . . μέλοι, 1.2) of the old? The poem provides two answers, the first being loss of interest. Old age does not care about love because it is preoccupied with other things, the "terrible worries" (κακαὶ . . . μέριμναι, 1.7) that destroy a man's capacity for love and joy. In fragment 2, which serves as a gloss on this expression, Mimnermus catalogues the many sorrows (πολλὰ κακά) of old age:

> For many sorrows are born in one's heart. One man's estate
>   is wasted away, and he faces a painful life of poverty.
> Yet another man is without children, and still longing deeply
>   for them he descends below the earth to Hades.
> Another has a life-destroying disease. And there is no one
>   to whom Zeus does not give an abundance of woes.
>
> (2.11–16)

As Griffith points out, the selection of evils here—poverty, childlessness (and with it the lack of an heir and *gērokomos*), and disease—is more Hesiodic than Homeric, and suggests the prolonged misery and the spiritual devastation of old age.[63] In 3.1–2 we read of the ill treatment the elderly receive at the hands of their children: for all the noble beauty of his youth the old man receives neither honor nor love from them (οὐδὲ . . . παισὶν τίμιος οὔτε φίλος). And in his prayer for euthanasia at age sixty he does not mention old age specifically but instead speaks of "diseases and burdensome cares" (νούσων τε καὶ ἀργαλέων μελεδωνέων, 6.1) as a virtual synonym for *gēras*.

The anxieties of old age, as Mimnermus lists them, describe a man's personal situation—physical, domestic, economic, and emotional—and are unrelated to his role as citizen or his responsibilities to the larger community. With old age a man becomes self-absorbed, his world small and impoverished. Unlike the wise counselors of Homer, who achieve at least in theory a deeper and less self-interested perspective on the affairs of the community, these men have woes and worries that serve to isolate them and cut them off from the commerce of public life, that network of transactions epitomized in the give and take of eros. Indeed, although Mimnermus focuses on illicit love, eros provides (as we shall see in Anacreon and others as well) a playing field of social relations, and Mimnermus' poem is framed as an exhortation to his peers to delight in the public sport of love. It is precisely the erotic interaction that the poet savors, and Golden Aphrodite is not only the moment of sexual union but the whole sequence that leads to it: "secret love, and the gifts which appease, and the bed" (κρυπταδίη φιλότης καὶ μείλιχα δῶρα καὶ εὐνή, 1.3).[64] For Mimnermus the distractions of old age are not only anti-erotic but antisocial, the antithesis of youth's engagement in the arena of love.

The poet provides a second account for the death of erotic interest in old age in his description of the prospect of rejection it offers. In Mimnermus Greek poetry for the first time speaks openly of the ugliness of the old man and its socio-erotic consequences. As we have noted above, in Homer bodily aesthetics are an index of class, and while he recognizes old age as a period of decline, he nowhere presents it in aesthetic terms. Homer focuses instead on the loss of strength that comes with age, as does the *Hymn to Aphrodite,* which describes the age of Tithonus as a loss of strength (κῖκυς, 237), not beauty. In Mimnermus, on the other hand, youth and age are carefully coordinated aesthetic categories; his description of old age emphasizes the changes it effects in one's appearance. In elegy 1 old age renders a man "ugly and base alike" (αἰσχρὸν ὁμῶς καὶ κακόν, 1.6), repulsive to those he might hope to love.[65] In fragment 5 the "flower of youth" is beautiful (καλόν, 5.3), and in 3.1 a man is most beautiful (κάλλιστος) in the season of youth. Old age is "grievous and misshapen" (ἀργαλέον καὶ ἄμορφον, 5.5), so disfiguring as to make a man "unrecognizable" (ἄγνωστον). It ruins his physical and his mental faculties, harming his eyes and clouding his mind (βλάπτει δ' ὀφθαλμοὺς καὶ νόον ἀμφιχυθέν, 5.7–8). The coming of old age is identical with the loss of youthful beauty, and the doom of old age becomes a sword of Damocles that hangs unseen over youth, spoiling preemptively its keen pleasures (5.5–6).

Old age thus makes a man an object of erotic scorn: as it is itself "at once hateful and dishonored" (ἐχθρὸν ὁμῶς καὶ ἄτιμον, 5.7), so with old age a man goes "hateful to boys, worthless to women" (ἐχθρὸς μὲν παισίν, ἀτίμαστος δὲ γυναιξίν, 1.9)—that is, the old man takes on the attributes of *gêras* itself. Mimnermus does not (as Anacreon will) provide a graphic account of the physical degeneration of age (hair, teeth, limbs). But this aesthetic sets in motion the process by which the aged male body becomes an object of social disapproval, subjected to the kind of aesthetic evaluation with which women had long been scrutinized.

Mimnermus grounds this perception of age not in his own feelings or experience but in nature and the gods, and assimilates the rhythms of human life to those of the natural world. Flower and sun here become consumate expressions of youth's beauty, brevity, and natural perfection. As old age cannot take pleasure even in the light of the sun (αὐγὰς . . . ἠελίου,1.8), in fragment 2 the season of youth is said to be fed by the rays of the sun (αὐγῆς ἠελίου, 2.2), and youth lasts only so long "as the sun scatters his rays upon the earth" (ὅσον τ' ἐπὶ γῆν κίδναται ἥλιος, 2.8).[66] In 1.4 the erotic pleasures of youth are flowers to be eagerly seized (ἥβης ἄνθεα γίνεται ἁρπαλέα). In 2.1–3 youth becomes the "flower-filled season of spring" (πολυάνθεμος ὥρη ἔαρος), and youth's flowers (ἄνθεσιν ἥβης) are the object of our short-lived (probably erotic) delight (τερπόμεθα 2.4, τερπνόν 1.1 and 5.3). At 2.8 youth itself becomes the "fruit of youth" (ἥβης καρπός), the brief harvest-season of enjoyment, and in 5.2 the speaker shudders to behold "the flower of my comrades, at once full of pleasure and beauty" (ἄνθος ὁμηλικίης / τερπνὸν ὁμῶς καὶ καλόν). In these metaphors of flowers and sun old age becomes the unspoken comparandum: the wilted flowers to be overlooked, the lengthening shadows of night and death (cf. Κῆρες . . . μέλαιναι, 2.5).

That nature (φύσις) in which Mimnermus grounds his aesthetics of old age is doubly present in the opening line of the second fragment (φύλλα φύει) where the speaker compares youth to the leaves that the spring puts forth, drawing upon Homer's well known simile:[67]

> As is the generation of leaves, so is that of humanity.
> The wind scatters the leaves on the ground, but the live timber
> burgeons with leaves again in the season of spring returning.
> So one generation of men will grow while another
> dies.
>
> (*Il.* 6.146–150: tr. Lattimore)

Homer finds in the cycle of the seasons and the continuity of the generative process some compensation for the ephemeral nature of human life.[68] Mimnermus, on the other hand, exploits the image for its implications regarding the individual life course:

> We, like the leaves which the spring puts forth, the season
>   full of flowers, when it waxes fast with the rays of the sun,
> like to these do we enjoy for only a brief span
>   the flowers of youth.
>
> (2.1–4)

While youth here becomes the leaves of a brief warm spring (2.1–2), the elderly become the shriveled leaves of autumn. Unlike Homer and Hesiod, Mimnermus ignores the cyclical and recurrent aspects of these rhythms to emphasize the brevity of youth and beauty; humans are described not as part of a self-replenishing collective but as individuals helpless before the designs of an indifferent nature.[69] Similarly, Mimnermus elsewhere attributes the character of old age to divine designs: it is the god (θεός) who has made old age so difficult, or Zeus who gives the old man so many troubles (2.16). In this way the poet's description of the life stages and the values he assigns them seem to represent not his own subjective appraisal but the given and eternal order of things, before which a man's only possible response is that helplessness (ἀμηχανία) with which he faces the other regretable aspects of life.

As "hateful to boys, worthless to women" (ἐχθρὸς μὲν παισίν, ἀτίμαστος δὲ γυναιξίν), the old man is identified as a thing of loathing to his erotic prospects both pederastic and heterosexual, and given the close relationship between Greek male sexual and social life, we should be careful not to underestimate the consequences of the desexualized old age Mimnermus describes. The balanced juxtaposition of "boys" and "women" in the line suggests the equality of hetero- and homoerotic relations in Greece and the importance of success with *both* categories of the beloved. As with "at once hateful and dishonored" (ἐχθρόν ὁμῶς καὶ ἄτιμον, 5.7), the predicates "hateful" (ἐχθρός) and "worthless" (ἀτίμαστος) are presented as different aspects of the same idea, each to be applied to either group of love objects. The reference to "boys" reflects the approved age-grading of homoerotic relations in aristocratic society, and therewith suggests the kind of social exclusion that attends erotic failure. The old man finds himself both in and out of the game of love, unable to win the favors of his beloved and maintain his dominance in such relationships, his honor and social standing—so identified with the erotic enterprise—now in question.[70] In establishing the aged male body as a thing of ugliness to be rejected, Mimnermus finds common ground between the experience of old men and women—as he says at 1.5, the delights of youth are to be plucked by men *and* women (ἀνδράσιν ἠδὲ γυναιξίν). But given the fundamental social distinctions between male and female, this shared experience constitutes a further assault on the old man, whose status is assimilated to that of woman, who becomes liable to the kind of abuse and invective traditionally visited on her, and who finds himself now dishonored among those who are themselves second-class citizens.

The social implications of old age are underscored in the complex of terms by which Mimnermus relates eros to broader concepts of friendship, enmity, and honor. In 1.9 the old man is hateful and worthless (ἐχθρὸς . . . ἀτίμαστος), and in 3.2 a father in old age is said to be neither honored nor loved by his children (οὐδὲ πατὴρ παισὶν τίμιος οὔτε φίλος). At 5.7 old age is itself "at once hateful and dishonored" (ἐχθρὸν ὁμῶς καὶ ἄτιμον), and at 5.5 youth (ἤβη) is τιμήεσσα—both "precious" and "honored." Mimnermus' diction is socially precise, and his notions of "honor" and "friendship" (τιμή and φιλία) retain their broader ethical force. As ἐχθρός rather than φίλος the old man becomes not merely "hated" by boys and women but becomes their "enemy" as well, marked for evil treatment in a culture whose Golden Rule is to "help one's friends and hurt one's enemies."[71] As ἀτίμαστος the old man is without that honor and esteem at the heart of Greek ethical life. Thus "hateful and worthless" suggests not only the lack of affection accorded old men by their would-be beloved but a breakdown in social relations that involves their standing in the eyes of their peers and the community as a whole.

In describing the old man as "ugly and base alike" (τ' αἰσχρὸν ὁμῶς καὶ κακὸν, 1.6), Mimnermus undergirds the aesthetics of male old age with its ethical deficiencies, and those who have rejected Hermann's emendation of the line have not appreciated the force of the claim the poet is making about old age.[72] In coordinating αἰσχρός with κακός, Mimnermus defines the old man, as it were, as "ugly without and base within," situating old age directly in opposition to that ideal of *aretē* as it is expressed in the notion of *kalokagathia*, which recognizes the inseparability of the aesthetic and the moral, the physical and the spiritual. This harmony of outward beauty (καλός) and inner excellence (ἀγαθός) was publicly enshrined in the generic *kouroi* which flourished in Greece during the time of Mimnermus. The *kouros* invites the beholder to contemplate "man" at the peak of his youthful and beautiful perfection, and whatever its origins its abstract and non-specific nature made it available for a variety of functional and symbolic uses; it was, as Hurwit puts it, "a kind of all-purpose iconographic blank," the idea of a man rather than a particular man, which assumed value only according to the context in which it was placed.⁷³ The aristocracy quickly appropriated this idealized image of youth as a symbol of its own moral and political *aretê*. The appreciation of "man" in his perfection became at once an artistic and a political statement, a celebration of a particular social order, and the conservatism of these *kouroi* and the resistance they offered to change made them an appropriate symbol for the traditionalism of the upper-class elite. The ideal of *kalokagathia* they embodied involved the promotion of the values of the aristocracy, who had the wherewithal to erect them and whose own economic and political situation was increasingly insecure.

Because he is so ardent in his advocacy of youth, Mimnermus is often regarded as a spokesman for the aristocracy and its claims, but this does not do justice to the complexity of his poetic idea and its ambiguous relation to the ideal of *kalokagathia*. It was apparently Mimnermus who first seized upon the idea of defining this concept more antithetically by developing a counterimagery of old age, which becomes not just removed from the perfection of youth but its very negation. In describing the old man as "ugly and base alike" (τ' αἰσχρὸν ὁμῶς καὶ κακόν), Mimnermus in effect establishes a corrolary of *aischrokakia* in which the physical ugliness of old age reflects the spiritual deprivation within, his physical appearance mirroring the "base cares" (κακαὶ ... μέριμναι, 1.7) and "many sorrows" (πολλὰ κακά, 2.11) that consume him. But by linking the celebration of youth with the denigration of old age Mimnermus problematizes the concept of *kalokagathia*. In literalizing the beauty of youth and developing a counterimagery of old age, Mimnermus takes what had stood as a symbolic affirmation of a *social* order and redefines it in terms of the movement of the *individual* through the life course. As ugliness is hallmark of the lower classes, he thereby characterizes old age as a passage not only from one stage to the next but also from one *class* to another. Old age thus deprives one of not just the sensuous pastimes of youth but of the entire social code that validates his existence. And while only the aristocracy by virtue of its wealth and privilege might be able to lay claim to *kalokagathia*, the horrid and loveless old age that is the counterimage of this ideal is the destiny of each and every man, a sign of a more universal helplessness (ἀμηχανία) before the grim necessity of nature. As the noble and wealthy now celebrate their own superiority, the symbol by which they do so now contains within itself the recognition that they too possess *aretê* only temporarily: every man, though he begins life an Achilles, with old age becomes a Thersites.

Because Mimnermus' elegies define themselves in opposition to the Homeric and heroic possibilities and (with the possible exception of fragment 14) do not, as in Solon or Tyraetus, seem to offer any new political ideal to replace it, they are often viewed as little more than reflections on the brevity of youth and exhortations to the individual pursuit of pleasure. Yet for Mimnermus, erotic success is an issue that is deeply involved with one's social identity. Where in the Homeric tradition the sexual lives of old men remain a private and domestic affair, Mimnermus relocates male old age within the public context, on the one hand placing it in competition for the favors of the young, on the other despising it for its failure to do so successfully.

GERONTEROTIC IDENTITIES: IBYCUS AND ANACREON

Mimnermus' claim that old age leaves a man disinterested in the business of love is contradicted by lyrics in which old men describe their own experience first-hand as subjects rather than objects. These poems use old age to create situations of erotic tension and dissonance, sometimes describing an ambivalence within the subject about his own desire, at other times pitting his amorous inclinations against an opposing set of social expectations. In a well-known poem by Ibycus of Rhegium (6th c. B.C.), we have a male speaker who is himself (as the scholiast observes) clearly old (πρεσβύτης):

> Once again Eros is giving me those melting looks
> from under his dusky blue eyelids
> and with every kind of love-charm there is
> drives me into Cypris' inescapable net.
> But I tremble as he comes my way
> like a horse in harness, a prize-winner now grown old,
> which goes with the swift chariot all unwilling to the race.
>
> (287)[74]

The speaker is summoned to a love affair that is at once enticing and frought with danger. The languid come-ons of Eros the hunter are the bait to lure him into Love's net, and the weakened condition of the speaker's will is implicit in the terms in which he describes his seductive demeanor. The dramatic situation is undefined; the object of his attention is identified only as a young man whose looks and nature become fused with those of the god himself. The speaker's experience is thus given a generic character, as he finds himself in a situation familiar to him. The poem focuses on his subjective response, both in his longing for love in the abstract (the Eros which hides behind the eyes of his beloved) and his hopes of seducing this particular boy on this particular occasion.[75]

The poem's strategy lies in the idea of repetition, introduced in the familiar motif of "yet one more time . . . " (αὖτε). The speaker trots out a series of erotic tropes—the sultry looks of Eros, the variety of his blandishments, the nets in which he and his Cyprian mother would entangle their prey—and these have their counterpart in the manifold experience of the veteran lover. Where Mimnermus is effusive in his celebration of the delights of eros, here the speaker's reaction at the prospect of a bout with love is decidedly mixed: while his desire is clear, the blunt "I tremble as he comes my way" (τρομέω νιν ἐπερχόμενον) is offered without explanation. The poem thus presents itself as a kind of riddle: Why should the speaker, or anyone, fear such an erotic encounter or an Eros who is portrayed so seductively? The answer is given epigrammatically in the final two lines. Like the horse that is "getting old" (ποτὶ γήρᾳ), the speaker has had his share of victories—he too is a prize winner (ἀεθλοφόρος). But despite his track record he shudders at the thought of returning again to the lists. In the juxtapositon of old (γήρᾳ) and unwilling (ἀέκων), Ibycus breathes new life into the topos that the lover loves by necessity, against his will and his better judgement, and always at the risk of rejection.[76] Love's compulsion is pitted against the speaker's self-consciousness of his age and its limits, and the compactness with which his predicament is presented suggests the extent to which the theme has already become typical. It is not clear whether the speaker is afraid of rejection or of being unequal to love's fervor: he is located not squarely in old age but only "near" (ποτί) it. As in Mimnermus, youth and old age are opposites that do not admit of a third term, and "middle age" has become that period when the lover begins to doubt his erotic ability.

The speaker's dilemma is crystalized in the image of the horse, nervously pawing the ground at the race track. As the horse finally goes, however unwilling, to the track, so the poem suggests that the speaker will likewise play love's game "one more time." The equestrian metaphor in matters erotic has a tradition in Greece going back to the *Iliad*, where Paris returns to the battlefield fresh from a bout of lovemaking with Helen like a beautiful horse galloping over the meadows to join the mares by the river (6.506–14). There Paris is a prize stallion full of youth and strength, running proudly and freely among the mares. The eroticism of that passage and its natural imagery contrast with the self-conscious old age of Ibycus' lover. Here the competitive aspect of eros could not be more striking, as love becomes the quintessentially aris-tocratic arena of contest (ἅμιλλα), the chariot race. The metaphor of the race lends love the character of a public event, with spectators who watch, who know one's track record, and who bet for or against one's success. Like the races at the great Panhellenic games, this is a moment where one's honor and standing in the community are in the balance. In representing himself as a yoke-bearing (φερέζυγος) horse, which does not direct itself but is obedient to the charioteer who com-petes in "the swift chariot race" (ὄχεσφι θοοῖς), the speaker compli-cates the equestrian metaphor and inverts the erotic roles it more typi-cally involves. As love affairs are more typically conceived in terms of the lover's domination and the beloved's submission,[77] the more appropriate hierarchy would be with the lover as charioteer, in the position of authority and control, and the beloved as the horse to be ridden. In Ibycus the lover assumes the role of the horse in harness, thus reflecting the confusion of erotic roles that attends the helpless old lover.

Anacreon, who was himself said to be long-lived and whose love affairs were legion, brought to poetic perfection the persona of the lover-in-old-age.[78] He too makes frequent use of the equestrian metaphor as a measure of the difference between the older lover and the younger beloved, whether of the power that the lover has (or would have) over the beloved, or of the ironic domination of the lover by the beloved. In the address to the "Thracian filly" (417), the taming of the energies of a young girl is described as the breaking in of a colt that prefers to frisk in the meadow rather than engage in a love affair with the speaker. She rejects him as though he knew nothing about love, but his years of experience have made him confident:

> Let me tell you, I could neatly put the bridle on you and with the reins in my hand wheel you round the turnpost of the race-course
>
> (417.3–4: tr. Campbell)

The metaphor of horse and rider suggests both the sexual act and the lover's domination of the beloved, which will be achieved all the more efficiently for the expertise of one so "clever and experienced at mounting" (δεξιὸν . . . ἱπποπείρην . . . ἐπεμβάτην, 417.6). In fragment 360, on the other hand, the speaker, as in Ibycus, becomes the horse in harness and tells the boy whom he loves that he is, albeit unaware, the "charioteer of his soul" (τῆς ἐμῆς ψυχῆς ἡνιοχεύεις, 3–4).

While in neither of these poems is the lover specifically referred to as old, the frequency with which Anacreon adopts the persona of the lover in old age suggests that age may be the cause of his rejection in these poems too. So too in 378, where love is described as a "being young together":

> See, I fly on light wings to Olympus in search of Love; for (the boy) does not wish to enjoy the fun of youth with me (συνηβᾶν).
>
> (tr. Campbell)

In other poems the speaker is explicit about the erotic defeat that comes with age and plays with its poetic possibilities. One fragment appears to be the beginning of a prayer: "hear an old man's prayer, you maiden of the lovely hair and golden robe" (κλῦθί μευ γέροντος εὐέθειρα χρυσόπεπλε κούρα, 418: tr. Campbell). The "maiden" is less likely the object of the speaker's affections than the deity (probably Aphrodite) whose help he would enlist,[79] and the reference to himself as *gerōn* suggests the nature of the request. As prayers formally begin with a review of one's service to the god, the speaker might well have gone on to describe a long life devoted to Love.

Although Anacreon frequently adopts the persona of the lover in old age, this does not make him diffident about his interest and abilities. Unlike Ibycus' old race horse that nervously hesitates at the edge of the race course, Anacreon more often challenges the prevailing assumptions about love and old age. As in the poem to the "Thracian filly" who cannot appreciate what the speaker's years of experience can bring to an affair, Anacreon opposes the view that would judge a lover's capabilities so simply on the basis of his age. There is a paradoxical quality to Anacreon's use of this theme. We have on the one hand a poet who is fully and completely at home with the culture of love and its conventions, and whose poetry is built upon an appreciation of the social subtleties that love entails, yet on the other hand one who points up their arbitrary nature. The result is a poetic personality that uses the figure of the lover in old age at times almost subversively, and seems less interested in arousing pathos than in producing insight into the cultural meaning of age.

Hair is for Anacreon a primary symbol of the interrelationship between age and culture; the status of one's hair is closely linked to erotic status and identity.[80] One fragment seems to poke fun at an old man's capacity for self-delusion: "once again bald Alexis goes wooing" (μνᾶται δηὖτε φαλακρὸς Ἄλεξις, 394b: tr. Campbell). In fragments 347 and 414 the speaker reacts to the cutting of the hair of Smerdies, Polycrates' favorite, which the tyrant ordered when the poet rivalled him for the boy's affection.[81] The speaker laments the cutting of the "perfect flower" of his "soft hair," which has ruined his beauty and altered their relationship. In fragment 420 the speaker describes his own transformation to *geron* as a time "when white hairs shall mingle with my black" (εὖτέ μοι λευκαὶ μελαίνησ᾽ ἀναμεμείξονται τρίχες: tr. Campbell). And in 395 the graying of the hair prefigures the passage to death itself. As Byl has noted, the effect is that of watching the speaker react to his image in a mirror:[82]

> My temples are already grey and my head is white; graceful youth is no more with me, my teeth are old, and no long span of sweet life remains now. And so I often weep in fear of Tartarus: for the recess of Hades is grim, and the road down to it grievous; and it is certain that he who goes down does not come up again.
>
> (395.1–12: tr. Campbell)

Where fragment 378 describes the ascent to Olympus as a search for love (διὰ τὸν Ἔρωτα), this poem offers the obverse: the descent to Tartarus signals the loss of eros, and old age becomes a movement away from the "sweet life" (γλυκεροῦ . . . βιότου) that the speaker so treasures, the negation of erotic joy that Mimnermus identified with life itself (1.1).[83] In Anacreon the cutting of the hair and the graying of the hair are twin aspects of a single concept, the destruction of erotic appeal and even life itself.

Anacreon often links the idea of hair with that of erotic rejection. In fragments 379 a–b the speaker tells how Eros with his "golden wings" (χρυσοφαέννων . . . πτερύγων) flies past him with his "graying beard" (ὑποπόλιον γένειον). In the well-known verses on the "girl from Lesbos," it is again hair, the fair hair of erotic youth and the anti-erotic hair of gray old age, which provides the axes of the poem.

> Once again golden-haired Eros
> throws to me his purple ball,
> and invites me out to play
> with a sweet young girl in fancy sandals.
>   But she, for she is from well-built
> Lesbos, is full of scorn
> for my hair (for it is white)
> and stares, mouth open, at some other . . . girl![84]

Discussion has fixated on the ambiguous and untranslatable last line: the girl from Lesbos "gapes after some other" (πρὸς δ' ἄλλην τινὰ χάσκει). The feminine termination of ἄλλην τινα has generated enormous controversy and two different approaches to the poem as a whole, which can be summarized briefly as follows.[85] Does ἄλλην τινα refer to "some other (hair)"—ἄλλην κόμην—that is, the hair of some other man the girl from Lesbos would prefer, thus coordinating the δέ clause of the final line with τὴν μὲν ἐμὴν κόμην of line 6? This interpretation takes the girl's rejection of the speaker at face value: he is old and gray-haired, and she quite naturally has eyes for some younger lover. Or does the line refer to "some other (girl)"—ἄλλην κόρην—a third party who is the true object of this girl's affections, and one whose sexual orientation is hinted at in the reference in 5–6 to her origins in "well-founded Lesbos" (εὐκτίτου Λέσβου)?

My preference is for this second construction of the final line and for the interpretation of the poem basically as described by Page: "The listener is ready to hear that she will turn from him [the speaker] to a younger man. But Anacreon, having prepared the way by the apparently casual mention of her native island, turns his rebuff to her discomfiture by the unexpected jest at the end—the real reason for her scorn is not that he is *old*, but that he is a *man*."[86] But I would qualify Page's description of the experience of hearing the poem in a small but significant way, which involves a more complicated model of the dynamics of listening to (or reading) the poem, and which the translation, whether successfully or not, attempts to capture. I suspect that the reader at first, on hearing the ἄλλην τινα of the last line, gives it the the first or "innocent" understanding ("some other hair"), coordinating the μέν of 6 with the δέ of 8, supplying κόμην as substantive. In doing so, the listener's expectations are obedient to the familiar conventions: the older lover loses, once again, to the younger.

However, this reading, once established, produces a certain tension and disatisfaction. The awkwardness of πρὸς δ' ἄλλην τινα (κόμην)—"after some other (hair)"—as an expression for πρὸς δ' ἄλλου τινος (κόμην)—"after (the hair) of some other"—prompts the listener to review the poem for another feminine substantive with which ἄλλην might agree. The clichéd nature of the convention makes the reader, especially the reader familiar with Anacreon, wonder if something more promising has been missed. As the reference to Lesbos in line 6 surrenders its initial Homeric and heroic overtones to the more contemporary nuances that might be associated with a "girl from Lesbos," the entire poem is suddenly given a reappraisal. While the refererence to white hair (λευκὴ γάρ) of line 7 suggests that the girl has rejected him for his age, the reason she has alleged are not her "real" reasons but a pretext. The "innocent" reading, I believe, is *meant* to sustain itself through the end of the poem, and to survive, albeit briefly, a first reading. It provides a logical and complete though somewhat disappointing meaning, which then gives way to the real account that the speaker offers for his rejection. Indeed, the Homeric allusion turns out to be something of a ruse, as the speaker has added the epithet "well-built" (εὐκτίτου) precisely in order to *delay* the associations between Lesbos and lesbianism that would be more immediate without it.[87]

The reading I give to the poem and the experience of hearing it depends precisely on the reader's discovery of the conventionality, even the banality, of the first reading and an initial readiness to embrace it: age defeated by youth, the gray-haired old man yielding to some younger rival. It is not only the girl from Lesbos who has been the object of the poet's machinations, but also the listener. Far from agonizing over his rejection or exploiting the situation for its pathos, Anacreon seizes upon its poetic and intellectual possibilities. Even the conventional "once again" (δηῦτε) in the opening line turns out to have a specific value: what might at first be understood as testimony to the age of the lover turns out to suggest the experience and the sophistication that will allow him to turn the tables on the one who jilts him.

As the speaker is revealed as more clever and resourceful, and manages so cooly to expose the real reasons for his rejection, he also shows that the prevailing ideas about love and old age are in this case merely a fiction. The poem employs a variety of structural and verbal devices to suggest the violence that is done when Eros is placed upon the Procrustean bed of these conventions. The first stanza captures the lightness and sophistication that characterize the culture of love in Anacreon, crystalized in the elegance of embroidered finery from the East—the girl's "fancy sandals" (ποικιλοσαμβάλῳ), the golden haired (χρυσοκόμης) boy-god and his pretty purple ball (σφαίρη . . . πορφυρῇ). Here as often in Anacreon love is play, or rather a "playing *with*" (συμπαίζειν): we have a parallel in 357, where the poet speaks of Dionysus as one with whom Eros, the Nymphs, and "purple (πορφυρῇ) Aphrodite" all join in play (συμπαίζουσι).[88] In 358 Eros summons the poet to play a game of ball and to enter his world of gentle play and careful protocol: love "invites" (προκαλεῖται), it does not demand, in keeping with sympotic *mise en scène*. The speaker is revealed as more than ready to play this love-game and is not in the least diffident about his attractiveness or erotic ability. In the second stanza the girl from Lesbos, for all her elegant appearance, is revealed as unequal to the delicate world to which she has been invited. Her protests ruin the triad of color in the first stanza (Love's golden hair and crimson ball, the delicate embroidery of girl's sandals), which oppose to the brilliant polychromy the dull antithesis of gray hair and dark hair and force the elegant diversity of eros onto the grid of crude archaic polarisms. Where love gently invites, the girl bluntly scorns (καταμέμφεται). Like the "Thracian filly" that will only play *alone* (παίζεις, 417.5) in the meadow, the girl would declare the partner Eros has chosen an unworthy playmate because of his age. In doing so she literalizes the metaphor that Anacreon elsewhere observes in describing love as a "being young together."[89]

In her refusal to join in the play of love, the girl from Lesbos is exposed not so much for her hypocrisy but as a kind of spoil sport, and the poet retaliates by showing that it is *she*, not he, who is to be driven from the game. Like the toss of the ball through which it is concretized, the verb "to play with" (συμπαίζειν) here implies the simple play of children. But Anacreon is aware that as with children the games that Eros plays can be fierce and competitive: "love's dice," he says in one fragment, "are madness and uproar: (ἀστραγάλοι δ' Ἔρωτός εἰσιν /

μανίαι τε καὶ κυδοιμοί, 398), and Love's game is elsewhere described as a wrestling match (πρὸς Ἔρωτα πυκταλίζω, 396).[90] In turning the tables on the girl from Lesbos and the clichéd notions of love and age that she would use against him, the speaker manages to exclude her from the game of love and to regroup the players around him.

CONCLUSION: AGED SEXUALITY AS A SOCIAL TEXT

Greek epic and lyric offer various configurations of age and sexuality in which the erotic status of old men becomes increasingly problematical: the aged male body is presented as an object of social concern and the relationship between old age and sexuality is invested with social significance in a number of ways:

1. *in the development of an age-graded aesthetics of the body*, in which erotic attractiveness and the ideals of beauty and moral goodness are appropriated to youth, and in which the outward physical signs of age become emblematic of a whole condition of ethical, social, and spiritual deficiency.

2. *in the portrayal of eros as a form of competition*, with young and old pitted against each other in pursuit of the same love objects; eros thus becomes understood in the context of a sexual game that involves winners and losers.

3. *in the application of categories of social value to sexuality*, so that erotic success and failure come to be seen as social and ethical categories involving one's honor (τιμή).

4. *in a change in the view of the aging process* from a gradual movement through a number of life stages to a simple and more antithetical opposition between *neotēs* or *hēbē* and *gēras*, with the polarities of youth-age assuming the dialectic characteristic of much of archaic thought.

5. *in the shifting of the locus of sexual activity from a primarily domestic context to a public and social one*, so that the pursuit of eros by young and old takes on the nature of a public spectacle in which success and failure become matters of public appreciation.

6. *in an increasing sense in which erotic identity is constituted by age*, in which the speaker regards his erotic predicament as that of an "old lover" and with the same kind of helplessness (ἀμηχανία) he suffers before such evils as disease, poverty, and death.

What are we to make of the importance with which early Greek poetry invests this theme? Foucault above others has emphasized the importance of discourse in understanding the defining role that sexuality plays in the relationship between what a culture deems sexually appropriate and other patterns of its social and conceptual organization. For Foucault, the various discourses of sexuality serve less as a battlefield between forces of repression and expression than as "an especially dense transfer point for relations of power"—that is, the representation of sexuality has to do less with overt sexual practice than with the way in which through it social groups are empowered or disempowered.[91] Foucault insists that it is especially through the medium of the body, and of the social meanings a culture attaches to it, that its members internalize the social order: it is through such mechanisms that "[power] reaches into the very grain of individuals, touches their bodies and inserts itself into their actions and attitudes, their discourses, learning processes and everyday lives."[92]

In the three published volumes of *The History of Sexuality* Foucault examines the crucial role of public discourse in the relationship between knowledge and power, idea and practice, and the significance of changes in discourse, in particular in the Western medical and scientific discourses of sexuality. His thesis finds interesting corroboration in Chudacoff's recent discussion of the history of age-consciousness, entitled *How Old Are You?*, which tracks the increasing importance of age norms in the history of American culture and the origins of social isolation of the elderly. Chudacoff notes that in early America "cultural expressions ignored the peculiarities or even the existence of old age," and that it was not until the end of the nineteenth century that American culture began to identify old age as a specific stage of life and define it as a period of sudden and inevitable decline.[93] The stages of life were also coordinated with changes in sexual behavior, and old age was defined as the advent of the "grand climacteric" in which the sexual lives of men and women came to an abrupt halt. The quote with which this chapter begins is one manifestation of the increased attention that the medical community in particular gave to the sexual character of old age. Equally important are the new attitudes that Americans adopted toward the elderly. As Chudacoff explains, "Heightened interest in behavioral and sexual characteristics of later adult life was part of a broader social trend: new consciousness of and new attitudes toward old age. . . . [A]s science and economic rationalization transformed the nation, attitudes toward the elderly shifted from ambivalence to disrespect and even to hostility."[94]

For the first time old age became identified with a host of physiological and psychological ills, the terms "senile" and "senility" took on negative and degenerative connotations, and the elderly began to be physically segregated in old-age homes.

The increasing emphasis on aged sexuality in early Greek poetry may be compared to the rise of the scientific discourses of sexuality that Foucault traces: in Greece "poetic knowledge" was admitedly partisan and open to challenge, but the kind of authority and social importance to which science has laid claim since the Enlightenment has its ancient counterpart less in science than in literature, especially in the archaic period. While the role of sexuality in the dominance of citizen males over disenfranchised groups (women, "boys," and to some extent slaves) is recognized, we also need to appreciate how *within* the dominant group, concepts of sexuality are organized in the service of power relations. Representations that impinge upon the sexual status of the ancient Greek are inherently laden with social significance, and images of aged sexuality provide a window into the political condition of old age. As Greek politics are conspicuously a politics of male sexuality, one in which sexuality is charged with powerful social meanings, representations that restrict or qualify the nature of male sexuality have a larger force than they might otherwise. Because Greek social identity is so closely linked with sexual activity, changes in the sexual lives of old men necessarily involve a reappreciation of their social status. I would suggest that these geronterotic images in archaic literature work intentionally and deliberately (in the Foucaldian sense of these terms) to that end, as an element in the "strategy" by which old age is established as a socially ambiguous category. To the degree that Greek poetic discourse desexualizes old age and defines it in opposition to full and successful male sexuality, the elderly correspondingly become socially disqualified and even politically disenfranchised. In singling out old men for their sexual incapacities and failures, these representations serve to establish old age as a distinct and problematical category that to some extent involves a corresponding social definition. The sexual and social impairment of old age become two sides of the same coin.[95]

To see the sexuality of old age as in some sense a metaphor for social participation is in keeping with what we know about the status of elderly men in Greece and their participation in the larger culture, or at least in Athens, to which most of our knowledge is limited. The

Greeks had no institutionalized concept of retirement, and men who worked typically did so as long as they could or had to. The Athenian male's military obligations ended with his fifty-ninth birthday, and as Greek males tended to marry at about age thirty, with the father (himself often then around age sixty) handing over control of the *oikos* to him, the son's coming into maturity, domestic authority, and economic independence roughly coincided with the time when his father was considered old. There would of course be continuity in their lives. They would continue to appreciate the cultural amenities of the polis, its religious and civic festivals, and enjoy the daily hum of politics and commerce in the agora. But the transfer of the family business and estate to their sons would strip them of much of their domestic authority and responsibilities.

Correspondingly, there seems to have been no important public office or function that old men held simply by virtue of their age.[96] A few priesthoods were reserved for the elderly, but this was not in general their prerogative; so too for seers, although they are often depicted as old in art and literature.[97] In more traditional societies, of course, one of the main functions of the elderly is to impart their memory and experience; old men allow the preservation of the past and the oral transmission of the cultural experience and values: we have seen the vestiges of such figures in Homer's wise counselors Nestor and Phoenix. But there is no corresponding figure in Greek social or political life. Kirk suggests that the introduction of the alphabet into Greece, probably in the late ninth or early eighth century, likely had important consequences for the status of old age. In preliterate Greece the knowledge of the past, of the authentic traditions and sacred truths, would largely have been the province of the elderly. But when literacy lifted the burden of memory, it was the poets and thinkers, not the elders and storytellers, who became the teachers of the culture, resulting in a blow to the proverbial wisdom of old age.[98]

As age did not necessarily connote wisdom, neither did it confer authority in any political or institutional sense. The governing Council in historical Sparta, to be sure, was in name and reality a Gerousia, with two kings and twenty-eight elders from the Spartan elite eligible at age sixty and elected for life; Tyrtaeus could truly say of his city that "the beginnings of counsel belong to the god-honored kings . . . and the revered elders" (4.3–5). But in this regard Sparta is clearly exceptional; in the variety of political constitutions that developed there is little evidence of gerontocratic institutions or practices.[99] While the evolution of the polis moved uniformly to reduce the hold of the aristocracy and to diffuse power more evenly, there is no evidence of structures through which the elderly wielded any kind of real political power. This does not mean that their participation was limited constitutionally. Van Hoof rightly observes that the elderly were not marginalized in any structural sense.[100] In Athens old men continued to sit in the Assembly and were eligible for election to the magistracies and Council—Socrates, who presided over the *Boulê* six years before his death, is case in point. The elderly also participated extensively in the Athenian court system: Aristophanes' *Wasps* caricatures the jury-mad old men who assembled at the law courts in the predawn hours to serve. Dover remarks that "a mass of old men sitting on a jury is the democratic equivalent of an immemorial feature of human society, the elders of the community sitting as judges."[101] But jury service implies neither great wisdom nor great power, and there are other reasons why these old men are so litigious. The *Wasps* plays up the poverty of the old chorus, for whom the three obol per diem for jury duty seems to have ensured a minimal subsistence level. It is also true that relieved of their domestic and military responsibilities, the elderly may have quite simply had little else to do: the displays of rhetoric and temper in the law courts may well have been the best show in town.[102]

There is little direct evidence that the elderly wielded political power in anything other than in ceremonial and vestigial form.[103] Aeschines (3.2–4; cf. 1.23) reports that Solon originally assigned the order of speaking in the Council and Assembly on the basis of age, the oldest first and youngest last, and that in the Assembly the herald began the proceedings by asking who of those over fifty wished to speak first; but the practice had been discontinued by Aeschines' day and probably much earlier. Garland notes that the aged were assigned specific powers in the appointment of the *probouloi* in 413 when the constitution itself was suspended, and rightly adds that "the prominence of thirty Athenian geriatrics at a time of almost unprecedented national emergency only serves to underline, however, how little their counsels counted for under normal conditions."[104] Demographics are also an issue here. While we know little statistically it is unlikely that there were ever more than a handful of old men in positions of influence at any one time.[105]

We may finally ask whether there was not a sense in which the underlying values of the emerging polis were antigerontocratic. Slater's analysis of Simmon's classic study of the aged in anthropologic literature of some seventy-one cultures suggests a strong correlation between a culture's attitudes toward old age and its social and political characteristics. "Societies in which the elderly have high prestige are generally authoritarian, totalitarian, collectivistic, and static," says Slater. "They are typically governed by monarchs, chiefs, or restricted councils of oligarchs. . . . In societies in which the aged have low prestige . . . government is by general assembly or some other democratic system. Individualism is prevalent and highly valued."[106] Slater's categories could well be applied to Greek political development. In conservative Sparta, where the authority of tradition and age was enshrined in the Gerousia, the elderly are spoken of frequently and deferentially. Tyrtaeus exhorts the younger warriors to defend their older colleagues, and reminds them that the man who fights bravely in youth "is distinguished among the citizens as he grows old" (12.38). But in the more democratic constitutions at Athens and elsewhere the principle of the authority of old age ran at odds with the whole tenor of the times: the egalitarian nature of the politics; the relocation of the male's identity from the patriarchal *oikos* to the polis; and the increasing valuation of reason over and against the authority of mere age.[107] In such cities, where politics served as an arena for individual competition, where the winds of social, intellectual, and political life shifted often, where "modernity" was a positive value, and where political success was often based upon one's rhetorical ability and adaptability to changing circumstance, the elderly were at a clear disadvantage. It is not surprising that it was in such an environment that the erotic glorification of youth and disparagement of age became social forces and literary commonplaces. The texts we have discussed provide oblique yet important perspective on the isolation and ineffectuality of old age and on the failure and ridicule the elderly risk in engaging in those social arenas increasingly dominated by the young.

CHAPTER 5

The Politics and the Poetics of Time: Solon's "Ten Ages"

How many horses have they got in this town? How many young men? Nobody knows! They haven't bothered to count 'em! That's peace for you! I've been in places where they haven't had a war for seventy years and you know what? The people haven't even been given names! They don't know who they are! It takes a war to fix that. In a war, everyone registers, everyone's name's on a list. Their shoes are stacked, their corn's in the bag, you count it all up—cattle, men, *et cetera*—and you take it away! That's the story: no organization, no war!

—from Brecht, *Mother Courage* (tr. Eric Bentley)

LATTIMORE translates Solon 27 as follows:

A child in his infancy grows his first set of teeth and loses them
   within seven years. For so long he counts as only a child.
When God has brought to accomplishment the next seven-year period,
   one shows upon his body the signs of maturing youth.
In the third period he is still getting his growth, while on his chin   5
   the beard comes, to show he is turning from youth to a man.
The fourth seven years are the time when every man reaches his
   highest
   point of physical strength where men look for prowess achieved.
In the fifth period the time is ripe for a young man
   to think of marriage and children, a family to be raised.   10
The mind of a man comes to full maturity in the sixth period,
   but he cannot now do as much, nor does he wish that he could.
In the seventh period of seven years and in the eighth also
   for fourteen years in all, his speech is best in his life.
He can still do much in his ninth period, but there is a weakening   15
   seen in his ability both to think and speak.

But if he completes ten ages of seven years each, full measure,
  death, when it comes, can no longer be said to come too soon.[1]

Critical discussion of Solon's verses on the "ten ages of man" has been extensive, but appreciation of the poem's hebdomadic analysis of the life course is largely divided: those who have focused on the poem's view of human growth and the aging process have regarded it favorably; those who have concentrated on its poetic qualities have found little to praise.[2] Schadewaldt, reacting to Wilamowitz and others who regarded the poem as little more than folk-poetry ("volkstümliche Merkvers"), studies it against the background of epic and lyric and finds in Solon's verses a vigorous Attic response to pessimistic notions of aging, particularly in Mimnermus.[3] Steinhagen sees in the hebdomads the artistic expression of Solon's true achievement: his recognition of life as a unified process of development capable of human measure ($\mu\acute{\epsilon}\tau\rho\text{o}\nu$).[4] Preisshofen, responding to both of these studies, appreciates the complicated relationship between Solon's stages of life and traditional motifs about youth and old age.[5]

Szemerényi, on the other hand, rejects the poem's authenticity altogether, finding the hebdomadic treatment incompetent and its language "so singularly gauche that only a beginner can be credited with it."[6] Campbell calls the poem graceless and monotonous, and complains that its structure "collapses" with the seventh and eighth hebdomads.[7] Adkins speaks of the poem's "absurdities and infelicities," concluding that "we can only regret that Solon invented or borrowed the scheme of hebdomads and decided to allot one couplet to each hebdomad."[8] The kind of split that has characterized critical treatment of the poem is implicit in Fränkel's judgement: "Artistically the rather dry poem is of no interest; what is notable is the calm and objective way in which Solon accepts natural development in its rise and decline."[9]

The relationship between the poem's philosophical and aesthetic dimensions can perhaps be illuminated in the context of its unique conceptual framework. Largely ignored in the discussion has been the literary and cultural significance of the hebdomadic structure, and its relation to other aspects of Solon's thought. Indeed, it might be easy for us to overlook precisely those features of the poem that are intellectually most distinctive. Because Solon's poem perceives life as a quantity capable of measure, organizing a man's threescore and ten years in a sequence of discrete and successive stages, we tend to read it in the context of a modern Western society that routinely regards human time in chronological terms and points of reference. For us, whose lives and mental habits are orchestrated by the mathematics of clock and calendar, and who are predisposed to regard life in terms of developmental stages, the kind of analysis upon which Solon embarks can be all too easily assimilated to our ways of thinking.

An analysis of the poem needs first to be set in the context of its conceptualization of human time and its complex and problematical relation to archaic Greek thought.[10] A fuller understanding of the poem—if we are to see it as other than a poetic eccentricity, isolated from the rest of Solon's work like a lost island, "wie ein verlorenes Eiland" as Schadewaldt put it[11]—ought first to appreciate the way in which the poet requires the reader to construct human time, what is involved in such a conception, and how this perspective relates to other aspects of Solon's poetical and political expression. It is toward establishing such a context that the following is addressed.

We can freshen our perspective on the poem's underlying *idea* in the context of more traditional perspectives on age. It is true, of course, that all cultures define the life course by dividing it into different social and linguistic categories, so that our perception of ourselves and others is always in the context of a limited number of life stages or age-grades.[12] Such classifications are an integral part of our understanding of what a person "is" and how we expect him or her to behave. Because these divisions are entrenched in both our cognitive processes and the social order, and because the passage between them may coincide in part with biological changes (e.g., puberty, menopause), age-grades are often regarded even today as reflections of the natural order rather than the cultural constructions they are.[13] Yet ethnographic literature serves to remind us of the enormous variety with which cultures construct the human life course: differences in the number and length of the age-grades, in the rituals and social markers that accompany the passage from one grade to the next, in the characterization of the age-grades and their relation to social life. For purposes of contrast, we might take a description of age-grading among the Masai of East Africa:

> For males, the grades are uninitiated youth (*ilaiyok*); young men or warriors (*ilmurran*), who are divided between junior and senior subgrades;

elders (*ilmoruak*), who are divided into junior, senior, and retired sub-
grades; and ancient elders (*ildasati*). There are thus seven effective age-
grades. For each there are well-established norms that prescribe the general lines of behavior, expectations, and obligations, both in public life
(community, political, and ritual affairs) and in private life (family, kinship, and interpersonal affairs).[14]

Moreover, in non-Western and traditional societies, chronological
concepts of age have at best limited social use. Fortes cautions anthropologists against identifying traditional age-grades in terms of our
chronological equivalents, noting that a social life "regulated by a cal-
culus corresponding to our schemes of chronological-age-linked rules
is totally lacking in preliterate tribal culture." He provides examples of
people who to our way of thinking do not "know" their age, not because they have forgotten or failed to take note of it, but because in
their culture the concept has little social value.[15]

There are some significant similarities between age-grading in traditional cultures and what we see in archaic Greek poetry. As we have
seen, the age structures embedded in Greek literature display considerable variety both in their number and linguistic expression.[16] But in
the characterization and interrelationship of the different stages, the
differences one observes are closely related to the social worlds of the
different works and genres. Implicit in Homeric epic is a distinction of
four male age-grades—that of the *pais*, the younger *neos* or *kouros*, the
mature male at the prime of life (Aristotle's *akmê*), and the *gerôn* or
presbys. In the *Iliad* these distinctions are articulated around the
matrix of heroic warfare, embodied respectively in those not yet warriors (like Astyanax), younger warriors at their physical peak like
Achilles and Diomedes, older more mature warriors and leaders like
Agamemnon and Odysseus, and elders like Phoenix, Priam, and
Nestor, who are partially or fully disengaged from the arena of war; the
Odyssey reflects the older three grades in the generational relationships of Telemachus, Odysseus, and Laertes. Hesiod's *Works and Days*,
as we have seen, makes a similar distinction on the basis of domestic
and agricultural function between nonproductive children, younger
and less productive workers, mature laborers and heads of the *oikos*,
and *gerontes* supported in old age by their sons. In erotic lyric, where
the criterion is often amorous success, life is often reduced to an opposition between two grades: the *neoi* who enjoy youth (*hêbê*) and the

pleasures of love, and the *gerontes* who (presumably) cannot. The representation of the grades thus differs according to whether the context is heroic, agricultural, domestic, erotic, and so forth, and allows the reader to assume correspondingly certain physical, social, ethical, and behavioral characteristics.

The poetic tradition, moreover, never describes an individual's age in chronological terms and (as teachers of inquisitive undergraduates will readily testify) is often intractable to the kind of age-related questions we routinely ask. In Homer, characters are identified not by age but in the context of their grade and generational relationships.[17] References to chronological age in Hesiod and lyric are few and general in nature, serving in maxims, as "notional" figures, or as statements about life expectancy.[18]

Even at this summary level there are obvious differences between the different age structures implicit in Greek literature and the self-conscious and explicitly systematic treatment of age we find in Solon 27. Where traditional age-grades are identified without reference to age per se, Solon's are identified quantitatively and chronologically; where traditional age-grades are of unequal duration and proportion, Solon's are equal in length, symmetrical in structure, and conceived in the context of a predetermined sum; and where traditional age structures are integrated into a system of social function and status, Solon's grades are characterized more abstractly and seem devoid of social information. Solon describes age not through the traditional literary nomenclatures but through an abstract chronology and the structure he works upon it here; thus Szemérenyi is to some extent right in claiming that the hebdomadic structure "does not fit into the mental climate of the sixth century,"[19] at least as a literary description of age. It would be a mistake then to approach the poem simply as one more variation within Greek literary concepts of age—as a system of ten stages rather than of three or four or five—since the very premise of the poem entails reconceptualizing age in an *untraditional* way.

Solon establishes the hebdomads as the poem's structural principle by allocating to each elegiac couplet, with the exception of 13–14, one seven year span, and by ending each couplet with a full stop. This purpose is also reflected in the poem's diction, which employs little of the conventional Greek vocabulary of age. Apart from the emphatic reference to infancy (παῖς . . . ἄνηβος ἐὼν ἔτι νήπιος) that begins the poem and makes the initial equation necessary to read it, and the reference in 4 to the onset of physical maturity (ἥβης . . . σήματα γεινομένης) that marks the end of childhood, the poem avoids the familiar age-specific words: *neos* or *neôteros*, *kouros* or *kouroteros*, *hoploteros*, *gerôn* or *presbys*, and so on. Solon uses the more generic *anêr* (8, 9,11), which strictly speaking does not imply age at all, and otherwise avoids words with age associations by using a variety of sentence subjects: god (θεός) in 3 and 4, pronominal "he" understood in verbs either expressed or to be supplied (12,13,15,18), non-personal subjects (5, 9,11,14, 16), and the semantically empty "one" (τις and πᾶς τις, 7,17). By eschewing the conventional vocabulary and describing age through hebdomads without a corresponding system of name-grades, Solon's poem locates itself outside of the literary and social contexts in which age is traditionally encoded.[20]

Solon's poem, moreover, not only employs chronological concepts of age but reorganizes them at the more abstract level of the hebdomad (ἑβδομάς), a word that appears here for the first time in extant literature and thus points up the novelty of the poem's framework.[21] That the poem does not introduce the term itself until the fourth couplet has sometimes been a point of criticism, yet part of the "problem" may be in Solon's attempt to establish a *sense* of the concept before introducing it as a technical term. Solon says "in seven years" (ἐν ἕπτ' ἔτεσιν, 2), and "the next group of years" (τοὺς δ' ἑτέρους . . . ἐναυτιούς, 3), and links these phrases to familiar terms (παῖς and ἥβη) before employing the hebdomad itself, first indirectly with "in the third" (τῇ τριτάτῃ, 5) and then directly with "in the fourth hebdomad" (τῇ δὲ τετάρτῃ . . . ἐν ἑβδομάδι, 7). Later he varies the pattern again with the curious "in seven and eight hebdomads, fourteen years from both" (ἑπτὰ . . . ἐν ἑβδομάσιν . . . ὀκτώ τ'· ἀμφοτέρων τέσσαρα καὶ δέκ' ἔτη, 13–14). But at no point in the sequence does he depart from the hebdomadic framework and proceed with a simple "then" or "and next." The results are inelegant, as with the unusual ἑτέρους in 3 for the second of a series, and in places even ungrammatical, as in 13–14, where the literal values of the cardinals (ἑπτά and ὀκτώ) cannot be sustained. But the overall impression is of an attempt to develop a numerical concept and structure heretofore unfamiliar in a literary context.

Accordingly, we should be careful not to underestimate the arithmetical operations involved in reading the poem and in applying it to oneself or others, an impulse I take to be as normal to the ancient reader as to us. To locate an individual in Solon's analysis, one begins with a chronological age and places it in its corresponding hebdomad (e.g., to which hebdomad does a man belong at age twenty-five? at fifty-three?), only then gaining access to the Solonian grade and its value. In order to determine the age span of a particular hebdomad (e.g., what ages are covered by the sixth hebdomad?), one converts the hebdomads to their chronological equivalents. Part of the idea of the poem is precisely in the process of reading—or rather computing—its contents. Solon's framework assumes a reader sufficiently numerate to appreciate its structure and to perform the necessary operations—and quickly too, if we understand its publication to have been primarily oral.

While this kind of numerical quantification is foreign to Greek literature, it is at home in the social world of sixth century Athens and the critical issues of property, sale, debt, and commerce. It is, moreover, typical of Solon's political thought, which addressed an astonishing range of social concerns in such quantitative terms. In contrast with Draco's liberal application of the death penalty, Solon established a more graduated system of fines, and as lawgiver (*nomothetês*) quantified the most diverse matters: dowries, funeral gifts, sacrificial animals, sumptuary practices, access to wellwater, distances between olive trees and beehives, even the sexual obligations of the husband of an *epiklêros* (heiress).[22] His economic and institutional reorganization is likewise conspicuous for its attention to numerical concepts. The reformulation of the Athenian system of weights and measures, probably from the Aeginetan standard to the Euboeic, and his alleged revaluation of Athenian coinage (from seventy-three to one-hundred drachmas to the mina), provided new exchange rates for the community.[23] The Athenian Council regroups four tribal "units" of one-hundred men each, and the nine *archai* may similarly have involved a primary election of ten from each tribe and a final selection by lot.[24] Especially noteworthy is his establishment of the *pentakosiomedimnoi* and of a system of property classes standarized around the unit of the "hundred-measure," which provides a corollary to the idea of the hebdomad and on which we will say more below.[25] In this sense the poem's chronological quantification reflects the intellectuality that characterized his political thought, so that the poem serves, perhaps not without a touch of humor, as an illustration of a "Solonian" approach to age and suggests the political context of the elegy itself.

Solon's poem likewise makes sense only in the context of a culture in which chronological age is an instrument of social organization and where people are at least to some extent regarded in such terms. This is borne out by the developmental patterns in more traditional communities where, to quote Fortes again, "chronological age becomes significant when the political and legal framework takes precedence over familial and kinship relations for determining citizenship."[26] That is, as persons in a given social order are increasingly regarded as individual citizens rather than as members of a family, so will they tend to be regarded politically and institutionally in terms of an impersonal and independent chronology rather than in terms of their kinship and generational relationships. While there is little evidence of the extent to which chronological age had previously been a principle of Athenian political organization, the social reorganization of the sixth century and the increasing encroachment of *polis* upon the affairs of *oikos* would necessarily have involved the establishment of chronological requirements for a range of institutions, in many cases for the first time, so that the poem reflects the increasing importance of chronological age in Athenian social life. In the classical period one was elegible for the archonship and the Council at thirty, requirements probably derived from Solonian precedents, and election to the lesser magistracies now open to the *hippeis* (horsemen) and *zeugitai* (teamsters) would certainly have involved age criteria. The organization of the cavalry and hoplite army must have fixed ages for training and active service and discharge, and participation in religious life and the enhanced state festivals would have been attended by a myriad of age-related requirements.

Mathematics and chronology thus become the vehicles by which Solon develops a more abstract model of the life course and dissociates it from the traditional classifications of age. Solon's poem requires the reader to reconceptualize the life course: to the degree that age is regarded in terms of a conventional vocabulary, Solon provides an alternative system of grades with a hebdomadic nomenclature; to the degree that socially age is increasingly regarded chronologically, Solon reorganizes these terms at the higher level of the hebdomads. Solon's framework thus serves both to defamiliarize conventional categories of age and to draw attention to its own system for the deliberate and "unnatural" creation it is.[27]

One must thus beware, in speaking as Bowra does of Solon's attempt "to discern an immanent order,"[28] not to imply that Solon's model is presented as an expression of a natural order that waited only for his discovery rather than as an artistic creation. Hudson-Williams criticizes the poem for corresponding imperfectly to the "natural" divisions of the life course: "This tenfold division is very rare, and the poet evidently found great difficulty in working it out: cf. vv. 13–14, where he is unable to distinguish between the seventh and eighth hebdomads; the fourth and fifth are naturally one period, so too the ninth and tenth."[29] But Solon's poem is conceived more with an eye to what will *work* than to what is *true*, and differs from the familiar literary models precisely to the degree that it acknowledges its own conventional and even arbitrary character. His use of the hebdomad as a system of measure, far from appealing to a philosophical or mystical authority, declares itself throughout as a product of human invention. The elegance and symmetry of the numerical axes (seven and ten) of Solon's analysis are the product not of nature but of artifice: the poem transforms the tradition that regards seventy as a normative figure for life *expectancy* into the idea of a "limit" that makes possible the poem's premise that life is capable of such a measure ($\mu\acute{\epsilon}\tau\rho\text{o}\nu$).[30] The elegy ends conditionally: "if one, having completed the tenth (hebdomad), should arrive at the measure (of the tenth)," it would not be "unseasonable" ($\ddot{\alpha}\omega\rho\text{o}\varsigma$) for him to die, that is, if he is not to commence an eleventh hebdomad and destroy the poem's axial structure. Steinhagen in particular has shown the extent of the poem's internal symmetry and balance, its pairing of hebdomads in order to capture the complementarity of the cycles of physical and intellectual growth and justify the particular $\mu\acute{\epsilon}\tau\rho\text{o}\nu$ (measure) he gives them.[31]

Solon also employs the concept of the hebdomad in somewhat different senses. It indicates primarily a *span* of time *within* which changes take place, marked by a dative construction: during the first seven years the *pais*, having grown teeth as a baby ($\nu\acute{\eta}\pi\iota\text{o}\varsigma$), loses them for the first time (1–2); during the third he sprouts a beard, his limbs grow, his complexion changes its hue. But the hebdomad can also identify a *point* in time at which a change occurs (marked by the accusative): at fourteen, with the completion of the second hebdomad ($\tau\epsilon\lambda\acute{\epsilon}\sigma\eta$, 3), one shows the signs of puberty; at the completion of the tenth ($\tau\epsilon\lambda\acute{\epsilon}\sigma\alpha\varsigma$, 17), one dies. Consider also the difference in the kind of "necessity" that governs the relationship between a given hebdomad and its contents: from the "must" that governs the physiological changes in the first four hebdomads; to the "should" that recommends

marriage and children at a time that is "seasonable" (ὥριον, the fifth);
to the "may" that describes the growth and decline of social and cognitive skills in the next four (where exceptions are never difficult to
find), to the aesthetic necessity that brings life to a conclusion with
the tenth hebdomad.

The relationship between the representation of age and poetic artifice is developed directly in Solon's so-called "reply" to Mimnermus
(20). Critics have typically read the passage as literary biography, seeing the "inconsistency" between the sentiment here and in 27 as evidence of a change of heart about the "proper" end (μοῖρα) of life or
even claiming the inauthenticity of the latter.[32]

> But if even at this late date you will still listen to me, strike that out
> (and don't be upset because I have put it better than you):
> change it and sing it like this, "Ligiastades":
> "may the fate of death find me at age eighty."
>
> (20.1–4)[33]

Schadewaldt and others are certainly right in seeing here an allusion to
Ionian pessimism about old age and aging,[34] but the point of the verses
seems as much one of poetics as ethics. Solon addresses Mimnermus
as the "clear-singer" (Λιγιαστάδης),[35] emphasizing the aesthetic
dimension of poetry. He reminds him of the place of revision in poetry
(μεταποίησον): he tells him to delete (ἔξελε) and edit, and to sing
(ἄειδε, continuing the play in Λιγιαστάδη) his song differently by
adopting a metrical equivalent: "eighty" (ὀγδωκονταέτη) for "sixty"
(ἑξηκονταέτη). Yet this would clearly be ridiculous in the context of
Mimnermus' general contempt for old age and of the particular verses
to which Solon alludes:

> May the fate of death find me, free from disease
> and burdensome troubles, at age sixty.
>
> (6)[36]

Solon's verses are less a moralistic request for revision or an argument
for the authority of his characterization of old age than a playful reflec-

tion on the way *poiêsis* and poetic convention are manipulated according to the aesthetics of genre and presentation.[37]

Like his "reply" to Mimnermus, Solon's other work illustrates the extent to which the representation of old age is shaped by generic convention and poetic context. In one context Solon uses his personal experience to develop the positive value of long life and describes old age at least potentially as a time of learning, ironically reversing more traditional attitudes that regard the elderly in their capacity as *teachers* and wise counselors:

> As I grow older I am always learning many things (γηράσκω δ' αἰεὶ πολλὰ διδασκόμενος, 18).[38]

In a different context the poet, using another image, contrasts a conventional notion of wealth with the more ordinary pleasures of life:

> For no man can take
> his immense wealth with him when he dies,
> nor by paying a price can he avoid death or grievous
> disease or the approach of evil old age.
>   (24.7–10)[39]

The figure of "approaching evil old age" itself recalls several passages in Mimnermus.[40] Yet Solon here reformulates the motif not in an opposition between youth and old age but to contrast the security of the simple life with the insecurity of great riches.[41] In another context Solon (if Plutarch is to be trusted), expresses in connection with his own old age an interest in the sensual pleasures more characteristic of lyric:

> Now I take up the pleasures of the Cyprian and Dionysus
> and the Muses, which make men glad.
>   (26)[42]

In the "ten ages," where the final stages make no mention of *gêras* at all and are developed with attention to the poem's symmetry and balance, the representation of old age is different once again. Solon neither praises old age on the basis of personal experience nor regards it in traditional terms as an evil, but characterizes it in the ninth hebdomad as a period of continuing ability *and* decline:

> He can still do much in his ninth period, but there is a weakening
> seen in his ability both to think and speak.
>
> (15–16: tr. Lattimore).

Throughout all these verses, Solon's characterizations of age are less a
position determined by their "objective nature" than the product of
his manipulation of poetical alternatives in different literary situations.[43] We need to appreciate poem 27 less as a distillation of Solon's
"views" on age and more with an eye to the poem's purposes: to what
end does Solon engage in this reformulation of age?

What the "ten ages" involves is a change of perspective, from
regarding the categories of age as natural and "given," to seeing them
as a self-conscious expression of human invention and the individual
artist. This kind of "perceptual shift" has an interesting parallel in
Solon's reformulation of the Athenian social classes, which effectively
replaced criteria described in terms of hereditary distinctions—consider the *eupatrids* or "men of good fathers"—with those described in
terms of agricultural product, where the best become the *pentakosi-
amedimnoi* or "five-hundred-bushel men," a title Solon himself may
have invented.[44] Such a reform involves not a nominal but a conceptual shift, from a notion of class wherein the ruling elite (δυνατοί) are
perceived genetically, to one in which such distinctions are economic
and where social structure is seen as a product of deliberation and
political process. While changes in the composition of the Areopagus
and the *archai* would surely have been slow, the change in the perception of those in power as quantitatively rather than qualitatively superior, and of the classes not as castes but as rungs on an economic lad-
der that can in theory be scaled, is a radical one.[45]

Alongside this social reorganization are Solon's poetic redefinitions
of its major concepts. He contrasts with the *dêmos* those who hold
power (δύναμιν) and are "wondrous in wealth" (χρήμασιν . . . ἀγητοί,
5.3), implying that the power of the latter is a product not of excellence but of money. In poem 23 he defines prosperity, calling the man
happy (ὄλβιος) who is not of great but of modest means, and claims
that equally wealthy (ἶσόν τοι πλουτέουσιν, 24.1) are those with great
riches and those who enjoy life's ordinary joys. In the same vein is his
declaration in poem 15 that "many bad men are wealthy, many good
men are poor" and the opposition it sets up between the vicissitudes of
wealth and *aretê*, which is ever secure and steadfast (τὸ . . . ἔμπεδον

ἀιεί), standing on its head the conventional association of wealth and excellence with the ruling aristocracy.[46]

In poem 27 Solon similarly reappropriates age from the natural to the political order, divorcing it from its familiar contexts and in the measure of number and quantity reconstructing it according to his own political ideals. The cool symmetry of the hebdomads and the poem's dispassionate language have led scholars to credit the poem with a special "objectivity," so that Fränkel speaks of its "gelassene Sachlichkeit" and Schadewaldt of its "Distanz" and "'philosophischen' Sehens."[47] Indeed, where lyric is more often characterized by the speaker's absorption in himself and the present moment, Solon's perspective appears transcendent and atemporal. But we need to appreciate this "objectivity" along with the poem's mathematical abstractedness as rhetorical techniques employed toward poetical ends. While the poem's abstract and unconventional character locates it outside the literary tradition, as though free from the narrower interests of the literary genres, Solon's redefinition of age is no less embedded in a set of social and political values. "Man" as the subject of the elegy is throughout an artifical and a political creation, conceived atomistically, with no family or lineage, no class or occupation, indeed without direct reference to the *polis* at all. Yet the perspective here is not so much "philosophical" as political: in the act of divorcing man from his kinship relations, from his occupational and generational relationships, from the narrow interests that distinguish one group from others, the poem reconstitutes him as individual citizen.

Solon's ten ages describe the unfolding of various abilities—physical, social, cognitive, and performative—that may seem obvious or natural but are carefully selected and structured. The changes in the first four hebdomads are primarily physical in nature, with an emphasis on bodily growth and its manifestations (σήματα, 4, 8) in teeth, hair, size, and strength. The fifth and sixth are primarily social and ethical: a man marries and provides offspring, his mind develops (or perhaps "becomes disciplined," καταρτύεται, 11), and he learns restraint and responsibility (οὐδ' ἔρδειν ἔθ' ὁμῶς ἔργ' ἀπάλαμνα θέλει, 12).[48] In the final hebdomads his intellectual and rhetorical capacities are at their peak for a full fourteen years and then decline. These various qualities involve a political world view consistent with the conception of man as individual citizen.[49] Man becomes the locus of those excellences valuable to the *polis*—physical strength, prudence, intelligence, speaking ability—and the provider of future citizens (παίδων . . . εἰσοπίσω γενεήν, 10). Hence the emphasis on the one hand on physical strength (ἰσχύν, 8) and on the *aretê* that it represents (7–8), qualities essential for the defense of the *polis*, and on the importance of marriage and offspring (9–10). Moreover, the poem develops the importance of mind (νόος, 11, 13), speech (γλῶσσα, 13, 16), and wisdom, (σοφίη, 16) which—far from being the province of poets or thinkers alone—suggest the wisdom, prudence, and speaking skill required in participatory citizenship. As the criteria by which these two kinds of *aretê* (8,16) differ, so a man will be excellent (ἄριστος, 7, 13) at two different stages of life. Solon thereby suggests the development of a political *aretê* parallel to that of physical *aretê*, and characterizes the second cycle of growth as that of the "great excellence" (cf. πρὸς μεγάλην ἀρετήν, 16). By combining the seventh and eighth hebdomads in one couplet he sustains the full expression of political *aretê* for twice the duration of one's physical prime, making the second cycle of development, and with it the qualities crucial for the citizen and statesman, the more emphatic. By assimilating the development of social and political abilities to physical development, which is rooted in the biology and whose signs (σήματα, 4, 8) are so conspicuous, Solon grounds them no less in "human nature" and establishes the *polis* as the arena in which such *aretê* is developed.

The poem thus constructs a model not only of time but of man himself compatible with the movement in which Solon played so large a part and which increasingly identified man as member of his *polis* first and of his *oikos* second. The poem nonetheless makes no direct reference to any specific social applications, military, political, or religious, leaving it to the reader to relate these life stages to the realities of Athenian social life. Indeed, Solon's age-grades correspond only vaguely to the institutional structures: military training begins somewhere in the third hebdomad, which is described simply as a time of physical growth; eligibility for political office begins in the fifth hebdomad, which is defined here (as in Hesiod *WD* 695–97) as a time for marriage. Indeed, Solon may have found the hebdomadal system attractive precisely because its transitional moments (ages 7, 14, 21 . . .) do *not* coincide with those of political or military life. By avoiding specific social allusions, his abstraction of man as individual citizen becomes more generic and thus more persuasive.

Solon's model similarly avoids contents specific to particular citizen groups, and can accommodate equally the farmer, merchant, craftsman, or aristocrat. Solon's broad conception of the human excellences implies no particular background, concerns, or behaviors as conditions on which *aretē* is attained. Formally the poem gives an impression of balance and fairness by allocating to each hebdomad one couplet (except for 13–14), so that the stages of life are given as it were equal treatment. This inclusive perspective is paralleled in other poems, in which poetic form itself expresses equality and impartiality.

> I gave the people as much privilege as they had a right to:
>> I neither degraded them from rank nor gave them a free hand;
> and for those who already held the power and were envied for money,
>> I worked it out that they also should have no cause for complaint.
> I stood there holding my sturdy shield over both the parties;
>> I would not let either side win a victory that was wrong.
>> > (5.1–6: tr. Lattimore)[50]

While the elite hold greater power and privilege, Solon regards each class with dignity: here remarkably even the *dêmos* is said to have its honor and privilege (τιμῆς, γέρας),[51] and a single couplet is afforded to each. Solon positions himself (ἔστην) apart from or above both groups, the image of the shield suggesting not so much his political power as the limitations of their more partial perspectives and the conciliatory nature of his role as reconciler (διαλλακτής). In another poem Solon dismisses the criticisms of both the *dêmos* and those "greater and superior in strength" (μείζους καὶ βίην ἀμείνονες), likening his position to that of a boundary stone between two armies (ἐν μεταιχμίῳ ὅρος, 37.9–10).[52]

The detached perspective developed in these spatial metaphors is achieved in poem 27 in the poem's mathematical balance, the simplicity of its diction, and its abstract and general character. In this regard Solon's approach contrasts with aristocratic lyric, which is characterized more often by the blatant *partiality* of its perspective and the exclusiveness of its world view.[53] Such poetry flaunts its privileged and restricted notion of excellence, and the speaker identifies himself precisely by the limits of his perspective, whether of class, wealth, or, as often, age. We read Mimnermus 1 as expressing aristocratic eros in self-celebration, and Anacreon 302 and 322 as instances of old men reflecting on old age. Other poems acknowledge the partiality of their perspectives: the mature perspective of Mimnermus 2 suggests the limitations in youthful experience, as Simonides 8.6–11 describes the naive perspective of youth and its delights.[54]

To the extent then that poem 27 involves a response to Ionian attitudes about youth and old age, the criticism is not only ethical but political, and consistent with the view expressed often by Solon (and remarked by Aristotle in *Ath. Pol.* 5) that the roots of Athens' social conflict lay in aristocratic wealth and conspicuous consumption. Yet here this response to the aristocratic perspective is achieved with particular reserve and subtlety, with Solon not so much arguing the case per se but changing the terms of the discussion. While aristocratic lyric idealizes youthful eros and denigrates old age, Solon does not deny the importance of eros (which is not mentioned) or of youth: it possesses one, though the lesser, of the two human *aretai*. Correspondingly, he offers no defense of old age per se, indeed does not even name it as such, but acknowledges its weakness and its abilities, though in reference now to the context of political *aretê*. To the extent that Solon suggests a new understanding of human nature and of *aretê* based on man as the individual citizen, the aristocratic perspective is not refuted but transcended within a more comprehensive model.

In bypassing the traditional conceptualization of age in favor of a mathematical and chronological approach, Solon addresses the idea of aging apart from the literary vocabularies and the assumptions they make about human growth and nature. In the graduated stages of the hebdomads, Solon develops a conception of excellence and human chronology consistent with his political and poetical thought and the terms in which it often finds expression: quantity and chronology, number and balance, an inclusive and conciliatory perspective. In this poetically radical represention of human time, Solon achieves a harmony of content and form such that they mutually reinforce each other. Far from being a "lost island" related to the rest of Solon's work only in its thematic interest in old age, the poem exemplifies much that is characteristic of this uncharacteristic poet and statesman.

Euripides and the Tragedy of Old Age: *Children of Heracles* and *Phoenician Women*

We are told that once at a festival in Athens, when an old man well on in years had entered the theater, nowhere out of all that great assemblage did his own citizens offer him a place. But when he approached some Spartan ambassadors who had taken their places in the seats reserved for them, it is said that they all rose up and offered him a seat. And when these men were applauded by the whole crowd again and again, one of them said that the Athenians understood what was proper, but were unwilling to practice it.

—Cicero, *De Senectute*

CICERO'S anecdote is frequently offered as evidence of the bad reputation that Athens had acquired for its shabby treatment of the elderly.[1] But if old people had a hard time finding a seat in the theater of Dionysus, the situation on the stage was just the opposite, at least to judge from Euripides. Indeed, had Aristophanes continued with his lambasting of Euripides in the *Frogs*, he might well have added to his criticisms of fallen women, pandering nurses, and royalty-in-rags a dig at the tragic poet's fascination with the elderly. All but two of the extant plays include among their dramatis personae aged characters,[2] and Euripides reveals a predeliction for those myths that allow him by tradition or innovation to employ elderly characters. In these dramas we find the aged in virtually every role the mythological and dramatic traditions allowed: king or queen, noble relative or friend, priest or herald, loyal retainer or slave. In a number of plays the protagonist is elderly: Iolaus in *Children of Heracles*, Hecuba in the play of that name and in *Trojan Women*, Jocasta in *Phoenician Women*. In others they play strong supporting roles: Pheres in *Alcestis*, Creon and Aegeus in *Medea*, Alcmene in *Children of Heracles*, Peleus in *Andromache*, Aethra and Adrastus in *Suppliant Woman*, Amphitryon in *Heracles*, Creon,

Oedipus, and Tiresias in *Phoenician Women*, Tyndareus in *Orestes*, Cadmus and Tiresias in *Bacchae*, even Papasilenus in *Cyclops*. In four of the plays the chorus is elderly (*Alcestis*, *Children of Heracles*, *Heracles*, and *Suppliant Women*), and weaving their way in and out of all of them are the aged servants who tend their masters and mistresses. The situation in those plays known only by title, summary, or fragment seems much the same, and it is significant that Euripides offered at his first competition in 455 B.C. *The Daughters of Pelias*, which told of their unfortunate attempt to rejuvenate their ancient father.[3]

The poet's fascination with old age—Kitto rightly calls it an obsession[4]—is of a piece with his other dramatic innovations. Aristophanes' Euripides boasts that he made tragedy "democratic" (*Frogs* 952); Euripides' extensive portrayal of the elderly, like his treatment of women and slaves, broadens the base of the genre: affording a more representative imitation of life and inviting our identification with "ordinary" characters more like ourselves.[5] There may also be a personal element at work. Euripides' extant work dates from the middle to end of his career: the poet was approaching sixty when he composed *Hippolytus*, seventy with *Trojan Women*, and eighty with *Bacchae*. While we are not, to be sure, to imagine him as identifying with his characters in a simple way, it is possible that his own experience with old age encouraged him to consider its artistic possibilities. But where Sophocles turns his full attention to the subject only at the end of his life in *Oedipus at Colonus*, Euripides is remarkable for his consistent focus on old age and the fullness with which he articulates its implications as a condition of life. His powers of observation need not have been restricted to himself, and it is tempting to see in his interest in old age a reflection of a broader interest in the subject in the late fifth century. Such would be an understandable consequence of the high profile the elderly were keeping. One of the paradoxes of the late fifth century is that this period of energetic intellectuality was largely dominated by elderly men: Sophocles, Gorgias, Protagoras, and Socrates, to name only the most obvious.[6]

Whatever the external reasons for his interest, Euripides must have been attracted to the subject primarily for its dramatic potential, for what he thought it could bring to his handlng of plot, scene, and character and the intellectual armature that drives them. Yet the implications of the theme for his art have attracted relatively little scholarly attention. De Romilly has observed the pessimistic character of his treatment of old age, set at one time against "the charms and innocence of youth," elsewhere in contrast with the imprudence of youth in illustration of what she aptly calls the Xerxes-theme.[7] Several studies have related the strained relations between young and old in Euripides to the generational strife of late fifth-century Athens.[8]

This chapter begins with some general observations on Eurpides' representation of the elderly, with emphasis on its overwhelmingly negative character and the striking ways in which this is achieved visually.[9] As a dramatist deeply involved with production as well as composition, Euripides was keenly aware of the relation of the elderly characters to tragic spectacle, what Aristotle calls *opsis*, and recognized that the elderly quite simply make for good theater. They are striking in appearance, immediately so in a masked theater,[10] and even the simplest actions are rendered more pathetic when performed by an old man or woman. Indeed, Euripides' stagecraft of old age is a dominant characteristic of his art, and his dramaturgy relies to a remarkable degree on his depiction of the elderly and his development of a repertoire of scene types and character types that involve them. Of interest here is the extent to which these larger general characteristics of his approach to old age cut across basic dividing lines: male and female, free and slave, major and minor character, even actor and chorus.

After this survey I will examine the issues of old age and gender in two specific plays, *Children of Heracles* and *Phoenician Women*, and the importance of the interrelationship of these two themes to their structure and meaning. In each of these plays Euripides examines the relationship between old age and gender and develops a set of opposing paradigms for elderly men and women. Here I hope to show how these typologies describe old age in terms of a kind of gender reversal, and how Euripides uses the exchange of masculine and feminine roles to raise questions about the interaction of the elderly with their families and societies. In examining plays from the beginning and end of his extant work that evoke such different responses in the audience, from the tragicomic *Children of Heracles* to the unrelievedly dark *Phoenician Women*, we see how within the limits of a single set of paradigms Euripides produces characters so varied as to inhabit fundamentally different dramatic universes.

EURIPIDES' STAGECRAFT OF OLD AGE

"Not everything in old age is bad," or so argues Jocasta in *Phoenician Women* (528). Yet although she points to the experience (ἐμπειρία) that comes with age and although other of Euripides' elderly men and women have moments of great wisdom, loyalty, and bravery, nowhere is it suggested that these consolations redeem the overall nature of old age, and no one ever sings the praises of *gēras*. Euripides' characters describe old age with adjectives that are dreary and critical: it is sorrowful (πένθιμον), heavy (βαρύ), accursed (δυσόνυμον), difficult (δυσπάλαιστον), bitter (πικρόν), hateful (λυγρόν), and even murderous (φόνιον).[11] He emphasizes, often graphically, the physical degeneration of old age and exploits its potential for pathos and humor. As his elderly characters hobble on or off stage, they typically rely on the assistance of attendants, younger characters, or each other.[12] The walking staff (σκῆπτρον, βάκτρον) is a standard property, and in five plays there are clear references to the staffs or staves that prop them up.[13] We may add to this group the dottering revelers Tiresias and Cadmus in *Bacchae*, whose thyrsoi will double comically as canes (363–65),[14] and Iolaus in *Children of Heracles*, who exits for battle likely limping along on his spear (327).

The speeches of the elderly are often a litany of their aged anatomy—gray hair, stooped backs, trembling hands, weary faces—and their halting entrances and exits are often announced with a reference to the "aged foot" (γέραιος πούς). Typical are the words of the old man in *Electra*:

> How steep is the climb to this house here for wrinkled old feet like mine to make. But for your friends you have to drag yourself along with doubled-over back and tottering knees.
>
> (489–92)[15]

In *Andromache* the chorus announces the agitated entrance of Peleus, "hastening hither his aged foot" (546), impatiently assailing Menelaus before he is fully on stage, and wishing only for a little of "the vigor of youth" (552–53) to speed his arrival. With Jocasta in *Phoenician Women* and Tyndareus in *Orestes*, both of whom make entrances "on aged foot," the effect is heightened by their masks with gray shorn hair and black clothes,[16] and with Tyndareus and the old man of *Electra*, the "where, oh where" (ποῦ ποῦ) of their opening words suggests their agitation and exhaustion. So too with the chorus in *Heracles*, which complains of its age and weakness as it limps on stage. Where the chorus in the parodos of Aeschylus' *Agamemnon* speaks of its "childlike strength" (ἰσχὺν ἰσόπαιδα, 74–75) as it is propped up on staves, it likens itself to a horse in harness pulling a load uphill. Its members exhort themselves to help one another (γέρων γέροντα παρακόμιζε, 125), comrades in old age no less than are young men in battle.[17]

A frequent motif is that of the aged apostrophizing some part of their own bodies (surely accompanied by some large gestures). In *Ion* the servant uses such an apostrophe to announce his exit, rousing himself to vengeance with a plea for rejuvenation:

> Come, my aged foot, and be young in your deeds if not in your years.
> March against your enemies with your mistress.
>
> (1041–43)

In *Children of Heracles* Iolaus concludes his comical exit for battle by reminding his arm (740ff.) of the service it once rendered Heracles; appropriately, the messenger says of his off-stage rejuvenation that one could see through the dusky mist "the kind of manly arms the young have" (857–58). In *Heracles* the coryphaeus reacts to the violence of Lycus: "Oh right hand, how you long to pick up a spear, your longing undone in your weakness" (268–69). Such apostrophes appear repeatedly in *Trojan Women*, where the heroine's references to her aged limbs form a kind of story in themselves. Hecuba delivers her opening words from flat on her back:

> Up from the ground, sad head, lift up the neck.
>
> (98–99)[18]

When Troy is set ablaze, she rallies her "aged foot" (1275) toward the citadel to bid it farewell. In her last words in the play, as she exits to the Greek ships, she sings

> alas, trembling limbs, bear my steps. Move on, unfortunate, to the life of a slave.
>
> (1327–30)

The body of Hecuba becomes a metaphor for Troy itself, weak, fallen and dismembered.[19]

Euripides' descriptions of the decrepitude of age at times approach the clinical. In moments of crisis the elderly faint or collapse on stage, and describe their own limbs and voices giving away. In *Children of Heracles* Iolaus faints with grief (602–3) as Macaria is led off to sacrifice, and he asks his young wards to prop him up against the altar and cover him up. In *Andromache* Peleus loses his voice, and his legs begin to buckle, when he hears the news of Neoptolemus' death (1078). In *Hecuba* the heroine collapses (438) as Polyxena is led off to die, and in *Trojan Women* Hecuba repeatedly faints or throws herself to the ground (462ff., 508–10, 1305).

Undercut so often by their own incapacities, the elderly in Euripides experience their bodies as a burden, as something alien and unequal to the powerful stirrings in their hearts—the chorus reminds Iolaus in *Children of Heracles* that "although your will is still young, your body is gone" (702–3). Their pleas for rejuvenation are not idle nostalgia but expressions of their own frustation. The sentiments of the chorus in *Heracles* are typical.

> Youth is something always dear to me, but old age lies upon my
> head a burden heavier than the crags of Aetna . . . (637–40).
> But baneful, murderous old age I hate (649–50).
> If the gods' wisdom and understanding were those of men, they
> would bestow a double span of youth as a clear sign of virtue (655–59)

In *Suppliant Women* Iphis, distraught at the deaths of Capaneus and Evadne, speaks similarly: he hates "difficult old age" (1108–9) and regrets that life does not consist of a second youth and second old age, where one might set aright one's previous errors (1080ff.). At times the aged not only long for youth but actively pursue it, even to comic effect. Cadmus and Tiresias claim to find a temporary reprieve from their years in Bacchic vigor, and we may imagine Tiresias' eagerness demonstrated in a lively step or two (188–90). In *Children of Heracles* Iolaus' prayers are answered off-stage when Heracles and Youth (Hebe) appear to make him young again. And in the final lines of *Andromache*, a revitalized Peleus, only minutes earlier distraught with grief, arranges a tryst with Thetis to collect both the youth and the immortality she has promised him *ex machina*.

Old age provides moments of pathos and high melodrama for the abuse it invites from others, and Euripides frequently characterizes an antagonist by his treatment of those who are old and helpless. In *Children of Heracles*, the herald Copreus throws Iolaus to the ground when he tries to protect the children, a sight that brings tears to the eyes of the elderly chorus (127–29). In *Iphigenia in Aulis* Menelaus brandishes his scepter and threatens to "bloody the head" of Agamemnon's old retainer (311). In *Bacchae* Pentheus bullies his grandfather and Tiresias, and has the seer's priestly chambers demolished (346–51). In *Hecuba* the Trojan matriarch clings desperately to Polyxena "like ivy to the oak" (397) when she is dragged off to sacrifice, and in *Trojan Women* Talthybius must have Hecuba restrained to keep her from throwing herself into the burning citadel (1282–86). Such scenes are extremely physical within the conventions of the Greek stage and are effective ways of evoking pity for old age and outrage for its assailants.[20]

Weak and vulnerable, the elderly depend on the protection of others. The opening tableaus of *Children of Heracles*, *Heracles*, and *Suppliant Women* present suppliant old men or women huddled around an altar holding boughs or tufts of wool, and in each case frightened children look to them for protection. Scenes of individual supplication involving the elderly are frequent, and while it is difficult to distinguish with certainty between those cases where the suppliant ritual is enacted in full and those in which it is largely figurative,[21] the sight of these aged suppliants provides moments of great pathos. In *Heracles* a suppliant father begs his own son to uncover himself to greet Theseus, appealing to him on the basis of his own old age (1204–10). In *Children of Heracles*, Iolaus begs Demophoon for protection for the children (226–31). Some plays offer several such scenes. In *Hippolytus* the nurse supplicates Phaedra at her bedside to reveal what destroys her and later begs Hippolytus to keep her passion secret. In *Hecuba* the protagonist begs Odysseus for Polyxena's life and later importunes Agamemnon for a chance to avenge the murder of Polydorus. In *Suppliant Women* we have scenes in which the chorus supplicates Aethra, old Adrastus supplicates Theseus, then finally the chorus and Theseus' mother Aethra supplicate him together to win burial for the fallen warriors. And in *Phoenician Women* Creon falls to his knees before Tiresias to save his son from the doom of death the seer has prophecied.

Euripides frequently contrasts youth and old age in bitterly dramatic confrontations that pit the generations against each other: Pheres and Admetus (*Alcestis*), Iolaus and Copreus (*Children of Heracles*), Amphitryon and Lykus (*Heracles*), Peleus and Menelaus (*An-*

dromache), Jocasta and Polyneices and Eteocles (*Phoenician Women*), Tyndareus and Orestes (*Orestes*), Cadmus and Tiresias and Pentheus (*Bacchae*). In every case the young are portrayed as spiteful and arrogant, and often abuse their elders specifically for their age. In *Children of Heracles* the herald calls Iolaus "an old man, a tomb, a nothing" (166–67). In *Andromache* Menelaus makes fun of the so-called wisdom of the elderly (645–46) and taunts Peleus for his years (678). As Tyndareus makes his exit in *Orestes* his grandson hurries him on, eager to address Menelaus free from the unpleasantness of his grandfather's old age (631). In *Bacchae* Pentheus is ashamed of the foolish old age of his grandfather (252). In *Alcestis*, where even the elderly chorus has shamed Pheres and his wife for refusing to die for their son (466–70), Admetus vows a monstrous revenge on his father:

> Better get going and have some kids, to take care of you in old age and dress you for death and lay out your corpse. These hands of mine will never bury you!
>
> (662–65)

Admetus threatens to deny his father the *threptêria* and refuse him burial, in Athens the rights of the elderly by law. He curses his father with endless old age (713) and in a final shameless blast tells his mother and father to "go and grow old like you deserve" (734–36). To be sure, the elderly at times seem to invite such treatment, and Euripides' choruses and characters complain of the disagreeable and meanspirited character of old age.[22] Admetus is cowardly and hypocritical, and in *Orestes* Tyndareus is openly vindictive toward his grandson; while both raise legitimate objections to the behavior of their younger interlocutors, neither has the moral authority to do so.

Despite their weakness, the aged will often stand up against their assailants. Amphitryon shrewdly tricks Lycus into going into to the palace to his own death. The aged slave in *Electra*, whom Orestes had dismissed as an "old scrap of a man" (554), proves a loyal supporter and artful deceiver, and it is he who conceives the plan of vengeance on Aegisthus. The old man in the *Ion*, though his vengeance is misguided and thwarted, shows himself a consumate actor at the banquet. We shall further discuss below the particular capacity for brutal revenge that Euripides' aged heroines show: in *Children of Heracles* Alcmene commands the execution of Eurystheus, violating his rights as prisoner-of-war, and tells her servants to "kill him and throw him to the dogs" (1051); in *Hecuba* the protagonist exacts a savage vengeance on Polymestor, anticipating her own metamorphosis as the "bitch of Cynossema."

But the elderly more often fall short of their ambitions, and their deeds meet with something less than success. In several of the poet's notorious sacrifice scenes the elderly step forward and bravely if incongrously offer their own lives—Iolaus for Macaria in *Children of Heracles*, Creon for Menoeceus in *Phoenician Women*—in spite of the fact that in each case it is specifically young and virgin blood that must be shed. At other times the disparity between their ambition and abilities is patently comic. In *Andromache* Peleus at one point threatens to bash Menelaus' head with his staff (588), and then as he frees the heroine and her son tries to reassure her with a dash of bravado:

> I'm still fit, not so old as you think. Why, if I get the chance to so much as look at him I'll be celebrating my victory, despite my age. A brave old man is better than a gang of the young. What's the use of a good body if a man's a coward?
>
> (761–65)

In *Heracles* the entire chorus rallies briefly against Lycus:

> O children of earth . . . will you not raise up these staffs that prop our right arms and bloody the head of this unholy man?
>
> (252, 254–56).

The gray-haired group brandish their staves, the emblem of their impotence, like weapons. In this chorus and others Euripides sustains the tradition at least at old as Aeschylus' *Agamemnon* whereby the old age of the chorus helps explain its passivity before the bullying ways of an Aegisthus, Copreus, or Lycus.[23] In a scenic tradition in which the chorus typically does not interfere with the stage action, and where indeed the very architecture of the theater may preclude physical contact between them, the playwright is faced with the task of explaining the passivity of the group before the scenes of violence that are played only a few yards from them. By composing the chorus of old men and other groups that almost by definition are weak, despised, and otherwise ineffectual, the poet naturalizes these "paradoxes of inaction."[24]

Here in *Heracles* as also in *Children of Heracles* the old men of the chorus bluster and threaten in anger, call for help, perhaps even make a token show of resistance, but they cannot really directly enter into the stage action. The effect of such scenes is quixotic rather than heroic, underscoring the impotence and frustration of old age. The elderly cannot act, but can only attempt to do so, propelled by fleeting and sentimental glimpses of their former glory.

What the elderly can do in tragic abundance is suffer, and seldom appreciated is the way in which Euripides specializes in depicting their suffering. His images of old age suggest the fragility of life and evoke a sense of catastrophe always lurking just beyond the scene. He plays repeatedly upon that most tragic of Greek reversals, epitomized in Homer's Priam, of happiness lost or nearly lost in old age, providing ample illustration of Solon's maxim to "count no man happy until he is dead." Indeed, the single most frequent scene in Euripides is that of the elderly in mourning over the bodies of their loved ones, be they wives, sons, daughters, or grandchildren: Creon over Glauce in *Medea*; Amphitryon over Megara and her children in *Heracles*; Hecuba over Polydorus in *Hecuba* and over Astyanax in *Trojan Women*; Peleus over Neoptolemus in *Andromache*; in *Phoenician Women* Jocasta over Polyneices and Eteocles (in the messenger speech), then Creon over Menoeceus, and finally Oedipus' fumbling grief over his wife and sons together; in *Suppliant Women* a funereal spectacular, with the aged mothers of the seven in mourning over their ashes, and old Iphis, who mourns both his son-in-law Capaneus and his daughter Evadne after her act of suttee; and in *Bacchae*, in the most macabre scene of all, Cadmus over the *disiecta membra* of his grandson.[25] Such scenes are the crowning piece of Euripides' stagecraft of old age. To achieve his effect the poet employs the details of Greek funeral ritual. The elderly beat their breasts, gash their cheeks, tear at their hair, and sprinkle dirt on their heads. They keen over the corpse, touching it fondly, describing its features and numbering its wounds, calling to mind past deeds and kindnesses. Given the public and formal nature of Greek mourning, the effect of such scenes must have been devastating. To many of these funeral scenes Euripides will add some detail to heighten the pathos and individualize the scene. In *Andromache* Peleus, at the end of his kommos over the body of Neoptolemus, dashes his scepter to the ground. In *Trojan Women* Hecuba buries Astyanax using Hector's shield and robes salvaged from Troy.[26] The words of Cadmus over

Pentheus, perhaps the finest example of this type, summon up the horrible prospect of childless old age:

> For the god has yoked all together in a common doom, you and him, to destroy this house and me, who childless, with no male heir, behold this shoot from your womb, killed most horribly, most foully.
>
> (1303–7)

The old man recalls moments of special tenderness:

> No longer will you stroke my chin, child, hug me, calling me "grandpa," and say "Who is wronging you or troubling you, old man? Is someone upsetting you, causing you pain? Tell me, grandpa, so I can punish the one who does this."
>
> (1318–22)

To some extent these tragic images may also be a reflection of the troubled times in which Euripides lived. There would have been few families untouched by the chain of misfortunes that rocked the city in those years: the casualties of the Peloponnesian War, the great plague, the catastrophic end to the Sicilian expedition. Although these disasters touched the whole city, the grief of the elderly, who had known the heights of Athens' earlier glory and had grown up in a time of expansion and prosperity, must have been especially keen, and to this extent Euripides is both historian of and spokesman for the suffering of the elderly.[27]

THE WRATH OF ALCMENE:
GENDER, OLD AGE, AND VENGEANCE IN *CHILDREN OF HERACLES*

Perhaps more than any other of the early plays of Euripides, *Children of Heracles* (produced in or around 429 B.C.) is characterized by abrupt and even shocking changes of mood and tone. Nowhere are these more striking than in the closing scene of the play. When Eurystheus is brought before Alcmene, she bitterly catalogues the abuse she and her family have suffered, wishing only that she could kill him more than once (959–60). When his rights as prisoner-of-war suddenly threaten to deprive her of the vengeance she savors, she confronts her Athenian protectors angrily, winning a concession shameful to both parties: she will kill him first, and they will have the body to do with as they please (1021–24). In her final words in the play, as if she had forgotten her own agreement, she orders her attendents to "kill him and throw him to the dogs" (1050–51). Alcmene's stark and brutal behavior effectively subverts the values and sympathies the play had worked to establish, throwing into darkness and disorder what might have seemed to that point a conventional suppliant play and a simple exercise in patriotism.[28]

Earlier scholarship saw the scene as an instance of the play's generally shoddy and episodic construction, like the melodramatic sacrifice of Macaria or the fantastic metamorphosis of Iolaus, its artistic shortcomings matched by the condition of a text Murray judged a *fabula misere mutila*. Grube reflects both points of view in maintaining that "no amount of additions or alterations can make this into a good play."[29] More recent criticism has tended to regard the play's discontinuities as characteristically Euripidean, and to appreciate the scene for the meanings and insights it generates rather than for the readerly (and Aristotelian) conventions it disappoints. While this approach has prompted readings of the play's historical, political, and social significance,[30] relatively less attention has been paid to its ethical dimension, in particular the implications of making Alcmene the vehicle for its dénouement. While it is true that neither she nor any of the play's personae are developed as fully individualized characters, neither is it necessary to regard them, as one critic does, as simply "masked abstractions."[31] The poet finds in Iolaus and Alcmene, who are identified insistently and repeatedly as *gerōn* and *graia*, an occasion to characterize old age more generally, and the play's dramatic form draws extensively on their elderly status.[32] To the extent that the poet develops Alcmene as in some sense a *typical* figure, her characterization takes on a significance that might seem obvious had it not gone virtually unremarked: that as Iolaus is emblematic of old age, it is more specifically of *male* old age, and the representation of Alcmene correspondingly involves a representation of elderly *women* in general. Although discussion of Iolaus regularly focuses on his age, critics have not appreciated Alcmene in her capacity as an old woman, nor have they illuminated the relationship we are left to draw between her age and her vengeance at the play's end.

Euripides develops Alcmene's character throughout in largely negative terms in relation to other characters, and reveals her as increasingly aggressive, authoritative, and almost "masculine" in nature. Ironically, this potential is latent in the very name Ἀλκ-μήνη, "strong in wrath," the elements of which are heavily gendered. In ἀλκ- is suggested male strength, defense, and battle, which Iolaus explicitly tells Alcmene is "men's work," just as childcare is women's (ἀνδρῶν γὰρ ἀλκή· σοὶ δὲ χρῆν τούτων μέλειν, 711).[33] In μην- is implied the epic and unforgiving wrath which, no less than the wrath (μῆνις) of Achilles or the gods, propels her: hers is, the chorus says, a frightening hatred (δεινόν . . . νεῖκος, 981–82) for Eurystheus, as earlier they had called it frightening (δεινόν) that Argos should harbor such rage (μῆνιν) against Athens (759–62). Like Medea, Hippolytus, and other Euripidean characters who realize the tragic potential of their names, Alcmene comes to be defined by this strength and wrath, and her conduct provides a focus for the play's reflections on the problematical relationship of gender, authority, and old age.

These themes are established in the prologue. Iolaus, Heracles' nephew and helpmate during his labors and a younger man elsewhere in the tradition, is here conspicuously superannuated.[34] The poet makes him of the generation not of Heracles' children but of his aged mother, and takes pains to establish the two elders as a pair. Iolaus introduces Alcmene with a military metaphor: "the retreat is being executed by a pair of oldsters" (δυοῖν γερόντοιν δὲ στρατηγεῖται φυγή, 39), where the duals present the two as a pair of generals in charge of the Heraclids' retreat.[35] He explains the division of their strategic labors (40–44): he (ἐγὼ μέν) outside the temple with the boys; she (ἣ δ᾽ αὖ) inside, sheltering (σῴζει; cf. σῴζω, 11) the girls (τὸ θῆλυ . . . γενός, νέας . . . παρθένους), lest they immodestly be exposed to public scrutiny. The poet provides in Iolaus and Alcmene parallel expressions of senectitude and cohorts of the same generation and experience, whose common history of suffering Iolaus rehearses in the prologue.

Alcmene is thus located in two frames of reference, as age-mate to Iolaus and as grandmother to the Heraclids. These relationships (noted at 445–46, 584, 630–31) are developed in her dramatic entrance at 646.

What's all the ruckus out here, Iolaus? Not another herald from Argos to push us around, is it? I may be weak, but you'd better get this, stranger: you won't touch these kids as long as I'm alive, or I'm not the mother of Heracles the great. If you so much as lay a hand on them, you'll have a glorious battle with this pair of oldsters!

(646–53)

With this scene the play divides roughly in two, and Alcmene's appearance sustains a number of earlier motifs.[36] As the play begins with the arrival of Copreus, Alcmene rushes out afraid that another herald (τις . . . κῆρυξ, 647–48) has come, and takes up her position over the children as had Iolaus. Her words recall those of her cohort. Her reference to her weakness (ἀσθενὴς . . . ῥώμη, 648–49) picks up Iolaus' lament at 636 (ἐρρώμεθα) and references to weakness at 23 and 274, just as her fear that Iolaus is again being assaulted (βιάζεται, 647) further develops the theme of Argive violence (βία).[37] She repeats several of Iolaus' expressions verbatim, describing herself and him as "a pair of oldsters" (δυοῖν γερόντοιν, 653; cf. 39) and vowing that the children will not be taken "as long as I'm alive" (ἐμοῦ ζῶντος / ζώσης ποτέ, 66, 650). The verbal echoes underscore the basic similarities in their situations, since each of them has the opportunity to speak, negotiate, and decide for the group. Each is served a restriction upon the field of action that brings about an aporia and threatens the group's safety: Demophon reports the oracles' demands, and the chorus declares Eurystheus' inviolate status. The poet thus effects a strong symmetry in the play, giving it an almost diptych structure and establishing its second part as something of a reprise of the first.

To this point, Macaria alone has appeared from inside the temple to represent the feminine world within. She enters with apologies for her boldness (θράσος, 474) and words that echo those of Sophocles' Ajax to his captive wife Tecmessa (293): "I know what is best for a woman: silence, and modesty, and to stay indoors quietly" (γυναικὶ γὰρ σιγή τε καὶ τὸ σωφρονεῖν/ κάλλιστον, εἴσω θ' ἥσυχον μένειν δόμων, 476–77). Macaria's demeanor toward Alcmene and Iolaus is tender and reverent. Her appearance is prompted by the weeping of Iolaus, whom she addresses politely as "old one" (γέρον, 501, 548; πρέσβυ, 560, 574), and in her farewell she admonishes her brothers to honor the old man and the old woman in the house (καὶ τὸν γέροντα τήν τ' ἔσω γραῖαν δόμων, 584).

Alcmene's appearance is striking for its contrast with Macaria's demure manner, heroic self-sacrifice, and dignified exit. As Macaria embodies the modesty (αἰδώς) that Iolaus and Alcmene seek to protect (cf. αἰδούμεθα, 43), Alcmene's boisterous entrance suggests her disregard for the canons of womanly deference and prefigures her protests later in the play. At precisely the moment when she refuses to abide by the Athenian *nomos* that protects Eurystheus, she rejects the constraints of her womanhood in terms that explicitly recall those of Macaria: "You can talk about my boldness (τὴν θρασεῖαν) and say I'm not behaving as a woman should (τὴν φρονοῦσαν μεῖζον ἢ γυναῖκα χρή), but I will kill him all the same!" (978–80). Both the chorus and Eurystheus respond by addressing her here, as nowhere else in the play, as woman (γύναι, 981, 983). Like Macaria, Alcmene recognizes that the crisis requires the suppliants to take responsibility upon themselves and actively affect the situation rather than passively accept it. But where Macaria's self-sacrifice wins her testimonies for her nobility and bravery (εὐγένεια, εὐψυχία), Alcmene's personal initiative toward the Argive king's death brings her "great blame" (πολλὴν . . . μέμψιν, 974)

The scene also strikes a contrast between Alcmene and Iolaus, who minutes earlier was crouched on the ground with eyes downcast, unable even to recognize the servant of Hyllus. Iolaus tells the servant that old age is a thing of weakness (γέροντές ἐσμεν κοὐδαμῶς ἐρρώμεθα, 636) and looks to him for a savior (σωτήρ, 640) from their ills. Although Iolaus has been successful in winning protection for the group, his old age has been characterized primarily by his physical weakness and utter dependence on the goodwill of others: as the chorus tells him, "your will may be young, but your body is gone" (702–3). For him old age brings insult (Copreus calls him "an old man, a grave, a nothing," 166–67) and even physical abuse: his manhandling by the herald brings tears to the eyes of the elderly chorus (127–29). When the oracles are reported, Iolaus founders as the play's action grinds to a halt. When Macaria saves the day, he applauds her noble sentiments but counters with the bathetic suggestion that they select the victim by lottery. Equal neither to the crisis nor its remedy, Iolaus balks at Macaria's request to stand beside her in death (464), collapses in a faint, and is propped against the altar and covered up.[38] His helplessness, at first pathetic, becomes outright comical when, in a parody of the traditional scene of arming, he exchanges his suppliant paraphernalia for spear and shield: Iolaus is unable to carry his own armor, and the servant, putting a spear in his one hand and supporting the other, "nursemaids" (παιδαγωγεῖν, 729) him off to war.[39] As Iolaus totters offstage he apostrophizes his own right arm, recalling its youthful glory in service to Heracles. Our expectations are reversed, of course, when Iolaus proves to be the hero of the battle and Eurystheus' captor, but this is achieved by virtue not of his old age but of its abeyance, in his miraculous metamorphosis into "a young man once again out of an old" (νέος . . . ἐκ γέροντος αὖθις αὖ, 796) and through the intervention of the gods themselves.[40]

Alcmene's spirited entrance begins her gradual appropriation of the dramatic situation, giving us theatrically as well as linguistically "dual protagonists" and defining each as the antithesis of the other. Male old age, as exemplified in Iolaus, is weak and infirm, and his relation to the events around him, for all his good intentions, is passive, ineffectual and at times slightly irrelevant.[41] Female old age, as embodied in Alcmene, is energetic and aggressive, and she wields such power and authority as she has purposefully and resolutely. Appropriately, while the theme of helplessness (ἀμηχανία) was a primary one earlier in the play (cf. 148, 329, 464, 472, 487, 492, 495), it does not recur while Alcmene holds center stage. Where Iolaus' development moves, broadly speaking, from "tragic" to "comic," Alcmene's is the inverse, and what begins as feisty high spirits is transformed into fearsome depths of self-will and anger.

Alcmene's confused and frightened state at first throws all into near-comic confusion.[42] She snaps at Iolaus for alarming her, pesters the herald for news of Hyllus, and abruptly disclaims interest as he describes the military situation (654–65). She is silent while Iolaus receives the report and suddenly insists on joining the battle. But with the herald offstage she minces no words: he is out of his mind to leave her alone with the children (709–10). Alcmene's earlier fears (cf. φόβου, 656) now find a new object, and for a second time Iolaus must calm them (cf. μὴ τρέσῃς, 654, 715).

> Al. And what if you die? What will happen to *me*?
> Io. Your grandchildren will survive to take care of you.
> Al. And if—god forbid—they are not so lucky?
> Io. Don't worry, our friends here won't abandon you.
> Al. Well, I'm glad you can be so confident, *I'm* certainly not.
> Io. And I'm sure that Zeus too is concerned for your plight.
> Al. Well. I'm certainly not going to badmouth Zeus, but *he* knows if he's done right by me or not.
>
> (712–19)

Alcmene's anxieties clearly center less on the group than on herself (cf. ἐγώ 712; ἐμοῦ 718; ἐμέ 719), and her earlier self-assertiveness begins to look more like sheer self-interest.

From his opening lines in the play, Iolaus espouses a set of values whose terms are consistently reiterated: family and kinship, friendship and loyalty even in adversity, gratitude for kindness, the individual's obligations to the group. He pledges his undying thanks to Athens and the idea finds scenic expression in the handclasp by which he joins Demophon and the Heraclids. He is ready to die for the group, and he commends Macaria's spirit of self-sacrifice. These values are reflected in his life of service as Heracles' trusty comrade (πιστὸς . . . παραστάτης, 125; cf. 88) and are emphasized linguistically in his extensive use of σύν and μετά and its compounds. He has shared Heracles' labors (μέτεσχον, 8) as his comrade on sea and land (σύμπλους, 216; σύμμαχος, 457). In the prologue he distinguishes the man who is righteous (δίκαιος) from the self-centered man who is "useless to the city and difficult to deal with" (συναλλάσσειν, 4) and says of his loyalty to the Heraclids: "I take refuge together with these exiled children, and as they suffer, so I together with them" (ἐγὼ δὲ σὺν φεύγουσι συμφεύγω τέκνοις/ καὶ σὺν κακῶς πράσσουσι συμπράσσω κακῶς, 26–27). His words reach a climax in his declaration that he will join the messenger "to share in strong battle with friends" (κἄγωγε σὺν σοί· ταὐτὰ γὰρ φροντίζομεν, φίλοις παρόντες, ὡς ἔοιγμεν, ὠφελεῖν. . . . μετασχεῖν γ' ἀλκίμου μάχης φίλοις, 681–83).

Where Iolaus defines himself in terms of his ties to others, Alcmene acts as an individual responsible only to herself; her responses correspondingly reflect her personal fears and desires. The poet reflects Alcmene's capacity for self-assertion in the patterns of her speech, which abound in singular references to "I/me/mine" (cf. 712–19 above) and culminates in a string of angry assertions of her right to execute her prisoner based only on herself. When the chorus objects that no one may kill Eurystheus, she counters "but *I* will, and I remind you that *I* am someone too" (ἔγωγε· καίτοι φημὶ κἄμ' εἶναι τινα, 973) . . . "and now that he has fallen into *my* hands (ἐπείπερ χεῖρας ἦλθεν εἰς ἐμάς, 976) . . . "the deed will be done, and *I* shall do it" (τὸ δ' ἔργον τοῦτ' ἐμοὶ πεπράξεται, 980). Her last two exchanges in the play similarly end in blatant appeals to her own interests: "By his death, he will pay me *my* punishment" (οὗτος δὲ δώσει τὴν δίκην θανὼν ἐμοί, 1025); and "don't expect that you'll live to drive *me* from my fatherland again" (μὴ γὰρ ἐλπίσης ὅπως/ αὖθις πατρῴας ζῶν ἔμ' ἐκβαλεῖς χθονός, 1051–52).

This contrast is sustained in the two characters' religious attitudes. Where Iolaus counsels trust in Zeus, Alcmene is convinced of his indifference (718–19).[43] Only in the hour of victory, and after dramatic evidence of the gods' concern, does she begrudgingly acknowledge them:

> *Cho.* O Zeus, giver of victory, now our terrible fear is gone and our freedom is restored.
> *Alc.* O Zeus, I guess you took some time to notice *my* suffering (τἄμα . . . κακά). But just the same I'm grateful for what you've done. For my part (ἐγώ), I never really believed my boy was with the gods, but now I know it well enough.
>
> (869–72)

Alcmene's skepticism has its foil in Iolaus' profound and prosaic piety, which is echoed in the sincere if occasionally platitudinous wisdom of the chorus. For Iolaus, Zeus' altar (βωμὸς . . . θεοῦ, 61) is a true sanctuary he hesitates to leave even when his situation is secure (344–47); he regards its violation as an affront (ἀτιμία, 72; ἀτιμάζων, 78) to the gods. These he imagines with unabashed anthropomorphism as potent presences. He rallies Demophon by reminding him that "our gods are every bit as strong as theirs" (347–52). When the oracle is delivered he accepts it as god's will (θεοῖσι . . . δοκεῖ τάδε, 437) and repeats it uncritically to Macaria (488–91), and he is careful even in her exit not to offend (δυσφημεῖν, 600) the deity. His defense is quite literally in Zeus, whose temple provides the armor he borrows for battle. When he opposes the chorus' advice to act his age and their insistence that he can never be young again (706–8), his strength of will is ultimately upheld by the gods themselves. His rejuvenation is clearly presented as a reward for his piety and loyalty, as evidenced by the scene's religious setting (beyond "godly Athene's holy hill of Pallene," 849–50), his prayer to Zeus and Hebe, and the astral epiphany of Heracles and Youth herself, who come to make him a fine specimen of youth (cf. ἡβητὴν τύπον, 857–58). His story finds a fitting epilogue in the trophy he erects to Zeus (936–37).

With the exit of Iolaus the dramatic focus moves fully to Alcmene. At the messenger's arrival she is again fearful (φόβος, 791) about receiving the news of who has lived and died. But where the chorus afterward celebrates the end of their fear (φόβου, 867), she has new

(and justified) reason to be apprehensive given the news of Eurystheus' survival:

> But what in the world was Iolaus' intent in sparing Eurystheus, and not
> killing him on the spot? Tell me. In *my* book this is none too smart—to
> capture your enemy and then not take your punishment.
>
> (879–82)

What Alcmene sees as foolish, Iolaus ironically had done in deference
to her (τὸ σὸν προτιμῶν, 883), affording her the opportunity to see
her enemy in defeat and to delight (τέρψαι θέλοντες σὴν φρένα, 939)
in the reversal of fortune that has befallen him.

 This reversal is described in terms of power and authority. The
herald had earlier characterized Eurystheus and the Argives as masters and rulers (τοῖς σοῖς δεσπόταις, 99; σοῦ κρατοῦντες, 100), making the suppliants like runaway slaves finally apprehended.[44] The
peripety reverses the metaphor: Eurystheus is described as "mastered
by your hand" (σῇ δεσποτούμενον χερί, 884) and Alcmene taunts
him imperiously: "so now you no longer rule but *are* ruled" (κρατῇ
γὰρ νῦν γε κοὐ κρατεῖς ἔτι, 944).[45] The inversion of the metaphor of
master and slave, however, is mediated in Alcmene's *domestic* authority over her servants, who address her as mistress (δέσποινα, 784, 928;
cf. 678) and whose freedom, we are twice reminded, lies in her hands:
Alcmene promises the messenger his freedom for the good news he
bears, and he later recalls her promise as a matter of noblesse oblige
(788–89, 889–91). Alcmene, however, in offering the servant his freedom, ironically asks him to free *her* (ἠλευθερῶθσαι . . . ἐλευθεροῖς,
789–90) from the fears that enslave her. Through these metaphors the
poet suggests the totality of her power over Eurystheus as well as its
lack of public or institutional sanction. She extends such power as she
has by sheer force of character and personality, and—important to
remember—in the absence of Iolaus and Demophon: it is hard to
imagine her debating and negotiating in their presence. Appropriately,
it is her servants (δμῶες, 1050) to whom she gives the order for the
execution.

 With Eurystheus' entrance, Alcmene's wrath is given free rein, and
in it she becomes an expression of pure hatred and revenge. She greets
him with abuse (ὦ μῖσος, 942; cf. 52) and gloats over her captive
(942–44). She reviews his persecution of Heracles in an abbreviated

version of his labors and his sacrilegious pursuit of her helpless family: "some old people, others still children" (956). She recognizes only one necessity, and as self-appointed judge she herself passes sentence: Eurystheus shall die and suffer in the process (958–60; cf. 874–75). Critics are near unanimous in their agreement that Alcmene and her arch-rival ultimately prove to be more alike than different.[46] The fear with which she has lived for years he admits to have been the driving force behind his persecution (cf. 996). He acknowledges himself a "sophist" (993) and provides a demonstration in the sophistry of his defense: he has acted simply out of policy. The hatred (νεῖκος, 986; δυσμένειαν, 991) for Heracles was a disease (νόσον, 990) Hera visited on him against his will; he has only praise for Heracles; he flatters Athens for its piety and discretion (1012–13). Alcmene counters his speech in the sophistry of the "compromise" by which she wins the unseemly collusion of the chorus (1020–25). He insists that she would have behaved no differently in his place, and she proceeds as though intent to prove him right.

Where Iolaus was deferential to his Athenian protectors, Alcmene argues her way into a full-blown confrontation with the chorus, and—heedless of Eurystheus' rights—rides roughshod over their objections. Where Iolaus' conduct is guided throughout by what people will say about him (cf. 28–30), his speech refering frequently to the norms of public opinion (αἰδώς),[47] Alcmene disregards public opinion. She refuses to be restricted by Athenian law (νόμος, 963, 1010), the will of Athens and its leaders (964, 1019), the apparent agreement of Hyllus (967–68), the proprieties of femininity (978–80), or the blame she will incur (974). So consuming is her anger that she is oblivious to the harm she thereby brings upon her own descendants, to the fact that Eurystheus' death will spoil her return to Argos (κακὸν . . . νόστον, 1042). When he reveals the oracle that will make his death a positive advantage to Athens, Alcmene will brook no delay (1045). She orders her servants to put him to death and ends with a final burst of spleen against her foe (1051–52).

Children of Heracles presents the reader with an image of the elderly female as not only active but aggressive and even frightening. The pathetic and at times comic old age of Iolaus is ultimately offset by the character of his larger representation—his piety and altruism, commitment to the common good, and strong will—so that in the end he is celebrated for his virtue (ὁ κλεινὸς Ἰόλεως, 859; ὁ . . . ἐσθλὸς

Ἰόλεως, 936). Where his piety and loyalty win him a divine reprieve from the laws of nature, Alcmene's hour of vengeance culminates in the image of a spiteful and domineering old woman, devoid of the proper femininity of the young Macaria, closer in character to the man who has been her nemesis. Alcmene's assertiveness and independence are vitiated by her selfishness, skepticism, and fanatical demand for revenge. In a sense, her character involves no less a metamorphosis than that of Iolaus. In her assault on Eurystheus she becomes something other than human, like the hydras and lions and hellhounds she adduces in evidence of *his* inhumanity (949–51), like the dogs to whom she would throw his corpse.

To what extent is this combination of femininity, old age, and vengeance anomalous? Although Greek literature presents only partial and occasional images of elderly women, there is evidence to suggest that Alcmene's capacity for vengeance is less in spite of her age than in some sense because of it. The association of old women and bitter expressions of vengeance finds frequent expression later in Euripides. In *Trojan Women*, Hecuba, so crushed by fortune that she is frequently prostrate on the ground with grief and age, is animated only once in the play, at the prospect of winning a revenge on Helen. In the agonistic form of Helen's impromptu trial, Euripides develops the quasi-legal atmosphere of Alcmene's judgement of Eurystheus (and Hecuba's denunciation of Helen is itself tempered by the presence of Menelaus). The protagonist of *Hecuba* identifies herself in her opening words as a helpless *graus* (59), "wretched for wretched old age" (δειλαία δειλαίου γήρως (156, cf. 203). Her helpless appearance, however, conceals enormous depths of hatred and a capacity for revenge that exceeds Alcmene's, both in its grotesqueness (where we are forced the watch the blinded Polymestor fumble about and serve as his own messenger) and in her unashamed use of deceit to win her revenge. In her future transformation into the "bitch of Cynossema" (κυνὸς ταλαίνης σῆμα, 1273), Euripides presents at last the literal counterpart to Iolaus' rejuvenation.[48]

Far from being peculiar to Euripides, the image of the vengeful old woman has a tradition going back at least to Homer. At the end of the *Iliad*, in a scene that bears more than a cursory relationship to our play, Hecuba tries unsuccessfully to dissuade Priam from his similarly unexpected decision to go the camp of the Greeks. Like Alcmene, she tells Priam he has "lost his wits" (24.201). As Alcmene worries for her future, Hecuba cautions Priam about the danger, and in a savage burst of temper against Achilles, wishes that she could "sink teeth into his liver and eat it" as vengeance for Hector's death (24.212–14).[49] Even more striking is the behavior of Eurycleia at the end of the *Odyssey*, in a pair of passages discomforting to modern readers. When she is summoned by Telemachus (she is addressed as γρηὺ παλαιγενές, 22.395) and sees the bloody corpses of the suitors, she is set to cry out in celebration, until her master forbids her such public expressions of joy and reminds her it would be unholy for her to gloat over the dead (22.408–12). She takes an almost sadistic delight in accusing the faithless servant women, telling them of the punishment that awaits them and leading them to their end. When she finally hobbles upstairs to awaken Penelope, she is described as actually "cackling" or "chuckling" (καγχαλόωσα, 23.1) with pleasure and is told by Penelope to contain her joy, at least for now (23.59).

The theme assumes cosmic proportions in Aeschylus' *Eumenides* in the portrayal of deities who are the very embodiment of vengeance. In developing the Erinyes as representatives of the "old order" (παλαιοὺς νόμους, 778, 808), Aeschylus makes them part of the earlier generation overthrown by the younger Olympians (οἱ νεώτεροι θεοί, 162). Athena acknowledges them as older (γεραιτέρα, 848) than she, and the Erinyes complain of the insult the upstart Apollo does their antiquity (πρεσβῦτιν, 731). But where divinity is otherwise considered by definition ageless, the Erinyes are themselves aged beings, "gray goddesses" (γραίας δαίμονας, 150), or again monstrous hybrids of old age and youth, "repulsive maidens, gray and aged children" (κατάπτυστοι κόραι, γραῖαι παλαιαὶ παῖδες, 68–69; cf. 150). Their lust for blood vengeance and the savage anger they display thus reflect both the antiquity of their mind (they call themselves παλαιόφρονα, 838, 871) and their status as old women. These aged deities threaten to engulf heaven and earth in their anger, yet ironically their vengeance proves less intractable and more open to accommodation than that of Alcmene.[50]

Euripides' representations of old age participate in a tradition of images of vengeful old women, and we need to appreciate the extent to which the poet both draws on and contributes to this literary stereotype. But the images also have a social dimension, and we may conclude by considering the extent to which images of aggressive and even frightening old women reflect larger cultural patterns. Anthropological literature points frequently to patterns of role reversal in old age and to a blurring of the gender boundaries, which among the younger distinguish behaviors deemed masculine from those that are feminine. A body of fieldwork points to patterns in which old men are "domesticated" and "effeminized" in old age, increasingly involved in the care of household and young children.[51] Correspondingly, there is evidence cross-culturally for an increase with old age in the freedom and independence of women whereby they assume a more assertive profile than before and wield greater power in and out of the home, their behavior less limited by the gender roles of their youth.[52] Gutmann notes the frequency of the so-called matriarchal shift and locates this change at the level of personality itself, suggesting that in both traditional and modern societies roughly opposite patterns of development obtain for men and women: where older men become increasingly passive and dependent, older women tend to give freer rein to their aggressive and egocentric impulses: "Across cultures and with age they seem to become more domineering, more agentic, and less willing to trade submission for security."[53] Margaret Mead, on the other hand, relates these changes to the arena within which power is exercised: "Old women are usually more of a power within the household than older men. Older men rule by ascribed and titular authority, but wives and sisters rule by force of personality and knowledge of human nature."[54]

Although the available data is scanty, such patterns of gender reversal and matriarchal shift find some corroboration among elderly women in Greece. It seems to be the case that old age brought Athenian women, particularly widows, greater freedom of movement in the city—as midwives, participants in festivals, and mourners even for those other than close relatives.[55] It was only in the immediate aftermath of widowhood, for instance, that the Greek woman won temporary control over her possessions.[56] As Slater and others have reminded us, however, images of female power and authority may be not so much public as domestic in their origin.[57] Elderly widows, their adult sons required by law to care for them, seem most often to have come under their authority (κυρίεια) and to have taken up residence with them, so that the *oikos*, perhaps earlier the scene of mother-son antagonism, might also have been an arena in which the mother struggled for domestic dominance with her son's young wife.[58] While nominally under the authority of their master or *kurios*, elderly widows might well have in their personal lives behaved effectively as their own *kuriai*.

Yet as one critic has noted in reaction to Gutmann's theories, displays of female assertiveness and independence may be less significant as evidence of real power or influence wielded than for the misogynistic reactions they provoke: such "power" as old women wield often wins them ill will rather than prestige, and the more virile character of their behavior is more typically turned against them.[59] The assertiveness, independence, and even the wisdom of older women often becomes a social liability, a perception that elderly women have a particular capacity for evil that is translated into local and negative stereotypes such as that of the crone, the hag, and the witch. Gutmann himself points to the frequency with which the "powers" of the aged woman make her an object of fear and hatred, and others have shown how male cultural dominance has perverted the archetype of the "wise old woman," so extensive across history and cultures, into a grotesque parody of itself.[60]

It is I think significant in this regard that that there is no corresponding figure for the wise old woman in Greek culture. The Greeks are clearly not unique in their contempt for old women, but it is striking just how extensive and pervasive is such stereotyping in Greek culture. Garland points out the Greeks' tendency to represent the monstrous and the horrible in the form of the spinster or unmarried old woman (Empousa, Medusa, Scylla, Lamia, the Graiai, Fates and Furies), evidence of the importance of childbearing and of the contempt for females who for whatever reasons fail to reproduce successfully.[61] We have observed in chapter 3 the development of sexual invective against the older woman at least as early as Archilochus, and in Athenian comedy the feisty, argumentative, and even sexually aggressive old woman becomes a staple.[62] These images seem less like evidence of the actual behavior of elderly women than of the same misogyny that makes a grotesque parody of other potentially positive images of female behavior. Alongside the images of the hideous spinster-monster and sex-starved crone we may locates Euripides' images of the vengeful old woman. Alcmene, and the literary stereotype she embodies, provide a Greek tragic version of such disparaging images of elderly women—images that have unfortunately been a part of their history, in literature and in life.

OLD AGE, TRAGIC ACTION, AND MOTHERHOOD:
JOCASTA IN *PHOENICIAN WOMEN*

In *Children of Heracles* Euripides develops his paradigms of male and female old age in two lesser known and almost homey figures and a legend of relatively minor standing. In *Phoenician Women* he examines the interrelationship of gender and age through a set of characters who are redolent of tradition and plays off his theme of gender reversal against a highly developed set of expectations. Produced most likely in 409 or 408 B.C., *Phoenician Women* provides a strong contrast to *Children of Heracles*. Where the plot of the earlier play, at least up to its final scene, is clear and straightforward, *Phoenician Women* seems cluttered and confused (the ancient hypothesis calls it "overfull and episodic"), and its unwieldiness has fueled efforts by textual critics to bring the play into more familiar proportions.[63] Where *Children of Heracles* provides clear objects for our sympathies and identifiable loci of good and evil, *Phoenician Women* is crowded with characters holding a range of conflicting ethical, political, and philosophical viewpoints.[64] And where the protection of Athens allows the children of Heracles to escape the designs of Eurystheus and his agents, the denouement of *Phoenician Women* is nothing short of catastrophic, its exodos a funereal extravaganza. As such, its setting, in contrast with that of *Children of Heracles*, provides an illustration of Zeitlin's characterization of theatrical Thebes as the anti-Athens, "the radical tragic terrain where there can be no escape from the tragic in the resolution of conflict."[65]

In its treatment of old age the play is clearly offered as a tour de force. As *Children of Heracles* opens with a strangely superannuated Iolaus, *Phoenician Women* begins by turning the more familiar chronology on its head: Jocasta did not, as in the tradition from the *Odyssey* to the Oedipus plays of Aeschylus and Sophocles, kill herself at the revelation of her incest.[66] As surprising as the sight of the aged matriarch is the way the entire house has grown old along with her. Creon, middle-aged in *Antigone* and *Oedipus the King*, is now a widower who describes himself as *gerōn* and his sister as *graia* (1318). As he is now "in the ripe time of life" (ἐν ὡραίῳ . . . βίου), he declares himself ready to die in his son's place (968–69), and Menoeceus excuses his father's protectiveness as what one would expect of an old man (994–95). Oedipus himself has still not left Thebes, his exile now deferred until after the death of his sons. He lives sequestered within the palace in what he himself describes as a morbid, ghostly existence (1543–45).[67] Antigone finally conjures him out, in a spectacular entrance that has something of the atmosphere of a *nekyia*:

> Oh woe, oh woe, leave your house, blind as you are, aged father. Reveal, Oedipus, your wretched age, you who cast murky darkness upon your eyes and drag out your long-protracted life within the house. Do you hear, as you wander through the courtyard on aged foot or sleep unhappy on your bed?
>
> (1530–38)

Jocasta, Oedipus, and Creon have become the peers of Tiresias, and their age is emphasized in their comments on the burdens of old age, the stagecraft of their labored movements, and the many characters presented as foils: Antigone, Polyneices, Eteocles, Menoeceus, even the chorus of maidens en route to Delphi, the pick of Phoenicia for their youthful beauty.[68] Virtually every scene involves the opposition of youth and age, from the *teichoskopia* of Antigone and the family slave to her final exit with Oedipus.[69]

That an older, wiser Jocasta should stand before us at first seems another of the fantastical what-if situations with which Euripides so often opens his plays. Yet here the superannuation of the cast is one dimension of a radical break with the tragic tradition: *Phoenician Women* defines itself in relation to its predecessors, opposes the Aeschylean and Sophoclean versions on the most basic points, and self-consciously subverts, supplants, or swallows up whole an enormous chunk of the dramatic tradition. Its *mise en scène* and prologue deny *Oedipus the King* and its ending in particular. Its central action absorbs into itself *Seven Against Thebes* yet differs from its model so outrageously as to border on parody.[70] Its exodus offers a new version (or as Conacher has suggested, a negation) of the *Antigone* and a kind of preview of *Oedipus at Colonus*.[71] Into all this the poet inserts, likely inventing for the occasion, the story of Menoeceus, which might in itself provide the core of a tragedy.[72] And the play locates this material within a larger perspective in a series of choral odes one may call Aeschylean in character for the way they enlarge the scope and force field of the play. In songs that reach back to the city's foundation by Cadmus, the Phoenician maidens provide a panoramic sweep of Theban history in which the present ordeal gradually merges with the struggles of the city's ancestral past.[73]

In Jocasta Euripides brings to culmination the type of the elderly heroine as he has developed it not only in Alcmene but in Hecuba in *Trojan Women* and *Hecuba* and to a lesser extent Aethra in *Suppliant Women*.[74] In all these plays there is emphasis on the maternal concerns of old women, their devotion to family, their determined and aggressive efforts on behalf of its survival (at times crossing the line that defines their lives between the public and domestic worlds), and their capacity for suffering, in plots that often move from conditions of misery to greater misery. On one level these heroines are all in their different ways exemplars of the "matriarchal shift"—of a female old age that is agentic, self-assertive, and public in contrast with a male old age that is passive, dependent, and inadequate in time of crisis. Yet these women are also traditionally female in their commitment to their families and in their efforts against those forces that threaten to destroy their families. As such, they remind us of the contingencies of the genre as a whole: tragic action is driven primarily by the young and the male (or those who choose to act as such).

Jocasta's relationship to this paradigm is clear. As protagonist she labors tirelessly to forestall another chapter in her family's violent history. Her maternity, emphatic throughout, is extended to include Menoeceus, for whom she has served as a kind of foster mother (986–89). As Loraux says, this Jocasta is "a mother to excess" in whom marriage and motherhood have been so mingled that she must die as a mother, that is, "die with" (συνθανοῦσα, 1282) Polyneices and Eteocles.[75] Her suffering is painfully highlighted: she ends her prologue, monody, and participation in the agon with references to her grief (86–87, 354, 618–19, 623–24); at the moment of her death she is described as ὑπερπαθήσασα, "super-suffering" (1456), the only use in tragedy of this rare word; and in the final reference to her in the play, Antigone says over her corpse "there she lies piteously, together with all her woes" (1696).

Jocasta's translation from *gynê* to *graia* is sketched in the prologue, which summarizes Theban history from Cadmus to the present. Particularly striking is how *passive* a role she has played until now, far more than was the case in *Oedipus the King*.[76] She presents herself as the submissive wife of Laius and the helpless victim of his drunken rape and its consequences. "He sowed a child on me . . . and he gave the baby to shepherds to expose," she says baldly (22–25), as if to suggest how little say she had in these life-and-death decisions. Advertised by Creon as prize for whoever would slay the Sphinx, she became wife of Oedipus and mother of their children, but she refers to her part in the marriage only in terms of their mutual ignorance (53–54). She apparently played no role in the discovery of the incest, nor in her sons' sequestering of their father and power-sharing arrangements. Jocasta's tone is dignified, even resigned (cf. 382). She does not dwell on her own misfortunes but emphasizes her role as mother: even Oedipus is referred to as "the labor of my travail" (30) and "my child" (33, 50; cf. 54–55), and the reference to her breast in line 31 (μαστοῖς) is the first of many such in the play.[77] Yet her last lines suggest the extent of her suffering.

> But Zeus, who dwell in the shining folds of heaven, save us, reconcile my children. It is not right for you in your wisdom to allow the same person (βροτὸν τὸν αὐτόν) to be wretched all his life"
>
> (84–87).

Jocasta views her fate indirectly and almost abstractly—it not clear if she is thinking of herself, Oedipus, or just impersonally—yet she holds to the hope for some happiness, if only late in life.[78]

Her emerging role as *graia* is revealed in her efforts to resolve her sons' conflict: "but I am attempting to end their strife and I have persuaded son to meet son under safety of truce before taking up arms" (81–82). Her change to a more active profile is suggested in the emphatic use of the first person (ἐγὼ δ' ἔπεισα) and her bold initiative in arranging for Polyneices and Eteocles the kind of face-to-face encounter that does not occur in Aeschylus. With the technical term for under truce (ὑπόσπονδον), Euripides suggests how she has crossed into an area normally reserved for men. Foley has noted how in her clear thinking and bold determination, Jocasta recalls Eteocles and Oedipus in the prologues to *Seven* and *Oedipus the King* respectively.[79] But she remains traditionally female in her priorities; whatever her concerns for the city her primary commitment is clearly to the preservation of her family.

Jocasta's maternity is developed in the poignant aria with which she greets Polyneices (301ff.), which prompts the chorus to comment on the awful power of parental love (355–56). She enters haltingly "on aged foot" (302–3), but she comes to life at the sight of her son,[80] and that tired body becomes the vehicle of deep pleasure as she takes her fill of embraces described in the most physical terms—breast, arms, cheeks, hair, neck. At a loss for words, she is inspired to dance and whirl all about him (περιχορεύουσα, 316).[81] She laments the long years since he left Thebes and tells how she has observed his absence in mourning, with black robes and white hair close cropped, and she sorrows that she could not play her rightful role in his marriage in Argos. She ends with a lament for the trials of the family: "Let it perish, whether it was the sword or strife or your father who was to blame, or some evil spirit which has revelled madly in the house of Oedipus. For it is on me that the pain of these troubles has fallen" (350–54). She does not indulge in speculation or soul-searching about the ultimate origins of the evil.[82] Her concern is the suffering it has brought the house and the special portion that is hers.

Oedipus is introduced as both foil to and cause of Jocasta's heightened profile in old age. In developing him as a paradigm of male old age, Euripides follows the Homeric tradition in which the hero remained king of Thebes even after the revelation of his incest.[83] His rule is interrupted when his sons, no more than boys when he blinded himself, mark their coming of age with an act that is the mirror image of his parricide and that adumbrates the theme of gender reversal. Jocasta notes that Oedipus had killed Laius when, "on coming into manhood with redish hair on his cheeks" (πυρσαῖς γένυσιν ἐξανδρούμενος, 32), he set out to Delphi to learn of his parentage. She says that when Polyneices' and Eteocles' "cheeks grew dark" (γένυς . . . σκιάζεται, 63),

> they hid away their father behind barred doors, so that his fate, which required so much cleverness to explain, might be forgotten. And he lives on in the house. Sick with his fate, he calls down on his sons the most unholy curses, that the two might divide this house with whetted sword.
> (64–68)

Rites of passage for young men are typically marked by their segregation and by some self-defining act directed against the maternal ties of youth and the effeminizing influence of women.[84] Oedipus' imprisonment looks like a rite of passage *manqué*, with acts of seclusion and symbolic violence literalized and deflected from their proper ritual object. The sons' embarassment at their father locates their behavior in the emotional turbulence of adolescence: by concealing (ἔκρυψαν,

84; cf. συγκαλύψαι, 872) him they avoid the contrived (πολλῶν δεομένη σοφισμάτων, 65) accounts they had offered for his condition. And as their act looks back to his parricide, so it also looks forward to his exile. Like those barred doors that protect the city (κλῆθρα, 114, 261, 1058) and shut out Polyneices, the doors (κλῆθρα, 64) behind which Oedipus is hidden make him exile and enemy within his own house. Although Jocasta reports Polyneices' and Eteocles' behavior without criticism, Tiresias condemns the two for their foolishness in concealing what the gods had contrived (σόφισμα, 871) to be an example to Greece: "For by denying their father his rights and not allowing him to leave, they made the poor man savage in his anger. Deranged (νοσῶν) and dishonored besides, he uttered terrible curses on them" (874–77). Helpless before the cruelty of his sons, Oedipus has become a kind of living skeleton in the family closet, his only recourse the bitter curses that he calls down upon them. Like Tiresias, Jocasta speaks of them as the product of a mind that is sick (νοσῶν, 66), and they are effective less for their inherent power than for the mistrust and fear they strike in his sons, a reaction that leads them first to cooperate and then to quarrel (69ff.).[85]

The greatness of Oedipus' past, suggested in the many references to his defeat of the Sphinx,[86] contrasts with the obscurity and helplessness of his present condition. Just as Jocasta has crossed the line that divides the worlds of male and female, entering the arena of war and diplomacy, Oedipus has become effeminized and literally domesticated in old age. His place is now within the house (ἐν οἴκοις, 66; δῶμα . . . τόδε, 68), the reserve of girls and women, and he is referred to repeatedly in terms that interrelate his age, blindness, and domesticity.[87] Although Oedipus was helpless to defend himself against their cruelty, his incarceration comes to seem almost self-imposed:[88]

> The blind old man in the house always clings to his tearful longing for the pair of you, now unyoked from the house. He jumps up for the sword for self-slaughter or to hang himself from the roof beams and groans out curses on his children. Always crying and wailing, he hides himself in darkness.
>
> (327–36)[89]

The description of Oedipus provides an interesting elaboration of behaviors associated with other of Euripides' old men (Iolaus, Amphitryon, Peleus) and has its Homeric prototypes in Priam and Laertes: their withdrawal from the public sphere into morbid grief and self-pity; their almost willful isolation and self-neglect; their helpless and enfeebled response to crisis. Oedipus vacillates between longing for his children, in the vein of Jocasta, and cursing them, between life and death by his own hand—itself a more typically feminine response to tragedy—and then again between different forms of suicide, the more manly death by sword and the more feminine by hanging.[90]

The darkness (σκότια, 336) in which Oedipus dwells, preparing us for his entrance later from darkness to light (ἐς φῶς . . . σκοτίων ἐκ θαλάμων, 1540–41), is like the darkness of death itself (σκότος 1453, σκοτίαν 1484). It is also fundamental to the gendering of space in the play. Jocasta's invocation of Helios and Antigone's description of the shimmer of the Argives' armor establish the outdoors as a masculine place of light; the palace, entered only by Jocasta, Antigone, and Oedipus, is represented as dark, domestic, and feminine.[91] Antigone emerges from the maiden's quarters of the house (παρθενῶνας, 89; δόμοις, 99) to view the troops and is afterwords told to return to her apartment (ἔσβα δῶμα καὶ κατὰ στέγας ἐν παρθενῶσι μίμνε σοῖς, 193–94); she will later be summoned out of house and chambers (δόμων, 1264; δομάτων, 1271; παρθενῶνας, 1275) to accompany Jocasta to the battlefield. Indeed, the references to the darkness in which Oedipus dwells seem to locate him directly in the *gunaikeia*, the women's quarters located in the darker and more remote areas of the house where doors were often bolted closed.[92] Oedipus' confinement becomes a striking statement of the feminine role to which age and grief have reduced him.

But as this is not just a house but the House of Oedipus,[93] the play draws upon its symbolic resonances to invest it with new levels of irony and paradox. The bed on which Oedipus lies "bed ridden" (λεχήρη, 1541), on which he was conceived (λέκτρα τἄμ' . . . ἐν δώμασιν, 14) and conceived in turn (ἐς μητρὸς . . . λέχος, 1609), is the bed of the dead Laius he defiles in *Oedipus the King* (λέχη . . . τοῦ θανόντος, 821) and the marriage bed (νυμφικὰ λέχη, 1242–43) on which Jocasta laments in that play. These are the chambers in which Jocasta gave birth to him, their womblike darkness completing the process by which he had sought to solve the mystery of his own engendering. The barred doors (κλῇθρα, 64) which now keep him within are those same doors through which he had forced his way into her chamber in *Oedipus the King* as well as the palace doors through which he was afterwards revealed to Thebes (κλῆθρα:1262, 1287, 1294). His confinement is also a return to the scene of his self-blinding, which was in itself an act of aging: in depriving himself of his sight and taking up the staff, Oedipus became that creature which walks on three legs, the third term of the riddle of the Sphinx.[94] He also assimilates himself to Tiresias, paradigm of aged blindness, who in *Oedipus the King* had prophesied that the murderer of Laius would leave Thebes blind and feeling his way with a staff (σκήπτρῳ, 456).[95] The darkness of these chambers literalizes the act that had prematurely aged him, the hero now in real old age and darkness, and Oedipus' blindness is elsewhere described in related terms: at 377 Oedipus is "he who sees darkness" (σκότον δεδορκώς), and at 1534–35 he has "cast the murky darkness" on his eyes (ἀέριον σκότον ὄμμασι σοῖσι βαλών). And as the act of self-blinding was also one of self-emasculation, the double-blindness of Oedipus in the dark completes the process of his effeminization.[96] In the darkness of the women's chambers Oedipus plays the role of the suicidal Jocasta of *Oedipus the King*, yet in his weakness and indecision is unable to bring the deed to completion. Family distinctions are further blurred, since in the shifting configurations of age and gender the father-brother and husband-son now reenacts the role of his wife-mother.

Oedipus' entrance at 1539 is clearly meant to evoke that in *Oedipus the King* following his self-blinding, but how different is the figure who stumbles from the palace from Sophocles' defiant hero. Broken by grief, this Oedipus does not act but only reacts. Passive before Creon's sentence, he rehearses the story of his misery in a speech that is pitiful if somewhat irrelevant (the hypothesis calls his final lyric "babbling"). He and Antigone assume the lyric burden in mourning the dead, a role that more properly belongs to women, as Antigone leads Oedipus first to the corpses and then off-stage into exile. Grief and age have left him so shattered that he sees no continuity between his past and present. When Antigone asks "where is Oedipus and his famous riddles," he replies, "Dead. One day brought me prosperity, another day destroyed it" (1688–89). When he recalls once more his glorious defeat of the Sphinx, Antigone, in what may well be the closing lines of the play, bids him to speak no longer of the good fortune of the past (1728–36).

Creon provides a second paradigm of the weakness of male old age. In his first appearance he attempts the role of wise counselor to

Eteocles.[97] Creon proves an able tactician; his advice is sound and his strategy practical, and here it is he, not Eteocles, who conceives the famous defense at the seven gates. More surprising is his failure to provide any kind of moral guidance to Eteocles, even when he speaks of his hope to meet and kill his brother in battle (754–56). This weakness becomes more pronounced in Creon's confrontation with Tiresias. In forcing the seer to declare his prophecy publicly and against his will, Creon tries on the role of Oedipus in *Oedipus the King* but fails miserably: it is as though Tiresias were thinking of the Creon of that play when he declares that "this man is no longer the same" (920).[98] Terrified by what he is told, he supplicates the seer by his "old man's beard" (923) and justifies his behavior with the bourgeois sentiment that "everyone loves his children" (965). His collapse is pathetic if understandable, and he is finally made to look foolish as Menoeceus dupes him into believing he will leave Thebes and sends him off to find money to finance his exile.

By the time of his second entrance Creon is so lost in personal grief that he is unaware of what has been happening elsewhere (1327–28). As in *Antigone* and *Oedipus the King*, he is again ruler by default (τὸν νεωστὶ κοίρανον, 1643) and issues edicts on the burial of Polyneices and the exile of Oedipus. But he does not present these orders as his own—he is only following instructions from Tiresias and Eteocles (1586–91, 1646)—and his concern for the marriage of Haemon is likewise at the direction of Eteocles (757–60). For a second time he retreats at a threat of violence to his son, this time Antigone's threat to kill Haemon. Unlike the Creon of *Antigone*, this Creon evinces a more traditionally female concern with the needs of family, yet only in the narrowest sense, as he is unwilling to extend to his nephew the rights which he claims are owed the dead (1320–21). In his privatism and his protectiveness of his children, Creon is finally cast in the type of the indulgent, gullible, and effeminate old father, less like the Creon of *Antigone* than his namesake in *Medea*.[99] As Eteocles' famous line "let the whole house go to ruin" (ἐρρέτω πρόπας δόμος, 624), showed his disregard of his house and family, Creon's "farewell, city" (χαιρέτω πόλις, 919), reveals his priorities as personal and domestic rather than political.[100]

Jocasta's movement in the play is more complex and can be charted in terms of an increasing masculinization of her behavior, a more public and aggressive effort on behalf of her family, and an intrusion both literal and symbolic into spaces more properly belonging to men, one adumbrated in her rejection of the womanly death tradition had assigned her. But Jocasta's behavior is presented in terms very different from that of Alcmene in *Children of Heracles*. Where in that play the increased assertiveness of the old woman is seen as transgressive and socially threatening, *Phoenician Women* yields a figure who is the obverse of this and in whom the same characteristics become expressions of a heroic maternity, rendering her character more sympathetic and more tragic. In each case the old woman's behavior is plotted in relation to that of the old man and as a response to a failure, real or perceived, to represent the needs of the situation effectively. In each case the old woman is constitutionally and temperamentally equipped to act outside the boundaries of traditional femininity to protect or avenge her children. Yet in the one, these energies are translated into negative stereotypes of vindictive and anti-social behavior: Alcmene crosses these boundaries with utter abandon and heedless of the scorn that will attach itself to her behavior. In the other, these energies remain harnessed within the family, and this hyper-maternity is the occasion for a character of more traditionally tragic and sympathetic composition: Jocasta crosses these same boundaries reluctantly and cautiously, only to discover the futility of doing so. Alcmene and Jocasta provide both the poles of Euripides' archetypes of aged motherhood and opposing constructions of her independence: the vindictive old woman, transformed figuratively or literally into the witch-monster; and the *mater dolorosa*, who wins tragic sympathy and social approval.

With each of her three exits from the house, Jocasta finds herself pulled further into the center of the play's action and away from traditionally feminine modes of behavior. Her opening speech reported the truce she arranged to bring her sons together and to save the house (δῶμα . . . τόδε, 68), and with her second exit from the house (πρόδομος, 296), Jocasta commences her active role in the negotiation process and formally assumes the role of reconciler (διαλλακτής). In a preamble (452ff.), she lays the ground rules for the arbitration sternly and professionally: the two are to deliver "considered speeches" (βραδεῖς . . . μῦθοι), must maintain eye contact with one another,[101] and will limit their remarks to the issue under discussion. Although she would prefer that one of the gods be "judge and reconciler" (κριτὴς . . . καὶ διαλλακτής, 467–68), Polyneices and the chorus make it clear that she must assume this role herself:

But mother, the resolution (διάλυσις) of these troubles rests with you.
Reconcile (διαλλάξασον) kindred brothers and rescue yourself and me
and the whole city from suffering. (435–37)
But look, here comes Eteocles for the reconciliation (διαλλαγάς).
It is your task, mother Jocasta, to give the kind of speeches by which you
can reconcile (διαλλάξεις) your children.

(443–45)

The concept of reconciiation (διαλλαγή), underscored throughout the play,[102] is at the heart of the counsel she offers in the agon. She
condemns the deities Eteocles worships, Ambition (Φιλοτιμία) and
Power (Τυραννίς), and recommends in their place the fair Equality
('Ισότης).[103] To Polyneices she stresses the importance of piety and
fatherland and the horror of waging war against the gods of his own
city. In her efforts to resolve strife (ἔρις) and enmity (ἐχθρά), in her
emphasis on fairness and reconciliation and the dangers of seeking
after "more" (τὸ πλέον) and "too much" (τὸ λίαν), Jocasta is cast less
as fifth-century democrat than as the archetypal reconciler Solon: like
the Athenian διαλλακτής she attempts to head off civil war, urging the
side that holds the power to yield and the side that would force such
change to consider the monstrous implications of fraternal violence.[104] A comparison with Alcmene is again instructive. Where the
more masculine character of her old age is manifested in her vengeful
spirit and spiteful rejection of proper legal procedure, Jocasta by contrast becomes both wise counselor and true politician: as she declares,
"I wish to give some wise advice to the two of you" (παραινέσαι δὲ
σφῷν τι βούλομαι σοφόν, 460).[105]
    Critics have noted the abstract quality of Jocasta's speeches and the
absence in them of emotional appeals to her own motherhood.[106]
They are in fact a combination of traditional ideas and current intellectuality, sophisticated arguments and forms of expression marshalled in support of conservative principles and against the sophis-
tries of her sons.[107] Far from being forced or out of character, Jocasta's
carefully reasoned and impersonal speeches underline the central
paradox of her role: in the interests of her children and in the absence
of a male figure to represent her, she must divest herself of her femininity, assuming a role and a rhetoric drawn from the male worlds of
science, philosophy, and politics. Yet even as she attempts to distance
herself from her motherhood, her themes remain expressions of her

maternal concerns. She begins her great speech by locating the source of her wisdom in life itself:

> Eteocles my child, not everything in old age is bad. But experience (ἡμπειρία) is able to speak more wisely than youth.
>
> (528–30)

The politics of Jocasta are in fact a mixture of the theoretical and the practical,[108] and suggest the application to the world of politics of just the kind of experience that might come from a lifetime of motherhood, and especially experience with the problems of jealousy, greed, and rivalry associated (however fairly) with siblings. In condemning ambition she points out the destruction it has brought to cities *and* families. She can draw on what she has seen of the changeability of human fortune in reflecting on the ephemeral nature of wealth. In her emphasis on equality and her warning to *both* sons to avoid foolishness (ἀμαθία δυοῖν, 584), political philosophy is blended with a mother's sense of what is fair—a commitment reflected in the balance of her speech, which she addresses to both sons, despite her partiality to Polyneices and the relative merits of his claim.[109] As Jocasta's plans collapse under her sons' obstinacy, and as the two display a different kind of equality in the stichomythia and antilabe they hurl at one another, she abandons her dispassionate role and cries aloud the dimensions of her suffering, finally begging them to avoid their father's Furies (618–19, 623–24).

In their relations with their aged parents, Polyneices is of the two brothers by far the more sympathetically drawn. Although he is no more open to reconciliation than his brother, he speaks of and to his parents with respect (288–90), at least inquires about his father's condition (376–77),[110] and asks to see him one last time (615) before bidding his mother a sad farewell (618). Eteocles, rude and impatient to his mother at his entrance, writes off the agon as a waste of time and dismisses her efforts as "long admonitions" (588–92). His character is revealed in the instructions he leaves Creon in the event of his death: he usurps his father's rights by making plans for Antigone's marriage and makes arrangements for his parents' needs in so perfunctory a manner as to offer a parody of the role of *gērokomos*.

> You are my mother's brother—why should I make a long fuss about it? Take care of her properly, for your sake and mine. But my father has

brought his foolishness upon himself, in blinding himself. I don't applaud him much for this. And it's he who will kill us with his curses, if it happens.

(761–65)

Jocasta's third entrance from the house (δομάτων . . . δόμων, 1067–68) begins the final phase of her efforts. Her inquiries of the messenger (first about Eteocles, then the city, and then Polyneices) and her grateful response at 1203 ("my children are alive and the land has escaped destruction") reflect her judicious balancing of the conflicting demands upon her. With the report of the imminent duel she determines to go at once "to the armies" (ἀνὰ στράτον, 1275) and to the very no-man's land between them (μεταίχμια, 1279) to supplicate her sons. Where in the agon Jocasta attempted to step out of her maternal role, she now resolves to take her motherhood into the violent heart of maleness and to supplicate the two by their mother's breasts (1567–69). The battlefield is the preserve of the male warrior-citizen, open only to men and those women who, like the Amazons, have renounced their femininity. The limit of a woman's world is the circle of the city wall, that threshold between city and battlefield on which, but never beyond, we find the women of the *Iliad*: Helen watching, Hecuba pleading, Andromache mourning.[111] One function of the *teichoskopia* in this play is to underscore the extent to which that line demarcates the proper boundaries of women's lives, and it is significant that when Creon arrives looking for Jocasta to manage the funeral for Menoeceus, traditionally a women's task, he is told she is out of the house (δόμων ἔξω, 1322). Yet here again Jocasta's intrusion into the battlefield does not represent a rebellion against the male order but her willingness to abandon the conventions of femininity for love of her sons. Nor does she hesitate to demand this sacrifice of others. Earlier we learned that it was specifically on her instructions that Antigone was allowed to leave the house briefly and only so far as the palace roof to view the troops. With due care Jocasta entrusts her daughter to the *paidagōgos*, who returns her forthwith and throughout the excursion is nervous that she will be seen in public (92–95, 196–201).[112] Now it is Jocasta herself who tells Antigone to come out of the house (δόμων, 1264) at once, leave behind her maiden chambers (παρθενῶνας, 1275) and girlish pursuits (παρθενεύμασιν, 1265), and go to the battlefield with her. When Antigone speaks of her reluc-

tance to expose herself to public view (αἰδούμεθ' ὄχλον, 1276; cf.
196), Jocasta tells her bluntly that her position does not allow for such
modesty. Antigone's respect for the proprieties of femininity recalls the
speech in *Children of Heracles* of Macaria, who also knows that maidens should remain inside the house (εἴσω . . . δόμων, 477); in addition
Alcmene had up to that point protected the modesty of the girls
(νέας . . . παρθένους αἰδούμεθα, 43), keeping them within (ἔσωθε,
42) and apart from public scrutiny (ὄχλῳ, 44). In accompanying her
mother to the battlefield, Antigone shows that she too is no less prepared to surrender her modesty in the interests of her family.

The description of Jocasta's death resumes the pattern of gender
reversal and provides a final conflation of her maternal goals and masculine means. There is predictable emphasis on her motherhood
with Jocasta bewailing the loss of "all the labor of her breasts" (τὸν
πολὺν μαστῶν πόνον, 1434).[113] Antigone addresses her brothers as
"supporters in old age of our mother" (γηροβοσκὼ μητρός) and betray-
ers of her own marriage (1436–37). When the two have breathed their
last, Jocasta dies a mother's death, impartial to the end: on whose sword
she slays herself we are not told (1456, 1577), and as she falls upon
their bodies she embraces them equally (1458–59, 1578). Antigone is
described as Jocasta's "shield-bearer" (παρασπίζουσα, 1435), casting
herself and her mother as a pair of warriors, and there is a martial over-
tone in Jocasta's final lament that she has arrived a "late helper"
(ὑστέρα βοηδρόμος, 1432).[114] The specifics of her death confound the
categories of gender: death on the field of battle (masculine), but by
her own hand (feminine); death accomplished by the sword (masculine), which she drives not through her chest but through the middle
of her neck (feminine).[115] Her death is an inversion of the role of Oedipus in a symmetrical and double sense: where in *Oedipus the King* he
invades the female quarters to punish himself for his crimes, doing the
deed with twin brooches taken from the robe of Jocasta, she enters the
male precinct of the battlefield and ends her life with a sword taken
from the bodies of her two sons; where in *Phoenician Women* Oedipus
remains within the house, unable either to live with the suffering he
has brought his sons or end his suffering by sword or noose, Jocasta
flees the house and ends her life decisively for the suffering her sons
have brought her.

The kind of reversals we have here, with Jocasta and Oedipus playing out and off against each other's roles, points to a larger paradox

that emerges from the treatment of age and gender in this play. In giving us an aged Jocasta and rejecting the denouement tradition had scripted for her, the poet defines the play in opposition to Sophocles. Yet in another sense this move is superficial, and in the ironies of its plot and destinies of its characters *Phoenician Women* is a reprise of *Oedipus the King* and its true sequel. As aged mother rather than noble wife, the protagonist is also translated from her role as passive observer of tragic action to active negotiator of its aftermath. But in assuming a more masculine role, the elderly woman exposes her efforts to the range of tragic irony and ambiguity. For all her valiant efforts, Jocasta becomes implicated in tragedy beyond the one she sought to forestall, and her efforts to alter the play's movement are undermined Oedipus-like by her own enlarged participation in the family's demise. As a rewriting of *Seven Against Thebes*, the tragedy of Polyneices and Eteocles is not only seen in relation to Jocasta's experience but becomes the terrifying culmination of her own efforts. It is in the Sophoclean idea that in the process of avoiding destiny one fulfills it that the play reveals its relation to *Oedipus the King*. As Oedipus had endeavored to avoid Apollo's prophecies only to fulfill them through his own efforts, Jocasta labors heroically to forestall the terrible consequences of his curses: but it is *precisely the truce that she herself has arranged* that backfires and becomes the occasion on which her sons freely choose to fight one another. *Phoenician Women* is presented as a kind of domestic version of *Oedipus the King*. In one the king takes up the ills of the city and achieves his goal, but at the cost of his own destruction and that of his family. In the other, the mother takes upon herself the ills of the family, but her efforts to save her sons only bring about their death and her own.

As in Sophocles' play, Jocasta's words and actions are charged with irony. Her prayer that the gods grant her sons a "coming-together" (σύμβασις, 85; cf. 71, 587, 590) finds a terrible literal fulfillment, and her plea that they respect Equality (ἰσότης), already ironic for the way in which kinship distinctions have been leveled in this family, is finally achieved in the grim equality of death (ἐξ ἴσου, 1402).[116] Similarly, the many references to Jocasta's breast cease to function as simple traditional expressions of maternal pathos, as her motherhood proves fatal to all who have enjoyed it. It was at her breast that Menoeceus was nursed (986–88), and he also undergoes a kind of gender reversal: in volunteering to die for the common cause, he plays what is more

properly in Euripides a maiden's role (Macaria, Polyxena, Iphigenia).[117] The play's greatest irony, however, is in the way the exodus
rewrites *Antigone* so as to involve Jocasta deeply in its action. As it was
she who conscripted Antigone to go with her to the battlefield, her
efforts have inspired her daughter to determine upon a similar course
of family commitment and public action, as she resolves upon another
bold excursion outside the city walls to accompany her father and
bury Polyneices "in the name of this, my mother Jocasta" (1665). Critics have sometimes puzzled over the absence of Ismene from this
drama, but she is in another sense present in the naive girl of the prologue, impressed by the sight of the Argive warriors but able to compare it only to what she has seen "in pictures" (130). It is clearly Jocasta's example that has transformed this sheltered girl into "the"
Antigone: a woman prepared to suffer for her family and to dispense
with both the restrictions and the rewards of her gender.[118]

It is not for nothing that we were told in the prologue that where
Oedipus had named Ismene, Jocasta had named Antigone and that she
herself had been named by her own father (12–13, 57–58). Antigone's
metamorphosis from Jocasta's foil to her likeness is reflected in her
two responses to Jocasta's opening prayer to the chariot of the sun: in
the *teichoskopia* in her invocation of the moon (175–76), and in the
exodus in her own prayer to the "four-horsed chariot of the sun"
(1562–63). Her own rapid defeminization begins with her departure
to the battlefield and continues as she joins the men of Thebes in the
funeral cortège into the city (1476–77). We may point briefly to the
most striking aspects of this process as it is brought to completion in
the exodus: (1) Her entrance, unveiled and with robes loosened, without the "maiden's blush" on her cheeks, her modesty now abandoned
(cf. αἰδούμεθα, 1276, αἰδομένα, 1489). As a "Bacchant of the dead"
(1489) she has no share in the maiden choruses of 786ff. with their
tuneful dancing and garlanded hair, but belongs instead to the horrid
fluteless revels of Dionysus' counter-face Ares.[119] In assuming the
image of the wild unfeminine mountain Maenad she brings back into
the city a role that belongs more properly *outside* its limits. (2) Her
defense of her father and pledge to bury Polyneices (although she is
willing to yield on the issue of burial), and her open defiance of Creon
and the justice of his edicts, despite his order to "return to the house
and act like a maiden" (κόμιζε σεαυτήν . . . δόμων ἔσω καὶ παρθενεύου,
1636–37).[120] (3) Her rejection of her betrothal to Haemon and threat

to become "one of the Danaids" (1675), man-slayers and misandrists par excellence, if she is forced to marry. (4) Her voluntary exile with her father, displacement from her home, and implicit assumption of the role of *gērokomos*, a task belonging more properly to her brothers (1436). (5) The distinction she draws between herself and other *parthenoi* as "most wretched of the girls in Thebes" (1716–17).[121] Antigone is cast as Jocasta's heir: she now shears her hair like her mother (1524–25), guides her father about as Jocasta had (1693ff.; cf. 1548–49, 1616–17), and like her mother refuses to be anything less than impartial toward her brothers. In demanding that Antigone join her and abandon her femininity, Jocasta has inadvertently involved her in another cycle of tragedy, and the journey from her house that should have marked the commencement of marriage and motherhood now will mark their loss.

Phoenician Women offers what is perhaps Euripides' grimmest view of old age, a pessimism in keeping with other late plays like *Orestes* and *Bacchae*. Yet the longevity of Euripides' personae lends to the premises of the play a certain wry humor, as though this tired old cast of familiar characters were being reassembled to run through this Theban material just one more time. In the densely allusive and self-conscious quality of its text, in its indebtedness to tradition and the freedom with which it plays with tradition, *Phoenician Women* shares in the metatheatrical and self-reflective character of Euripides' other late plays.[122] This is most striking in his use of the convention-busting devices for which he was notorious: his demuring with an account of the commanders at the gates (751–52) only to produce it later is only one of many instances of this.[123] Of particular interest are the many references to Dionysus and choral singing and dancing, culminating in the image of Antigone as a "Bacchant of the dead" (1489). Podlecki has observed how the metaphor points up the paradox of tragic performance: a joyous celebration for Dionysus becomes the occasion for witnessing the tragedy of Thebes, the birthplace of the god.[124] Yet one might also point to the chorus and the way it seems to suggest the reading or viewing of tragedy itself. In bringing into the story women en route from Phoenicia to Delphi, at once foreigners and yet related to these events, detached and yet familiar with the tradition on which the story is based, involved in the events and yet at a critical distance from them, the poet comes close to reproducing the condition of his spectators, for whom tragedy is necessarily a kind of interlude, a stopping along the way to somewhere else. At once involved and detached, emotionally engaged yet helpless to intervene, using its own knowledge of the tradition and observing relationships between past and present to puzzle out the meaning of it all, the chorus in its song cycle replicates the peculiar way in which ancient viewers attached meaning to the events unfolded before them and came to share in a grief that was not properly their own (ὧν μέτεστί μοι πόνων, 249).[125]

Sophocles' version of the Theban hero in old age has come to overshadow that of his rival so totally that it is easy to underestimate the enormous popularity *Phoenician Women* enjoyed in antiquity. Yet it is possible that the old age theme here also reflects a certain frustration with tragedy as a whole and its repetitious returns to the Theban cycle: revivals of Aeschylus' *Seven Against Thebes*, the many Theban plays of his contemporaries and rivals (like the *Oedipus* by Xenocles which defeated his *Trojan Women* in 415). If Euripides' desire was not just to finish the story but to finish it off, he would have occasion to laugh: not of course at Sophocles' *Oedipus at Colonus*, which he would not live to see, but at himself only a year or so later when he would find himself hard at work on an *Oedipus* of his own.

CHAPTER 7

The Unpolished Rock:
Sophocles' *Oedipus at Colonus*
and the Lessons of Old Age

... not only a man's knowledge or wisdom, but above all his real
life—and this is the stuff that stories are made of—first assumes
transmissible form at the moment of his death.
> —Walter Benjamin, "The Storyteller"

Old age and the passage of time teach all things. (γῆρας διδάσκει
πάντα καὶ χρόνου τρίβη.)
> —fragment from Sophocles' *Tyro*

IF it is true that *Oedipus at Colonus* represents the reversal of the Oedipus that was offered a few years earlier in *Phoenician Women*, with
Sophocles restoring to heroic stature the broken old man in Euripides,[1] it is also true that the difference between the two plays does not
declare itself at once. Indeed, Sophocles develops the opening scene of
Oedipus at Colonus by playing more against his own tradition than
against that of Euripides. It is significant that each of the so-called
Theban plays begins in a similar way and with a convention that distinguishes them from the rest of the poet's extant work. The protagonist addresses another character in familial terms and with questions
that establish a situation of need or crisis. The pattern culminates in
the opening lines of the last of the plays.

Antigone, child of the blind old man, to what land, to whose city have we
come? Who on this day will receive with some small gifts Oedipus the
wanderer, who asks for little and gets even less, although even this is
enough for me? For my sufferings, and time, my companion for so long,
and thirdly nobility have taught me to be content. But child, if you see
somewhere to sit, some public place or sacred grove, stop and sit me
down, so we may find out where we are. Coming as strangers, we need to
learn from the townspeople and do what they tell us.

(1–13)

From a sister's urgent questions in *Antigone*, to a king's attempt to comfort his people in *Oedipus the King*, we come to the simplest and most helpless of questions: Where are we? Who will feed us? Where can I sit? From the proud and self-confident protagonists of the first two plays we move to a hero who proclaims his willingness to acquiesce, to learn, to obey.

In the opening lines of *Oedipus at Colonus*, or even earlier as the hero first hobbles into the theater, Sophocles locates his hero in three primary frames of reference: he is blind (τυφλοῦ, 1); he is old (γέροντος, 1); and he is an outsider, a wanderer (πλανήτην, 3). Each of the terms of this metaphorical matrix is elaborated linguistically and scenically in the lines that follow. As Oedipus enters, he is so tired he must find somewhere to rest. "It has been a long road for an old man (ὡς γέροντι)," says Antigone, and he replies, "sit me down now, take care of the blind man (τὸν τυφλόν)" (20–21). As strangers (ξένοι, 13) themselves, Oedipus and Antigone must hail a stranger (ξεῖνε, 33) to tell them where they are. Blindness, exile, old age. The figures work together so effectively, are interwoven so seamlessly, that they seem hardly metaphors at all. All are expressions of the hero's destitute condition, his dependency on others for the most basic of his needs. All are sources of the suffering (πάθαι, 7) he has endured for so long and that Antigone recognizes in her first words (πάτερ ταλαίπωρ' Οἰδίπους, 14). All mark him visually as different; the shocking sight of his foul rags and grim visage provokes comment from every character in the play.[2] Most important, these figures, individually and cumulatively, mark Oedipus as a person of no consequence, as something less than a man, and thus vulnerable to the disregard and dishonor (ἀτιμία) that attached itself to such people in the Greek world. Already in the prologue we see how Oedipus anticipates the kind of rejection that his condition invites. When he tries to find out from the local man where he is, he begs him "do not dishonor (ἀτιμάσῃς) me, wanderer though I am" (49–50). Even in the privacy of his prayers he recognizes his insignificance. He asks the Eumenides, guardians of the grove on which he has trespassed, for passage from this life "if I do not seem to be of too little account" (104). As he supplicates the goddesses and Athens, itself the most honored (τιμιωτάτη) of cities, his abject condition becomes the basis of his appeal: "Have pity on this pathetic ghost of the man Oedipus. For this is not the body (δέμας) that once was his" (109–10). As in the opening lines of the play, the hero refers to himself in the third person, imagining himself as others see him.

The worthlessness of Oedipus is of course superficial, for *Oedipus at Colonus* invites us to consider the relation between his loathsome aspect and the enormity of the gift he offers, what Whitman called "the everlasting contradiction of inner and outer value."[3] The riddle is no less puzzling to the old riddle-solver himself. When Ismene reports on the new oracles, he scoffs aloud, "how could anyone's prosperity possibly depend on such a one as *me*?" (391). The theme is a familiar one. As the heroic nature could be hidden in the young woman's body of an Antigone or in the crippled limbs of a Philoctetes, it is here concealed in the body (δέμας) of Oedipus and is again elaborated in the antithesis of appearance and reality.[4] This body of Oedipus has become a ghost of itself, so weak that he must plead with his daughters not to leave him alone because it does not have the strength (οὐ. . . ἂν σθένοι τοὐμὸν δέμας, 501) to get about without help. In *Oedipus the King* the hero spoke with loathing of "my wretched body" (τοὐμὸν ἄθλιον δέμας, 1388), wishing only that he could deprive it of its hearing as well as its sight. Now this same body, which elicits revulsion or pity in those who behold it, is the gift that Oedipus offers to Theseus.

> I have come to give to you my wretched body (τοὐμὸν ἄθλιον δέμας), a gift which is not worth looking at. But the good it offers is greater than beauty.
>
> (576–78)

Oedipus' body has become a paradox, at once itself and its opposite, like the "light that is no light" (φῶς ἀφεγγές) of which his body takes its final leave at the end of the play (1549).

The paradox that is Oedipus, however, need not apply only to the value that he will have when he is dead and the protection that will belong to those who possess his corpse. In a pattern that is seen first in the prologue, one that will be repeated again and that adumbrates the structure of the play as a whole, first impressions about the value of the blind old beggar prove misleading. The local man whom Oedipus asks not to dishonor him (ἀτιμάσῃς) says that he will not make him dishonored (ἄτιμος, 52). He tells Oedipus where he has come and allows him to speak of the "great gain" that he brings to Theseus. And although he remains incredulous of what benefit can possibly come "from a man who does not see," he arrives nonetheless at a different appreciation of this trespasser:

> Hear me now, stranger, so that you do not come to harm. For you are clearly noble, as I can see, apart from your fate.
>
> (75–76)

There is a neat irony in the stranger's idiom that he can *see* (ἰδόντι) that Oedipus is noble, since in fact his appearance suggests just the opposite. It is only in the course of *speaking* with Oedipus and in the dialogue they exchange that the stranger is able to glimpse the nobility concealed beneath his squalid exterior.

An examination of old age in relation to this paradox is justified not only because this theme tends to be less appreciated than the other two but because the nature of old age and what it means to be an old man are, I think, central to its design and interpretation.[5] *Oedipus at Colonus* considers the *value* of old age: what good, if any, is long life to this man or to any man as an individual and in his relations with others? Oedipus' own words provide the starting point for such an assessment. When told of the gods' sudden interest in him, he dismisses their efforts as belated and almost unbecoming: "it is a cheap favor to raise up an old man who fell in his youth" (395). Oedipus considers the distance between youth and old age, between the man he was and what he has become, and in light of his depreciation finds the gods' attempt at recompense inadequate.

Knox has commented on what a bold stroke it was to cast an elderly Oedipus as protagonist, given the unflattering treatment of the elderly elsewhere in tragedy, especially in Euripides.[6] Here I would like to extend this approach and consider Oedipus as an old man against the backdrop of other representations of old age in Greek literature. The play, I suggest, invites us to appreciate its protagonist in the context of the literary traditions on old age, tragedy in particular, and the overwhelmingly negative character that they take. This tradition, already at work as we form our first impressions of Oedipus, finds its most cogent and explicit statement in the third stasimon, where the chorus describes old age with a string of privatives: "old age is *inf*irm, *un*friendly, *loveless*" (ἀκρατὲς, ἀπροσόμιλον, γῆρας ἄφιλον, 1235–37). For the chorus, old age is worthless, and Oedipus would seem to provide a graphic portrayal of the features they regard as so hateful: its weakness and dependence on others, its social isolation, the neglect and abuse to which it is vulnerable. Oedipus himself at times seems to second this view. At one of the emotional high points of the play, as Creon attempts forcibly to abduct Oedipus, the hero can find no greater curse to hurl at him than this:

> May Helios, the god who sees all, grant to you and your family to live the kind of old age that I have had.
>
> (868–70)

No less than those around him, Oedipus sees in his old age an epitome of human suffering. The play does not deny the tragedy of Oedipus' old age nor of old age in general. To the contrary, in the interweaving of the figures of age, blindness, and destitution, in the final sufferings through which it puts the hero, it seems to offer proof positive of the horrors of old age.[7] Yet even as it acknowledges the dimensions of Oedipus' tragedy, it challenges the tradition that regards old age as unredeemed misery and identifies it also as a source of positive value. It develops in its hero another conception of old age, one that questions the traditional interpretation and offers a different paradigm in its place.

At a symbolic level the hero-cult that will survive Oedipus at Colonus suggests the kind of power that is concealed beneath the decay of old age and the vital contribution that the elderly make to their culture. Yet in regarding Oedipus in terms of the value that he possesses as an old man, I will be speaking more to the point that Easterling makes when she insists that "Sophocles throughout the play takes pains to present Oedipus *as a man*, a man who behaves in a characteristically human way."[8] This is not to deny the uniquely religious dimensions of Oedipus' character, or the relation between certain aspects of his character and his imminent transformation from mortal to *hêros*.[9] *Oedipus at Colonus* provides a hero who is located in both human and divine space, who to use Segal's metaphor stands at the intersection of both a horizontal and a vertical axis and whose passage partakes of both the religious and the social.[10] Yet although the play culminates in the revelation of Oedipus as something greater than a man, it is also true that Sophocles gives us until that moment a remarkably coherent and consistent picture of a *gerôn*, one whose behavior may be understood largely without recourse to a supernatural essence that acts through or takes shape in him. To the extent that the play is successful in developing Oedipus as a man and a figure who is in some ways exemplary of old age in general, it also suggests that his greatness resides not only in his extraordinary destiny or in the unique status he will have in death but also in his capacity as a man; Oedipus' greatness in other words is at least in part not despite his old age but precisely *because* of it. As such, the theme sustains the ironies that permeate the play, as it combines in the same figure a kind of worst case scenario of old age and what is arguably the most compelling defense of old age to be found in Greek literature.

The old age of Oedipus is underscored throughout the play, and the poet develops and organizes his personae so as to further highlight the theme.[11] Oedipus and Theseus provide old and young representations of heroic nobility and responsibility, men who in the prime of life rule (or ruled) great cities. In Creon and Polyneices we have old and young antagonists who attempt to manipulate Oedipus to their own selfish ends, and who are kindred spirits in their hypocrisy and willingness to use force and violence to achieve their own selfish means. A third group consists of Antigone and Ismene and the elderly chorus, figures who support Oedipus and who, within the physical limits imposed on each by virtue of gender or age, work on his behalf. Thus, we have a triangular grouping of the dramatis personae, with an older and a younger tier linked by broad similarities of characterization, affording a multiplicity of perspectives on old age.

THE POET AND THE LIFE COURSE

One place to begin an examination of old age is in relation to the traditions that have come down concerning Sophocles' life. *Oedipus at Colonus* was almost certainly the last of the plays on which Sophocles worked, and the poet himself did not live to see it produced (by his grandson, we are told, in 401 B.C.). The date traditionally assigned its composition, around 405 B.C., would make the playwright almost ninety years of age and in the last year of his life—a tribute to his creativity and longevity. Like both Aeschylus and Euripides, Sophocles here leaves us a striking example of "old age art," to use Kenneth Clark's unglamorous phrase: the distinctive, innovative and problematical creations that come with the fullness of age.[12] The circumstances of the play's creation invite us to make some connection between old age and the literary imagination, between the work of art and the place of the artist in the human life course. What kind of concerns occupy the poet at the end of a long and rich career?

Oedipus at Colonus has been described as "personal to the point of betrayal,"[13] and the parallels between the poet and his protagonist are striking if somewhat obvious. Like the hero, Sophocles was approaching the end of a long and eventful life. Colonus was his birthplace and probably his home, and the play reflects his knowledge of its topography and local cults as well as his affection for the land and its beauty. Having served his city in a variety of religious and political capacities he, no less than the hero, was aware of the legacy that would survive his death. Critics have often taken these kinds of correspondences as an invitation to read the play as a kind of autobiography. Wilamowitz and Lesky, among others, have suggested that the unhappy picture of old age in the third stasimon reflects Sophocles' unpleasant experience of old age.[14] Others have argued that Oedipus' curses on Polyneices grow out of the poet's conflicts with his own son, or that the entire scene was conceived as an act of revenge, a clumsy insert in a play that was never fully completed.[15]

Yet rather than view these correspondences, actual and alleged, as instances of simple self-expression, a kind of spilling over of the playwright's "personal life" into his art, we may see them as attempts to lend to the work a distinctive character as a final, culminating effort. In *The Life of the Poet* Lipking reminds us of our strong tendency to locate the individual creative work in the larger *oeuvre* and to see in the pattern of the artist's life's work a "fulfilled poetic destiny." It is in Virgil, Lipking recognizes, where we first see the poet as self-conscious maker and shaper of his own poetic career, whose clear and deliberate ascent to the "higher" genre, the longer work, the greater depth of inspiration and gravity of purpose would provide a template against which later poets would chart their movement.[16] But this does not mean that earlier poets did not also attempt to set their late work in a distinctive relationship to their earlier.[17] There are good reasons to regard *Oedipus at Colonus* (perhaps not accidentally the longest of the extant tragedies) as a kind of poetic last will and testament. It draws much of its power from its retrospective character, in particular to *Antigone* and *Oedipus the King*, to which it clearly forms a kind of sequel,[18] and the return to the Theban material provided an opportunity to respond to Euripides' recent efforts in his *Oedipus* and *Phoenician Women*. In *Oedipus at Colonus*, the wealth of cross-references to the tragic tradition, the correspondences between protagonist and playwright and the unparalleled intrusion of the author into the world of his own play all help lend the play a special standing.

We get one indication of Sophocles' approach to old age in this play by looking at it in relation to the testimony, albeit anecdotal, that has come down about the poet in old age. One piece, from the first book of Plato's *Republic*, is put in the mouth of the self-satisfied old Cephalus. Asked by Socrates to describe what it is like to be so old, he responds with a reminisence:[19]

> I was once present when the poet Sophocles was asked by someone: "Tell me, Sophocles, how are you when it comes to sex? Are you still able to make love to a woman?" And he said "Say no such thing, my friend! Why, I couldn't be gladder to have escaped from that. It is as if I had run away from a cruel and savage slave master."
>
> (329 b–c)

The second anecdote appears among other places in Cicero's *De Senectute*, which reports how the playwright's sons had once indicted their father on a charge of senile incomptence. As Sophocles was so devoted to his art, he seemed to neglect the management of his estate, and they, hoping to divest him of his authority, took him to court with a claim that he was no longer compos mentis. Cicero describes the poet's dramatic self-defense, in which

> . . . the old man recited to the judges the play which he had in hand and had last written, *Oedipus at Colonus*, and asked whether the poem seemed the product of an incompetent mind. After the recitation, he was acquitted by the verdict of the judges.
>
> (*De Sen.*22)

As Cicero tells the story, the point is simply the play's poetic excellence, which rendered the charge of senility patently false. But there is a deeper irony in the content of the recitation and in the parallels between the poet and his protagonist: an old man, his heroic struggle in the Attic deme that had been Sophocles' birthplace, shamefully abused and manipulated by his sons, but ultimately protected by the fairness of the Athenian people, to whom he would leave a great gift that would forever survive his death.[20]

What these anecdotes have in common is their appreciation of the difference between old age as it is commonly perceived and as Sophocles claims to have experienced it. In the first, old age is dreaded for its physical deterioration and the waning of sexual appetite. Sophocles admits the fact but contests the evaluation, perhaps with an eye to the lyric tradition and its preoccupation with the sexuality of old age. In the second anecdote, the poet suggests that what others see as evidence of his mental infirmity is really proof to the contrary, and that the distraction and self-absorption that his sons would attribute to senility are in fact testimony to his genius. In each of these instances Sophocles instructs his listeners on the nature of old age, showing them that popular assumptions may be wide of the mark, the product of misperception and misevaluation. As Aristophanes insists in *Frogs*, the Athenians expected their tragic poets to be teachers (διδάσκαλοι), to speak with authority on political and moral questions both in and out of their works. In these anecdotes Sophocles attempts to educate the public on what it is to be an old man and uses his own life as evidence.

The historical value of these anecdotes is dubious and perhaps ultimately not significant. Indeed, it seems to me quite possible that it was *Oedipus at Colonus* that inspired a tradition about Sophocles as the critic of traditional assumptions about old age. In the play as in the anecdotes Sophocles suggests that old age is not a simple thing capable of objective description but a complex experience that can be understood in different ways. It is not just that attitudes will differ from the "inside" as opposed to the "outside," since the elderly may themselves subscribe to that view of old age which is held generally. The point is rather that the perception and the very experience of old age is shaped by a body of shared assumptions about it. *Oedipus at Colonus* can be regarded as an exercise in cultural criticism that challenges the popular construction of old age. It suggests that this conception, even when put in the mouths of the elderly themselves, is defined too negatively, that individual experience may be at odds with conventional wisdom, and that the literary and specifically tragic traditions on old age are at best partial and incomplete.

CIRCLES OF ELDERS

Jones has commented on the strong sense of locality that characterizes the later plays of Sophocles, what he calls "a kind of interdependence of man and place."[21] The stagecraft of the opening scenes of the play is crucial to the definition of Oedipus as an old man, and the *mise en scène* establishes a complex topography that is at once physical and spiritual, leading us to regard the play as a whole in a certain way, and made all the more impressive for the economy with which it is accomplished: with the possible exception of a simple prop or two Sophocles draws only on language and the basic architectural resources of the Greek theater, yet achieves some of the most vivid *skēnographia* to be found in tragedy.[22]

Oedipus has traveled a "long road (μακρὰν . . . ὁδόν), for an old man" (19), simple words that suggest several kinds of journeys: the day's march, about to come to an end; the many miles from Thebes to Athens and the years it has taken to walk them; the road that has been Oedipus' life and that for him will here come to an end.[23] The place to which they have come is both a terminus and a resting place (ξενόστασιν, 90), a passage to something greater, just as Colonus leads to Athens, and as the Bronze Threshold (χαλκόπους ὁδός, 57; cf. 1590–91), which we are to imagine as being deep within the grove, leads to the nether world. The locale is particularly suited to the liminality of this aged hero, poised as Homer would say "on the threshold of old age" (ἐπὶ γήραος οὐδῷ) and located on so many borders and boundaries: spatial, chronological, political, and religious.[24]

After Antigone has described the beauty of the place to which they have come, she invites her father to "bend your limbs here on this unpolished rock" (τοῦδ' ἐπ' ἀξέστου πέτρου, 19), a simple prop that we can imagine to be located to the spectator's left and approached by Oedipus from the parodos that represents the road away from Athens; yet the rock is also close to the grove (of which the *skēnē* is a part) and is itself within the sacred precinct (τέμενος, 136) of the Eumenides, as becomes clear first from the horrified reaction of the stranger who finds Oedipus sitting there and then from the shock of the chorus, who at once declare him "out of place" (ἐκτόπιος, 119).[25] Oedipus refers to the spot again after he has discovered its sacred nature. He must have been led there by the goddesses themselves, for otherwise "I would never have taken my place upon this holy unhewn seat" (σεμνὸν . . . βάθρον τόδ' ἀσκέπαρνον, 100–101). The diction in each case is remarkable—"unpolished" (ἀξέστου) is extremely rare, and "unhewn" (ἀσκέπαρνον) is unattested elsewhere. The moment at which Oedipus actually takes his seat is highly dramatic, perhaps unique. *Oedipus at Colonus* is the only extant tragedy in which a character actually sits on stage, and while it is not clear how long he remains seated there (he may rise at some point during his address to the stranger), the spectacle of a character delivering his lines from a seated position lends the moment a special character.[26]

The image of the unpolished rock calls to mind two passages in Homer in which old men are seated on stones.[27] In book 18 of the *Iliad*, in the scene depicted on the shield of Achilles of the city at peace, we are told of a trial that has convened to settle a quarrel resulting from a case of homicide: "the elders were in session on benches of polished stone (ἐπὶ ξεστοῖσι λίθοις) in the sacred circle and held in their hands the staves of the heralds who lift their voices" (503–5). In book 3 of the *Odyssey* we hear how on the morning after Telemachus' arrival Nestor "went outside and took his seat upon the polished stones (ἐπὶ ξεστοῖσι λιθοῖσι) which were there in place for him in front of the towering doorway, white stones, with a shine on them that glistened" (3.405–8). Nestor sits in the ancestral seat from which his father Neleus had presided, scepter in hand and surrounded by his six dutiful sons. The difference between the polished stones on which Homer's elders consult and the unpolished rock on which Oedipus rests is in one respect a measure of the difference between them: their prosperity and his destitution; their vigorous participation in the life of the community and his homeless condition; their authority, symbolized in the scepters that they hold, and Oedipus' dependence on his daughters, whom he even calls his scepters (σκῆπτρα, 1109; cf. 848).

The scenes in Homer provide idealized and archetypal representations of elders engaged in their traditional duties: deliberating over the problems of the community, sharing the wisdom of the ancestral tradition and the results of their accumulated experience. These are both sacred assemblies: the *gerontes* of the *Iliad* arrange themselves "in a sacred circle" (ἱερῷ ἐνὶ κύκλῳ); the stones on which Nestor's group sits are dripping with oil (408), a sign of their sanctity. The sacred circle suggests both the solidarity of the group and their integration into the community gathered around them. By contrast, the rough-looking rock on which Oedipus rests, exposed to the elements and set apart from human civilization, suggests his own unprepossessing exterior, his asocial status, his isolated and neglected situation. In sitting on this single rock, in laying claim to it as his final destination, Oedipus partakes of its solitary character. It is significant that in the third stasimon, when the chorus pities Oedipus for his wretched old age and the series of misfortunes that assail him, they compare him with a striking image to a rock: "just as in the winter some northern headland is driven, beaten on every side by the waves, so too this man . . . " (1240ff.). In a classic expression of Sophoclean heroism, the rock alone in the world of nature becomes a symbol of the isolation and endurance of the hero, surrounded and buffeted relentlessly by the waves of destruction.[28]

But as we track this line of imagery through the prologue and parodos, we find a path that leads from the unpolished rock toward Homer's elders. Like the "sacred circle" in which they sit, the rocky seat where Oedipus rests is in a sacred area: it is clearly a holy place (χῶρος . . . ἱερός, 16, 54) as Antigone declares at once; the stranger further explains that the entire vicinity is sacred (χῶρος . . . ἱερὸς πᾶς ὅδ' ἔστι, 54). This rock is unpolished and unhewn not only because of its natural condition but because it is sancrosanct and may not be touched by human hands: it is unpolished and unhewn in the same way that the grove itself is untouched (ἄθικτος, 39) and untrodden (ἀστιβές, 126). Oedipus takes refuge deep within this area, that is, in the *skene* itself—"away from the road . . . down in the grove" (113–14), as he says. And when the chorus finally coaxes him upstage and out of the grove, he is relocated on yet another rocky surface. They tell him "there: go no further than that step of natural rock" (τοῦδ' αὐτοπέτρου βήματος, 192).[29] And when Oedipus asks whether he can sit, the chorus answers precisely: "yes, go to the side, squat down low on the edge of the rock (ἐπ' ἄκρου λάου)" (195–96). This "rocky step" is harder to identify precisely, but it is clearly located at some distance away from the *skene* and in the direction of the orchestra—the chorus tells Oedipus to move so that a great distance (πολλὰ κέλευθος) is put between him and the grove (162–63)—and probably represents the formal boundary of the *temenos* proper. This rocky ledge may be another stage property, although if we assume the existence of a raised platform or *logeion* in front of the *skênê* from which the actors speak, it may in fact have been represented by nothing more than its front edge or perhaps the first of a flight of steps that lead from the platform to the orchestra.[30] The rock, on which Oedipus will be seated for much of the rest of the play (it is possible that he does not actually leave this seat until his magnificent exit into the grove at 1555), is frought with significance—as Seale says, "the seated, oracular figure of the blind Oedipus is the dominant visual impression."[31]

The diction is equally interesting. "Natural" (αὐτοπέτρου) is also a *hapax* in Greek, and like "unpolished" and "unhewn," the epithet defines the location as other than the work of human hands. Vidal-Naquet has observed the significance of the description of this rock as a "step" (βῆμα), which otherwise describes the raised platform for pubic speaking, the rostrum, and calls to mind that most famous *bêma* on the Pnyx, which was itself fashioned out of the slope of the rock.[32] In introducing the image of the *bêma* , for the Athenian citizen a foundation of his cultural and political life, the poet brings with it the idea of social interaction and political participation. Indeed, in locating such a *bêma* within the scenic area, the poet lends the setting a bold metatheatrical quality and literally doubles his own image by providing one speaking area within another: here the actor, who by his very nature speaks to the community from the platform of the stage, is given within that space a second platform from which he addresses the community within the world of the play. At the same time the figure of the "rocky step" is a kind of oxymoron in the way it juxtaposes the worlds of nature (αὐτοπέτρου) and culture (βήματος), a tension expressed spatially in the location of the step in the area between the sacred grove and the chorus, whatever more specific location we assign it.

The rocky step provides Oedipus, presumably for the first time since his exile, with a space from which he can engage in speech with a human community.[33] Oedipus moves from a sacred area in which he must refrain (ἀπερύκου) from speaking to one where he can add his speech (λόγον) to the chorus' conversation (λέσχαν) and where speech is "permitted to all" (πᾶσι νόμος, 166–69). It is hardly accidental that the first community into which the hero is introduced is composed of old men like himself. The poet takes great care in the definition of this group, local men from Colonus (78) whom Antigone describes on their approach as old (χρόνῳ παλαιοί, 112).[34] In her insightful treatment of the chorus in this play, Gardiner stresses two aspects of their characterization, both closely related to their age.[35] The first is the piety of these reverent (αἰδόφρονες, 237) men, as reflected in their distress over Oedipus' trespass of the grove, their horror at his polluted condition, and their knowledgeable description of the rites of appeasement, which they describe in such vivid detail we can almost see them being performed; their songs throughout, with their frequent allusions to local worship and cult practice, suggest their deep reverence for the gods. The second is their compassion for and loyalty to Oedipus. Once they have resolved the issue of his trespass, they are vigorous and unwavering in their support. Gardiner speaks of an "alliance of the old," as the chorus takes up the part of the hero first before Theseus and then against Creon and then finally, although at first reluctantly, against Polyneices. She observes how deeply these elders are involved in the structure of the play as a whole, as reflected in the number of *kommoi* and odes they sing and their extensive use of dialogue.[36] Similarly, Burton calls attention to the emotional nature of their songs and the absence in them of moral and intellectual comment: "they are essentially simple countrymen, not elders of a city, and they are moved above all by a heartfelt love of their deme and its wider setting, a deep sense of awe and duty as guardians of a sacred place, and the natural sympathy of old age for old age."[37]

Yet we should also appreciate how remarkably *typical* is this chorus of elderly men. To the extent that one can speak of such choruses of elders in Greek tragedy as a type—there are seven in the extant plays—this chorus is perhaps the most representative.[38] The themes of the first three odes have parallels in the choruses of Euripides' *Children of Heracles* and *Heracles*, and all are appropriate to a chorus of old men: their hymn of praise to the beauties of Colonus and Athens and to the deities who will keep their city safe forever; their nostalgic song as the fight against the Thebans rages offstage, in which they only wish that they could be present at the battle; and their reflections on the hardships of old age and of human life in general.[39] Like other elderly choruses, this one is characterized by its inability to interfere physically with the stage action, in keeping with the convention dating back at least to *Agamemnon* by which tragic "paradoxes of inaction" are rendered more realistic by choruses composed of the elderly or of women, who must watch helplessly as foreigners from without or tyrants from within violate the orderly process of law and constitutional government.[40] The elders of Colonus bluster and threaten before the violence of Creon and his men, and even make a token show of force, but must wait for the arrival of Theseus to stop the crime. And just as the choruses of Euripides' *Children of Heracles* and *Heracles* are characterized by their support for Iolaus and Amphitryon, the elders of Colonus develop a deep solidarity for Oedipus. In general, we may note the conservative nature of such choruses, which place a high value on tradition, stability, and legitimate authority, a conservatism reflected in this chorus' recommendation that Oedipus adapt himself to the practices and traditions of Athens: "undertake to hold in contempt whatever the city has grown to dislike (τέτροφεν ἄφιλον) and to reverence what it loves (φίλον)" (184–87).

That the poet employs so many of the conventions of the aged chorus is not for lack of imagination. Sophocles begins the process of the hero's social and political reintegration by having him confront, address, and gradually assume membership in a community of elders, one which is traditionally defined and closely identified with the conventions of tragedy.[41] As the chorus enters the orchestral area, singing what we assume will be a traditional parodos, we can imagine its members in distress and disorder as they look about anxiously for the "old wanderer" (122–23): the action is not unlike that of the chorus in the desperate search scene of *Ajax* 866ff. When they cannot find him, the voice of Oedipus coming from inside the grove confounds our expectations: this parodos, we realize, will take the form of a *kommos*. The shape of this interchange symbolizes the beginnings of the hero's participation in this circle of elders, as he is first engaged in song with them, then negotiates an agreement with them, and cautiously and reluctantly inches away from the *skênê* toward them.[42] Two long passages by the chorus (118–37, 150–69) give way to a more balanced interchange between Oedipus and these elders, as the chorus and then Antigone persuade him to move away from the area of the unpolished rock and to take a new place upon the rocky step (192ff.). In the areas that belong to the grove and the chorus the play sets off sacred and secular space, with Oedipus seated on the threshold between them.[43] But in another sense the setting opposes one kind of sacred area against another: the *adyton* of the *skênê* and the grove it represents against the orchestra with the altar at its center; the space that is sacred because the gods have revealed it as sacred and have claimed it for themselves against the space that is sacred because humans have deemed it so and reserved it for cultural expression. As with the process of his dialogue, the stagecraft provides a representation of the symbolic process by which Oedipus moves away from one sacred area toward another and finally locates himself exactly in between the two. Oedipus leaves the grove to approach the aged chorus, whose fifteen members will at times be arranged around this circle, a circle that literally both includes and does not include the hero.

THE LESSONS OF OEDIPUS: I

Like the polished stones on which Homer's elders sit, the rocky step locates Oedipus in a sacred space from which he can speak within a circle of elders and demonstrate his own talents as elder. His assumption of this role is integrated with the theme of instruction, which is developed almost programmatically in the prologue. There Oedipus speaks repeatedly of what he has learned or needs to learn: from his own destiny (διδάσκει, 8), from Antigone (διδάξαι, 23), and from others (μανθάνειν, 12; μάθω, 26; ἐκμάθω, 114). He concludes the prologue with a gnomic reflection:

> It is by learning (μαθεῖν) that we are cautious in the things we do.
> (115–16).

While Oedipus will show himself on occasion a willing student, he is also revealed in the course of the play as teacher in his own right, one whose words provide instruction on a variety of subjects, including old age itself.[44] In developing Oedipus as a kind of wise counselor, the play draws on the tradition that values the elderly for what they have learned and can share with others, and that sees them as venerable fonts of such wisdom. In speaking of the wisdom of Oedipus, I am not speaking of what we might call revealed truth: of what he knows from oracles and the growth in him of his own increasing prophetic power, although we should not minimize the inductive effort this requires nor the intelligence with which Oedipus pieces together old and new oracles with what he sees happening about him.[45] Nor am I referring to the instruction he gives in regard to the mysteries of his death and the destiny that is uniquely his. To the extent that Oedipus possesses this kind of absolute knowledge, he is set apart from ordinary mortals and becomes, like the blind old Teiresias, the mouthpiece of the gods. I am speaking instead of what Socrates in the *Apology* calls human as opposed to divine wisdom, of the kind of knowledge on which social and ethical life is based, and of the tradition that sees the elderly as precious repositories of such knowledge.

The notion of such a tradition itself requires some qualification, since as we have seen, the figure of the wise old counselor, ubiquitous in more genuinely traditional societies, appears in Greek literature only in a limited way. The assumption that wisdom comes naturally with old age is in fact infrequent in Greek literature, which is more often intent on undermining the connection between the two, and so it is worthwhile to review briefly just what this tradition amounts to. The figure of the wise counselor is central to the *Iliad,* embodied in Nestor and Phoenix and the Trojan city-elders (*dēmogerontes*). But already in Homer this role is frought with ambiguity. The authority of these elders is far from automatic and often contested, and their success as counselors is at best mixed. Their advice, though earnestly given, is frequently unsolicited, unheeded, and widely off course. They have their counterpart in the second book of the *Odyssey* in Halitherses and the other old Ithacans who try in vain to talk some sense into the young suitors. That the youthful protagonists of epic should disregard the advice of the elderly is in one a sense a precondition of their own tragic greatness, but the overall impression that elderly counsel is also by and large failed counsel is warranted. In the later tradition the figure of the wise old man becomes more submerged. A fragment of Hesiod reassigns the function of counsel from old age to middle age and replaces it with piety: "deeds belong to the young, counsel to those in the middle, and prayers to the old" (321 West). Archilochus (or someone writing in his tradition) recommends that the elderly live a life apolitical and socially disengaged: "an idle life (βίος ἀπράγμων) is good for old men, especially if they happen to be simple in their ways or prone to be stupid or talk nothing but nonsense, which is typical of old men" (330 West). Nor does Solon, reflecting the political realities of Athenian citizenship in his poem on the "ten ages of man" (27 West), associate old age and wisdom in any special way. Like Hesiod, he sees "middle age" (43 to 56) as the acme of male life and old age as a period of relative decline: "in the ninth [hebdomad] he still has some ability, but his speech and his intellect are feebler in respect to great excellence" (15–16).

The old counselors of Greek drama are characterized by a similar kind of ambivalence. There are a number of occasions, especially in Euripides, where old men offer advice to the young: Pheres to Admetus (*Alcestis*), Creon to Eteocles (*Phoenician Women*), Tyndareus to Orestes (*Orestes*), Cadmus to Pentheus (*Bacchae*). Yet these men serve in a familial capacity, not by virtue of a recognized social role. Their efforts are typically unsuccessful, and their moral and intellectual authority is often so undermined by their own selfishness, folly, and vindictiveness that they are not entitled to give the advice they offer. The figure of the wise old counselor in tragedy is a minor and occasional one: the old *paidogogus* in the opening of Sophocles' *Electra*, whose advice Orestes solicits and accepts (23–31, 81–85); the old servant at the beginning of *Hippolytus*, whose master disregards the good counsel he is offered. The theme of aged wisdom, when it is raised, is used more often to discredit the elderly, as in *Andromache* when Menelaus says in exasperation of Peleus: "why would anyone say that old men are wise and that the Greeks once thought them so intelligent" (645–46).[46]

In developing his protagonist as a source of wisdom and instruction, Sophocles breathes new life into this beleaguered tradition.[47] In his exchange with the stranger in the prologue, Oedipus has said (in Jebb's translation of 74): "in all that I speak there shall be sight"; as the play unfolds we see that this is not limited to the mysteries surrounding his death and burial. The living Oedipus and his human knowledge become valuable sources of enlightenment, and the play provides a number of opportunities both formal and informal in which he can share this. *Oedipus at Colonus* provides a number of opportunities in which Oedipus addresses issues of importance, and clarifies and resolves situations of confusion and impasse. As such, his conversation and interaction with the characters within the play parallel the larger pattern of the reintegration of the hero into society, a schema that applies to the dead hero of *Ajax*, the living hero of *Philoctetes*, and in both respects to the hero of *Oedipus at Colonus*. The process of Oedipus' social and political reintegration is carefully charted in this play: from his encounter with the stranger in the prologue; through his revelation to the chorus that he is without a city (ἀπόπολις, 208; cf. ἄπολιν, 1357); and culminating in Theseus' granting to Oedipus the rights of full citizen (χώρᾳ δ' ἔμπολιν κατοικιῶ, 637).[48] Oedipus' developing status as wise counselor provides a social role within which that political reintegration is accomplished, one that is tied to the theme of reciprocity that is both ethically and politically at the heart of the play and that is especially necessary given the ambiguous and dangerous aspects of Oedipus' character: as Segal poses the question directly, "How can the ordered structures of society confront and incorporate their negation?"[49] In the wisdom Oedipus offers his new community we see that what he offers in return for the protection he is provided is not limited to the boon of his death.

Unlike Homer's elders, whose authority is shored up by their position and prestige and who sit in impartial judgement on the matters before them, Oedipus is himself at the heart of the issues under discussion. And unlike that wisdom that comes from the ancestral and institutional traditions of the community, Oedipus' wisdom has been won in solitude as the product of his own tragic experience. In his opening speech he presents his unique qualifications as counselor, describing his teachers and giving one example of what he has learned.

> For my sufferings, and time, my companion for so long, and third my nobility have taught me to be content. (στέργειν γὰρ αἱ πάθαι με χὠ χρόνος ξυνὼν μακρὸς διδάσκει καὶ τὸ γενναῖον τρίτον. 7–8)

There is heavy irony here at work, as we see the Sophoclean hero schooled in this most un-Sophoclean virtue στέργειν—acquiesence, patience, contentment.[50] Some have suggested that Oedipus' own behavior, his temper and passionate anger, is positive proof that he has learned no such lesson.[51] To be sure, it is clear from his first confrontation with the local man (35ff.) that for Oedipus στέργειν does not imply a wilingness to "take" whatever he is given. He tells Antigone that he has learned to yield to what is truly necessary (μὴ χρείᾳ πολεμῶμεν, 191), and throughout the play we see him distinguish between his own inevitable destiny and the kind of treatment that others would mete out to him.

Yet as important as this lesson is the process by which the hero claims to have learned it. Oedipus describes his education in almost mathematical terms, the elements of which suggest the form of an equation (D = A ı B ı C), as though the subtraction of any of the three factors would result in less than the desired total. Indeed, the formula that Sophocles offers here seems a kind of final statement on the nature of true learning and the elements of which it is compounded. The first are the many sufferings (πάθαι) of Oedipus in Thebes and the long years of his exile. The educational value of suffering was articulated at least as early as the Aeschylean dictum of wisdom through suffering (πάθει μάθος), and the theme also appears in Sophocles' *Women of Trachis* (142–43). Yet there is nothing automatic about the process as Oedipus describes it; here suffering requires time in which to reflect upon it.[52] That time is both teacher and testing ground of the hero is another Sophoclean motif, in *Electra* and *Philoctetes* in particular, and in this play too we have in Polyneices an instance of the "late learning" (ὄψ' ἄγαν ἐκμανθάνω,1264) that is so

frequent in tragedy.[53] Yet Oedipus here speaks specifically of *long* time
(χρόνος . . . μακρός) in which he has reflected on his past, and like the
fragment from the lost *Tyro* with which this chapter begins, the reference seems to point to the special insight that has come with old age.
The last factor is Oedipus' sense of his own nobility (τὸ γενναῖον),
what he brings with him to his experience. Throughout the play nobility describes the essential content of one's character, the dignity and
demeanor that defines a man or woman in relation with others, as
when Oedipus praises Theseus for his nobility (τὸ σὸν γενναῖον, 569,
1042; cf. 1636); or encourages his daughters at his death to show
theirs (1640); or makes his own nobility manifest to the stranger (76)
and denies to the chorus that he is evil by nature (κακὸς φύσιν, 270).

The challenge that faces Oedipus in drawing wisdom out his own
experience is complicated by the fact that doing so forces him to suffer
once again the pain of his past. We do not see Oedipus indulging in the
kind of reminiscence that is such a valuable source of self-esteem and
reintegration for Homer's Nestor or Priam—he speaks of the past only
when he is forced to, whether by the curiosity of the chorus or the
provocation of Creon. Oedipus effectively has no past to which he can
refer, and his pollution cuts him off from the functions of memory and
recollection in which the elderly typically and willingly indulge.[54] As
Oedipus shares the lessons he has learned in long reflection on his
painful past, his task is not simply to deliver his knowledge but to
transform it, to take what he has learned in the cauldron of suffering,
time, and nobility, and convert it into more generalizable principles.
Oedipus' wisdom is revealed in the application of his knowledge in
particular concrete situations. In one sense, the process he represents
is nothing less than the paradox of tragedy itself, with its endless and
repetitious stories of the sufferings of the Labdacids and Atreids and
Heraclids. How does one translate such personal experience and private grief into wisdom, how does the personal come to have social
application? This paradox crystallizes in Oedipus in that what he
comes to share in the play is derived so much from his solitary experience in exile, in isolation from the community that would normally
give it shape.

Oedipus finds a first opportunity in the dilemma his arrival has
created. The chorus succeeds in coaxing Oedipus out of the sacred
grove with a promise that "no one shall ever move you away from this
place of rest against your will" (176–77). But when the shuffling on

stage has ended and the chorus' desire to learn (ἐκπυθοίμαν, 206) his identity tears from him the revelation that he is "wretched Oedipus," they recoil in utter horror. He must get out of their land (ἔξω πόρσω βαίνετε χώρας, 226), even "leap" out at once (234), lest the city incur some liability (χρέος, 235) from contact with a person who is polluted and clearly hateful to the gods.[55] When Oedipus protests their breach of the agreement, they argue that they are only repaying him in kind.

> Fate does not punish a man who avenges himself for what was done to him first. One deceit deserves another: it wins for the deceiver a return of grief, not kindness.
>
> (229–33)

Antigone intercedes with an eloquent lyric appeal for pity, pleading by all that the chorus considers holy and presenting her father's condition as a result not of sin but of ineluctable fate. Although they are disposed to listen, their fear of "the things from the gods" (256) keeps them from reconsidering.

Oedipus' response (258–291) is the first long address he makes to any character other than Antigone, and the change from lyrics to iambics marks the shift from an emotional to a more reasoned appeal. His speech elaborates two arguments, one directed at them and the other at himself, which fold in upon each other. The first is that by driving him away they show their city's reputation (δόξα, κληδών, 258) for piety and compassion to be a false one. Athens is reported to be "most god-fearing" (θεοσεβεστάτας, 260)[56] for its treatment of suppliants and strangers, but by expelling him from his refuge they reveal this reputation to be a myth. They should remember that the gods are not blind (ἀμαυρούς, 278) and that they keep watch on the holy and unholy man alike. The implication is twofold: not only should they beware the gods' punishment on themselves, but they can be assured that if Oedipus himself is guilty the gods will see to his punishment. Oedipus' second argument is that their fear of him (δείσαντες 265, ἐκφοβῇ 269; cf. τρέμοντες, 256) is unwarranted. His so-called deeds (ἔργα, 266) are better understood as things done to him (πεπονθότα) rather than as things he did (δεδρακότα, 267). He is in fact innocent of the murder of Laius, whose killing was under provocation and so clear an instance of retaliation that even had he known the man was Laius he would not be evil (κακός, 272) for killing him. As it was, however, he was totally ignorant of whom it was he met at the crossroads. As such, his "deeds" do not reveal him to have a base nature (270) and he bears no guilt for what he has done. To the contrary, he is himself "holy and pious" (ἱερὸς εὐσεβής τε, 287) by virtue of the gift he bears and which he shall shortly reveal. To the contrary, it is *they* whose deeds are unholy (ἔργοις . . . ἀνοσίοις, 283) and harmful to Athens, *they* who will prove evil (291) if they remove him.

In a lucid analysis of this speech, Slatkin has shown how Oedipus' argument involves a fundamental critique of the relation between piety and morality as the chorus understands it.[57] In assuming the guilt of Oedipus and their own competence to judge it they have failed to look to the man himself and the harm they do the city by driving him out. As "for these reasons" (ἀνθ' ὧν, 275) shows, Oedipus' argument is based not only on the protection that suppliants are guaranteed and the agreement they had struck with him but also on the specific self-defense that he has provided. By forcing the chorus to look at him, to consider the meaning of piety in respect to his own individual suffering and destiny, Oedipus forces them to extend their notion of reverence into social relations. The challenge Oedipus presents to the chorus, suggests Slatkin, indicates that the benefit (ὄνησιν, 288) he brings to Athens is not limited to the protection he will offer from the grave: just as the oracle that Ismene reports says that Oedipus will be needed "living and dead" (390), so here he "offers the Athenians the opportunity to make their values real by accepting him."[58]

The length and the depth of this argument take the chorus by surprise. His reflections (τἀνθυμήματα), delivered "in no few words" (λόγοισι . . . οὐκ . . . βραχέσι), have stricken them with awe and dread (ταρβεῖν, 292–94). Their decision to allow him to remain on the step for the time being and to defer the matter until Theseus' arrival is a virtual agreement with him, for they do not bring up the issue when the king arrives nor does it come up in the play again. One reason Oedipus has been persuasive is that his defense is constructed around values that the chorus has already upheld—reverence toward the gods and the well-being of the city (cf. πόλει, 236); his argument employs many of the commonplaces that are used in suppliants' pleas for safety (the chorus' duty to the gods, their pledge to him, Athens' reputation).[59] But Oedipus complicates the issue by introducing a distinction between true and false piety, between the appearance of holiness and its reality, which is already implicit in his first words about Athens' reputation (δόξα, 258). Oedipus develops parallels between the situation of the chorus and his own experience of people's reaction to him. He suggests that what the chorus truly fears is neither his body (σῶμα) nor his deeds (ἔργα, not deeds at all), but only his "name" (ὄνομα, 265–66), that is, the reputation that is inseparable from his notorious name (301, 306). Oedipus' name here connotes the popular understanding of the man and his life and functions as a virtual synonym for δόξα. This name, he proceeds to explain, is a false one, as a true understanding of the circumstances of the death of Laius reveals. He finds a second illustration of the difference between appearance and reality in his own body:

> Do not, as you look upon this ill-looking face, dishonor (ἀτιμάσῃς) me. For I have come here a holy and pious man and with a benefit for these citizens.
>
> (285–88)

Oedipus' face, at first sight of which the chorus had recoiled in horror (141, 150ff.), is itself evidence of his argument that things are not what they seem, and he promises to reveal shortly the piety concealed beneath it. Just as popular tradition mistakes the name of Oedipus for his real condition, just as the chorus mistakes his outer aspect for his true holiness, they need to be careful lest they drive a wedge between what Athens is said to be and is.

The chorus attempted to justify its reversal by an appeal to the principle of reciprocity—as they were deceived by Oedipus, they are entitled to deceive him in return (229–33).[60] Oedipus embraces this principle in arguing that his killing of Laius was really an instance of retaliation: having suffered a wrong at the hands of Laius, he only returned in kind (παθὼν . . . ἀντέδρων, 271). Yet Oedipus again complicates the issue by introducing the crucial aspect of knowledge. His own experience at the hands of Laius shows that before returning like for like one must have a complete knowledge of the situation, lest such retaliation prove horribly wrong. He came to the crossroads not knowing (οὐκ εἰδώς, 273) whom he met and would not have retaliated as he did had he known (although he insists that the provocation was sufficient—even *had* he known he would still not be guilty). At the time of his birth and exposure, on the other hand, although he had done no wrong to Laius, he received one from him, who had full knowledge of what he was doing (εἰδότων, 274). Oedipus' experience yields a double application. On the one hand it suggests the possibility that the chorus does not yet know who *he* truly is and should be wary of applying the principle of retribution, lest they later find themselves in his own unfortunate position. On the other hand it suggests that for them to expel him once they do learn who he is would be as unfair as Laius' exposure of him as a helpless baby.

In this presentation to the chorus Oedipus shows his general adherence to the traditional values and ethical code to which the chorus subscribes, so that the two parties meet on a common ground of piety. At the same time, he introduces an understanding of religion that is remarkable for the degree to which it requires not only obedience and knowledge but also depth of insight and understanding. The chorus has defined its religious principles in its application of the prohibitions and restrictions it involves, one which is captured and sustained in the negatives and alpha privatives that characterize the chorus' language throughout the play.[61] Oedipus, on the other hand, stresses the need for *interpretation* in matters of religion and shows the inadequacy of so literal-minded and fearful a piety. Their contrasting views of religion are further developed in the advice the chorus gives him later in the scene, when they share with him their expertise on the rites of appeasement to the Eumenides: "I wish to advise you now on what is best for you" (464). Here for the first time in the play Oedipus officially addresses the chorus as friends (φίλτατε, 465).[62] "In what way, teach me" (διδάσκετε, 468) says Oedipus, and later "teach me further" (προσδίδασκε, 480). They promise that if he will perform the rites they will continue to support him, but if he does not they will be fearful (δειμαίνοιμι, 492) for him.

In serving here as teachers to Oedipus, the chorus both acknowledges the counsel he had provided them and establishes a pattern in which they instruct each other, employing that principle of reciprocity that they earlier had used against him. Yet this in turn provides the occasion for another lesson in piety. The instructions they give Oedipus on the rite are punctilious and exactingly correct, and they hint that if he is unable to perform them another may make the prayer in his place (488). The kind of substitition they would approve has plenty of precedent in Greek tragedy, but when Oedipus authorizes Ismene to act on his behalf he adds a crucial qualification:[63]

> For I think that one person can make this payment for thousands, if he
> approaches with good intention (εὔνους).
>
> (498–99)

While it has been objected that Oedipus' liberal sentiment here is no
more than a justification for Ismene's acting on his behalf (he cannot,
of course, leave the stage himself), it also characterizes a more flexible
view of religious matters generally: for Oedipus the efficacy of a rite
performed on behalf of another depends on one's spiritual condition,
one's motives and intentions.[64] As we watch Ismene and Antigone
arrange their respective duties and care for their father, it is clear that
Oedipus' more liberal approach to ritual matters derives from his own
experience, from the care these "friends" have grown accustomed to
ministering to one another. Oedipus extends the principle on doing
on behalf of others from the merely personal into the religious. Ismene
expresses her need to learn (μαθεῖν, 504) from the chorus the proper
location for the rites, and they in turn offer to help her with anything
else she may need. In the *kommos* that follows we hear Oedipus present a more emotional self-defense against the charges of parricide and
incest when the chorus, perhaps emboldened by its secure relationship with the hero, expresses its desire to inquire (πυθέσθαι, 511),
hear (ἀκοῦσαι, 518) and learn (μαθεῖν, 543) about his past. They are
able to extract this account from Oedipus only with difficulty; they
ask him to yield (στέρξον, 519; cf. 7) and obey (πείθου, 520) and
finally win their wish by appealling again to that reciprocity on which
they have built their relationship.

The arrival of Theseus provides another opportunity for Oedipus
to serve as wise counselor, and the construction of their exchange is
similar to that of Oedipus and the chorus. Theseus delivers a long
speech (551–68) in which he asks Oedipus to declare what he wants,
establishing in the process both his authority and humanity. He and
Oedipus enter into a dialogue in which Oedipus reveals the situation,
although only partially and obscurely. Oedipus' reference to future
hostilities between Athens and Thebes occasions a long speech in
which he expounds on the mysteries of change in human affairs. This
demonstration of wisdom and goodwill wins praise from Theseus and
further guarantees of his safety.

As is often remarked, Theseus provides as perfect an example of
noble virtue as is to be found in tragedy and serves as an idealized

image of Athens itself. His concern for the suppliant is demonstrated in the prompt attention he gives to the report of Oedipus' arrival. He declares his pity (οἰκτίσας, 556) for Oedipus, recalling his own experience as a stranger and the hardships he once endured: because of his special sympathy, no stranger shall ever be denied his protection. Theseus is also conspicuous for his confident attitude toward his own intelligence. Even as he provides a detailed description of the appearance of Oedipus (551ff.), he boasts to have inferred his identity even as he was en route to Colonus, thereby eliminating the need for Oedipus to make a long introductory speech. His language is characterized by the force and frequency with which he uses verbs to know (ἔγνωκα 553, ἐξεπίσταμαι 554, οἶδα 562, ἔξοιδα 567) in his first speech alone. Indeed, in his compassion, agility of mind, and readiness to act swiftly and decisively he calls to mind Oedipus himself as he was presented at the beginning of *Oedipus the King*, both of them clear-headed and effective leaders in the prime of life.

What Theseus clearly expects from Oedipus is a conventional suppliant's request (προστροπήν, 558), and he is confident of his ability to understand and save (συνεκσῴζειν, 566) his suppliant. What he gets instead is a baffling series of riddles and half-answers complicated by politics, the mysteries of the gods, and Oedipus' own character. In their long exchange one senses Theseus' mounting frustration as he attempts to understand the nature of Oedipus' summons. Theseus tells his guest to instruct him in his needs (δίδασκε, 560), and as Oedipus builds to an answer, he declares again "teach me this now, that I may learn" (τοῦτ' αὐτὸ νῦν δίδασχ' ὅπως ἂν ἐκμάθω, 575). But Oedipus proves a trying teacher. He defers an explanation of the nature of his gift until his death: Theseus will learn "in time" (χρόνῳ μάθοις, 580). The favor Oedipus requests (that he be buried in Athens) seems so small as to be hardly worth the asking, and when Theseus learns of Thebes' efforts to bring Oedipus back and calls him a fool for his stubborn refusal to return, Oedipus tells him to hold his criticism until he understands (μάθῃς, 593), which prompts yet another request for instruction (δίδασκε, 594). When Theseus assumes that the evils (κακά, 595) Oedipus mentions refer to his parricide and incest, he is told in essence "of course not, everyone already knows about that" (597). Then Oedipus stymies the king once again with his prophecy that Thebes will someday be "beaten down" (605) by Athens.

Theseus has impressed us with his intelligence and his worldly experience. He begins and ends his opening speech with references to time: to the past (ἔν τε τῷ πάρος χρόνῳ, 551) and what he had heard about Oedipus, and to the future (τῆς εἰς αὔριον . . . ἡμέρας, 567–78) that is no more secure for one man than another. But when Theseus inquires how relations between the two states could become bitter (πικρά, 606), Oedipus exposes the limits of the young king's world view and the advantages of the perspective provided by age and long time (ὁ παγκρατὴς χρόνος, 609; ὁ μύριος χρόνος, 618–19). He addresses him almost paternally and calls him his friend (φίλτατε):[65]

> Beloved son of Aegeus, the gods alone know neither old age nor death, but all else is confounded by all-powerful time. The earth's strength wanes, that of the body is weakened, trust withers as mistrust flourishes, and the spirit never stays the same, neither among men who are friends nor between cities. To some now, to others at some later time, things of joy become bitter and then once again kindly.
>
> (607–15).

"Bitter" (πικρά, 615) returns to Theseus' question (606) and looks specifically at the relationship of Athens and Thebes.[66] In old age and death humanity meets those conditions that distinguish it from divinity. For Oedipus, the phenomena of time and change are seen as dreadful intrusions but also as part of a larger process that applies to all aspects of life, material, political, and spiritual. He reveals these vicissitudes as a source of wisdom, and by beginning with a reference to old age and death—for him not vague abstractions but present or imminent realities—he lays claim to a personal experience with the lessons that he gives. He knows firsthand of the degeneration of the body (σώματος, 610; cf. 266), of the death of trust and the flourishing of mistrust (πίστις . . . ἀπιστία, 611; cf. 950), though he allows the listener to supply the evidence that makes his speech credible, his own treatment at the hands of his friends and city.

As striking as his betrayal and banishment by Thebes are the changes that time has brought to his own consciousness and his attitude toward his own guilt. His earlier words on the aftermath of his self-punishment have less to do with "reconciling" the play with *Oedipus the King* than with showing the change of heart he has undergone, and they provide a parallel mediation on the themes of time and change:

... for during the immediate period, when my anger was seething, it was my deepest desire to die or be put to death by stoning, but no one seemed willing to help me with what I wanted. But after a time (χρόνῳ), when my grief had mellowed and I learned (ἐμάνθανον) that my anger had gotten away from me and my punishment was greater than my crimes, it was then the city forced me out of the land, after all that time (χρόνιον).

(433–41)

There is no more dramatic illustration of the kind of change that has come from the meeting of long time, suffering, and nobility than that which Oedipus himself has undergone, as he has come to distinguish in himself the difference between what one critic has called ceremonial as opposed to moral guilt.[67] Ironically, Oedipus will provide an exception to the principles of time and change he preaches in the eternal protection he will afford from his grave. When later he prepares to instruct Theseus in the sacred mysteries, he gives the young ruler further instruction in the mysteries of time: "I will teach you (διδάξω), son of Aegeus, what is appointed for this city, things not to be marred by age (γήρως ἄλυπα)" (1518–19), as if to contrast the gift he offers and the aged body that is its vehicle. The protection Oedipus offers Athens is like that of the olive tree, which also stands outside the world of time and corruption: no one young or old (οὐ νεαρὸς οὐδὲ γήρᾳ συνναίων, 702–3) shall ever destroy it, for it stays under the watchful eyes of Moirian Zeus and Athena. In this way the mysteries that Oedipus will describe to Theseus as being immune to age and that will be located in the wooded grove are linked with the sacred olive groves that protect the city and are themselves untouched by age and time.[68]

Oedipus' dialogue with Theseus is no less impressive than his earlier exchange with the chorus. They speak for a second time in wonderment, telling Theseus of "the kinds of things like this" Oedipus has been promising and vouchsafing for his intent to carry through with them (629–30). Theseus, not to be outdone by this tour de force, responds to Oedipus' goodwill (εὐμένειαν, 630–31) not with words but deeds, offering Oedipus not only the protection due an ally or suppliant but the rights of a citizen (ἔμπολιν, 637). In the process of their dialogue Oedipus and Theseus establish a mutual relationship, and the counsel Oedipus offers is the more striking for the intelligence and self-sufficiency with which Theseus is characterized. In the following scene with Creon, Theseus will be again characterized primarily as a man of action and will in fact so characterize himself (1143–44),[69] a role more traditionally associated with the young. That role is anticipated here when Theseus puts a limit on Oedipus' instruction and a halt to his nervous questions about his security: "do not teach me what it is necessary to *do*" (μὴ δίδασχ' ἃ χρή με δρᾶν, 654). When Oedipus objects that "you do not know (οὐκ οἶσθα) the threats . . . " (656), Theseus reacts in a short speech that is the mirror of the first: as if to emphasize what he *does* know, he uses the verb οἶδα (I know) three times (656, 662, 666) to describe the protection he guarantees. At the end of the play Oedipus will briefly resume his political education of Theseus. With Thebes again clearly in mind he speaks of the ease with which so many cities become violent (καθύβρισαν, 1535; cf. 960) and of how the gods never fail to catch a man who "disregarding religion turns toward madness." Yet even as he warns Theseus to eschew such behavior, he allows that "you already know such things as I would teach you about" (ἐκδιδάσκομεν, 1539).

THE LESSONS OF OEDIPUS: II

As Burton has noted, the tranquil imagery of the first stasimon, which sings of the beauty and blessings of Colonus and Attica, recalls the atmosphere of the opening scene when Antigone first described the beauty of the grove.[70] In addressing its song to Oedipus (ξένε . . . ἵκου, 668–69), the play reaches a point of rest and effects a kind of closure. The hero's social and political reintegration is firmly established, his security has been guaranteed, and vital new human relationships have been built. Theseus has left him under the watchful eye of the chorus, whose friendship with the hero is no less secure than that with the king. In what remains of the play, as Oedipus is confronted in turn by Creon, Polyneices, and finally death itself, we may watch him with an eye to how old age reacts to such misfortune. Nowhere in the play is the subject of old age addressed so directly as in the third stasimon (1211–48), which comes in the middle of this series of crises. As Oedipus awaits the appearance of Polyneices, one more in this series of griefs, the chorus looks on with pity and reflects on the burdens of old age.[71] When they first saw Oedipus, they declared him "unhappy in life, long of life" (δυσαίων μακραίων τε, 151–52), and this ode draws out the relationship between the two ideas. They begin the strophe (1211–23) in a manner appropriate to their characterization, appealing to the traditional maxim of the proper measure (τοῦ μετρίου, 1212; τοῦ δέοντος, 1220). The man who hopes for a greater portion of life than is fitting is a fool, they observe, for the "long days" (μακραὶ ἁμέραι) of a long life simply lay up a great store of griefs (πολλὰ . . . λύπας ἐγγυτέρω), and the old man can no longer see life's delights (τὰ τέρποντα). To such a man death, joyless and impartial to all alike, comes as a final deliverance from life's sufferings (ὁ δ᾽ ἐπίκουρος ἰσοτέλεστος . . . θάνατος ἐς τελευτάν, 1220–23).

In the antistrophe the chorus extends the argument from long life to existence as a whole: here old age concentrates and epitomizes the misery that is the human condition:

> Not to be born is best by every possible account. But once born, to go back as quickly as possible from where one came is easily second best. For once a man leaves behind youth and all its carefree frivolities, what pain, what trouble stays away? what suffering is not at hand? murder, faction, strife, battles, and envy. And then last comes his portion of despicable old age: infirm, unsociable, loveless, wherein dwell together all the worst of ills.
>
> (1225–38)

The stanza is remarkable for its negative and degenerative view of life, which takes the form of a survey of the male life course in three stages. Youth (τὸ νέον) is best, but only because it is ignorant of the true horror of life and is busy expending its energies in trivial pursuits (κούφας ἀφροσύνας).[72] The stage that follows, which we can identify generally as manhood, suddenly finds itself plunged into life's hardships, here offered in a depressing little catalogue the terms of which are particularly appropriate to the fortunes of Polyneices and Eteocles.[73] The stanza comes to a climax in its account of contemptible (κατάμεμπτον) old age: it is infirm, unsociable, loveless (ἀκρατὲς, ἀπροσόμιλον, ἄφιλον). The string of privatives that modifies gêras links old age in the antistrophe with death in the strophe, where the "fate of Hades" (Ἄιδος . . . μοῖρα) is similarly described as "without the wedding song, the lyre and dancing" (ἀνυμέναιος, ἄλυρος, ἄχορος, 1222–23). Neither here nor anywhere in the play does the chorus say anything positive about old age. Like death, to which it is a prelude, old age is regarded only in terms of its deprivations and is home to the pick of life's evils (κακὰ κακῶν). As we have seen, the use of such negative epithets to locate the essential and unchanging features of old age has a long tradition in epic and lyric.[74] In tragedy Euripides' describes *gêras* as "gray," "bitter," and "sorrowful," and Sophocles himself elsewhere describes old age as "baneful" and "white."[75] Yet for sheer poetic effect the triple anaphora of these paralleled epithets is perhaps unsurpassed.

Because the sentiment of the third stasimon—best is not to be born, second best to die soon—is frequent in Greek literature, and because it is expressed with chilling beauty here, it is often given a wide application. In the *Birth of Tragedy* Nietzsche generalized from the third stasimon to the whole of Greek culture: "the Greek knew and felt the terror and horror of existence," a vision that gave birth to the need for Greek tragedy. Similarly, the verses are often said to represent the play's "view" of old age or the feelings of the aged poet himself.[76] But it is crucial to keep these verses in context. Just as the piety and patriotism of the earlier *kommoi* and odes are carefully fitted to the character of the chorus and to the situations in which they were sung, the reflections on old age are also the product of a particular chorus at a particular dramatic moment. Indeed, the text itself seems to insist on this. The language is marked by the conventions that have characterized the chorus and the descriptions of Colonus throughout, in particular the use of alpha privatives and triplets, so that the triple anaphoras used of death and old age are linked as closely as possible with the place and the idioms of the chorus.

The chorus begins its reflections on old age by declaring the subjectivity of the view it offers—the man who hopes for long life is a fool "in my eyes" (ἐν ἐμοί, 1214). And in the transition to the second strophe the chorus refers to itself again: "in this [old age and its evils] this man here is wretched, not I alone" (ἐν ᾧ τλάμων ὅδ'—οὐκ ἐγὼ μόνος, 1239). The relationship that the chorus sees between itself and the protagonist calls to mind the fourth stasimon of *Oedipus the King*, which is sung upon the revelation of Oedipus' parricide and incest. In that ode the Theban chorus finds in Oedipus a model of human existence (παράδειγμα, 1193) that has altered their view of life and shown that happiness is nothing more than a seeming to be so: "with you and your fate as my model, wretched Oedipus, I count no mortal happy" (1194–96). In *Oedipus at Colonus* the chorus again finds in the hero a model of old age that applies to them.[77] Yet the relationship between Oedipus and the paradigm he represents is in an important sense reversed from that in the earlier play, and the language of 1239 reminds us that this conception of old age is not one that they discover in Oedipus and then apply to themselves but rather one that they *have brought to Oedipus from outside*. The model of old age is in fact the one by which these elders already regard themselves as wretched (τλάμων), and which they here determine fits his circumstances as well. This difference between the two odes reflects the relationship between the chorus and Oedipus in each play. In *Oedipus the King*, the chorus of Theban citizens is defined in terms of the distance between itself and their king, who to this point might otherwise have seemed a model of happiness and good fortune. In *Oedipus at Colonus* these elders regard themselves and Oedipus by what they have in common, and their sympathy in the present ode is another demonstration of their solidarity with him.

As in other respects this chorus typifies the conventions of the elderly chorus, so we must look to tragedy for the context of this ode, and here again there is much that is distinctively Euripidean. In this version of the adage that "not to be born is best" one hears echoes of Euripides' *Bellerophon*: "I say for my part that I agree with what people say everywhere, that it is best for a man not to be born."[78] The reflections on old age are reminiscent of several passages in Euripides. A character in the lost *Oenomaus*, presumably the play's namesake, says that "any mortal who wishes to arrive at accursed old age (δυσώνυμον . . . γῆρας) does not reason well. For long life (μακρὸς . . . αἰών) gives birth to countless miseries."[79] In *Suppliant Women*, old Iphis speaks of his hatred of old age and of those who seek to prolong life unnaturally through potions and charms (1108–13). The sentiment and context recall in particular the second stasimon of Euripides' *Heracles*. As with Oedipus' treatment by Creon, the chorus of elders stand helpless before the violence that Lycus does to Amphitryon, Megara, and the children, and they too make a token attempt at resistance (253–57). And when Heracles then like Theseus here comes to the rescue in the nick of time, they sing of the hardships of old age in terms that are clearly meant to apply to both themselves and Amphitryon.

> Youth is a thing I hold dear (φίλον). But old age lies ever upon my head like a burden heavier than the rocks of Aetna, and its darkness is a veil upon the light of my eyes. I would not choose the wealth of Asia's king-

doms or palaces filled with gold before youth, best in wealth, best in poverty. But miserable and murderous old age I despise (τὸ δὲ λυγρόν φόνιόν τε γῆρας μισῶ). Let it go beneath the waves and come no more to men's houses and cities but instead be borne aloft on wings high in the air.

(637–54)

In the second strophe the chorus finds some compensation for old age in the joy of their own musicmaking: they will never stop singing of the Graces and the Muses and Memory, or again of the victory of Heracles, despite their age, as long as they have wine and the lyre and the flute. Like the "old swan" that sings from "hoary throat" (κυκνὸς ὣς γέρων ἀοιδὸς πολιᾶν ἐκ γενύων), they will sing on in praise of Heracles (692–94).

The chorus' view of old age in *Oedipus at Colonus* is if anything even more pessimistic.[80] Yet here as always in Sophocles we must inquire precisely what kind of *value* we are to put upon this reading, what kind of weight we are to give the tragic construction of old age that they offer. Although the chorus believes that Oedipus illustrates its concept of old age, we need to keep in mind the limits of their perspective and the extent to which it is embedded in its own character and a particular set of tragic conventions. As a repository of traditional beliefs the Sophoclean chorus often reveals the limitations of its assumptions and values. Whitman, speaking of the Sophoclean chorus generally, describes it as a "symbol of the inadequacy of everyday morality to judge the ultimate questions," and Bowra suggests that the chorus in this play represents "ordinary uninstructed opinion."[81] We have seen how the chorus' traditional and literal view of religion,[82] similarly expressed in negative terms, is contrasted with the beliefs and practices of Oedipus and prompts lessons in piety from him. We should not take the construction of old age as "infirm, unsociable, loveless" at simple face value but instead ask what kind of response Oedipus and the play as a whole make to this characterization. The series of encounters in which Oedipus faces Creon, Polyneices, and finally death itself respond in so direct and sequential way to the terms of the chorus' lament that the triplet can be regarded as a key to its structure. A closer examination of these epithets and their relation to this dramatic sequence allows a reading of the hero that does not simply deny the chorus' perspective but reveals it as a partial and inadequate reading of the events that occasion it.

It is in the wake of the conflict with Creon that the chorus describes old age as weak or infirm (ἀκρατές): a scene in which Creon tells them to their faces "do not give orders where you have no power" (μὴ κρατεῖς, 839); in which he seeks to execute his plan to locate Oedipus' corpse where he will have no power over himself (σαυτοῦ κρατοῖς, 405); and in which Oedipus, his daughters, and the chorus itself all become victims of Creon's violence. The theme of the weakness of old age is not otherwise prominent in Sophocles.[83] On the other hand, it is emphatic in the male characters of Euripides as we saw in the previous chapter—indeed, there is perhaps no better exemplar of this tradition than the enfeebled old hero of *Phoenician Women*. In *Oedipus at Colonus* the hero's physical weakness has been emphasized repeatedly in the play's stagecraft and in his own words (501–2), and the scene with Creon repeatedly speaks of the elderly in terms of their inability to *do* (δρᾶν). At the approach of Creon and his escort the chorus seeks to comfort Oedipus: "though I may be old, the strength of this country has not grown old (γεγήρακε σθένος)" (726–27). Creon, quick to size up the situation, sees their anxiety and assures them that he comes "not wishing to do anything (δρᾶν τι), for I am an old man and I know that I have come to a city that has great strength (σθένουσαν)" (732–34). Directing his remarks not at Oedipus (patronizingly referred to as "this man here" at 735) but the chorus, Creon uses his age as a *captio benevolentiae* and trots out his credentials. Referring again to his long life (τηλικόσδε, 735), he emphasizes the fact that he is the appointed representative "of all the Thebans," sent on this embassey to persuade Oedipus to return to Thebes.[84] He addresses Oedipus in words that echo those of Antigone (ὦ ταλαίπωρ' Οἰδίπους, 740, cf. 14) and appears to respect his age (γέρον, 745), and he delivers a speech full of sympathy and an invitation to come home quietly to those who will take care of him.[85] It is hard to decide whether this show is put on entirely for the benefit of the chorus or whether Creon actually expects that age has made Oedipus gullible enough to swallow it. In either event, Oedipus begins his lengthy response by calling Creon a sophist in everything but name, exposing Creon's wise and diplomatic manner as nothing but a mask for his cruel manipulation.[86]

Creon's disclaimers about the inability of old age to *do* belie the violence that is already at work off-stage against Ismene and that is then turned against Antigone and Oedipus, first signaled in Oedipus' challenge to Creon to seize him "against the will of (βίᾳ) his allies"

(815). The following lines are filled with references to Creon precisely as a doer (ἔργῳ 817, πράσσεις . . . εἴργασαι 825, δρᾷς 829, 835). On the other hand, the elderly chorus, faced with Creon's violence and Oedipus' desperate plea, "what will you *do*?" (τί δράσετε, 823), pushes up against the limits of Greek scenic convention and comes closer here than anywhere else in tragedy to making physical contact with the actors.[87] In the exchange at 833–42, the chorus threatens resistance as Antigone is dragged away. Helpless by reason of Creon's power, their old age, and the paradox of inaction that circumscribes their role, they issue a desperate call to arms and cry out that the city is being attacked by force (σθένει). The theme is sustained in Antigone's cries that she is helpless (οὐδὲν σθένω, 846) before Creon's force (πρὸς βίαν, 845). It is a mark of his shamelessness that he attempts to exploit the theme even as he would drag off Antigone and Oedipus: it is Oedipus, he claims, who is acting (δρᾷς . . . εἰργάσω), he who is working "against the will of (βίᾳ) his friends" (854). As the chorus tries to block his exit, and Creon threatens to abduct Oedipus himself (πεπράξεται, 861), his own words point up the contradiction he has tried to sustain: "I shall drag him away by force (βίᾳ), even if I am alone and slow with age (χρόνῳ βραδύς)" (875). As he publicly acknowledges the *hybris* (883) of which he is guilty, the action reaches a second crescendo and the chorus concludes with yet another alarm.

But the episode also strikes a contrast between the weakness of old age and the wisdom that in some sense compensates for this. Creon uses this countertheme as the basis for his introduction, in which he makes a clear bid for the role of elder statesman and wise counselor, and the idea is picked up at 791 when Oedipus exposes Creon's real intentions and challenges him: "am I not wiser (ἄμεινον . . . φρονῶ) than you in the affairs of Thebes?" Creon retaliates with the charge that whereas old age *ought* to bring wisdom with it, Oedipus is still as foolish as ever:

> You fool! Not even after all these years (τῷ χρόνῳ) do you seem to have developed any wisdom (φρένας). Or do you live to be an insult to old age (λῦμα τῷ γήρᾳ τρέφῃ)?"
>
> (804–5).

Creon proceeds to ridicule him for his scant intelligence (νοῦς, 810). It is telling that Theseus, before Creon has said a word in his defense, condemns him as a disgrace to both his city and his age: "your many years have made you both old and foolish" (γέρονθ' ὁμοῦ... καὶ τοῦ νοῦ κενόν, 930–31). Accused by Theseus of having committed (δέδρακας, 911) indignities against Oedipus, Creon attempts the argument Oedipus had earlier used with the chorus (266–67, 271): he was not so much doing as retaliating (πεπονθὼς... ἀντιδρᾶν, 953; cf. 959) for the wrong Oedipus had done him in cursing him. He concludes with a play for sympathy by presenting himself as the underdog, one who though old (τηλικόσδε, 959), weak and alone will try to fight back (956–59), and later when he is ordered to lead the way to the girls he even complains of his own weakness (1018).

Oedipus begins his passionate self-defense, his longest speech in the play, by referring to the cruelty with which Creon has brought up the charges of parricide and incest.

> Oh you shameless arrogance, which old man do you think you are insulting in this, me or yourself?
>
> (961–92)

Oedipus here makes explicit what language and stagecraft will have already suggested—that he and Creon are "rival" elders, each arguing their cases before the chorus of elders for the "prize" of Oedipus himself.[88] The hero rightly argues that whatever Creon can find to say about him, he is himself the more disgraced for the effrontery with which he charges it. Creon's wisdom is finally shown to be as shallow as his sympathy. It is telling that at one point Oedipus contests his claims about the murder of Laius by challenging him to "teach" (δίδαξον, 969) him otherwise, and that he closes his speech by referring to the lesson that Creon will learn (ἐκμάθῃς, 1012) about the kind of a city he has come to in attempting to steal a suppliant old man (τὸν ἱκέτην γέροντ' ἐμέ, 1008).

The violence to which Oedipus is subjected evokes the chorus' feeling for the infirmity of old age and the weakness of the individual *gerôn*, a response not unlike that of the elderly choruses of *Children of Heracles* or *Heracles* to Lycon's abuse of Amphitryon or Copreus' violence against Iolaus. Yet it is significant that the play as a whole does not regard strength (σθένος) or power (κράτος) in terms of age but defines them and their cognates throughout in social and political terms. When Ismene first reports the recent oracle that tells of the

power (cf. κράτη, 392) Oedipus will have over his enemies, he is confused and at first understands the reference in terms of physical
power.[89] Yet it is this political sense of power that informs the play: the
power of the kingship of Theseus coveted by both Creon and Oedipus'
sons; the power due to the city that has control of Oedipus' body in life
and in death; the military might by which Theseus prevails over Creon
and that Polyneices will bring from Argos to Thebes.[90] The power that
Theseus brings to bear against Creon is only that which he wields as
leader of the community, the city's ageless strength (σθένος) with
which the chorus attempted to reassure Oedipus (726–27). It is a crucial difference between this play and the others cited that Oedipus is
assaulted not by a young man but by an elder like himself, one who for
all his rhetoric about the weakness of age relies openly on the force of a
group, not on his own individual strength.

Creon has been called "the one thorough villain in Sophocles."[91]
While it is true that one will look in vain for redeeming features in his
character, it also has more depth and complexity than is appreciated
and the importance of his age is not often observed. This old man, so
quick with disclaimers about his weakness and so fluent in the
rhetoric of old age, is still thoroughly beholden to force and quick to
call upon it. Unable either to adapt to the limits that age brings or like
Oedipus to draw upon the spiritual potential that is in it, he takes
refuge in a kind of brutality that is only the exaggerated strength and
vigor of youth. Creon's tyrannical behavior is not only hypocritical but
also a denial of the impotence of his old age. *Oedipus at Colonus* is not a
play that simply pits the strength of youth against the weakness of old
age but one in which the power of the community is shown to be used
by young or old justly or unjustly—it is not Oedipus' age that has
endangered him but Creon's misuse of the power of Thebes, just as it is
the strength of Athens that saves him. Oedipus' alleged weakness,
moreover, belies other more subtle strengths than those kinds of physical or political power that have been emphasized in the play. There is
of course the power of his curses and of the fate that has left him blind
but not speechless (cf. ἄφωνον, 865; ἄναυδος, 1274). There is the
power he has by the sheer force of his own Promethean will, and I use
the word advisedly: he will not allow others, whether it be Creon,
Polyneices, or even Theseus himself, to interfere with the course on
which he is set, even if all he can do to enforce it is to lay claim to a
place to sit and refuse to move from it.[92] There is the simple strength of

the truth by which Oedipus reveals Creon's hypocrisy and accounts for the real circumstances of his expulsion. And there is the strength that he has from those who have remained or become his friends, and who have not only protected him but listened to him and simply loved him in return.

That old age is constitutionally unsociable and disagreeable (ἀπροσόμιλον) is a frequent theme in tragedy. Sophocles draws upon it in *Ajax*, where the grief that the hero's aged parents will feel at the news of his death is set against the anger Telemon will vent on the hero's brother. Standing over the body of Ajax, Teucer imagines the abuse that is in store for him on his return to Salamis:

> And I suppose that Telamon, your father and mine, will greet me with a happy face and kind looks when I come without you? Of course not. Why, even when things are going well it is not his way to smile. . . . Those are the sort of things which that irascible man, so difficult in old age , is going to say, one whose anger brings him to quarrel over nothing.
>
> (1008–18)

But "unsociable" especially calls to mind the ill-tempered nature of Euripides' old men, the nastiness and small-mindedness that he develops with such skill in Pheres in *Alcestis* and Tyndareus in *Orestes*. It is behind Agave's complaint in *Bacchae* about how "disagreeable and scowl-faced old age makes men" (1251–52), and the chorus' comment in *Andromache*, in the middle of the agon between Peleus and Menelaus, that old people show no self-control and are hard to control because of their sharp tempers (727–28; cf. 689).[93]

By the time the chorus sings the third stasimon it has experienced the volatile temper of Oedipus. Oedipus himself has referred to the excesses of his temper (θυμός, 434, 438), and Theseus felt its sting when he called Oedipus a fool for clinging to his anger (θυμός, 492). Its power was unleashed against Creon, who warned that Oedipus' rage (ὀργή) has always been his ruin and that "in time" he would come so see how he was harming himself (852–55). But even more striking will be the hero's anger when he is instructed by Theseus (cf. δίδασκέ με, 1154) of the newly arrived suppliant. Oedipus speaks of Polyneices with the utmost anger and contempt (στυγνός, 1173; ἔχθιστον, 1177), refusing to see him and asking Theseus not to force him to "yield" in this (1178; cf. 1184, 1201). He finally gives in, but only after

Theseus and Antigone have appealed to him directly. Antigone, who had earlier given her father valuable advice (171–73), again assumes the role of "young counselor" in order to persuade her father (πιθοῦ μοι, κεἰ νέα παραινέσω, 1182), a role the more striking for his earlier admonition that she and Ismene keep their account of their abduction short since "brief speech is sufficient for girls of your age" (1116).[94] Antigone reminds him of his obligations as father and argues that whatever his son's behavior these take precedence over his desire or right to retaliate. She reminds him of his bad temper (θυμὸς ὀξύς 1193, κακοῦ θυμοῦ 1193) and points to his blindness as a permanent reminder of its unfortunate consequences. She compares Oedipus to other fathers who have both bad sons and sharp tempers but manage to keep at least the latter under control.

The third stasimon is sung while Polyneices is en route, and although the chorus knows something of Polyneices from Oedipus' earlier speech to Ismene (337ff.), they will certainly feel that as son and suppliant he is deserving of at least a hearing. Oedipus' hard-heartedness here may well have struck them as an expression of the ill-temperedness and disagreeableness of old age and an instance of a type of father familiar to the theater. One function of the scene is to show that there is far more to Oedipus' anger than this, and that however excessive we find the curses with which he dismisses Polyneices, his anger springs from something far deeper and more immediate. Winnington-Ingram's careful study of the anger of Oedipus explains the hero's retaliation against his sons not only in relation to his destiny as *hêros* but also as "a wrathful passion rooted in human motive." In its human aspect it is "grounded in past experience," and the suffering he has endured evinces a retaliation that is not only within his rights but even to be expected within the structures of Greek morality; in its divine aspect this anger is given effective tragic shape in the way that Oedipus' fate is linked to the Erinyes-Eumenides, those spirits of vengeance in whose grove the hero will find his resting place and whose implacable nature the hero assumes.[95] But as Hester observes, when Oedipus curses his sons "he calls on the gods as a curser naturally does, not as a fellow-spirit, and his motivation is essentially human and personal."[96]

The scene with Polyneices is developed so as to emphasize the reasons for the old man's wrath, where his attempts to elicit sympathy not only provoke his father but rapidly prove an exercise in self-conviction. His speeches repeatedly if inadvertantly draw attention to the very issues for which his aged father has put on his "unapproachable, inexorable face" (τὸ δυσπρόσοιστον κἀπροσήγορον στόμα, 1277) and that are at the root of the "heavy wrath" (μῆνιν βαρεῖαν, 1328) he bears against him. The first sight of his father provokes a graphic description of his appearance:

> Oh, what am I to do, girls—weep first for my own misfortunes? or for those which I see in my aged father here, whom I find in exile in this foreign country with you two, dressed in rags whose horrible filth has grown old along with him, rotting to his side, his hair uncombed and blowing in the breeze atop his sightless face. And to complete the picture he carries his day's rations, his poor belly's need, along with him. Poor me, I learn all this far too late. And I testify that I come here the basest of men for the manner of your life: you need not ask of others what I am.
>
> (1254–66)

Polyneices' disgust at his father's condition strikes a strong contrast with the opening speech of Theseus, who treats Oedipus with pity and even deference. Easterling, who studies the scene in detail, notes how the "extraordinary tastelessness and artificiality" of this language suggest Polyneices' own uneasiness.[97] That he is so overwhelmed at the sight of Oedipus is clearly meant to suggest, as he himself admits, his long neglect of his father. It also serves to show us how far we have come in our own estimation of the hero: where Polyneices can see Oedipus only for his squalid exterior (like Creon, he speaks at first *about* Oedipus and in the third person, turning to him only at 1265), we have come to regard him more for his inner resources.

Polyneices' self-consciousness is reflected in his revealing references to care and nurturing (θρεπτήρια 1263, τροφαῖς 1266), which clearly allude to his own failure in regard to *gêrotrophia*, provision of the care he owes his father. As in his earlier speech to Ismene (337–52), Oedipus again dwells at length on the theme of *trophê* (nurture) and the gender reversal that has taken place in this respect between his sons and daughters:

> For it was you who fed me (ἔντροφον) with this suffering, you who drove me out, and because of you that I wander and beg from others what I need from day to day. If I hadn't had these two daughters to take care of me (τροφούς), I would be dead as far as you are concerned. But it is these two

who are my saviors, they my caretakers (τροφοί), they who are not women but men for sharing my suffering.

(1362–68)

Polyneices' and Eteocles' failure to render the kind of filial support that Athenians required by law involves a fundamental breach of the social order, and a failure to appreciate the cultural weight of this institution may lead us to more sympathy for Polyneices than is properly the case.[98] Yet Oedipus' anger at his sons involves more than their failure to meet their familial obligations. As his words make clear, it is not only the nurture itself but the symbolic value of the contract that concerns him. When Oedipus had earlier commented on his expulsion, he complained of how his sons "so dishonorably forced the one who begat them out of his fatherland" (τὸν φύσαντ᾽ ἐμὲ οὕτως ἀτίμως πατρίδος ἐξωθούμενον, 427–28). Here again Polyneices practically puts the words in his father's mouth. He makes the mistake of asking him not to dishonor him (ἄτιμον, 1278) and says that he is making war against Thebes because he "deemed it right" (ἠξίουν) that he rule because he was the older and his brother the younger "in birth" (γονῇ . . . γεραιτέρᾳ . . . φύσει νεώτερος, 1294–95).[99] In the heat of his anger Oedipus extracts from both these themes—the principle of seniority and the importance of honor—a more general lesson. In words that directly reflect the language of Polyneices, he says that he will lay his curses on them

so that the two of you may deem it right (ἀξιῶτον) to reverence your parents (τοὺς φυτεύσαντας) and not to dishonor (ἐξατιμάζητον) them, even if you are offspring (ἔφυτον) of a father who is blind. For these girls here did not treat me so.

(1376–78).

The issue arises again when Antigone attempts to persuade Polyneices to give up the expedition. When she asks him how *he* can be so angry (θυμοῦσθαι, 1420) as to destroy his own city, he reveals his sensitivity to the subject of age and honor.

It is shameful (αἰσχρόν) to live in exile, and though the older (πρεσβεύοντα) one to be laughed at like this by my brother.

(1422–23)

Ismene's earlier account of the brothers' quarrel also emphasized the importance of age, with the younger brother displacing and exiling the older (ὁ . . . νεάζων καὶ χρόνῳ μείων γεγὼς τὸν πρόσθε γεννηθέντα, 374–75).[100] Critics have often noted that unlike in *Phoenician Women*, where Polyneices is the younger, and *Seven Against Thebes* where the sons are perhaps to be considered twins, Sophocles makes Polyneices the older of the two. It has been suggested that the result is to make Polyneices more tragic and sympathetic here at the expense of our feelings for Oedipus.[101] This is true as far as it goes, but the effect is ultimately to undercut the very position that Polyneices is taking here. Even as his anger leads him to make war against his own city for the dishonor done him by someone younger, he has himself violated the honor of the elder who most deserves it.

Yet for Polyneices the issue of honor is a self-righteous smoke screen for his ambition, for the "scepters and thrones" (425, 448–49, 1354) that the brothers equally covet.[102] For Oedipus the issue of *trophê* is inseparable from that of the honor he is owed, and it is the dishonor (ἀτιμία) to which he has been subjected that fuels this mighty rage.[103] Indeed, what is perhaps most distinctive about the old age of Oedipus is his insistence on being treated with that same dignity with which he continues to conduct himself, that nobility that he applauds in Theseus and his daughters (569, 1042, 1640) and that is still so striking in him that it drew comment even from the stranger (75–76). In Euripides the helplessness of the elderly often makes them an object of shame even to themselves, reluctant to expect anything but pity and help from others. Oedipus repeatedly acknowledges his dependence on Antigone, so complete that she has become not only his caretaker but his "gerontagogue" (γερονταγωγεῖ, 348). Yet despite his abject situation Oedipus demands that he be treated honestly and respectfully. We have seen him stand up not only to his enemies but to the chorus and even to Theseus, whose criticism of him provoked a strong reaction (592–93). It is significant in this regard that Polyneices assumes precisely the opposite about him. In his attempt to evoke sympathy, he says that "you and I both live by *fawning upon* (θωπεύοντες) others" (1336–37). Yet we have seen Oedipus do nothing of the sort, and he comes closer to the truth when he says to Creon: "to you it is dear to *fawn upon* (θωπεῦσαι) the good name of Theseus" (1003). Oedipus' denunciation of Polyneices is, as Winnington-Ingram says, "a crescendo of human passion" in which

Oedipus speaks "not as a dispassionate judge but as an ill-used man brimming over with *thumos*."[104] It is no display of peevish old age, but an expression of anger at the neglect and dishonor he has received instead of the care and reverence he is owed, and in this respect it is very much the rage of an old man. One of the ironies of Creon's speech is his claim that "anger stops not with old age but only with death" (954–55).[105] Creon's claim is very much the truth—to be angry is but to be alive—but as the sentiment points there to the hypocrisy of his own anger it also looks ahead to the righteous anger Oedipus displays in response to what he sees as an assault on his dignity. When the chorus expresses their displeasure with Polyneices and asks him to leave at once (1397–98), we may perhaps infer that they have been moved by the ferocity of Oedipus' argument and the spirit of self-respect that is behind it, and we may be less willing to attribute the anger of Oedipus to disagreeable old age.

With the exit of Polyneices come the omens that herald Oedipus' death, where Oedipus' calm reaction to the thunder contrasts with the chorus' superstitious panic.[106] Here no less remarkable than his earlier anger is the courage with which Oedipus faces his end, the steadfastness with which he commits himself to his appointed destiny, and the composure with which he describes its terms to Theseus. In the final moments of life, Oedipus links his death to the will of the gods and speaks of it in terms that recognize it as god-decreed (θέσφατος, 1472), necessary (χρή, 1521), and fated (μοῖρα, 1521, 1546). Unlike the chorus, he does not allow the end of life to subsume its meaning as a whole. It is significant that where the chorus sees death as a deliverer (ἐπίκουρος, 1220) and sees in it for Oedipus a final escape from a lifetime of suffering (cf. 1556–78), Oedipus himself nowhere regards it as such. Oedipus' attitude toward death is revealed to stunning theatrical effect in his exit when the blind man becomes the leader of the leader (ἡγεμών, 289, 1542), as Theseus, Antigone, and Ismene follow him into the grove.[107]

In calling old age "unloved" (ἄφιλον) the chorus underscores the idea that it is despicable (κατάμεμπτον), even as the chorus in the *Heracles* spoke of youth as something beloved (φίλον) and of their hatred of old age (γῆρας μισῶ, 650). But the epithet speaks to the related point that in tragedy the elderly are so often alone and unprotected, without friends and loved ones (φίλοι) to defend them from abuse, neglect, and assault by others, a condition that provides the starting point of *Children of Heracles* and *Heracles* as well as *Trojan Women* and *Suppliant Women*. The theme of *philia* (love/friendship) is especially prominent at the end of the play and is expressed in terms that bear directly on the chorus' charge that old age is unloved. The chorus summons Theseus to come quickly with the news that Oedipus is preparing to return a kindness to his friends (φίλους, 1497). In the last words he delivers in person, Oedipus addresses Theseus as "most beloved of hosts" (φίλτατε ξένων, 1552) and blesses the man, his land, and his people. The theme comes to a climax in the messenger's speech. Just as the hero has bequeathed to his sons his hatred and curses as their proper portion (γέρας, 1396), he enfolds his daughters in his arms to share with them a final lesson:

> Children, on this day your father's life comes to an end. My time here is finished, and you will no longer have the hard task of taking care of me. It was difficult, children, I know. But all these labors are cancelled by a single word: love (τὸ . . . φιλεῖν). There is no one from whom you have so much love as from me. And now you will live the rest of your life without me.
>
> (1611–19)

The lines are testimony to the depth of his affection for his daughters, so clear throughout the play, and are a counterweight to the ferocity of his anger in the prevous episode. Yet as has been noticed, they leave us with a riddle. How can Oedipus can speak of the love he has given his daughters as adequate recompense for *their* suffering (μοχθήματα)? It is certainly not for being unaware or unappreciative. He has described their labors repeatedly and at length (344–56) and here admits that the care (τροφή) they have provided has been toilsome and difficult (δυσπόνητον, σχληράν). He has called his daughters his eyes and his walking staff. He has depended on them for his physical survival, advice, and comfort, news of Thebes and the latest oracles. He speaks of his love for them in almost gushing terms when Theseus returns the two safely to him, and their love for one another is often expressed in the most physical terms: kissing, embracing, lifting, and seating. Ismene has herself observed that children must complain of the labor they do for their parents (508–9). We have just had described for us the care they take in bathing and clothing their father in preparation for his death, a familiar task invested with a new meaning. What does he mean when he says that all their efforts are repaid by the love he gives them, cancelled out (λύει) in a single word?

The pattern we have observed in this play, in which Oedipus extrapolates from the data of his own experience to develop lessons for life, leaves us with one possible answer: that reflection has taught him the same lesson, and that he has felt in the love given him by his daughters a boon equal to the enormity of his suffering. We have seen how Oedipus can dismiss the gods' willingness to restore him in old age as a "cheap gift" (395). There is nothing he can be given in old age or death that can balance against what was lost in his fall from greatness. Yet in a final paradox Oedipus seems to suggest that in the small circle that encompassed him and his daughters and in the love they exchanged with each other there was recompense for his and their suffering. There is no need to look to other traditions to understand what Oedipus means here by "love," for the idea is located squarely within the ethic of reciprocity, of helping one's friends and harming enemies, which is at the heart of his dealings with others in life and death. Yet in a play in which so much emphasis has been placed on what friends (φίλοι) should *do* for each other, Oedipus here seems to suggest that the simple affection and gratitude he has given his daughters—indeed the only thing that he has been able to give them[108]—was itself a kind of doing and a fair return for all the palpable good they have done him. By focusing on the kind of substance love has in itself and in the ability of love to balance against even the most miserable life, Oedipus deepens the conventional ethic and extends the notion of φιλεῖν (love) beyond its customary bounds. In this enlarged ethic, love is not a zero-sum game but a mystery in which those who love (φίλοι) receive more for their love than it costs them.

It is not accidental that in the very next words we hear from Oedipus he addresses Theseus again as his friend (ὦ φίλον κάρα, 1631), nor that in the wake of the messenger's speech the dialogue is filled with references to φίλος and its cognates. As the daughters begin a final *kommos* for Oedipus, the characters reaffirm the bonds of love that unite them in their relationships: the chorus for their countrymen (φίλων, 1667), Antigone for the chorus (φίλοι, 1677), Ismene for Antigone, and Antigone for Ismene (φίλα, 1716, 1724), and the chorus twice for both girls (φίλαι, 1721, 1737), and even for Oedipus himself. Antigone gives a testimonial to her continuing love her Oedipus that is filled with new insight and mystery:

> And now I see that can be a kind of longing even for what was bad. For that which was in no way loved (φίλον) *was* loved (φίλον), as long as I kept him in my arms. Oh father, my love (φίλος), shrouded in eternal darkness beneath the earth, not even there shall you ever go unloved (ἀφίλητος) by me.
>
> (1697–1703)

As Oedipus' message of love has prompted these demonstrations, it has also engendered a deeper understanding of the relation between love, suffering, and commitment that Antigone clearly has taken to heart. She sees that precisely what was disgreeable about her father, that toil (πονή) that Ismene had said children owe their parents (508–9), which Oedipus agreed was difficult (δυσπόνητον, 1614), and for which she had given her life and her maidenhood, was itself even pleasant in that it became an opportunity to love her father. To the chorus' charge that old age is unloved (sustained in Polyneices' complaint of the "unlovely" old filth that clings to the old man (ὁ δυσφιλὴς γέρων γέροντι . . . πίνος, 1259–60), Antigone's speech provides a double response: not only was Oedipus much loved despite his age, but even in those aspects of his nature that seemed difficult (κακά)—old age, blindness, helplessness—love was at work. Oedipus' counsel represents a powerful exhortation to the daughters to continue to love, and one that is not just personal but also social in its implications. This is clear in the explosion of love among the characters at the end of the play and is implicit in Antigone's decision to return to Thebes to help her city and her brother. Thus while Oedipus' curses upon his sons will ultimately and ironically bring in their train the death of Antigone,[109] we are able to read her final exit as a statement of her own devotion to her loved ones rather than as an expression of tragic doom.

A NEW PARADIGM

In all of this it seems to me that Oedipus' behavior is rooted in a different paradigm of old age and himself as an old man than that assumed by the chorus, tragedy, or Greek culture generally. It is significant that nowhere in the play does Oedipus himself complain about old age. Crucial again are his words to Theseus: "the gods alone know neither old age nor death, but all else is confounded by all-powerful time" (607–8). Oedipus recognizes that human existence involves corruption and death. To rail against the necessity of such change is futile and foolish: like the gods, Oedipus does not battle against necessity (μὴ χρείᾳ πολεμῶμεν, 191). But as the hero embraces the human condition, so in old age paradoxically he yields to its limits and constraints. In setting the sufferings of old age in a different conceptual framework, this paradigm represents the transformation and the spiritualization of that passivity regarded by the chorus with such disgust. We have seen Oedipus suggest that the vicissitudes of life can be instructive and point to the lesson of contentment (στέργειν) that suffering, time and nobility have taught him (6–7). This contentment is not simply the realization of the treatment that he, as destitute beggar, must allow in order to live from day to day. This quality of acceptance and resignation in the face of what truly must be also lies at the heart of the attitude to old age he embodies, one that puts him in sharp contrast with the aggression and violence of Creon.

Throughout the play we have seen Oedipus come to terms with his past. As with his imminent death no less than his tragic past, the oracles he receives are the outward sign of the necessity of the fate that has been his. Oedipus has come to accept this destiny, even to identify with it. In his prayer to the Eumenides, he asks them not to be "ungracious to Apollo and me" (Φοίβῳ τε κἀμοί, 86), linking himself with the god and the oracles that have been at the source of his suffering.[110] Although he has reconciled himself to his fate, he continues to insist on the essential dignity of his life. Twice to the chorus and again before Creon and Theseus he defends himself against charges of parricide and incest. He recognizes his defiled condition, which keeps him from so much as touching Theseus in gratitude (1130–35), but he will not assume personal guilt for his deeds or allow himself to be publicly shamed for them. Defending himself against Creon's slander, he says that he will speak of these matters only because

> I will not be spoken of ill in this marriage or in the murder of my father
> for which you keep charging me and reproaching me so bitterly.
>
> (988–90)

Oedipus' repeated arguments for his innocence show how the aged hero has achieved, at painful cost, a sense of the essential integrity and inevitability of his own life.

Oedipus at Colonus supplants for a paradigm of helpless dependency one that acknowledges the passivity of old age but reserves for it a full measure of dignity and a relationship between the elderly and their community that is meaningful and mutual. The paradigm embodied in Oedipus we may call heroic, though not in the sense that it is restricted to the heroes of tragedy or is meant only to point up the distance between the heroic temper and the stuff of which ordinary mortals are made. The principles that guide the hero in his old age are not specific to the hero alone but are available to all. There is a real sense in which the passage through old age is a crisis that all must face and to some extent resolve. In a thoughtful essay on "The Virtues and Vices of the Elderly," which draws heavily on Eriksonian psychology, William May identifies the virtues, neither automatic with old age nor exclusive to the elderly, which provide the strength that is required to deal with the adversity of age and to flourish in the midst of them. May's list reads like a description of Oedipus and the resources on which he draws in the play: *courage*, which is not simple fearlessness but the ability to keep one's fears under control for one's own good; *patience*, which is not to be confused with passivity but is rather "purposive waiting . . . taking control of one's spirit precisely when all else goes out of control"; *wisdom*, which in respect to memory "characterizes the person who remains open to his or her past, without retouching, falsifying, or glorifying it"; and *integrity*, which is nothing less than the moral structure of the whole person:

> Persons of integrity, undivided and upright, do not say one thing while intending another. At one with themselves, they do not need to dissemble with others or deceive themselves.[111]

So too, Erikson himself in speaking of old age has described the condition simply as "integrity," a term that characterizes the successful completion of the life cycle. He identifies as its attributes the very qualities we have seen in Oedipus: an acceptance of one's destiny, an assumption of responsibility for one's life, and a defense of the dignity of one's life against all threats.[112] None of this need diminish the unique status of Oedipus in the classic Sophoclean sense. Indeed, the terms in which Oedipus completes his destiny are a further measure of the degree of his greatness, and his unwillingness to conform to his culture's assumptions about old age provides yet another index of that heroism.

So too, I cannot but believe that the urgency and passion that characterize Oedipus in this play are the product not only of his own nature but also of the imminence of his own death, which he declares even as the play gets under way. The knowledge that he will shortly die makes it incumbent on him to order his life not only for himself but for what he will leave behind. Oedipus seems to me, in a way that I find quite understandable, to be intent upon the story that will survive him—that it will be right, and will represent him fairly. One thing that is striking about the end of the play is the way it leaves us with two traditions: the ineffable mysteries of Oedipus' death and burial, those apocrypha which are for Theseus and his descendents alone to understand (cf. μαθήση, 1527; μανθάνειν, 1644), and a more general wisdom, one reflected in Oedipus' final words to his daughters on the value of love, which is published for all. And these two traditions correspond in turn to the two scenic areas, the unpolished rock and the rocky step, the sacred grove and the circle of elders. Indeed, in the very conventions of the messenger speech the poet shows how this second kind of wisdom becomes tradition, what the messenger himself calls a myth (μῦθος, 1581), as the teachings of Oedipus are given to Antigone and the messenger and in turn to the chorus and of course to us. And as we are treated to the spectacle of tradition in the making, we are reminded in this case of its origin in one who was both poet and elder himself. There is a final and delightful irony as we see the protagonist, intent to the end upon the tradition that will survive him, and the playwright who in the act of creating him shapes his own life, careful of the story that will be told of him and the denouement of which is the writing of the play itself. As a playwright who was enormously successful throughout life from his first competition at the age of twenty-eight until his posthumous victory with this play, Sophocles would hardly have made the case that wisdom belongs exclusively to the elderly. But as we remember the anecdotes about the poet in old age, it is not unreasonable to suggest that in the final year of his own life, as he recognized and confronted the obstacles which his culture and tradition placed before the resolution of the life course and the limits these put on life's possibilities, he found quiet opportunities for heroism in the act of poetry itself.

Epilogue

Indeed when I consider old age, I find four reasons why it is regarded
as a misfortune: first, because it keeps one from public activities; second, because it makes the body weaker; third, because it deprives one
of almost all physical pleasures; fourth, because it is not far removed
from death.

—Cicero, *De Senectute* , 15

IT is ironic that the discipline which is heir to the oldest extant study
in gerontology should have been so slow to take up the study of old
age and the elderly in classical antiquity. Gerontology and Classics
have always maintained something of a nodding acquaintance with
each other, due largely to the prestige enjoyed in both fields by Cicero's *De Senectute*. Historians of gerontology know to begin their studies of the discipline with discussion of this work, with a quotation or
two from the venerable Roman almost de rigueur. And classicists tend
to take a certain unwarranted satisfaction in the influence that Cicero's
work has had on this upstart discipline, an attitude that has an ana-
logue in Whitehead's famous description of the history of philosophy
as but a series of footnotes to Plato.

Although the scholarship on old age suggests not so much a field
as the foundations on which a field is currently under construction,
one is certainly better equipped to examine the subject now than was
the case even a decade ago. A spate of recent work has made it possible
to define boundaries, establish areas of common knowledge and
points of controversy, generate bibliographies, and propose research
agenda. Little of this material has been directly influenced by work in
gerontology, and this insularity is related to the resistance of classicists
to theory in general and to recent critical theory in particular: its models tend to be literary and historical and its methods so second nature
as not even to be thought to be methods. Yet here too classicists, like
other humanists, are becoming increasingly aware of the interdisci-
plinary nature of the subject and the need to look at materials and
methods outside the discipline as it is normally practiced.

It is hoped that this volume, both in its successes and its shortcomings, will serve to illustrate the enormous potential that this subject holds for classicists and perhaps even inspire a few to take up the subject first hand. The problems of studying old age and the elderly in classical Greece are the same as those that bedevil the study of socially marginal groups likes slaves or women, where we are also heavily reliant upon literary sources. This is offset somewhat by the abundance of the testimony of the ancients themselves, so that a view of old age in antiquity can be had in large part "in their own words." As we have noted, that this should be the case is itself something of a paradox. The elderly in ancient Greece, as a class if not as individuals, were at a distance from the traditional centers of power (political, legal, military), and the high profile that the subject carries in Greek literature shows that it was clearly an issue of both literary tradition and social concern. While we are fortunate in the sensitivity and depth of insight such ample first-person testimony affords, the purposes and the imaginative nature of these materials are often at odds with historical reconstruction, and we must avoid the temptation of assuming that what may be unique or even idiosyncratic views of old age necessarily reflect popular practice or perceptions. We need to move beyond models which assume that texts "reflect" the "attitudes" of their authors and beyond interpretations which explain one text simply by looking for an earlier source that has "influenced" the later. What is needed are ways of getting at the social implications of the sources, textual or material, and an effort to ask what kind of *meanings* these representations carry and to see their relation to other aspects of life: political, familial, spiritual.

The previous chapters have attempted to make some contribution to this end. The argument of this book has been that Greek representations of old age comprise a category of analysis that is fundamentally related to the poetic traditions and the social environments in which they are embedded, and that different treatments of old age are determined by the nature of these contexts as well as by the projects of specific works. As such, these texts are part of an ongoing conversation about old age, one that begins at least as early as Homer and that continues unabated until the end of the classical period. As I hope has been clear, there is no special immediacy nor any automatic kind of understanding that comes through literature, poetry in particular—indeed, the imaginative nature of these sources and the complexities of establishing their context make the task of interpretation all the more difficult. Yet taken as a whole, certain patterns within the tradition emerge. In Homer the representation of the elderly, who stand upon "the threshold of old age," is ambivalent; the grim prospects associated with old age are offset by some redeeming qualities, in theory if not always in practice. In Hesiod and the Homeric *Hymns*, in the lyric and elegiac tradition, and in Greek tragedy, the picture ranges with few exceptions from bleak to horrid. And the very pessimism of this tradition helps us to appreciate the iconoclastic force of Sophocles' *Oedipus at Colonus*, which attempts to fashion a portrait of old age that both recognizes the hardships of this life stage and locates on a different plane a new set of virtues and values that the tradition had not allowed.

There can be no doubt that the negativity of this tradition is related to serious cultural concerns about the nature of old age and the status of the elderly, and the changing character of these representations tells a kind of story in itself. The ambivalence in Homer's treatment of the elderly suggests the shifting status of old age in the emerging polis, as Greek culture distanced itself from its traditional and more conservative roots and as the political systems, formerly more inclusive in nature, revealed their implications for traditional constructions of prestige and authority. In Greek lyric we have noted the way in which the themes of sexuality and eroticism provide a set of metaphors for social participation: for old men, where the erotic disadvantage under which they attempt to love corresponds to their marginal political and social status; and for women, where the disparaging treatment of the sexuality of aged and aging females, one that is finally challenged in Sappho, suggests the kind of double exclusion under which aged Greek women lived. And in fifth century tragedy the frequency with which the elderly become paradigms of suffering may be connected to the kind of suffering that touched all Athenians but perhaps the elderly with special poignancy, as the city reeled under the vicissitudes of war and intellectual upheaval.

In the end, of course, one cannot but be struck by the frequency with which the elderly in Greek poetry become paradigms of suffering and offer the spectacle of human happiness shattered, stolen, or compromised. The idea finds epic representation in Homer in Priam, Phoenix, Nestor, Hecuba, Chryses, and Laertes; in lyric and elegy in the pathos and ridicule of their erotic predicament; and in the late fifth century in the distillations of tragic suffering provided by Sophocles and especially Euripides. But we also want to keep in mind the symbolic value of these scenes and their relation to the Greek vision of life as a whole, in particular in its competitive and agonistic dimension. The Greeks were clearly moved by the idea of tragedy in old age and the loss of happiness near the close of life. It is as though life were a kind of footrace: even though one might take the lead and hold it almost to the end, if one should stumble the whole race is lost. According to Herodotus (1.30–33), Solon's insistence that we look only to the end of life was such that he was willing to rank the elderly Tellus or the youthful Cleobis and Biton the happiest men he had known, men who had the good fortune to meet the end of their lives quickly and were honored by their communities. Greek poetry, on the other hand, treats us repeatedly to the spectacle of human happiness lost or nearly lost in the final stretch. In Greek poetry we have compelling images of how precarious a thing is human happiness and a logic that was both aesthetically satisfying and in keeping with the Greek vision of life as a whole.

Notes

INTRODUCTION

1. Cole and Gadow 1986.5.
2. For recent treatments of the anxiety of age in American culture, see Chudacoff 1989 and Cole 1992.
3. Eyben 1989 and Suder 1991 offer detailed bibliographies on old age in antiquity. General discussions of old age in Greek culture can be found in Haynes 1962, Kirk 1971, de Beauvoir 1972, Finley 1981, Bremmer 1987, Minois 1989.43–76, and esp. Garland 1990.242–87; there is still much of value to be found in the 1969 reprint of Richardson 1933. A number of relevant essays can also be found in the collections in Bertman 1976 and Falkner and de Luce 1989.
4. "Rabbi ben Ezra" 1–3.
5. See esp. the studies by Golden 1990 and Garland 1990.
6. See, e.g., Herzfeld 1985.xiv–xv and 10–11.
7. See, e.g., Gulliver 1968.157–62, La Fontaine 1978.1–20, Baxter and Almagor 1978.159–60, and Östör 1986.281–304.
8. Translation is from the Penguin edition by W. K. C. Guthrie (1956).

CHAPTER 1

1. Cf. Wade-Gery 1952.281: "The minstrels' tradition, centuries old in Greece, foundered beneath the *Iliad*"; Redfield 1973.145: "The composition of the *Iliad*, therefore, initiated the decline of epic poetry. . . . The *Odyssey* looks less original, if only because it is clearly a sequel"; Clay 1983.26: ". . . in a sense, the *Iliad* is the canon against which the *Odyssey* measures itself."

Other work speaks less in terms of sequence and sequel than of the overall complementarity and dynamic relation between the poems. Compare, for example, Nagy 1975.41, who regards the poems as "parallel products of parallel evolution," and Pucci 1987.18, for whom the poems "presume each other, border and limit each other, to such an extent that one, as it were, writes the other." See also Thalmann 1984.157–84. The following analysis assumes the responsivity of the *Odyssey* to the *Iliad* in some form, whether as fixed text or more fluid tradition.

The text throughout is that of T. W. Allen, *Homeri Opera*. Vols. I–V (Oxford 1902–12), with book numbers of the *Iliad* and *Odyssey* indicated by Roman and Arabic figures respectively. Where noted translations are from R. Lattimore, *The Iliad of Homer* and *The Odyssey of Homer* (Chicago 1951 and 1965).

2. Redfield 1973.145.
3. On the concept of time in the poem, see esp. Whitman 1958.287 ff. and Bergren 1983.

The life stages or age-grades in Homer, as is generally true in traditional societies, are suggested not in terms of chronology but by a range of terms and a character's physical maturity, social status, behavior, or generational relationships. On age in general in Greek thought, see Nash 1978.

Implicit in both poems is a distinction of four male age grades—that of the παῖς, the younger νέος or κοῦρος, the mature male at the prime of life (as Aristotle would say, ἀκμάζων; on the inconsistencies with regard to Greek concepts of and terms for maturity or middle-age, see Nash 1978.4–5), and the γέρων or πρέσβυς. In the *Iliad* these distinctions are articulated around the matrix of heroic warfare, embodied respectively in those not yet warriors (such as Astyanax); younger warriors at their physical peak like Achilles and Diomedes; older, more mature warriors and leaders, such as Agamemnon and Odysseus, and elders like Phoenix, Priam, and Nestor. In the *Odyssey* the older three grades are embodied by Telemachus, Odysseus, and Laertes.

4. Cf. Whitman 1958.290: "even as the circular pattern was appropriate to the *Iliad*, as a poem of heroic being, the linear movement of the *Odyssey* is wholly inevitable for a poem of becoming."

5. where the temporality is enhanced by his belated and urgent assumption of the responsibilities of young manhood. On the *Telemachia* as "initiatory paradigm" and *rite de passage*, see Eckert 1963.

6. Little has been written on the Homeric representation of old age. For the most thorough treatments, see Schadewaldt 1960.44–50 and Preisshofen 1977.20–42. Also helpful are Kirk 1971.126–38, Querbach 1976, Byl 1976, Stahmer 1978.31–34, and MacCary 1982.196–216 *passim*.

I shall speak throughout of "Homeric society" without implication to its historicity, although in general I would agree with Murray 1980.38 that "there is a historical basis to the society described in Homer, in the poet's retrojection of the institutions of his own day." For a similar conclusion and review of the problem, cf. Rose 1975.131–32. In any event, my working assumption is that of Finley 1965.43: that "essentially the picture of the background offered by the poems is a coherent one" and that it can sustain a cultural analysis.

7. 24.211, 225, 233, 249, 255, 387 (bis), 389 (bis), 390, 394, 406, 451.

8. Page 1955.101–36, followed by e.g., Kirk 1962.204–8 and 244–52.

9. See in particular the arguments by Stanford 1965, Erbse 1972.166–244, Moulton 1974, J. Finley 1978 *Appendices* I and II, Wender 1978.45–75, and Murnaghan 1987.26–33.

10. The survey by Cowgill and Holmes (1972) identifies this as a cultural universal: "All societies have some system of age grading. In all societies some people are considered 'old.'" Cf. Holmes 1983.23–25, 117–18. For some interesting examples, see e.g., Gulliver 1968.157–62 and LaFontaine 1978.1–20. Gulliver's examples include cultures that have several categories for the aged.

11. First developed in Cumming and Henry 1961. Although disengagement was presented as a "universal" theory of aging, most gerontologists now see it as culturally determined and applicable only to certain aspects of modern urban and industrialized societies. See the valuable critiques by Havighurst 1968 and Cowgill and Holmes 1972.

12. A good review of the anthropological literature on the status of the elderly and the factors that affect it most directly may be found in Holmes 1983.11–17.

13. Simmons 1945.79; the data is usefully analyzed in Slater 1964.231–34. Until relatively recently, Simmon's cross-cultural gerontology found few followers among

anthropologists; see Clark 1968. For a survey of some of the work since, see Holmes 1976 and 1983 and Kertzer and Keith 1984.19–61.

14. Simmons 1945.105–130.

15. See e.g., Gulliver 1963.25–65 and Spencer 1965 chs. 4–7.

16. Simmons 1945.131–76.

17. Maxwell and Silverman 1970.

18. Gutmann 1976.89; the fieldwork is synthesized in Gutmann 1987.23–46. Although I respect the empirical nature of Gutmann's findings, I have reservations about his claims to universality and to an inherent psychological basis for the patterns he discerns.

19. See esp. Gutmann 1987.82–97.

20. Gutmann 1977.308. In the Old Testament great old age was considered a sign of divine blessing and virtue, as evidenced by the abundance of aged patriarchs, a view that still characterizes much of Middle Eastern culture (cf. Patai 1959.229–33).

21. Weber 1947.346.

22. Fortes 1984.119–120.

23. Cf. Redfield 1975.110–113.

24. Roussel 1951.

25. The formula πρότερος γενόμην (γεγόνει) καὶ πλείονα οἶδα (ἤδη) is used to describe the superiority of Zeus over Poseidon (XIII.355), Odysseus over Achilles (XIX.219), and Poseidon over Apollo (XXI.440). Agamemnon similarly calls for Achilles to give up his anger "inasmuch as I can call myself the elder" (IX.161), and at XXIII.396 ff. Antilochus defers to Menelaus by reason of the latter's age and his own impetuous youth. Antenor praises the economy of Menelaus' speech, "even though he was only a young man" (III.215). Iris reminds Poseidon that the Furies "forever side with the elder" (πρεσβυτέροισιν Ἐρινύες αἰὲν ἕπονται, XV.204), and Zeus calls him πρεσβύτατον καὶ ἄριστον (presumably, after himself) at 13.142. But in none of these passages is the reference specifically to *old* age.

The heroic practice of fighting in pairs is age-graded, with the younger warriors linked with older more experienced ones, on the premise that the impulsiveness of the youth (cf. III.108–10, XX.407–12, XXIII.589–90, 602–4) will be restrained by the company of someone older; cf. Nash 1978.7. But the older of the two need not, of course, be elderly, and Nestor plays this role only temporarily with Diomedes in Book VIII.

26. Cf. Chantraine 1968.216, s.v. γέρας; Plutarch approves the etymology in *Mor.* 789f.(= *Should Elders Take Part in Public Life?* 10). For other examples of the change in vowel grade in -es- stem neuter nouns like that in γῆρας-γέρας, see Schindler 1975.262. The formula occurs at IV.323 and IX.422, though in the latter γερόντων describes members of Council generally; see note 38 below. Nestor not surprisingly intends it in its literal sense. Chantraine rejects the connection some (e.g., MacCary 1982.209) would make between γέρας/γέρων and Nestor's epithet Γερήνιος.

27. Segal 1971 discusses Nestor's astute perception of the quarrel and of the culpability of Agamemnon. Cf. also Donlan 1979, who distinguishes leadership based on "position-authority" from that based on "collective authority." While Donlan does not discuss the elderly as a special group, they can be regarded as spokesmen for the consensus of group values.

Schadewaldt 1960.45 observes a symmetry "von Vörzügen und Mängeln auf beiden Seiten," and Preisshofen 1977.24 finds in young and old a reciprocity of word and deed: "so wie die Jugend auf den Rat der Älteren, so sind die Alten auf die Tatkraft der Jüngeren angewiesen."

28. E.g., Preisshofen 1977.35, and LSJ 348 s.v. γῆρας. On the metaphor in λιπαρόν, see Frisk 1970. II.126 f.

29. Cf. 4.210, 11.136, 19.365, 23.284.

30. On his character see Redfield 1975.92–98 and Donlan 1971. Agamemnon's abuse of Chryses is so explicit in its tone and language that I fail to understand the categorical claim at Preisshofen 1977.23: "An keiner Stelle in der Ilias äussert oder verhält sich ein Jüngerer abfällig gegenüber einem Älteren . . . und nirgends klingt in dem Wort γέρων—ob in einem Bericht oder als direkte Anrede gebraucht—eine abfällige Nuance mit."

31. Priam is described with γέρων, γεραιός, or γῆρας forty-four times in Book XXIV; his only companion is the κῆρυξ . . . γεραίτερος (149,178), and his age is set off against the ἥβη of Hermes (376) and the beauty of Achilles (630).

Macleod 1982.33–34 notes the following similarities: XXIV.501–2, I.12–13; XXIV.555-57, I.18–20; XXIV.560, I.32; XXIV.569–70, I.26, 28; XXIV.571, I.33; XXIV.780–81, I.25. Whitman 1958.259 discusses the "geometric" relationship of the two books, but sees the restitution of Hector to Priam as corresponding mainly to the seizure of Briseis. On the symmetry between the two scenes, see most recently Minchin 1986.15 and n.23.

32. On the significance of the seating arrangements referred to at 515, 553, and 597 to Achilles' behavior throughout the scene, see Frazer 1976.

33. Griffin 1980.108 comments on how despite their brevity the brief obituaries that accompany these passages convey deep emotion.

34. As Cameron 1971.90 observes, the reciprocal nature of the institution is illustrated by Plut. Sol. 22 who reports that in Athens a son, who would otherwise be disenfranchised for failure to render the θρεπτήρια, was exempt from this obligation if his father had failed in his duty to teach him a trade (on which see Diog. Laert. 1.55). On the legal and social background of the θρεπτήρια, see Lacey 1968.116–18, Richardson 1969.55–58, Powell 1988.381 and n.258, and Garland 1990.256–58, 261–62.

35. Cf. VIII.517 ff., where Hector takes the exceptional measure of assigning the young and πολιοκροτάφους . . . γέροντας temporary battle stations, and the similar scene on the shield of Achilles (XVIII.514–15). M. Finley 1965.89 says of Nestor, "his value to the army was only moral and psychological."

36. οὖρος Ἀχαίων: VIII.80, XI.840, XV.370, 659; 3.411.

37. On the centrality of skill in warfare to the Homeric notion of aretê, cf. Jaeger 1945.5–14, Adkins 1960.31–34, Donlan 1980.3–6, 23–24 (who cites Finley 1965.19: "Everything pivoted on a single element of honor and virtue: strength, bravery, physical courage, prowess. Conversely, there was no weakness, no unheroic trait, but one, and that was cowardice and the consequent failure to pursue heroic goals").

38. For γέροντες as counselors see II.21, 53, 404; IV.323, 344; IX.70, 89, 422, 574; XV.721; XVIII.448; XIX.303, 338.

39. The simile suggests the myth of Tithonus (Hom. Hymn. Aphr. 218–38), whose advanced old age is frail and helpless, his speech childish prattle, and who (in other versions) is metamorphosed into a τέττιξ; see esp. King 1986.

40. The allusion is heightened by III.147, which identifies among the dēmogerontes

three of Priam's brothers, where Tithonus is conspicuous in his absence (the four are named together at XX.237–38).

Schein 1984.171–72 comments on the discrepancy between the titular authority of the elderly and their actual power.

41. See note 38, above.

42. Nestor underscores his point later in the speech when he instructs the young (κούροισιν) to take their stations by the earthen rampart and then instructs Agamemnon to rule (ἄρχε), as he is most kingly (βασιλεύτατος, IX.66–69).

43. The principle is sometimes used by others (e.g., Agamemnon to Diomedes at IV.372 ff.), but only Nestor claims to embody the superiority of the past. Querbach 1976 points to the resentment such claims engender in the young and to how Diomedes in particular repeatedly points up the weaknesses in Nestor's counsel.

44. Cf. Holmes 1983.119–21.

45. Gutmann 1977.315–16: "societies that sponsor an egocentric, self-seeking spirit in the population will be lethal to young and old alike. But societies which sponsor altruism, and the formation of internalized objects, provide security to these vulnerable cohorts. . . . By keeping his object status, the older person avoids becoming the *stranger*, and is thereby protected against the fear and revulsion aroused by the 'other.' There is a much noted tendency for the aged to reminisce, and even to relive their earlier life. Though taken as a sign of egocentricity, this may be an adaptive move to escape the lethal condition of 'otherness.' As they reminisce, the elders seem to be saying, 'See me not as I am, but as a total *history*, and as someone who was once like you.'"

46. Cf. Butler 1963.66: "a naturally occurring, universal mental process characterized by the progressive return to consciousness of past experiences, and, particularly, the resurgence of unresolved conflicts." For some literary applications of Butler's model, see Woodward 1986.

47. Edwards 1987.182.

48. Cf. Preisshofen 1977.26, Donlan 1979.53 and esp. Austin 1966.301–3. While I agree with Austin on their paradigmatic function, I see their self-referentiality as psychologically and socially revealing.

49. Cf. Edwards 1987.67, 182.

50. Querbach 1976.55–56 observes that it is only Nestor's uncontroversial suggestions (e.g., II.337–68, VII.327–44, IX.52–78, X.191–93) that are heeded. Kirk 1971.129 calls his counsel obvious; cf. M. Finley 1981.163.

51. See esp. Pedrick 1983, who notes how the speech in running counter to several of the regular conventions of such paradeigmata signals that Nestor's advice "balances dangerously between glorious victory and disaster."

52. Scodel 1982.

53. Donlan 1979.53.

54. On the ambiguities surrounding age, kingship, and Laertes' retirement, see M. Finley 1965.89–90 and Kirk 1971.131. On Athenian practice, see Lacey 1968.116–18.

One is tempted to see in the birth of Telemachus the occasion for the succession: perhaps the combination of Laertes' age and the availability of a mature son and a grandson made possible the transfer of rule to the next generation. It is precisely the absence of someone old enough both to claim and hold the kingship in Ithaca that creates the crisis that threatens Telemachus and the city, which has gone twenty years without calling the people to assembly (2.26–27).

55. Hecuba questions the soundness of Priam's φρένες at 24.201. Both ἔμπεδος and ἀεσίφρων are used elsewhere in Homer in relation to behavior and age. Helen complains of Paris' immaturity that "this man's heart (φρένες) is no steadfast thing, nor will it be so ever hereafter" (VI.352); Penelope similarly complains of Telemachus' immaturity (18.215). At XXIII.603 Menelaus says that Antilochus has not in the past been ἀεσίφρων, as his youth has made him now.

56. See I.19, II.37, 332, 373, 803; IV.18, 290; VII.296; IX.136, 278; XII.11, 15; XIII.14; XVI.448; XVII.160; XVIII.288; XXI.309; XXII.165, 173, 230, 251.

57. E.g., I.255; II.160,176, 304; III.288; IV.28, 31, 35, 47, 165, 173; V.535, 614; VII.386; VIII.552; XX.306; XXII.453; XXIV.28, 37.

58. In addition to Hector, Helenus, Deiphobus, and Paris, we hear of Laodice, III.124, VI.252; Democoon, IV.499; Echemmon and Chromius, V.159; Gorgythion, VIII.302; Isus and Antiphus, XI.101; Medesicaste, XIII.173; Cassandra, XIII.366; Cebriones, XVI.738; Polydorus, XX.407 ff., Lycaon, XXI.34 ff.; Lycaon and Polydorus, XXII.46.

59. E.g., at II.414, 788; VI.242, 245 ff.; VI.316–17; VII.346; XIII.176; XV.551; XXII.478.

60. IV.47, 165; V.464; VI.283, 449, 451; VII.427; VIII.552; IX.651; XI.197; XIII.460; XV.239; XVI.738; XXIV.117, 145, 217, 299, 373, 386, 405, 477, 483, 552, 634, 659, 803.

61. Cf. the similar contrast between the reference to γέρων Πρίαμος at XIII.368 and Idomeneus' sarcastic reference to Δαρδανίδη Πριάμῳ at XIII.376.

62. III.148, 203; VII.347. Like Priam, Antenor loses many sons, legitimate and illegitimate, to the Greeks, although his son Agenor is saved from Achilles by the gods just before Hector is deceived by them.

63. On the misconception that there is an essential connection between prophecy and old age, see M. Finley 1981.163–64.

64. This understanding of the γήραος οὐδός was first suggested to me by Professor Martin Ostwald, whose insight I gratefully acknowledge. Hesiod uses the formula at WD331 where κακῷ ἐπὶ γήραος οὐδῷ seems to indicate old age in general.

That the threshold is old age itself is recognized by Walter Leaf's commentary ad 22.60 and in Cunliffe's Lexicon though in a different sense, the latter understanding the threshold to be architecturally part of the μέγαρον itself, in which case the phrase becomes merely epic periphrasis.

65. See Clay 1983.141–48; on the formula, see Janko 1981. The meaning is developed most explicitly at 5.218, where Odysseus says to Calypso of Penelope: ἡ μὲν γὰρ βροτός ἐστι, σὺ δ᾽ ἀθάνατος καὶ ἀγήρως.

66. On the relationship between heroism and death, see esp. Schein 1984 chap. 3.

67. Gutmann 1977.314; cf. Gutmann 1987.229: "Older men, because of their special access to the gods, to the myth-embracing past, and to the spiritualized ancestors, become the living exemplars of the legend. It is they who bypass the time gap between then and now, bringing the two into conjunction. Via the elders, the mythic past and the mundane present are interpenetrated, and the climate of mythic origins is brought forward, into the here and now."

68. Schadewaldt 1960.48: "Die einfache naturgemässe Auffassung gesunder Völker."

69. The poet anticipates the formula in introducing the hero with the alternate for-

mula for dawn, Ἠὼς δ᾽ ἐκ λεχέων παρ᾽ ἀγαυοῦ Τιθωνοῖο/ ὄρνυθ᾽, ἵν᾽ ἀθανάτοισι φόως φέροι ἠδὲ βροτοῖσιν (5.1–2), which suggests the complex relationship of old age, death, and immortality. The idea is also implicit in Thetis' complaint to Hephaestus that she alone of the Nereids was married to a mortal who lies in his halls γήραι λυγρῷ . . . ἀρήμενος (XVIII 434–35), and in Zeus' lament that a team of horses ἀγήρω τ᾽ ἀθανάτω τε (XVII.444) were given to Peleus.

70 See, for example, Adkins 1960.30 ff.

71. See Turner 1967.96–97 on the liminal status of initiates in traditional rites of passage: "The essential feature of these symbolizations is that the neophytes are neither living nor dead from one aspect, and both living and dead from another. Their condition is one of ambiguity and paradox, a confusion of all the customary categories."

72. See A. P. Edwards 1985.51–52 and MacCary 1982.196 ff.; MacCary suggests a connection between Phthia and φθίω/φθίνω as suggestive of "destructive old age."

73. See Arthur 1981 on the walls of Troy and the Scaean Gate as a kind of threshold between (female) city and (male) battle.

74. On the relationship between death in manhood and the rhetoric of youth, cf. Nash 1978.12 and n.253, who notes how in death Patroclus too leaves behind ἀνδροτῆτα καὶ ἥβην (XVI.857).

75. Cf. Kirk 1971.134, 137–38.

76. 23.121–22. Cf. also 2.96, 2.324, 331, 13.425, 16.248, 250,18.6, 21.310, 22.30, 24.131; at 14.60–61 Eumaeus refers to the suitors as ἄνακτες . . . νέοι.

77. Preisshofen 1977.33–34. "das Bild eines . . . geschlossenen Kreises jünger Männer."

78. The later tradition develops Nestor's fits of rhetorical abandon: in the Kypria, when Menelaus invites him to join the expedition, Nestor apparently treats him to four separate epyllia.

79. Cf. Clay 1983.184: "Menelaus with his Helen lives on in embalmed splendor, no longer a casus belli, while the noble relic, Nestor, now recounts incidents from the Trojan War rather than his youthful exploits. Neither is capable of heroic enterprise."

80. This is how I understand ἐν ὠμῷ γήραι θῆκεν at 15.357: that Anticleia's death "placed him in a raw (i.e., premature) old age." Cf. Hes. Op. 705. Preisshofen 1977. 37–39 notes apropos of the Laertes episode that the Odyssey pays more attention to the physical details of aging than does the Iliad.

81. Austin 1975.102 finds in Laertes "the clearest example of orientation in space as an expression of psychological condition. . . . In the autumn of his life he has moved both outward and downward."

82. Cf. A. P. Edwards 1985.54–59 and J. Finley 1978.206–7.

83. Murnaghan 1987.26–30 discusses Laertes' dress and appearance as constituting "a kind of disguise" from which he, like other members of Odysseus' household, must be recovered; she observes how this disguise combines elements appropriate to his grief ("mourning as sympathetic imitation" of the dead) and features reminiscent of Odysseus' disguises in Phaeacia and Ithaca.

84. Homer uses πρῶτ᾽ ἐξερέοιτο ἕκαστά τε πειρήσαιτο in the same way in its only other occasion in the poem (4.119), when Menelaus, confounded by Telemachus' bursting into tears upon being welcomed, wonders if he should inquire into the reasons for it. Murnaghan 1987.22 relates the pattern of identification, testing, and emo-

tional reunion to other recognition scenes in the *Odyssey*. Katz 1991.163 notes Odysseus' weighing of alternatives and how the decision to test his father first recapitulates his earlier decision with regard to Penelope (13.333–38) and complements Penelope's similar decision to withhold recognition from Odysseus in Book 23.

85. On this sense of κερτόμιος, cf. Macleod 1982 *ad* XXIV.649.

86. For interpretations of the scene, see Lord 1960.170 ff., Clarke 1967.25, Stanford 1968.60–61, Thornton 1976.116 ff., and Wender 1978.56–57.

87. Fenik 1974.47–50 suggests that "the criterion of functionalism has almost no value in interpreting scenes of identification in the Odyssey," and singles out the pointlessness of Athena's deception of Odysseus in Book 13.

88. M. Finley 1965.90 (footnote) is troubled by what he sees as an inconsistency between the condition of Laertes here and as described earlier. But this is precisely Odysseus' objection: there seems to be no *reason* for his neglect. Cf. Kirk 1971.131–32 and Wender 1978.52–53.

89. Cf. Redfield 1975.111: "Because successful inheritance is the completion of the householder's social task, each householder is (in effect) dependent on his heir."

90. Compare Whitman 1958.304–5 and Wender 1978.60–62. Katz 1991.178–79 observes how in each of the "truth-tales" by which Odysseus reveals himself to Penelope (the bed) and his father (the orchard), recognition is extended because identity as husband or son is not so much proved as instantiated.

91. Foley 1978.15–16 notes the active role Ithacan kings play in agriculture and sees in the recognition with Laertes Odysseus' revitalization of the process of economic reproduction. Walcot 1970.18–19 suggests that Homeric heroes generally were skillful in both warfare and farming. But most of his evidence comes from the line of Laertes, and there are no parallels elsewhere to the depth of Odysseus' agricultural interests or the unusual attention given them.

92. Hygin., *Fab.*95; cf. also *Kypria* p.103 (Allen); Lykophron 815–18; Apollod. *Epit.* 3.7. There is no tradition of Odysseus as warrior before the Trojan war.

93. 18.368–86. Particularly striking is the competitive context of the references to farming and the contrast between Odysseus' pride in such work and Eurymachus' derisive offer to hire him (18.356–64). Compare the ploughing scene on the shield of Achilles (XVIII.541–72), where the mood is peaceful and cooperative rather than competitive.

94. On the simile, cf. Foley 1978.11.

95. On Cicero's association of λιστρεύειν with fertilizing, see Boscherini 1969. On the association of κόπρος and rebirth, see esp. Schwartz 1975.

96. Kirk 1971.132–33.

97. Xenophon describes agriculture and warfare as complementary forms of *aretê* that involve the whole community (*Oecon.*20.2.5). The tradition is also implicit in the *Contest of Homer and Hesiod* in opposing the poet of war and violence to the poet of farming and peace. Cf. Walcot 1970.1–4.

98. Simmons 1945.47, 58, 85, 102, 105–6, 113, 175, 212. See also LeVine and LeVine 1985.30–32, who include among the essential characteristics of agrarian societies the "lifelong loyalty of children to their parents" and the hierarchical nature of their age-grading: "The later years—for those relatively few who reach them—bring more social power, public esteem, and personal choice."

99. The expression is related to ὠμῷ γήραι at 15.357; see above note 57.

100. Nagy 1975.35–36. On the *Odyssey*'s inversion of the terms of heroic κλέος, see Segal 1983; on κλέος in this scene, cf. Edwards 1985.51–52.

101. On the prophecy of Tiresias, see Hanson 1977, Nagler 1980, and Peradotto 1986.

102. Lattimore reads "Death will come to you from the sea." On ἐξ ἁλός as "away from" rather than "out of" the sea with a review of the ancient and modern testimony, see Hanson 1977.42–48.

103. Cf. Whitman 1958.290: ". . . in some sense, the *Odyssey*, overshadowed by the prophecy of Tiresias, never really ends." On the "proleptic perspective" of Tiresias and its relation to Odyssean narrative technique, see Bergren 1983. 50–54. On the prophecy of Tiresias as it relates to the conflicting demands of mythic narrative and *Märchen*, see Peradotto 1986.444–46 and 450–54.

104. 14.37, 45, 122, 131, 166, 386, 508; 16.199, 273, 456; 17.202, 337; 18.10, 21, 53, 74, 81; 24.157.

Compare the many references to Odysseus' ragged clothes (e.g., ῥάκος ἄλλο κακὸν βάλεν ἠδὲ χιτῶνα, /ῥωγαλέα ῥυπόωντα, 13.434–35) and Laertes' κακὰ εἵματα (11.191), ῥυπόωντα . . . χιτῶνα ῥαπτὸν ἀεικέλιον (24.227–28).

The beggar's nostalgia for his own "past abilities" assumes multiple ironies when he wishes only that he were as νέος as Telemachus or Odysseus himself and could avenge the hybris of the young suitors (16.99–104).

105. Dornseiff 1937 sees in the ἀθηρηλοιγός the magic word (erlösende Wort) that breaks the power of the sea (as symbolized in the oar) over Odysseus. Gutenbrunner 1950 suggests ethnic humor at the expense of inland peoples for whom the stem *lopat-* indicated a winnowing shovel by seafarers for whom it signified an oar or rudder. Hanson 1977.34, 41–42 sees in the motif generally a dramatic way of marking the end of the journey and notes that the planting of the oar need not be an aetiological reference to a Poseidon cult but simply a sign that Odysseus has no more use for it.

106. Cf. Bertman 1968.121–23.

107. See, for example, Mackail 1936.8, who remarks that beginning with Book 21 ". . . the handling weakens a little, as though from some ebbing force in a poet who has felt the touch of age."

CHAPTER 2

1. Text for Hesiod is from Solmsen, Merkelbach, and West, *Hesiodi Opera* (Oxford 1970), with WD and Th. indicating the *Works and Days* and *Theogony* respectively; where noted translations are from R. Lattimore, *Hesiod* (Ann Arbor 1959).

2. Walcot 1961.4–7 and 1966.81–86 (cf. also C. W. Querbach 1985.1–12, which elaborates upon Walcot's pattern of ring composition); West 1978.172–77; Vernant 1965.19–47 (= 1983.3–32). A review of the history of interpretation of the passage and helpful bibliography can be found in P. Smith 1980.

3. Kirk 1970.234 and 1971.135 relates the references to a pattern of immaturity, maturity, and hypermaturity. Vernant 1965.40–41 sees the sequences as three pairs of races characterized by youth, maturity, and old age, respectively. On Eastern and Asian versions of the myth, which associate the final race with early senescence, see West 1978.174–75 and Fontenrose 1974.2–3.

P. Smith 1980 also discerns a developmental pattern in the sequence, arguing that "the character and the actions of each of the races are presented in such a way as to suggest a stage—or the unconscious memory of a stage—in a man's life." Smith's attention to age differs from mine both in its purpose—a "psychological" reading of the sequence as "a symbolic expression of personal growth" (145) as opposed to the cultural reading I offer—and its analysis. He equates the Golden race with an unconscious memory of earliest childhood, whereas I argue that the Golden race is conceived of in terms of adulthood and and its self-awareness. He sees the Heroic race as largely imposed upon the sequence and merely "an echo and a pendant to the Bronze race," and reads the Iron race as inclusive of the whole of adulthood. While disagreeing with some of the particulars of Smith's interpretation, I do feel that an anthropological understanding of the sequence in no way precludes an appreciation of its psychological significance. The Golden race, for instance, might reflect a nostalgia for childhood experience and yet be articulated in terms not drawn from childhood itself and that have a different cultural significance.

4. On Hesiod's use of this mythic type as an *aition* in his "gospel of work," see esp. Fontenrose 1974.5–16. On his originality in conceiving of the Gold (and Silver) race, see Baldry 1952.

5. On the nonchronological and cyclical notion of time in Hesiod, cf. Vernant 1965.22–23. Although I disagree that the values associated with the races are timeless (the periods of human life can come of course in no other order), the life course model I suggest is not incompatible with Vernant's suggestion that the races represent a "renewable cycle" that implies at new beginning at its conclusion.

6. Cf. Garland 1990.14. On the structure of the life course in Greek thought in general, see Hudson-Williams 1926.129–30, Boll 1950.161–83, Gomme 1972.105, Nash 1978.4-5 and notes, Mette 1982, Vilchez 1983.63-95, and especially Garland 1990.1–11 and *passim*.

7. Where in modern Western culture aging is conceived in the context of chronological age and a fixed dating system, such is rarely the case in preliterate and nonindustrial societies, where age is understood rather in relation to biological, generational, and social factors; see esp. Fortes 1984.99–122.

8. With the omission of the παῖς (as is often the case), Hesiod uses the same division in fr. 321. The locus classicus on the grades of νεότης, ἀκμή, and γῆρας is Aristotle *Rhet*.2.12–14.

9. The relation is explicit in Hesiod's caution regarding the accidental emasculation of twelve-year-old boys (*WD* 750–52).

10. which for instance Aristotle, *Hist. Anim.* 581a, puts at age fourteen; cf. the discussion in Garland 1990.167–68.

11. M. Finley 1981.159–60. Finley distinguishes the biological achievement of manhood, the passage to civic manhood (as for instance in Athens with the δοκιμασία of the ephebes at age 18), and the virtual end of childhood several years earlier in peasant cultures.

On the significance of the regulation of the life course by a chronology governed by the state, see esp. Fortes 1984.

12. That there is no single or consistent term for men for what we would call "maturity" (ἀνήρ, unlike γυνή, is not age-specific) does not imply that the Greeks did not distinguish it as a life stage. Nash 1978.4–5 and 19 n.13 notes the terminology

problems and comments on a variety of expressions for "middle-age" (to which we can add Hesiod's use of μέσος, "in the middle," in frag. 321). The explanation lies in part, I suspect, in the fact that "maturity," as our own expression suggests, has a *normative* relation to the other grades and serves as the perspective from which one looks on age in general, so that one is νέος or γέρων in relation to the stage in between. But as J. Winkler observes in *Rehearsals of Manhood: Athenian Drama and the Poetics of Manhood* (forthcoming, Princeton), Greek culture is also conspicuous for the relative absence of more traditional rite of passages into manhood, which he links with a more precarious and less final sense of "manhood" that is never fully and finally achieved. (Cf. the seminal work by Herzfeld 1985 in this regard.) The lack of such a term for "mature man" may be related.

13. Cf. the description of Phaethon as τόν ῥα νέον τέρεν ἄνθος ἔχοντ' ἐρικυδέος ἥβης (*Th.* 988).

14. Solon's "ten ages" (West 27) first applies the term ἀνήρ to the fifth hebdomad (age 28–35) and recommends attention to marriage and offspring at that age; cf. Plato *Rep.*460e, *Laws* 772e, and Aristotle *Pol.* 7.15.10, and see below chap. 5. On age and eligibility for military and public service in Athens and Sparta, see e.g., Garland 1990.242–45, 282–84.

The predicament of the elderly is closely related to the patterns of retirement and inheritance in the *oikos* and to the generational transfer of authority. On the Boeotian *oikos* in general, see Lacey 1968.71–72, and esp. Arthur 1973.19–26; on patterns of retirement in Athens (with some interesting demographical speculation), see Strauss 1993.68–70.

15. in the two different ritual structures at Athens, the entry into the phratry or family clan at age sixteen with the sacrifice of the κουρεῖον at the feast of the Apaturia, and the military and civic ephebia that began at 18. On the relation between the two and significance of both as rituals of status-transition, see Vidal-Naquet 1986 chaps. 5–6 and Winkler 1990a.25 (with helpful bibliography in n.7).

16. For two examples, see Gulliver's study of the Arusha (1963.25–66) and Spencer on the Samburu (1965.80–101). In each case the passage from the lower grade of manhood to elders occurs at the end of young manhood (approximately age thirty), and largely coincides with marriage and domestic responsibilities.

17. In anthropological discourse "gerontocracy" does not, of course, necessarily denote old age. The practice has a loose parallel in the Homeric γέροντες who serve in the Council of princes regardless of their literal age, but where broadly speaking those who are older lay claim to being wiser and to "know more."

18. West 1978 *ad loc.* notes that nine and forty are to be considered formulaic or "notional" figures.

19. Clay 1981–82 observes that the formula is not a hendiadys: the gods are both deathless *and* timelessly frozen in the radiance of youth or maturity, effected by a preservative diet of nectar and ambrosia. Cf. also Preisshofen 1977.6–8.

20. Cf.*Th.* 277, 305, 949, 955; in the fragments see 23.12 and 24, 25.28, 229.8. At *Th.* 955 note the reference to the divinity of Heracles, whose agelessness is underscored by his winning of Ἥβη as bride.

21. Cf. *WD* 113–14, *Th.* 225, 604; other negative expressions appear at *WD* 331, 705.

22. which may however be intended as a gloss not on Nereus' being called

γέροντα but on the name Nereus itself; cf. West 1966 *ad loc.* Cf. also Preisshofen 1977.10–13.

23. If the fragment represents a παροιμία, we are probably to assume a balance between the three functions; such is in keeping with archaic thought in general, where prayer represents a form of action rather than passive resignation. Homer associates old age and prayer in the references at *Il.* 6.87, 113, 270, 287, but prayer is in no sense age-specific, and the prayers of the elderly appear no more efficacious than those of others.

Kirk 1971.125–26 and 134 characterizes Hesiod's attribution of wise counsel to the period of middle-age as "perhaps an eccentric view" and as arising from the fact that in a state run by βασιλῆες there is not the same need for wise or aged counsel.

24. On the offspring of Night and the inner structure and meaning of the catalogue see Ramnous 1959.64–72, who groups old age and its three siblings under the common theme of ruin. Old age was occasionally represented as a daimon: the vase by the Geras painter in the Louvre shows a balding and shriveled old man being clubbed mercilessly by the youthful Heracles; on Heracles as a symbol of youth and life in conflict with old age and death, see Kirk 1974.188ff.

25. On the representation of women in *Th.* see Marquardt 1982, who speaks of Hesiod's "tendency to view universal ills, such as old age and death, in a feminine context," as well as Sussman 1978, Loraux 1978.43–87, and Arthur 1973 and 1982.

26. following West on the meaning of ὠμῷ (although the comparable phrase at *Od.* 15.357 seems capable of bearing quite the same meaning: Anticleia's death aged Laertes unnaturally).

27. On the economics of the period in general, see Starr 1982.422–35, and M. Finley 1981a *passim.* More detailed studies of Boeotian agriculture and the economics of Hesiodic thought include Detienne 1963.22–25, Murray 1980.chs. 3–4, and Sussman 1978.32–41.

28. Cf. Kirk 1971.134.

29. Not to mention that the *oikos* with just one son keeps one clear of the kind of quarrels over inheritance in which Hesiod and Perses were embroiled; cf. Golden 1990.119–20.

30. disagreeing with West, who reads the ἕτερον παῖδα as a grandson rather than a second son.

31. Cf. Pucci 1977.84–85, who stresses "the theme of man's identity with his original form throughout his life . . . identical to the form he took as he sprang from the earth." On the condition of hands and feet as indices of age and suffering, cf. *Od.* 11.497 and 19.359.

32. As West notes *ad loc.*, this is the meaning of Hesiod's claim that gods and mortals ὁμόθεν γεγάασι, i.e., "that they started on the same terms."

See also Vernant 1965.40–41, who seems mistaken in linking the races of Gold and Silver as representing what he simply calls "youth." The race of Silver, as I suggest below, is not about youth, but about the childhood of the παῖς, which the Greeks distinguished from the young manhood (νεότης) that begins with the arrival of ἥβη. The Golden race is clearly regarded, like the Olympians themselves, as in maturity. While it is true that both races are exempt from old age, this hardly characterizes them both as youthful in any useful sense of the term.

33. As West notes *ad loc.*, Ὀλύμπια δώματ᾽ ἔχοντες normally suggests the Olympians, and is secured by the reference to Ζεὺς Κρονίδης in 138. The formula is used more loosely in 110 and qualified with the reference to Cronus in the following line. Cf. Fontenrose 1974.11–12, who suggests that the transition from Gold to Silver is occasioned by the new rule of Zeus, which puts an end to the race of Gold and establishes a new order of work.

34. Other instances of νήπιος are always in the latter sense: WD 286, 397, and 633 (of Perses); 40, 218, 456; and fragments 33a.28 and 61.

Golden 1990.5 mentions the extended childhood of the Silver Age in evidence of the negative qualities that the Greeks in general attributed to childhood.

35. Cf. Kirk 1970.136: "The purpose might be to stress the absurdity of life, however long and free from suffering, if it includes no period of maturity."

36. Cf. West *ad loc.*

37. Cf. the Okeanides at *Th.*347, Hekate at *Th.*450–52, Eirene at *WD* 228. That the preclassical meaning of κοῦρος is of the youth who has just come into manhood is proved by Harrison 1912.11–12 and Nilsson 1950.547.

Vernant 1965.32–34 suggests that, as in a number of myths, the Bronze race is born autochthonously (and therefore asexually) as young warriors.

38. For illustrations and very different interpretations of the exclusion of women from male initiatory rites, see Bettelheim 1954.117–19, 227–38, Eliade 1958.4–10, and Reik 1960.123–24. On literary reflections of such ritual behavior, see e.g., Eckert 1963.50 and 52 on Telemachus, in whom we see the Homeric version of several of the Hesiodic motifs: of the παῖς whose childhood is protracted and who has not assumed any responsibiity for the *oikos*; of the κοῦρος who comes of age physically (cf. his stringing of the bow), and as a warrior and defender of the *oikos*; but who still (e.g., in his leaving open of the door to the armory at *Od.* 22.154–56) falls somewhat short of the maturity of the older ἀνήρ.

39. Cf. Vernant 1965.23, who notes that there is nothing in the text (apart from the decrease in the value of the metals) to suggest that Hesiod means to characterize the Bronze race as inferior to the Silver. The point again justifies Vernant's general argument that the sequence involves not progressive degeneration but discrete stages that occur in a cyclic order.

40. In many cultures the mention of warfare itself implies the young men who are charged with the defense of the people. Cf. Gulliver 1968.157–58, who observes in many cultures a particular concern with the age-grade of the adolescents and young men who provide the militant warrior grades because of their problematic relationship to the community.

41. Cf., e.g., *Il.*4.321, 393; 5.807; 9.68, 86; 12.196.

Hesiod refers to Peace as κουροτρόφος (228), contrasting it to war, which here becomes by implication the destroyer of κοῦροι.

42. Cf. 3.108–10, 20.407–12, 23.589–90, 602–4.

43. Nagy 1979.156–60, 172–73, although his coordination of the Bronze and Heroic races as aspects of the epic tradition seems to me more successful than that of Gold and Silver as parallel expressions of heroic cult.

44. Cf. above note 15.

45. By characterizing the kind of warfare that the Bronze race indulges in as the

"deeds of Ares," the poet indicates this race's interest in only the destructive aspects of war; there is no reference to Ares in the description of the Heroes.

There may be a further link between youth and hybristic violence in the poet's description of Typhoeus at *Th*. 820–68, which represents a final resistance to the civilizing patriarchy of Zeus. The birth of Typhoeus after the Titanomachy, as well as the opposition between Typhoeus and the Titans in 820, characterize the rebel as younger than Zeus, and his description as ὁπλότατον (821, i.e., most fit for ὅπλα—cf., e.g., *Il.* 3.108, 4.323, 9.58) links youthfulness with martial superiority. There are also a number of verbal echoes between the strength, physicality, and invinciblity of Typhoeus and that of the Bronze race.

46. *Rhet.* 2.12.3–16. Cicero likewise distinguishes the *ferocitas iuvenum* from the *gravitas* of maturity (*De Sen.* 33).

47. My reading of the Heroes differs from that of Vernant 1965, who sees in them a different version of the same age-group as that of Bronze. Kirk 1971.136 likewise attempts to link the Bronze and Heroic races in what he sees as a lack of justice and of a sense of responsibility that "bedevils" them both. I see no evidence for such criticism of the Heroes in the text, which explicitly identifies them as more just and better; West *ad* 161 also suggests that Hesiod presents the destiny of the Heroes in a more favorable light. Von Fritz 1947.233ff. appreciates the difference between the Bronze and Heroic races, but reads them as different perspectives on the legendary past.

48. On δίκη and ὕβρις respectively as "legal process" and "violence," see Gagarin 1973.81–94. Solon likewise attributes to maturity (in the sixth hebdomad, age 36–42) the peak of a man's intellectual powers and self-restraint from lawless behavior: τῇ δ' ἕκτῃ περὶ πάντα καταρτύεται νόος ἀνδρός,/οὐδ' ἔρδειν ἔθ' ὁμῶς ἔργ' ἀπάλαμνα θέλει (11–12). Cf. Nash 1978.7.

49. Cf. Nash 1978.7.

50. Marital status is one expression of Achilles' conflict with Agamemnon: he rejects the latter's marriage offer, discusses his marriage prospects in Phthia at 9.393–94, and has apparently spoken of marrying Briseis (19.297–99). He calls Briseis his bride at 9.340, which serves precisely to underscore the difference; see above chap. 1.

51. See esp. Walcot 1961.4–5 and 1966.81–82, who sees in the similarity of the Isles of the Blessed to the Golden Race evidence of ring composition that ends the traditional sequence at line 173. On the contrast between the description of Pandora's intent (ἐμήσατο κήδεα λυγρά, 95) with the Golden and Heroic races, see Pucci 1977.84–85 and cf. C. W. Querbach 1985.2–3.

52. Cf. Fontenrose 1974.9.

53. Cf., e.g., *Il.* 22.74, 77, 24.516; *Od.* 4.317, 499. At *Il.* 8.518 Hector mobilizes the πολιοκροτάφους . . . γέροντας to assist in guarding Troy.

54. Cf. *Il.* 9.366, 23.261; *Od.* 21.3, 81, 24.168. That Hesiod speaks of μέλας . . . σίδηρος at 151 may be in part to reserve πολιός and its overtones for the Iron race.

55. Hesiod might have developed the Iron race by characterizing it in terms of certain criticisms commonly made of old age—its garrulousness, nostalgia, and pessimism—but these are not the vices by which he would characterize his own times. Aristotle catalogues the deficiencies of old age in *Rhet.* 2.13.

56. χειροδίκαι, like δίκη δ' ἐν χερσί below (192), implies the rejection of legal process and the use of violence in dealing with conflict; cf. Gagarin 1973.90.

CHAPTER 3

1. For discussion and illustrations of the *Lebenstreppe*, see Chew 1962.148–49 and figs. 101–2, and Cole 1992.24–25, 110–19.

Text is cited as follows: Homer and the Homeric *Hymns* from T. W. Allen, *Homeri Opera*, Vols. I–V (Oxford 1902–12); where noted translations are from R. Lattimore, *The Iliad of Homer* and *The Odyssey of Homer* (Chicago 1951 and 1965). Hesiod from Solmsen, Merkelbach and West, *Hesiodi Opera* (Oxford 1970), with *WD* and *Th.* for *Works and Days* and *Theogony* respectively; where noted translations are from R. Lattimore, *Hesiod* (Ann Arbor 1959). Archilochus from M. L. West *Iambi et Elegi Graeci ante Alexandrium Cantati* (2 vols., Oxford 1971). Sappho from D. A. Campbell, *Greek Lyric I* (Harvard 1982), with his translations as noted; Campbell's enumeration for the most part follows that of E. Lobel and D. L. Page, *Poetarum Lesbiorum Fragmenta* (Oxford 1955 = *PLF*).

2. Cf. for instance R. A. Levine: "The cultural vocabulary and normative structure of age-related behavior is so different for men and women . . . that no single description of the ideal of typical life course would suffice. It seems that even in the simplest societies, men and women measure their lives against radically different standards." (Cited in Hagestad and Neugarten 1985.38.)

Holmes 1983.129, surveying the cross-cultural work in anthropology and aging, says categorically: "It is universally true that *old age does not have the same meaning or involve the same circumstances for men as for women*" (his italics).

3. Cf. Coles 1992.24–25.

4. On the structure of female life course in Greece, see esp. Garland 1990.1–16.

5. There is no appreciable difference of meaning between the two terms, both of which like γέων can be pejorative; it is noteworthy that both are used metaphorically of things that are wrinkled, shriveled, or otherwise ugly: the skin of boiled milk, the folds of skin below the navel, a kind of seacrab, a locust, etc. (cf. LSJ *ad loc.*).

6. On the relations between the stages of life and woman's reproductive and domestic activity, see e.g., Cantarella 1987.20–23. She suggests that the fact that women pass through only the stages of *parthenoi* and marriage is anticipated in prehistoric initiation rites for Spartan and Athenian women, which likewise revolved around their responsibilites as "weavers and bakers and organizers of family life."

In this connection cf. the important essay by Ortner (1974). Ortner attributes the "universal" devaluation of women to the tendency to regard them, because of their reproductive function and domestic responsibilities, as more closely bound to nature, and as inferior to men, who identify themselves with the community and the transcendence of culture over natural and domestic concerns. Cf. Spelman 1982, who relates the contempt for women in Plato and Aristotle to their disdain for the body in general ("somatophobia") and the association of women with work that involves the mundane needs of the body.

7. Cf. Bremmer 1987.206.

8. Garland 1990.17.

9. On the Greek preference for barely pubescent women, see Garland 1990.212–13 ("an unhappy mixture of sexual politics, male pride, and medical ignorance"); cf. Slater 1968.23ff.

10. On the age of menopause, see Amundsen and Diers 1970 and Garland

1990.249–50.

11. Bremmer 1987.192ff. Likewise Garland 1990.244: "Ironically the independence which women now achieved should probably be seen as a reflection not of their
enhanced *status* but of their diminished *value*. Since women past menopause are no
longer capable of supplying heirs, there was not the same need to ensure their protection as when they were of childbearing years." Bremmer and Garland both cite Hyper-
eides fr. 205 Blass: "a woman who leaves the home ought to be at a stage of life when
those who come across her don't ask whose wife she is but whose mother she is."

On the freedom of the older woman women in Greece, see below n.15 and chap. 6.

12. de Beauvoir 1972.84.

13. Cf. Winkler 1990.163: "There was available a common understanding that
proper women ought to be publicly submissive to male definitions, and that a very
great pressure of propriety could at any time be invoked to shame a woman who acted
on her own sexuality."

14. On the seclusion of women see Lacey 1968.158–62, Pomeroy 1975.79–84,
Cantarella 1987.46, and Keuls 1985.206–10.

15. Interesting in this regard are cross-cultural studies suggesting that the
increased freedom and independence of older women allow them sexual licenses for-
bidden earlier. Holmes 1983.129 says of the old woman, "In some respects, her status
may be likened to that of a prepubescent girl in that in many societies she is free to
ignore a number of repressive taboos and regulations." Gutmann 1987.161–62 speaks
of the "power" of "the sexy older woman" who can play out "immodest and even
obscene behaviors." Yet the evidence offered on behalf of such "sexual liberation"
consists almost exclusively of such activities as telling bawdy jokes, drinking in public, sitting with men, or gossipping with other women—*not* her taking the sexual initiative directly. There is a parallel in the Greek tradition of the aged Baubo (identified
with Iambe in the Homeric *Hymn Dem.*), the ugly and aged daimon known for her
lewd behavior (display of her genitals) and obscene talk; cf. esp. Olender 1990.

16. On older prostitutes as *fellatrices*, see Krenkel 1980.81, Jocelyn 1980, Bremmer
1987.203, and Keuls 1985.180–82, 200–2.

17. There is a hint in the *Iliad* that old age brings women a special cultic or religious role. Helenus tells Hector to instruct their mother to gather the aged women of
Troy (γεραιάς, cf. *Il.* 6.270, 287, 296) in Athena's temple to ask for her protection, and
Athena's priestess Theano, wife of old Antenor, is perhaps herself (despite her epithet
καλλιπάρῃος, 6.302) an elderly woman. On the cultic activities of elderly women as a
measure of their relative freedom of movement, see Bremmer 1987.194ff. and cf. Garland 1990.258.

18. There may be a similar edge to Paris' complaints about Antenor's proposal at
*Il.*7.358.

19. πολυήρατος, "much to be desired," is used earlier when Helen presents
Telemachus with a beautiful robe and tells him to lay it up for "the lovely occasion of
your marriage" (πολυηράτου ἐς γάμου ὥρην, 15.126); marriage is also described as
"blooming" (θαλερός) at 6.66 and 20.74; cf. *Il.* 3.53. The *Iliad* suggests a similar perspective in its joyful descriptions of unmarried young men and women together,
ἠίθεοι καὶ παρθένοι, twice on the shield of Achilles (18.567, 593; cf. 22.127–28).

20. There is also an interesting complementarity in the descriptions of Athena and
Hermes, who appear in disguise to help Odysseus: she in Phaeacia "in the likeness of a

young girl, a little maid" (παρθενικῇ ἐικυῖα νεήνιδι, 7.20), he "in the likeness of a young man with beard new grown, which is the most graceful time of young manhood" (νεηνίη ἀνδρὶ ἐοικὼς, πρῶτον ὑπηνήτῃ τοῦ περ χαριέστατος ἤβη, 10.278–79); cf. also Athena at 13.222. Here similarity of age is underscored by similarity of narrative function.

21. For a discussion of the narrative and linguistic parallels, see Belmont 1967, though the argument is vitiated by the author's insistence that the two are derived from a "single archetypal character."

22. The complexities of the subject are well represented in Foley 1978.

23. Cf. Winkler 1990.129ff. *passim* and 164–65.

24. Hesiod speaks of the κούρη only at WD 783, 785, 794, where it is used in the sense of daughter.

25. In WD the maiden's place inside the house (δόμων ἔντοσθε, 520, ἔνδοθι οἴκου, 523) and beside her mother (φίλη παρὰ μητέρι, 520) recalls the "foolish children" of the Silver race who live inside (ᾧ ἐνὶ οἴκῳ, 131) for a hundred years beside their mothers (παρὰ μητέρι κεδνῇ, 130).

26. On the destructive power of female sexuality and seductiveness, see Th. 205, WD 65–68 and 373–75.

In WD the evils of old age and women are also connected in the vignette of the "bad wife," the perfect leech (δειπνολόχης, 704) who can "burn" her husband without fire and drive him to "raw" old age, that is, age him prematurely: εὔει ἄτερ δαλοῖο καὶ ὠμῷ γήραι δῶκεν (705). On women in Hesiod in general see esp. Marquardt 1982, Sussman 1978, Loraux 1978, and Arthur 1973 and 1982.

27. On Archilochus' relation to the traditions of preliterate song, see esp. Dover 1964.199ff. and Russo 1973–74.711ff.

28. In 48 the speaker describes the perfumed charms of some women, probably *hetairai*, who were "so fragrant in their hair and bosom, that even an old man would have loved them" (ἐσμυριχμένας κόμην / καὶ στῆθος, ὡς ἂν καὶ γέρων ἠράσσατο): while old men are sluggish in regard to sexual arousal, the beauty (or perhaps the number) of these women would suffice.

29. Henderson 1976.159 suggests a tradition of song in which men report their sexual experience with women of various ages and social backgrounds.

30. On the Roman material, see esp. Richlin 1983.109–16 and 1984. For a helpful if polemical study of the figure of the crone in the Western tradition, see B. Walker 1985.

31. Richlin 1983.110.

32. It may be significant in this regard that Percles on each occasion uses γρηῦς ("old biddy"), which is slightly more pejorative than γραῖα.

Plutarch also reports the story at Cim. 14.4.

33. Plut. Per. 189–90, Cim. 480.5–481.7. The themes are merged in Ar. Lys. and Thesm., where the women take their sex lives and the city's affairs into their own hands.

34. Neoboule is "older" in the Cologne epode and perhaps in the reference to the γεραιτ[έρην as restored in 63 = Pa. Ox. 2312. On Lycambes, Neoboule, and other Archilochean versions of "stock characters" in generic situations, see West 1974.25–33, Dover 1964.205–12, and Nagy 1976.193. Lefkowitz 1976 cautions against the historical value of any biography gleaned from Archilochus' verses and the traditions that developed around them.

35. E.g., Hor. Carm. 1.25, 3.15, 4.13; Anth. Pal. 5.298.

36. On Penelope's skin, see *Od.* 2.376, 4.749–50, 18.172, 179, 19.204. ἀπαλόχροας παρθενικάς also occurs at *Hymn Aphr.* 14.

37. Page 1964.139–40 notes the Homeric echoes in κάρφεται (cf. *Od.* 13.398, 430, where the verb is used to describe the withering of Odysseus' good looks) and in the second line of the fragment in general.

38. Cf. Henderson 1976.164–65 ("To the archaic mind the bloom of youth disappears with an excess of libido or sexual experience") and Brown 1984.

39. Campbell 1976.155 observes the support this supplementum receives from Alcman, who speaks at 120.9 of a man who married πρὶν τὸ γένηον μέλαν ἔμμεναι.

40. Henderson 1976.159–60 suggests the convention of the "clever seducer" in relation to the Cologne poem.

41. On the language of defloration throughout the poem and in particular in relation to the Διὸς Ἀπάτη of *Il.* 14, see Henderson 1976; cf. the floral imagery in Archilochus 30.

42. That the phrase suggests a perfect "dream girl" is suggested by Hipponax 119W: εἴ μοι γένοιτο παρθένος καλή τε καὶ τέρεινα. That Homer uses τέρην not of people but of skin (as observed by Campbell 1976.154) serves to contrast the young and sexually attractive skin (νέον . . . χρόα, 49–50) of the sister with the dry and wrinkled skin of Neoboule (cf.188.1–2). Henderson 1976.164 connects Homer's use of τέρην for plants with the vegetal imagery throughout the poem.

43. For παρθένος of "unmarried women who are not virgins," see LSJ s.v. παρθένος 2. On the technical boundaries of virginity, see esp. Sissa 1990.

44. The *Hymn to Demeter* 108 describes the daughters of Celeus as ὥστε θεαί, κουρήιον ἄνθος ἔχουσαι, and Hesiod 132M–W speaks of a girl who "lost her tender flower because of hateful lust" (εἵνεκα μαχλοσύνης στυγερῆς τέρεν ὤλεσεν ἄνθος). Herodotus uses ἀπορρέω specifically in connection with fallen fruit: μὴ ἀπορρέῃ ὁ καρπὸς φοίνικος (1.193). Cf. Campbell 1976.152–53 and Degani 1974.122.

45. Hesychius glosses the word as a synonym for γραῖα, but at Theoc. *Id.* 7.120 the young man Philinos is said to be ἀπίοιο πεπαίτερος, "riper than a pair," and losing his youthful bloom (καλὸν ἄνθος); cf. Marcovich 1975 *ad loc.*

46. Cf. Ussher 1973 *ad loc*, who notes that the metaphor is anticipated at 884 when the young woman calls her "rotten" (σαπρά).

47. On the frag. see Carson 1990.145–46. I cannot agree with the argument of Brown 1984 that the woman's degeneration is a result of *deprivation* of sex: the adjectives κυυζή and πέπειρα as they appear elsewhere clearly suggest active or excessive sexual indulgence.

48. The language recalls his abuse of a courtesan at frag. 17 in which Πασιφίλη, "friendly to all," is the rocky fig tree that feeds many crows (πολλὰς κορώνας); here the "friendly" Neoboule is the ripe fruit and can "go to the crows" (ἐς κόρακας ἄπεχε, 31). For a similarly sexually suggestive use of φίλη, cf. Anacr. 389.

49. DuBois 1988.27; cf. DuBois 1984 for a similar appreciation of the Helen exemplum in Sappho 16.6–11, which presents Helen not in the traditional narrative and Homeric pattern of passive object/goal but as desiring subject, "actant," in her own right.

50. For a careful analysis and attempted resolution of the theoretical and historical problems involved in the assumption that such a female perspective can be formulated and survive in an androcentric culture, see Skinner 1993, who describes Sappho's

expression as the historical consequence of "women-among-themselves speaking (as) woman."

51. On the critical violence that has been done to Sappho's poetry by discussions that are overtly or or implicitly hostile to it because of its status as "woman's poetry" or its homoerotic context, see especially Lefkowitz 1974 and Hallett 1979.

52. Stigers 1981.46. My discussion of Sappho is indebted throughout to her thoughtful essay.

53. See e.g., Giacomelli 1980b.137 and n.5.

54. Cf. Stigers 1981.46: "Eros or Aphrodite is the universal, eternal sexual longing which can never be mastered, while the individual provoking it is only a temporary focus of the longing, the prey or prize which loses its allure once the man has captured it."

55. Aphrodite's smile is the subject of dispute. Snyder 1989.15–16 rightly observes that it does not, as others have suggested (e.g., Page 1955a.15–16, Stanley 1976.313–16), indicate amusement or derision but rather the "power, benevolence and serenity" of the Archaic smile. Gentili 1988.85, 89 describes Aphrodite's tone as "now calm and serene, now impatient; but her impatience is always kindly, without any trace of anger or remoteness," and contrasts her smile with "the fixed, immobile smile" of the Aphrodite φιλομμειδής of epic poetry.

56. Giacomelli 1980b has argued that in verses 21–24 Aphrodite consoles the speaker not by promising a change of heart by the girl who now rejects her, but by reminding her that justice will ultimately be done when this girl suffers the role of the older lover and finds herself similarly rebuffed. But this argument assumes that the structure of female homoerotic relations as Sappho represents them parallels the practices in male poets and that the age-grading of these relationships is necessarily similar: "*It is plausible* that there were parallel sentiments among Greek women who engaged in homosexual relationships, and that Sappho could expect to be liberated from her desire for this particular girl as soon as that girl became *obviously too old* to play the role of beloved. Aphrodite's words in verses 21–24, then, are a promise to Sappho of release from *erotic tyranny*" (141; emphases mine). We need more evidence on the age structures of female homosexuality and their relation to patterns of dominance and submission. As Fränkel 1973.183 says, "[Sappho] surrenders with that knowledge of helplessness which is characteristic of Greek lyric." I see no indication that Sappho regards love as tyranny.

57. Especially if, as has been suggested, the purposes of these poems and the institution that produced them was to prepare these young women to cross the line between girlhood and womanhood. For various views of the relations between the poet Sappho and her *thiasos*, the public and private nature of activities and its relevance to the question of audience, see Merkelbach 1957, Russo 1973–74, Calame 1977, Hallett 1979, Rösler 1980, and especially Burnett 1983.211–28, Gentili 1988.72–89, and Skinner 1993. The view of Sappho as headmistress of a girls' school, still widespread, originated with Wilamowitz (1913.17–78), though without textual evidence.

58. Gentili 1988.75–76; cf. Merkelbach 1957.4–16.

59. There is an interesting point of comparison here in Archilochus' use of vegetal imagery in relation to age and sexuality in the Cologne epode, which opposes the flower (ἄνθος, 27), the virginal ideal, to the women, the overripe (πέπειρα, 26) fruit.

Sappho, despite the virtual gardens of floral imagery in which she festoons her beloveds, finds the expression of the ideal of erotic perfection not in the impossible delicacy of the flower but in the sweet apple itself (γλυκύμαλον, 105.1), overlooked and difficult to reach; on the sexual symbolism of the image of the apple, see Winkler 1981.79 and notes.

60. Winkler 1981.69 (= 1990.175). Giacomelli 1980b.140–41 relates the conception of time to other archaic and classical Greek expressions of justice.

61. See e.g., fragment 9 ("as long as I live"?), 88 ("for I shall love as long as there is (breath) in me," 15, and φιλήσω, 24. Cf. also fragment 15, which in its references to the vicissitudes of one particular affair suggests a fullness of narrative.

62. Schadewaldt 1950.115–19.

63. Gentili 1988.84.

64. Burnett 1983.290.

65. Burnett 1979.18–19.

66. Cf. Stigers 1981.52. In response to the description by Page 1955a.83 of the verses as merely "a long list of girlish pleasures," Winkler 1981.82 draws attention to the contrast between the beloved's δεῖνα πεπόνθαμεν (4) and the speaker's κάλ' ἐπάσχομεν (11): where the perfect tense focuses on the experience of loss in the present, the imperfect appreciates the duration of love over time. Burnett 1979.18 observes how the description of their lovemaking as it is to be remembered is "removed from history, from narrative, and from any contact with the mundane world." On the various levels of time in the poem, see also Schadewaldt 1950.114–19 and McEvilley 1971.8–9.

67. Cf. Stigers 1981.49. Lanata 1966.63ff. identifies such χάρις as a distinguishing quality of those who have reached the age of love.

68. Cf. Preisshofen 1977.57 n.153.

69. Winkler 1990.167.

70. Burnett 1983.224–25; cf. 216ff. on the didactic and instructional qualities of Sappho's verse generally.

71. Correspondingly, in the one fragment of Sappho that has invective force (55), she attacks a women not on the basis of her body or her erotic failure but for her lack of culture and education: since she "has no share in the roses of Pieria" there will be no memory (μναμασύνα) of her after her death. Because she has no access to the lyre, apparently as singer or song, her life has no meaning and is already a kind of death. To be miserable for Sappho is not simply to be unsuccessful in eros but to be without access to the revitalizing power of erotic reflection, whether as singer or song.

72. The fragments are discussed most recently in Preisshofen 1977.57–64 and Di Benedetto 1985, with complete references. Although I share many points of agreement with these two discussions, it is striking that neither makes any mention of the importance of Sappho's womanhood to the theme or of the poetic traditions as they relate the meaning of age for women.

73. We do well to recall the remarks of Alcaeus on the beauty contests held in Lesbos (130B.17–18; cf. schol. A on Il. 9.129).

74. Snell proposes some form of κάρφω in 6, but Di Benedetto 1985.145, cautioning that this may be too "crude" a word for Sappho, suggests perhaps a form of ἰάπτω, drawing attention to Od. 2.376. If so, Sappho may be intentionally using a verb associated with the aging of Penelope rather than Odysseus (cf. Od. 13.398, 430).

75. Di Benedetto 1985.146 points to Mimn. 5.8 and 1.7, *Hymn Aphr.* 244, and Pind. *Pyth.* 4.158; Snell's emendation νόον ἀμφιβάσκει in 7 also finds support in Mimn. 5.8.

76. Di Benedetto 1985.146 suggests [κἄμεθεν πόθ]ος πέταται διώκων.

77. The connection between old age and song in the two fragments is noted by Stiebitz 1926; cf. Preisshofen 1977.59. Di Benedetto 1985 notes the negative associations of age and song in Hor. *Carm.* 3.15.13–15.

78. Cf. Treu 1976.169. ἰόκολπος is used of a bride at 30.5. Alcaeus applies the epithet to Sappho herself in frag. 384.

79. On ἤδη as a poetic convention, see Preisshofen 1977.59 n. 138.

80. Di Benedetto 1985.147–49, who holds out the possibility of either βαθυκόλπων (Stiebitz's emendation) or ἰοκόλπων in 11, restores 11–12:

> [γεραίρετε Μοίσαν   ]κόλπων κάλα δῶρα, παῖδες,
> [λάβοισαι] φιλάοιδαν λιγύραν χελύνναν.

81. Noted by Stiebitz 1926.1259ff. Stehle 1990 relates the myth of Eos and Tithonus here to other mythological references in Sappho that describe "a goddess desiring a young, beautiful, mortal man whom she hides away in an enclosed place far from civilization" as ways in which the poet creates a space for a distinctively female erotic fantasy.

82. Page 1955a.130 n.1.

83. Di Benedetto 1985.151–52 proposes Τίθωνον at the beginning of 21 as the object of φέροισα, and αὖ]τον (still referring to Tithonus) as the object of ἔμαρψε.

84. It is significant, for instance, that both κάλλιστον and λάμπρον appear in poem 16.

85. Cf. Treu 1976.59, 156, Preisshofen 1977.62–63, and Di Benedetto 1985.154–56 (who reads ἔρος ἀελίω).

86. Preisshofen 1977.62; Di Benedetto 1985.155.

87. Di Benedetto 1985.156–160 suggests that in speaking of the "love of the sun" Sappho invents "un nesso nuovo ed atipico," which corresponds to her discovery of "una dimensione nuova dell' animo umano" in proclaiming her will to live despite old age. In this way Sappho not only breaks with the negative poetic tradition of old age but replaces the "objective" view of old age that is found for instance in Mimnermus with a subjective reappraisal.

88. Schadewaldt 1950.160–61.

89. Campbell 1982 *ad loc.*

90. We recall, for instance, the fiercely independent appraisal of what is κάλλιστον in 16.3.

91. ἄβρος is clear at 2.14, 44.7, 100, 128, 140.1, less certain at *LPF* 25.4 and 84.5; the substantive appears only here. On the importance of the word and concept, see Treu 1976.171–72, 176–77, Di Benedetto 1985.154, and Preisshofen 1977.56, 61 and 64.

92. Gentili 1988.87. Preisshofen 1977.63–64 points to the highly abstract nature of the closing lines, as reflected in the substantive ἀβροσύνα and the string of substantive adjectives that follows (he would add to τὸ λάμπρον and τὸ κάλον also τῶδυ, accepting Gundert's emendation in 25 τῶδυ δὲ] τοῦτο.

93. Winkler 1990.202–6 (discussing an unpublished paper by E. Stehle), groups Sappho's use of the Tithonus myth with that of Endymion and Selene (199), Phaon

and Aphrodite, and Adonis and Aphrodite, as "four versions of the same exemplary tale. He whom a goddess loves ceases to be a phallic man, enters instead a state of permanent detumescence." Winkler suggests that in frag. 58 Sappho may be comparing herself to Tithonus in being carried off by the Dawn and given the gift of endless speech ("though I will die, my songs will live on forever"), but he neglects the negative force that the exemplum seems to carry in the fragment as in the tradition.

94. Gentili 1988.87.

CHAPTER 4

1. From the Penguin translation of W. Hamilton (1951).

Text is cited as follows. Homer and the Homeric *Hymns* from T. W. Allen, *Homeri Opera*, Vols. I–V (Oxford 1902–12); where noted translations are from R. Lattimore, The *Iliad of Homer* and *The Odyssey of Homer* (Chicago 1951 and 1965) and A. Athanassakis, *The Homeric Hymns* (Baltimore 1976). Hesiod from Solmsen, Merkelbach and West, *Hesiodi Opera* (Oxford 1970); where noted translations are from R. Lattimore, *Hesiod* (Ann Arbor 1959). Mimnermus from M. West *Iambi et Elegi Graeci ante Alexandrium Cantati* (2 vols., Oxford 1971). Ibycus and Anacreon from D. A. Campbell, *Greek Lyric II* and *Greek Lyric III* (Harvard 1988 and 1991), with his translations as noted; Campbell's enumeration follows that of D. Page, *Poetae Melici Graeci* (Oxford 1962).

2. Alcibiades discusses Socrates' amorous nature at *Symp*.216d and 223a, and throughout likens Socrates to a Silenus, whose age and lecherous tendencies were proverbial and celebrated in satyr plays like *Cyclops* and *Ichneutai*; it is significant that at 216a–b he declares that he could sit and listen to Socrates until *he* grows old (καταγηράσω). Socrates and Anacreon are linked as amorous old men in Anac. 503.

3. *Phdr*.227c. Socrates goes on to describe a host of physical and emotional defects that the younger beloved must tolerate in his older lovers (240b–e). On the famous ancedote in which Sophocles talks about sex and old age in *Rep*. 329b–c, see chap. 7.

4. For other sexual situations in Aristophanes involving old men, see *Birds* 668–69, 1252–56, *Ach*. 990–99, *Thesm*. 59–63, *Wasps* 1342–45; cf. *Gêras* frag. 140 Edmonds. On old women and sexuality in Aristophanes, see above chap. 3.

5. So Seneca on a *controversia* he claims to have heard Ovid deliver (*Contr*. 2.2.10).

6. Bertman 1989 surveys the theme in ancient poetry. For Greek New Comedy see McCary 1971 and for the *Greek Anthology* Esler 1989. Houdijk and Vanderbroeck 1987 provide useful commentary on the relation of the literary materials to Greek and Roman sexual attitudes.

On the theme in Western literature, see the interesting essays by Fiedler 1979 and 1986.

7. For bibliography on the physiology and sociology of sexuality in old age, see Gordon et al. 1976.324–25 and Whaton 1981. Discussion of some of the contemporary issues can be found in Butler and Lewis 1976.

8. On fifth century Athens as phallocracy, see Keuls 1985.

9. On age and marriage, see Garland 1990.210–13 and notes.

10. On age-grading in erotic relations, see Dover 1978.73–91, 100–9, 153–70, Buffière 1980.185–86, Giacomelli 1980b.137 and n.5, and Garland 1990.187, 208–9.

11. Houdijk and Vanderbroeck 1987.58.

12. Johnson 1982.31: "In the Greek idea of lyric, then, the business of the lyric

poet is to provide a criticism of human passion that will indicate which passions are to be embraced and which are to be shunned: the purpose of this demonstration is the education of the hearer, a process of education that functions not by the poet's stating what must be done or learned but rather by his showing what sorts of behavior, what configurations of identity, are possible or preferable." Cf. Fränkel 1973.151 n. 50: "The 'I' who passes judgements in archaic lyric is always intended as a representative."

13 On the absence from the Homeric epics of overt reference to homosexual relations, and on the relation of Achilles and Patroclus in particular, see Dover 1978.196–99 and Halperin et al. 1990.86 and notes.

14. Cf. Donlan 1980.6, 20–22 and Nagy 1979.262–63. Russo 1974 wisely cautions against attributing to Homer too simple an association between aesthetic beauty and moral goodness.

15. as when Hector criticizes Paris (Il. 3.39–57) or Odysseus lectures Euryalus (Od. 8.167ff.); cf. Donlan 1980.6–7. It is noteworthy that although the adjective καλός is used widely in Homer, the noun κάλλος is reserved for a handful of conspicuous men and women (among them, in the Odyssey but not the Iliad, Odysseus).

16. In the Odyssey Nestor sleeps beside his "grave wife" Eurydice (3.403, 451–52). The aged Antenor, among the wisest of the dēmogerontes, is married to Theano, who is described as "beautiful cheeked" (καλλιπάρηος, Il. 6.298, 11.224) and "brilliant" (δῖα, 5.70).

17. Cf. Alc. 347. On old age as a time of dryness when the vigor of youth and male sexual force (regarded as a fluid μένος) begin to dissipate, see Onians 1951.214–15, 219–21, Giacomelli 1980a passim, Carson 1990.137–45, and Garland 1990.248 and references; on menos in early poetry in general, see Nagy 1974.265ff. On Anchises' fear that his tryst with Aphrodite will leave him ἀμενηνός (HymnAphr. 188), see below.

Cicadas were noted for their dryness and their serpent-like ability to slough their γῆρας; cf. Arist. HA 5.549b25, Onians 1951, King 1986.24–26, and Garland 1990.248, 267. The relation between desiccated skin and old age, frequent in erotic lyric, is implicit in Hesiod WD 702–5, who warns that a bad wife can age a man prematurely: (εὗει ἄτερ δαλοῖο καὶ ὠμῷ γήραϊ δῶκεν, which may have a sexual connotation: see Carson 1990.141); cf. also Il. 9.115–16, where Phoenix declares to Achilles that he will not be left behind without him, "not were the god in person to promise / he would scale away my old age and make me a young man blossoming (γῆρας ἀποξύσας θήσειν νέον ἡβώοντα). Here old age is seen as a dry encrustation to be "scraped off" the real (i.e., youthful) person beneath; see van der Ben 1986.

18. See e.g., Rankin 1977.59–60.

19. See Lacey 1968.41–42, 112–13 and Keuls 1985.267–73, who observes a reference in Lysias On the Murder of Eratosthenes 31 that assumes a man's right to kill anyone he caught in flagrante with his pallakē.

20. Cf. Devereux 1955.92 and 1973.43–44; the interpretation is accepted by Scodel 1982.103. One can add to Devereux's arguments Phoenix's remark that the gods "were bringing to completion" (ἐτέλειον, 9.456) the curses; given the time frame of the episode (cf. 9.470), proof of this could only have been in his failed sexual performance. There is nothing in Phoenix's personal history to suggest that he ever had occasion to put a curse of childlessness to the test.

21. Schein 1984.111–12.

22. Scodel 1982.

23. Cf. Preisshofen 1977.37–39.

24. On the visual acuity of youth, cf. *Il.* 23.476–77.

25. Odysseus expresses a similar idea in a passage that combines nostalgia for the past, a reference to the dryness of old age, and his own penchant for agricultural metaphor (see above chap. 1). As he dissembles to Eumaeus, he suggests the *aretē* hidden beneath his shabby appearance.

> I took for myself a wife from people with many possessions,
> because of my courage, for I was no contemptible man, not
> one who fled from the fighting; but now all that has gone from me,
> but still, I think, if you look at the stubble (καλάμην) you see what the corn was
> like when it grew, but since then hardship enough has had me.
>
> (14.211–15: tr. Lattimore)

26. So strong is the suitors' desire for Penelope that when they see her their "limbs were loosened, and their hearts enchanted by love" (τῶν δ' αὐτοῦ λύτο γούνατ', ἔρῳ δ' ἄρα θυμὸν ἔθελχθεν, 18.212; hence the irony of λύτο γούνατ' and λελῦτο δὲ γυῖα at 18.212, 238). On their desire being in some sense reciprocated, if only unconsciously, see Devereux 1957.

27. On ἀνήνωρ as a synonym for ἀμενηνός in the sense of "unmanned, impotent," see Giacomelli 1980.17 and n. 51, who cites *Th.* 750–52, where Hesiod cautions against accidentally making one's twelve-year-(or twelve-month?) old son ἀνήνωρα. On other myths that suggest the emasculating effects on a mortal of sex with a goddess, see Winkler 1990.202–4.

28. As Stehle 1990.95–96 observes, Odysseus' "escape" from Circe and Calypso allows the poem to sustain the hierarchy of male over female over and against the hierarchy of divine over mortal that grants each goddess, either potentially or temporarily, sexual domination over the male.

29. Clay 1981–82.116 observes that in preparation for the climax with the suitors Athena applies ambrosia cosmetically to Penelope (18.188–96), the original significance of which was as a retardant of age and physical decay.

30. Hdt. 2.53.2. rightly observes that Homer and Hesiod gave to the Greeks their gods' genealogies, epithets, offices, and forms. On the gods as literary figures, see e.g., Whitman 1958.221 ("Like the characters of the *Iliad*, the gods of the *Iliad* are refashioned, within the limits of their assigned spheres, to fit the poem, and there is no reason to believe that they would not be different in a different one"), but cf. Gould 1985.25.

31. Otto 1954.127–28.

32. See Clay 1983.141–48.

33. For different structuralist readings of the *Hymn*, see Segal 1973, Smith 1981, and King 1989. Clay 1990.189 says of the themes of mortality and aging, "By the end of the hymn, all the possible combinations of these two categories will have been presented to form a complete system."

34. Janko 1982.179–80 suggests that the *Hymn* was composed between *Th.* and *Hymn Dem.* and argues (169) for a date in Hesiod's own lifetime between *Th.* and *WD.*

35. Cf. Byl 1976.235–36.

36. *Il.* 3.139, 446, 14.328, *Od.* 22.500.

37. Smith 1981.40 describes the embarrassment of the Olympians and later Aphrodite herself as the result not of their yielding to the power of sexual desire but of

the way "it has involved them in a kind of miscegenation, a painful contact with mortality and so with death."

38. On Anchises' urgency as an expression of the irresistable nature of erotic *ananke*, see Parry 1986. Clay 1989.172 notes that at *Il.* 3.54 the lyre is listed as one of Aphrodite's gifts to another passionate Trojan lover, Paris.

39. and where the casual juxtaposition of the homoerotic and heteroerotic interests of the gods reflects the lack of any absolute cultural distinction between them; it is significant that Ibycus 8 similarly groups the myths of Tithonus and Ganymede.

40. Cf. Clay 1990.185.

41. Smith 1981.78–82 emphasizes how the three moments of Tithonus' biography are analogous to the stages of mortal life, "youth, gray-haired maturity and extreme old age."

42. Clay 1981–82.115. Smith 1981.79 observes that Tithonus' double diet—bread and ambrosia—symbolizes the way Tithonus unites in himself the opposition of mortality and immortality.

43. Smith 1981.81 notes the effect of the switch to the present tense in ῥέει (237)—"His voice is flowing on *now*"—and is probably right in characterizing his talk as mere babbling. Again, there may be a connection between Tithonus and his brothers among the Trojan *dēmogerontes* in their idle and ineffectual speech (perhaps reinforced through the cicada simile of *Il.* 3.151–53). Van Eck 1978 *ad* line 237 argues that ῥέει ἄσπετος refers to the power of his speech, which flows "unspeakably great," but I see no support for this in the *Hymn* or in the cicada simile of the *Iliad*.

44. Smith 1981.83: "His picture of Tithonus is of a man in the end utterly without human connections."

45. On the assimilation of the very old to the very young, see King 1989.72–73, 82. Noteworthy in this respect is Plato *Laws* 929d–e, which recommends that an old man convicted of παράνοια or senile incompetence will no longer be master of his estate but "will dwell in his own household as a *pais* for the rest of his life"; cf. Garland 1990.262.

On old age as involving a gender reversal for old men, see Gutmann 1987.94ff.: "The general pattern is that older men are increasingly like women and with women. Becoming more domestic in their interests, they also retire into domestic space, the inner space of women." See Chap. 6.

46. Clay 1990.190–91.

47. See Giacomelli 1980 and Scodel 1982.

48. It seems equally possible that the hymnist has suppressed any reference to the *tettix*, given the emphasis in the Homeric tradition on the humanity of heroes and its exclusion of fantastic and supernatural elements in the myths; see also Clay 1990.189 and n.128.

49. Smith 1981.47–48 describes Anchises as "untypically concerned with his old age and with the future of his family," but Clay 1990.174 provides Homeric parallels. Anchises' concern for the prosperity of his lineage (θαλερὸν γόνον, 104) may suggest a particularly Trojan value (cf. Hector at *Il.* 6.476–78).

50. On the crosscurrents between the different versions of the myth, see Smith 1981, Di Benedetto 1985, and King 1986. The fragment would fit well thematically in that portion of the "Nanno" collection preserved in fragment 12, which deals with Helios, Eos, and the never ending toil of the sun.

51. See e.g., *Il.* 2.46, 186, 5.724, 9.413, 13.22, 14.238, 18.370, 24.88; in *Th.* ἄφθιτος

is used three times of Zeus' imperishable counsels (545, 550, 561) and three times of Styx and its water (389, 397, 805).

52. Gentili 1988.46 says of the fragment, "The immortal old age of Tithonus is the symbol of eternal misfortune worse than death," with useful discussion on the function of myth in lyric.

53. Cf. e.g., King 1989.80 on the version in the *Hymn* (i.e., without the metamorphosis into a tettix): "To be fully mortal, to experience the aging which destroys, is better than to be like the aging but undying Tithonus. . . . Aphrodite creates a model in which the normal condition of mankind, between the eternally young Ganymedes and the eternally old Tithonus, seems something to be desired."

54. On Mimnermus and old age, see Bowra 1938.17–24, Fränkel 1973.209–13, Schmiel 1974, Griffith 1975, and Preisshofen 1977.86–90

55. τίς δὲ βίος, τί δὲ τερπνὸν ἄτερ χρυσῆς Ἀφροδίτης;
   τεθναίην, ὅτε μοι μηκέτι ταῦτα μέλοι;
   κρυπταδίη φιλότης καὶ μείλιχα δῶρα καὶ εὐνή,
     οἷ' ἥβης ἄνθεα γίνεται ἁρπαλέα
   ἀνδράσιν ἠδὲ γυναιξίν· ἐπεὶ δ' ὀδυνηρὸν ἐπέλθῃ
     γῆρας, ὅ τ' αἰσχρὸν ὁμῶς καὶ κακὸν ἄνδρα τιθεῖ,
   αἰεί μιν φρένας ἀμφὶ κακαὶ τείρουσι μέριμναι,
     οὐδ' αὐγὰς προσορῶν τέρπεται ἠελίου,
   ἀλλ' ἐχθρὸς μὲν παισίν, ἀτίμαστος δὲ γυναιξίν·
     οὕτως ἀργαλέον γῆρας ἔθηκε θεός.

56. For the simple twofold opposition between young(er) and old(er) see e.g.: *Il.* 2.789, 9.36, 258, 14.108; *Od.* 1.395, 3.24, 362–63, 4.720, 8.58, 16.198; Tyrtaeus 9.27, 37, 41–42. At *Od.* 23.212 Penelope laments that she and Odysseus could not "enjoy their youth together and come to the threshold of old age" (ἥβης ταρπῆναι καὶ γήραος οὐδὸν ἱκέσθαι).

57. Kirk 1971.140 says regarding Mimnermus 6 that "he was ready . . . to stretch the technical limits of youth when it came to the point." But the distinction has some precedent at *Od.* 8.137, where Odysseus (who is well into what we would call middle age) is said not to be lacking in ἥβη (the strength of youth).

58. Cf. Bowra 1938.21.

59. Κῆρες δὲ παρεστήκασι μέλαιναι,
   ἡ μὲν ἔχουσα τέλος γήραος ἀργαλέου,
   ἡ δ' ἑτέρη θανάτοιο· μίνυνθα δὲ γίνεται ἥβης
   καρπός, ὅσον τ' ἐπὶ γῆν κίδναται ἠέλιος.

60. Griffith 1975.78–79.

61. Κῆρες δὲ παρεστήκασι . . . θανάτοιο in Mimnermus 2.5–7 and κῆρες ἐφεστᾶσιν θανάτοιο / μυρίαι at *Il.* 12.326–27.

62. Schmiel 1974 comments on the self-conscious appraisal of youth from "the vantage point of experience" that characterizes Mimn. 2 and Simon. 8, and how here, in contrast with the brevity of youth, old age is a prolonged misery. Yet I disagree with his comment on the Kers of old age and death that "[t]he former is surely evil, the latter evidently good." As 2.4–5 suggest, youth is unaware of both good and evil, and as Gerber 1975.265 says, "For Mimnermus real happiness consists in not realizing that one is happy, in not knowing that good and evil exist in separate categories." Youth is

unaware of both the good it presently has, and of the evil that is to come—to wit, the old age and death that are described in the following lines. Although it is clear in 2.9 and 1.2 that old age is a greater evil than death, old age is not therefore to be considered ἀγαθόν. This surely is the case in Semon. 29.8 (which Schmiel cites as a parallel to Mimn. 2), which says that when a man is young he is also foolish, "for he does not expect to grow old or die." Cf. Griffith 1975.78–79.

63. Griffith 1975.80. Schmiel 1974.288 too notes how the poet suggests that unlike the brevity of youth, old age drags on. Mimnermus' view of old age as a time of weakness, poverty, and disease is anticipated to some extent in the *Odyssey* in the figures of Laertes and Odysseus himself in his disguise as aged beggar.

64. Adkins 1985.100 suggests that line 3 is a rhetorical tricolon, and that all three of the pleasures the speaker mentions (κρυπταδίη φιλότης καὶ μείλιχα δῶρα καὶ εὐνή) refer to the physical enjoyment of eros, but I prefer to read μείλιχα δῶρα as a reference to the gift–giving by which the lover would seduce his beloved, and Mimnermus as suggesting the delight to be had not just in the receiving of gifts but in the whole social transaction of love.

65. On Hermann's emendation αἰσχρὸν ὁμῶς καὶ κακόν (which is accepted in the editions of West, Campbell, and Gerber) in relation to καλοκἀγαθία, see below.

66. I agree with Campbell *ad loc.* that 2.8 likely means "as brief as a sunrise." ἠέλιος is a metrically appropriate substitute for the Ἠώς of the Homeric formulas he notes. Mimnermus may also be drawing on the associations with the Eos–Tithonus myth and the (relative) brevity of Tithonus' youth.

Note also the importance of the sun in fragment 12, also from the "Nanno," which may have been offered in an erotic context. As Bowra 1938.35 notes, the sun is the most frequent single image in Mimnermus.

67. That leaves and flowers are metaphorically coextensive is suggested by the epic formula φύλλα καὶ ἄνθεα γίνεται ὥρῃ (*Il.* 2.468 and *Od.* 9.51).

68. Cf. Griffith 1975.77 and 81, and Bowra 1938.19–20.

69. Griffith 1975.77 observes that where in Mimnermus the φύλλα are only the object of the verb φύει, the passive products of nature, in the Homeric simile they are alternately subject and object of their verbs.

70. Houdijk and Vanderbroeck 1987.59–60, speaking in general of male old age and Greek sexual practice, insist that because no external restrictions prohibited him from the pursuit of sexual relations, "the old man was not put in a marginal position." I would suggest that it is precisely in the *lack* of restrictions that their situation becomes marginal, since the old man is required to define his sexual identity in the same terms as those of the dominant youth.

71. For examples of the injunction to help one's friends and hurt one's enemies, see Archil. 23.14–15, Solon 13.5, Theog. 869, Pind. *Pyth.* 2.151, Aesch. *Cho.* 122, Eur. *HF*585, *Ion* 1046, *Med.* 809, and Pl. *Men.* 71e.

On the social force of φίλος and ἐχθρός, see Goldhill 1986.79ff.

72. E.g., Schmiel 1974.286 n.1. Adkins rightly notes of κακόν that its sense is "inferior" rather than "immoral" or "unjust" (1985.98 and 224 n.15).

73. On the relation between the *kouroi* and the aristocratic ideal of *kalokagathia*, see esp. Hurwit 1985.197–202 and Stewart 1986.60–63. Stewart coordinates the circumstances under which these *kouroi* were sculpted with places and periods in which aristocratic power and prestige were on the rise.

74. Ἔρος αὖτέ με κυανέοισιν ὑπὸ
βλεφάροις τακέρ' ὄμασσι δερκόμενος
κηλήμασι παντοδαποῖς ἐς ἄπει-
ρα δίκτυα Κύπριδος ἐσβάλλει·
ἦ μὰν τρομέω νιν ἐπερχόμενον,
ὥστε φερέζυγος ἵππος ἀεθλοφόρος ποτὶ γήρᾳ
ἀέκων ὄχεσφι θοοῖς ἐς ἅμιλλαν ἔβα.

(287)

75. On the poem's imagery and presentation of conflict beween the lover's attitudes toward love in the abstract and toward the particular object of his affection, see Stigers 1981.47–48, although she does not (as the scholiast does) associate the age of the horse with that of the speaker. On the unwillingness of the horse (cf. ἀέκων) to race as an expression of the ἀνάγκη that binds the lover (though never the beloved), see Giacomelli 1980a.138.

76. On the theme of erotic ἀνάγκη, see Schreckenburg 1964.59–60 and Giacomelli 1980a.138–39 and notes 9–12.

77. On the fundamentally asymmetrical and hierarchical nature of power relations in love, cf. Halperin 1990.30.

78. According to some accounts Anacreon lived to be eighty-five, and he is traditionally referred to as old in the testimonia: cf. Campbell 8, 9, 11, 12, 13. The tradition of the amorous old man is sustained in Anacreonta1.6–7, 7, 39, 43.15–16, 47, 51, 52b, 53.7, 59.11–13, 61b.

79. Gentili 1973a.

80. Cf. Maximus of Tyre (18.9): "his poems are full of the hair of Smerdis and the eyes of Cleobulus and the youthful beauty of Bathyllus" (tr. Campbell).

81. The relevant testimonia are given by Campbell with frag. 414; Smerdis may also be the "beautiful–faced boy," καλλιπρό[σ]ωπε παίδ[ων, of 346 fr.1.2. One wonders if Polycrates' object in having his hair cut was not only aesthetic but symbolic as well. Since the cutting of the hair often occurs in rites of passage from the male's status as παῖς to that of κοῦρος (at Athens the ceremonial cutting of the hair was called the κουρεῖον), Smerdies' haircut may have the effect of a status transition, from an age when one is appropriately the object of such homoerotic affection to an age where one is not.

82. Byl 1976.242. The author of Anacreonta 7 seems clearly to have the poem in mind, although the speaker there offers a good deal more resistance to the image that his mirror offers.

83. Giangrande 1968.109–11 suggests too ingeniously a salacious double-entendre in the final line, arguing that ἀναβῆναι refers to the capacity for erection and that the poem's real complaint is that the dead can no longer make love.

84. σφαίρη δηὖτέ με πορφυρῇ
βάλλων χρυσοκόμης Ἔρως
νήνι ποικιλοσαμβάλῳ
συμπαίζειν προκαλεῖται·
ἡ δ', ἐστὶν γὰρ ἀπ' εὐκτίτου
Λέσβου, τὴν μὲν ἐμὴν κόμην,
λευκὴ γάρ, καταμέμφεται
πρὸς δ' ἄλλην τινὰ χάσκει.

85. For recent defenses of each of these two main readings of the poem and excellent reviews of the extensive literature on it, see Woodbury 1979 and Marcovich 1983 respectively. Like almost all modern editors and critics, I reject as unnecessary Barnes' attempt to replace the ἄλλην of the MSS with the masculine ἄλλον. And for reasons that are well marshalled in the articles by Woodbury and Marcovich, I reject the readings of the poem imposed by Giangrande 1973 and Gentili 1973, which read ἄλλην τινα as "some other hair" (that is, the pubic hair of the poet or some other) and identify the girl from Lesbos as a *fellatrix*.

86. Page 1955.143 n.3.

87. ποικιλοσαμβάλῳ in v.3 also would trigger an association between the girl and the ἁβροσύνα that characterized the aesthetics and the life-style of Sappho and her circle; see chap. 3. Woodbury 1979.282 suggests quite aptly that the reference to "well-built Lesbos" connotes the elegance and sophistication for which Lesbian women were known, though he would connect this with their fastidious and discriminating taste in the selection of lovers—hence the girl's rejection of the speaker because of his age.

88. Note also frag. 374, where Anacreon gives musical accompaniment as he tells Leucaspis to "enjoy the fun of youth" (ἥβᾳς).

89. Cf. συνηβᾶν, 378, 402a.

90. Cf. Campbell 1983.22 on Anacreon 396 and 398: "In all these cases Eros plays games of a competitive nature such as a young boy might play. . . . "

91. Foucault 1978.103, with general discussion by Halperin 1990. By "power" Foucault intends not the juridical sense in which we are accustomed to identify its exercise—power as law, sovereignty, prohibition—but as "the name that one attributes to a complex strategical situation in a particular society" (1978.93)

92. Foucault 1980. He explores the continuities between classical Greece and the later tradition in the second volume *The Use of Pleasure* (1986) where he finds a common ground in the way that sexuality became for the Greeks no less than for us a focus of moral solicitude and ethical concern. Regrettably, Foucault did not pursue his investigation of ancient sexuality into any of the poetic testimonies available, and the second and third volumes of *The History of Sexuality* are limited to philosophical and ethical texts.

93. Chudacoff 1989.25.

94. Chudacoff 1989.54.

95. Winkler 1990.26ff. does well to remind us in regard to the interpretation of dreams that the ancient idea of sexual symbolism tended to be the inverse of our own Freudian based view: where we regard the non-sexual as manifest content for a repressed sexual meaning, the ancients saw sexual themes and images as symbolic of the nonsexual and specifically the social and political.

96. Arist. *Ath. Pol.* 53.4 notes certain judicial arbitrators (διαιτηταί) aged sixty and above who presided over cases settled out of court and who served nonrenewable terms of one year.

97. Aristotle recommends that old men serve as priests (*Pol.* 7.1329a31–34); see Finley 1981 and Garland 1990.281.

98. Kirk 1971. On the loss of status that accompanies education and literacy, see Cowgill 1974 and Holmes 1983.14, 179–180.

On the wisdom of old age, see above chap. 7.

99. Powell 1988.9 suggests that "in Greek societies, as elsewhere, the influence of the wealthy and of the old tended to be very great." But apart from Sparta, always the

exception, the sources he cites (p.29 n.52) have nothing to say about the political power of the elderly.
100. Van Hoof.1983.
101. Dover 1972.128.
102. This is not to say that they did not take their charge seriously. Forrest 1975 notes that where the younger generation (those, like Alkibiades, born in 450 B.C. or later) had come to take the Athenian constitution largely for granted and could weigh its merits with theoretical detachment, the elderly continued to regard it as an issue of vital public interest and the idea of participation in the machinery of the democracy could still excite their passions. The youth's intellectual theorizing about alternate constitutions and lack of political experience led to the oligarchic revolution of 411.
103. Garland 1987.18 says in respect to Plato's statement at *Rep.* 5.465a that it is universal for older men to rule and younger men to submit, that "whatever the answer on the domestic level, certainly on the pubic level and most notably in the sphere of Athenian democracy, no such obligation existed."
104. Garland 1990.206 and 283 points to the debate and vote on expedition itself, which was divided closely along age lines (Thuc.6.8–27).
105. On life expectancy and longevity, see Garland 1990.245–47 and Strauss 1993.68–70.
106. Slater 1964; cf. Glotz 1929.96–97.
107. Cf. Reinhold 1970 and Strauss 1993 *passim*. In Socrates' criticism of democracy at *Rep.* 562e–563b, Plato observes that under such constitutions the young are thought to be the equals of the old, and the old mimic the young in their behavior and beliefs.

CHAPTER 5

1.   παῖς μὲν ἄνηβος ἐὼν ἔτι νήπιος ἕρκος ὀδόντων
       φύσας ἐκβάλλει πρῶτον ἐν ἔπτ᾽ ἔτεσιν.
     τοὺς δ᾽ ἑτέρους ὅτε δὴ τελέσῃ θεὸς ἔπτ᾽ ἐνιαυτούς,
       ἥβης ἐκφαίνει σήματα γεινομένης.
     τῇ τριτάτῃ δὲ γένειον ἀεξομένων ἔτι γυίων
       λαχνοῦται, χροιῆς ἄνθος ἀμειβομένης.
     τῇ δὲ τετάρτῃ πᾶς τις ἐν ἑβδομάδι μέγ᾽ ἄριστος
       ἰσχύν, ᾗ τ᾽ ἄνδρες σήματα ἔχουσ᾽ ἀρετῆς·
     πέμπτῃ δ᾽ ὥριον ἄνδρα γάμου μεμνημένον εἶναι
       καὶ παίδων ζητεῖν εἰσοπίσω γενεήν.
     τῇ δ᾽ ἕκτῃ περὶ πάντα καταρτύεται νόος ἀνδρός,
       οὐδ᾽ ἔρδειν ἔθ᾽ ὁμῶς ἔργ᾽ ἀπάλαμνα θέλει.
     ἑπτὰ δὲ νοῦν καὶ γλῶσσαν ἐν ἑβδομάσιν μέγ᾽ ἄριστος
       ὀκτώ τ᾽· ἀμφοτέρων τέσσαρα καὶ δέκ᾽ ἔτη.
     τῇ δ᾽ ἐνάτῃ ἔτι μὲν δύναται, μαλακώτερα δ᾽ αὐτοῦ
       πρὸς μεγάλην ἀρετὴν γλῶσσά τε καὶ σοφίη.
     τὴν δεκάτην δ᾽ εἴ τις τελέσας κατὰ μέτρον ἵκοιτο,
       οὐκ ἂν ἄωρος ἐὼν μοῖραν ἔχοι θανάτου.

Text for Solon is cited according to M. L. West *Iambi et Elegi Graeci ante Alexandrium Cantati* (2 vols., Oxford 1971), with iota in the long diphthongs written subscript. In 27 I read ἐκφαίνει in 4 (with Campbell and others) and retain the σήματα of the MSS in 8.

Translation as indicated is from R. Lattimore, *Greek Lyrics* (Chicago 1949).

2. A review of the considerable literature on the poem can be found in Steinhagen 1966.599–600.

3. Schadewaldt 1960. Cf. Lesky 1963.127: "We take the poem to be a deliberate rejoinder to Mimnermus' gloomy picture of old age." Wilamowitz 1893.314–15 defended the poem's authenticity against Porson and Usener, but remarked, "Er hat nichts individuelles." Byl 1976.244 describes the poem as a "leçon d'optimisme."

4. Steinhagen 1966.

5. Preisshofen 1977.81–85.

6. Szemerényi 1964.137–38.

7. Campbell 1967.247.

8. Adkins 1985.132. Both Adkins and Campbell 1967 contrast Solon's piece unfavorably with Shakespeare's "Seven Ages" (*As You Like It* 2.7), an unfortunate comparison in that it invites one to regard the poem as a kind of "genre piece," though there is no evidence that it was conceived according to any existing literary type.

9. Fränkel 1973.232.

10. The poem's hebdomadal structure was earlier attributed to Pythagorean or astrological influence and to the significance of the "mystical" number seven; see Roscher 1906 and Boll 1950. Even if it is true that astrological influence provided the point of occasion for the poem's composition, this would tell us little about Solon's understanding of such a concept and the particular ends to which he puts it here.

11. Schadewaldt 1960.42.

12. See, for instance, Gulliver 1968. I.157–62, La Fontaine 1978.1–20, and in the same volume Baxter and Almagor 1978.159–60.

13. La Fontaine 1978.2–3 observes the differences in the ways such "facts of nature" are perceived and how the cultural impulse to ground the conventions of age in nature can invent biological differences where they do not exist.

14. Gulliver 1968.157.

15. Fortes 1984.99–101.

16. On Greek age classifications, see above chap. 2 n.6.

17. The Homeric poems maintain a rough internal chronology and frequently mark the passage of time in years; cf., e.g., *Il.* 2.134, 239, and *Od.* 2.175 (the first of many allusions to Odysseus' return "in the twentieth year"), 3.306, 7.259–61, 13.377. But Homer does not invite the reader to compute age numerically, and sometimes confounds our chronological sense, as when Helen observes at *Il.* 24.765 that twenty years have passed since she left Sparta.

18. Hesiod expresses caution regarding the accidental emasculation of twelve-year-old boys (*WD* 750–52), where δωδεκαταῖον may have a religious context. Other references to age are approximate: a man should marry μήτε τριηκόντων ἐτέων μάλα πόλλ' ἀπολείπων/ μήτ' ἐπιθεὶς μάλα πολλά (696–97), and hire a τεσσαρακονταετής (441) to plow for him. These references, like that to the nine-year-old bulls (ἐνναετήρω, 436) that are strongest in their youth (ἥβης μέτρον ἔχοντε, 438), are characterized as formulaic or notional figures by West 1978 *ad loc.*

19. Szemerényi 1964.137.

20. Interesting in this regard is the system attributed to Pythagoras (Diog. Laert. 8.10) of four twenty-year stages. While it presents some parallels to Solon's idea, it differentiates each chronological stage by a corresponding term (the παῖς, νεηνίσκος,

νεηνίης, and γέρων respectively), and according to Diogenes assimilates them to the movement of the seasons.

The same is true of later hebdomadal divisions of the life course, like that of "Hippocrates" in the *De Hebdomadibus,* which identifies the seven ἡλικίας of man's nature as παιδίον, παῖς, μειράκιον, νεηνίσκος, ἀνήρ, πρεσβύτης, and γέρων; see West 1971.

21. The term (or its equivalent) may have been familiar in nonliterary contexts; "counting by" a given numeral was likely common enough, at least commercially. Concepts like the ἑκτήμοροι, whatever the exact meaning of the term, show the application of number to social problems.

22. Plut. *Sol.* 20–24 *passim.* On the tenor of the laws as a whole, cf. Murray, 1980. 189: "Throughout the legislation runs a sense of the application of reason to social problems, and of a controlled freedom from tradition." Certainly the character of the legislation is related to its self-conscious composition in writing, which Solon stresses in 36.18–20 (θεσμοὺς . . . ἔγραψα).

23. See Aris. *Ath. Pol.* 10 and Plut. *Sol.* 15.4. On the many questions regarding these issues, see for instance Ehrenberg 1973.73–74, Jeffrey 1976.92, and Hammond 1986.159–60. Interesting in this context is Plutarch's remark (*Sol.* 2.1) that Solon had been a merchant in his youth.

24. Cf. *Ath. Pol.* 8 and Plut. *Sol.* 19.1.

25. *Ath. Pol.* 7. On whether Solon himself assigned to the *hippeis, zeugitai,* and *thêtes* the values of three hundred, two hundred, and less than two hundred respectively as in *Ath. Pol.* 7, and whether the medimnos was a literal or symbolic valuation, see Ehrenberg 1973.66–67, Jeffrey 1976.92–93, and Hammond 1986.160–61 and below n.44. For a more critical treatment on the extent to which the division into property classes was original with Solon, see Sealey 1976.115–19.

26. Fortes 1984.114.

27. Aristotle implies a distinction between a hebdomadal and a "natural" division of the life course at *Politics* 7.15.11: οἱ γὰρ τοῖς ἑβδομάσι διαιροῦντες τὰς ἡλικίας ὡς ἐπὶ τὸ πολὺ λέγουσι οὐ κακῶς, δεῖ δὲ ᾗ διαιρέσει τῆς φύσεως ἐπακολουθεῖν; what he means by a "natural division" is clear from the rest of the discussion in the *Politics* and *Rhetoric* (2.12–14), where he works within a traditional framework of νεότης, ἀκμή, and γῆρας and undergirds this order with chronological points of reference. Aristotle sets the arrival of puberty at age fourteen (*Hist. Anim.* 581a).

28. Bowra 1938.100.

29. Hudson-Williams 1926.129; cf. Campbell 1967.248. Steinhagen 1966.603–4 suggests that in combining the seventh and eighth hebdomads Solon produces the odd number of couplets required by the poem's particular structure and symmetry.

30. Herodotus has Solon remark to Croesus: ἐς γὰρ ἑβδομήκοντα ἔτεα οὖρον τῆς ζόης ἀνθρώπῳ προτίθημι (1.32.2; cf. Diog. Laert. 1.55). But as Preisshofen remarks (1977.81 n. 237), the motif may itself be derived from the poem.

31. Steinhagen 1966.602–4.

32. Bowra 1938.101 calls the higher term "a pardonable exaggeration." Steffen 1955.42–47 suggests that the poem was occasioned by Mimnermus' sixtieth birthday. Kirk 1971.141 says that ". . . [Solon] ironically chooses to chide Mimnermus, rather than himself, for the miscalculation." Adkins 1985.131: "but poets are not necessarily consistent, and in 27W Solon may be using someone else's scheme of ten hebdomads as a framework for his thought." West 1974.73: "[Solon] may not have meant his

poem as a genuine communication for Mimnermus' ears, but it takes the form of one . . . "

33. ἀλλ' εἰ μοι καὶ νῦν ἔτι πείσεαι, ἔξελε τοῦτο—
    μηδὲ μέγαιρ', ὅτι σεο λῶιον ἐπεφρασάμην—
    καὶ μεταποίησον Λιγιαστάδη, ὧδε δ' ἄειδε·
    "ὀγδωκονταέτη μοῖρα κίχοι θανάτου".
                                                (20.1–4)

34. Schadewaldt 1960.43; cf. Fränkel 1973.217.
West 1974.181–82 suggests that Mimnermus 6.2 was quoted by Solon, and reads τοῦτο in 1 understanding ἔπος in the sense of "verse" as antecedent.
35. Bergk emends this to Λιγυαστάδη, with reference to the entry in the *Suda* on Mimnermus; Campbell, following Diels, reads Λιγυαστάδη. In any case the derivation from λιγύς and ἄστης (ᾄδω) seems secure.

36. αἳ γὰρ ἄτερ νούσων τε καὶ ἀργαλέων μελεδωνέων
    ἑξηκονταέτη μοῖρα κίχοι θανάτου.
                                                (6)

37. Fränkel 1973.230 aptly characterizes the spirit of Solon 20 as symposiastic; cf. Preisshofen 1977.84. It is noteworthy that Lucian *Makr.* determines that anyone who lives to age eighty may be called μακρόβιος.
38. Plutarch's two references to the famous line (*Sol.* 2.2, 31.7; cf. 29.6) assume that it refers to Solon's old age, as have most readers since. But as Young 1971.12 n.39 points out, it is possible that γηράσκω is being used idiomatically and that the sense of the line is simply that "as long as I live I continue to learn."
Snell's edition follows that of Diehl in considering West 20, 21, and 18 as sequential fragments of a single poem; those of Bergk, and Gentili and Prato do not. Campbell 1967.249 says that they need not neccesarily be from the same poem.

39.   τὰ γὰρ περιώσια πάντα
    χρήματ' ἔχων οὐδεὶς ἔρχεται εἰς Ἀίδεω,
    οὐδ' ἂν ἄποινα διδοὺς θάνατον φύγοι, οὐδὲ βαρείας
    νούσους, οὐδὲ κακὸν γῆρας ἐπερχόμενον.
                                                (24.7–10)

40. Mimnermus speaks of κακὸν ἄφθιτον . . . γῆρας at 4; cf. also 1.5–6 and 5.6.
41. Cf. Schadewaldt 1960.56.

42. ἔργα δὲ Κυπρογενοῦς νῦν μοι φίλα καὶ Διονύσου
    καὶ Μουσέων, ἃ τίθησ' ἀνδράσιν εὐφροσύνας.
                                                (26)

Plut. *Amat.* 5; cf. Fränkel 1973.218.
43. One might similarly contrast the lush imagery of ἥβη in poems 24 and 25 and their context of homosexual love with the description of youth in poem 27, which makes no reference to eros, and again with Solon's strict legislation in regard to pederasty (cf. Aeschines 1.14).

Solon shows a similar freedom in the treatment of old age within his legislation. Aeschin. 3.2–4 speaks of a law of Solon's (long fallen out of practice) which gave the right to speak first in both the *Boulê* and Assembly to the eldest of the citizens (τῷ πρεσβυτάτῳ τῶν πολιτῶν) and then in turn to others in order of age, and suggests that meetings of the Assembly began with the herald's call "who of the men over fifty years old wishes to speak?" On the other hand, Plut. *Sol.* 22 reports that Solon exempted a son from his obligation to render the θρεπτήρια, normally grounds for loss of citizenship, if his father had failed in his duty to teach him a trade (cf. Diog. Laert. 1.55)

44. Jeffrey 1976.93, cf. Ehrenberg 1973.67: "If the name of the *pentakosiomedimnoi* was in earlier use, it could only have been as a kind of nickname for the most wealthy. What was completely new was that Solon used the four groups as a basis for constitutional rights, and that the military divisions as well as the *pentakosiomedimnoi*—the latter for the first time officially recognized—served on account of their economic standing."

45. Also interesting in this perspective is the revision of the Athenian calendar attributed to him (Plut. *Sol.* 25.3). Solon addressed the incompatibility of systems of temporal measure based on solar days and lunar months by designating the transitional days as ἔνη καὶ νέα or "old and new" and appointing the following day as the official beginning of the new month. He also renumbered the days of the month, counting backward again from the twentieth. Like the restructuring of the life course, the solar and lunar rhythms here provide natural "objects," which become the occasion of self-conscious manipulation and mathematical organization.

46. Cf. Fränkel 1973.232 and Ehrenberg 1973.64. The attribution is contested since the same lines appear at Theog. 315–18.

47. Schadewaldt 1960.58 also speaks of "die Sprache der Distanz und des sach- und seinsgemässen Sehens."

Preisshofen 1977.84 comes closer when he observes that the poem in its very denial of traditional motifs of age reveals no less of a one-sidedness than that of Mimnermus: "Überzeugend kann die Elegie, die ihre Grösse der streng durchgehaltenen Distanz verdankt, nur für einen distanzierten Hörer sein."

48. On the range of possible meanings for ἀπάλαμνα ("immoral," "foolish," "impractical"), see Campbell 1967.248.

49. Cf. Adkins 1985.132.

50. δήμῳ μὲν γὰρ ἔδωκα τόσον γέρας ὅσσον ἐπαρκεῖν,
         τιμῆς οὔτ᾽ ἀφελὼν οὔτ᾽ ἐπορεξάμενος·
      οἳ δ᾽ εἶχον δύναμιν καὶ χρήμασιν ἦσαν ἀγητοί,
      καὶ τοῖς ἐφρασάμην μηδὲν ἀεικὲς ἔχειν·
      ἔστην δ᾽ ἀμφιβαλὼν κρατερὸν σάκος ἀμφοτέροισι,
      νικᾶν δ᾽ οὐκ εἴασ᾽ οὐδετέρους ἀδίκως.
                                                                              (5.1–6)

51. Murray 1980.185 appreciates γέρας as an expression of the honor of Homeric nobility.

52. Cf. Murray 1980.190: "It was no coincidence that the image of the marker-stone recurs in his poetry, for all his work was concerned with boundaries, and the arbitrator is himself in essence 'a marker-stone in boundary land.'" Solon also uses a spatial metaphor when he defends himself from the personal attacks on him, where

the demos and its enemies become dogs and he the wolf at bay: ὡς ἐν κυσὶν πολλῆισιν ἐστράφην λύκος (36.27). On the subject in general, see Will 1958.

On equality as a Solonian principle, cf. Plut. *Sol*.14.2 who says that his dictum τὸ ἴσον πόλεμον οὐ ποιεῖ won approval by rich and poor alike, the former assuming that τὸ ἴσον would be based on worth and excellence (ἀξία καὶ ἀρετῇ), the latter on measure and number (μέτρῳ καὶ ἀριθμῷ). Poem 27 in a sense does both. ἰσόν τοι πλουτέουσιν is also the controlling idea of poem 24.

53. The distinction between "aristocratic" and "bourgeois" lyric is well developed in Arthur 1973.37–39.

54. On the self-conscious appraisal of youth from "the vantage point of experience" that characterizes Mimnermus 2 and Simonides 8, see Schmiel 1974.

CHAPTER 6

1. The story is also told in Plut. *Mor*. 235d–e (= *Sayings of Spartans* 55) and Val. Max. 4.5., which both place the incident at the Panathenaea (although this does not rule out the possibility that the setting was the Theater of Dionysus). Hdt. 2.80.1 observes that the Spartans were unique among the Greeks in yielding their seats to the elderly. On the ethic of disrespect for the elderly by which the Athenians were distinguished from the Spartans, see Garland 1990.276–80; cf. Powell 1988.222.

Except where noted, text for Eurpides is cited as follows: *Children of Heracles* from the Teubner edition of Garyza (1972); *Phoenician Women* from the Teubner edition of Mastronarde (1988); other plays from the Oxford editions of Diggle (Vol. 1, 1984 and Vol. 2, 1981) and Murray (Vol. 3, 2nd ed. 1913).

2. The exceptions are *Iphigenia in Tauris* and the suspect *Rhesus*.

3. See among the fragments in Nauck^2: 25, 282, 291, 453, 508, 509, 575, 619, 637, 805, 1080.

4. Kitto 1939.251, troubled by the protracted reflections on old age by the chorus of *Heracles*; cf. Byl 1975.136.

5. Gouldner 1965.110–15 suggests that Greek tragedy in composing its choruses of "dependent-subordinate personages who give voice to weakness, such as old women or men, slaves, suppliants, lower-class men, or fallen gods," and Euripides in featuring such characters in his plays, invite an identification with a model of the self that runs counter to the culturally sanctioned (and socially problematic) models of individuality.

6. On longevity and creativity, see M. I. Finley 1981.160ff.

7. de Romilly 1968.158–70.

8. Reinhold 1970; Thury 1989.

9. For general comments on Euripides and the conventional representation of old age in Greek tragedy, see Byl 1975, esp. 135–39, and Kaimio 1988.12–14 and *passim*.

10. Pollux describes tragic masks for old and mature men and women in detail at *Onom*. 4.133–42, though fifth-century masks were certainly not so stylized as in second century A.D.

11. Cf. respectively *Alc*. 623; *Alc*. 672; Nauck^2 575; Nauck^2 252, 282.11; *Supp*. 1108; *HF* 649 (where Wilamowitz reads φθόνερον for φόνιον). On the negative and abusive language applied to old age throughout Euripides, see Byl 1975.136–37.

12. Attendants to elderly or assistance in walking: *Alc*. 612, *Med*. 335, *Andr*. 551,

747, *Hec.* 59ff., *Supp.*1104, *Ion* 738ff., *Or.* 474, 629, *Phoen.* 834ff.; they are certainly present though not referred to in other scenes. Cf. also *Ion* 725ff., *Tro.* 506–7, and *Bacch.* 193, where Cadmus says of his support for Tiresias: γέρων γέροντα παιδαγωγήσω σ᾽ ἐγώ; the paedagogic metaphor appears at *Heracl.* 729.

13. *HF* 108 (cf. 254), *Ion* 743, *Andr.* 588, *Phoen.* 1539, 1548, 1719, *Tro.* 276.

14. On the tone of the scene, see Kaimio 1988.15–16; Winnington-Ingram 1969.138 suggests that the poet's penchant for humor here resulted in a scene "not perfectly assimilated to the grand design."

15. The old man's exhaustion takes on added significance if we assume that the "steep approach" is represented not by the parodos but by a flight of stairs leading to a raised platform or *logeion*; so too for the old servant at *Ion* 738ff., Tiresias at *Phoen.* 834ff., and the old chorus at *HF* 119ff. See Arnott 1962.27ff.

16. *Phoen.* 303–4, 322–26 (cf. also γεραιὸν πόδα of Oedipus' entrance at 1537–38); *Or.* 456–58; cf. Hecuba's shorn head at *Tro.* 480.

17. The old men also comment on Amphitryon's sluggish and sorrowful entrance at 1039ff. and describe him (as they had themselves) as an ὄρνις (110, 1039).

18. So Murray's text for 98–99. Diggle reads ἄνα, δύσδαιμον· πεδόθεν κεφαλὴν ἐπάειρε δέρην <τ᾽>.

19. Cf. also *Hec.* 169, *HF* 268; de Romilly 1961.80–83 notes the frequency with which κεῖσθαι is used of the elderly in Euripides; cf. Byl 1975.137.

20. The theme receives its comic treatment in *Cyclops* 581ff., where Papasilenus becomes an unwilling Ganymede who is dragged into the cave by his drunken suitor.

21. For the distinction between "complete" and "figurative" supplication, see Gould 1973.77. For a study of the status of each of the supplication scenes in tragedy, see Kaimio 1988.49–61.

22. See e.g., *Andr.* 727–28, *Bacch.* 1251–52.

23. Cf. Byl 1975.131–32.

24. I borrow the phrase from Kirk 1970.2. These situations provide a dramaturgical problem whether we regard the separation of the chorus and actors as rooted primarily in convention or as physically enforced by a raised *logeion*; on the existence of a raised stage, the opposing positions are well represented by Pickard–Cambridge. 1946.69ff. and Arnott 1962.1–41.

This is not to suggest that in every case the age of the chorus alone provides a complete or a "realistic" account for their passivity. For attempts to show the relationship between the inaction of the chorus in *Agam.* and other aspects of their characterization and themes in the play, see Wills 1963.260–62, Gantz 1983.82–83 and esp. Winnington-Ingram 1983.208–16.

25. On the extensiveness of the theme of ἀπαιδία in Eurpides, see Byl 1975.139 n.1.

26. Consider also the *Hec.*, where the queen sends off a servant woman with a pitcher to fetch water for Polyxena's burial, and the *HF*, where Amphitryon shushes the chorus lest their singing wake the sleeping hero.

27. We get an idea of the suffering of the elderly in the Funeral Oration of Pericles, whose only consolation to them is to suggest that they can hold onto the memory of earlier and happier years and remember that it will not be long until death ends their grief (Thuc. 2.4).

28. Burian 1977.15–16 calls the ending "a brief coda that unflinchingly reverses every major theme of the play, reopens every question, challenges every conclusion."

Burian's account of the play's dramatic form offers a superior reading of the play as a whole and one with which I am largely in agreement, although I would argue that the violence of the play's ending is carefully anticipated in Alcmene's representation throughout. Reinhardt 1979.195ff. *passim* also appreciates the play as an example of suppliant drama but criticizes what he sees as its patriotic and episodic character in comparison with the fuller and more forceful treatment the genre finds in *OC*.

29. The literature on the play is usefully reviewed in Burian 1977.1–3, and the textual questions are reconsidered most recently in Lesky 1977. The best defense of the integrity of the text remains Zuntz 1947. The quotation is from Grube 1941.174.

30. See, e.g., Delebecque 1951 ch. 2, Zuntz 1955.33–38 and 81–88, Vellacott 1975.183–86, Burnett 1976, and Taylor and Brooks 1981.5–7 and 15–22.

31. Burnett 1976.4.

32. Iolaus is described or addressed as γέρων or γέραιος at: 39, 75, 80, 86, 129, 166, 333, 343, 466, 501, 548, 572, 584, 630, 636, 653, 793, 796, 956; as πρέσβυς at 461, 560, 574, 843. Alcmene is similarly described at 39, 446, 584, 653, 654, 888, 911, 956. Their age is underscored by the many references in the play to ἥβη, νέος and other words for youth, by Iolaus' rejuvenation, and in staged productions by masks and appropriate gestures. In the elderly chorus (cf. πρέσβυς,120), Euripides is clearly drawing upon the tradition of the *Marathonomachoi* as representatives of traditional virtues of Athens' past.

33. Cf. πόλιν . . . Μυκήνας . . . πολυαίνετον ἀλκᾷ, 759–61; ἀλκίμου μάχης, 683; ἀλκίμου δορός, 815.

34. Cf. Avery 1971.553–55. Burian 1977.13 n. 36 minimizes the significance of Iolaus' senescence, noting that no one refers to it explicitly in the drama. But Euripides could hardly have emphasized his age more in the play than he does, and while the audience would surely have "granted" him this license, it requires nonetheless an adjustment from the more familiar legends of Heracles.

35. νῷν 640. The two are spoken of as a pair at 584 and 630–31, and Alcmene refers to them as τοὺς . . . γέροντας (956). The pairing of Iolaus and Alcmene reflects other instances of doubling in the play: Demophon and Acamas as δισσοὺς . . . Θησέως παῖδας (35); Hyllus, who offstage leads the older brothers described as οἷσι πρεσβεύει γένος (45), and Macaria who, οὐ ταχθεῖσα πρεσβεύειν γένους (479), leads the girls within the temple and may well be the eldest among them (her talk of marriage at 523–24, 579–80, and 591–92 implies that she is of marriageable age); the Argive herald Copreus and Eurystheus in their appearances at the beginning and end; and Heracles and Hebe in their capacity as twin deities of youth. Cf. Burnett 1976.5 n.4.

36. Lesky 1977.235 observes that the messenger's entrance halts Iolaus' κάτω ὁδός and turns it toward the coming rejuvenation. Grube 1941.171 suggests that the dark tones of this scene anticipate Alcmene's vengeance later.

37. On the theme of βία, see Burian 1977.6 and Burnett 1976.23.

38. Lesky 1977.234–37 suggests a discrepancy between Iolaus' position as described at 603–4 and that shown in 633–35, to be explained by the loss of an intervening scene reporting Macaria's death; cf. Cropp 1980.

39. The dialogue repeatedly opposes verbs of doing to expressions of wishing, wanting, and seeming: cf. 692 and 731–37. Zuntz 1955.29 speaks of the passage as "almost Aristophanic ridicule," and Burian 1977.11 labels it as "perhaps the most overtly comic in extant tragedy."

40. As Burian 1977.12 n. 33 observes, the relation between Iolaus' onstage weakness and offstage vigor is one of "total contrast."

41. His remarks at 297–303 on the importance of marrying within one's station are somewhat off the point, as is his kind but useless (γενναῖα . . . ἀλλ' ἀμήχανα, 464) suggestion to Demophon that he be delivered to the enemy (cf. 466–67). Zuntz 1955.28 notes Iolaus' tendency toward moralizing generalizations.

42. Zuntz 1955.36 describes her entrance as being "like a chicken in a thunderstorm." Lesky 1977.237 compares the comic character of the drunken Heracles in *Alc.* and Clytemnestra's address to Achilles at *IA* 819ff.

43. Burnett 1976.8, comparing Creusa and Apollo in *Ion*, notes the comic overtones in the aged Alcmene's complaints of ill-treatment by her lover.

44. So Iolaus, on his knees in formal supplication of Demophon, puts himself totally at his mercy: "be a kinsman to these children, be their friend, father, brother, master (δεσπότης)" (229–30). The word is also used of Athena, who is the city's "mother, guard and δέσποινα" (772).

45. Cf. Burian 1977.16 n. 43. The point is even stronger if we accept the emendation κρατοῦσα in 884.

46. Zuntz 1955.36–37: "How alike they are. . . . The law of lawlessness has been used against her and she uses it in return when her chance comes." Fitton 1961.457: "Alcmena . . . seems spiritually hardly better than her persecutor." Avery 1971.560: "Alcmene takes on some of the bad qualities which had been attributed to Eurystheus earlier." Burian 1977.17: "In effect she has become another Eurystheus. She puts into practice here the same unrelenting hatred of the enemy that he practiced so long."

47. Iolaus refers to αἰδώς, αἰσχύνη, and behavior that is αἰσχρόν at 6, 43, 200, 223, 460, 541, 700.

48. Cf. Segal 1990.127: "The most fearful metamorphosis of the play, then, is not the future change in Hecuba but the way in which the two enemies come to resemble one another in the present. As Hecuba moves from just venger to monster, she will become literally a stranger to herself; she becomes one with her own hatred, trickery, and murderousness." For a discussion of the heroine of *Hec.* in relation to Freud's notion of the "uncanny" (*unheimlich*), see Rabinowitz 1993.114–24.

49. The passage recalls Hera's readiness to "eat Priam and Priam's children raw" to appease her anger (3.34–36), thereby associating Hecuba's anger with the terrible χόλος of Hera.

50. The theme is perhaps also implicit in Hes. *Th.* in the representation of Earth, to the extent that she is in a sense "old" by reason of her antiquity if not her appearance. It is Earth who initiates the violent revenge (τίσιν, 210) on Sky and who later (though the passage may be interpolated) produces Typhoeus, who attempts a kind of last revenge on the new order of Zeus.

51. For summaries of the fieldwork on the feminization and domestication of older men, see Holmes 1983.129–32 and Gutmann 1987.94–96.

52. Gutmann 1987.155–84; Holmes 1983.129–32.

53. Gutmann 1977.309. Also interesting in light of Gutmann's own fieldwork is the frequency with which elderly men achieve heightened religious power and/or prestige as priests and mediators between the divine and human worlds (see above chap. 1), qualities Iolaus evinces if not in an official capacity in his deep piety and the favor the gods show him; cf. Gutmann 1987.220–24.

54. M. Mead, "Ethnological Aspects of Aging" (cited in Gutmann 1977.311). De Beauvoir 1972.488 remarks that old age is often a liberating period for women: "All their lives they were subjected to their husbands and given over to the care of their children; now at last they can look after themselves."

55. On the subject in general, see Lacey 1968.116–17, 175 and notes, Bremmer 1987, Garland 1990.257–58 and above chap. 3.

56. Cf. Lacey 1968.22 and n.20.

57. On the Greek mother-son relationship as one of conflict and tension, see esp. Slater 1968.28ff.

58. That Plato (*Laws* 775e–776b) recommends against the practice suggests his awareness of the ill-will it created.

Alcmene is necessarily under the κυρίεια of some male, whether of Hyllus or, if he is to be considered a minor, of Iolaus as his guardian. In this context, the anxious exchange between Alcmene and Iolaus (712–16) also suggests her apprehension for her legal and social status in the event of his death.

59. A. Michelini in a review of Falkner and de Luce 1989, *Newsletter* of the Women's Classical Caucus, vol. 17 (spring 1992): 40–44.

60. Gutmann 1987.173–79. An interesting if excessively polemical study of the devolution of the figure of the crone can be found in Walker 1985, esp.125–44.

61. Bremmer 1987.203–4 and Garland 1990.258–59.

62. See Henderson 1987. Garland 1990.270 notes that the comic masks mentioned in Poll. *Onom.* 4.150 suggest the stereotyping to which old women were subjected: γράδιον ἰσχνόν ("little old shriveled woman"), γράδιον λυκαίνιον ("she-wolf"), γραῦς παχεῖα ("obese old woman"), and γράδιον ὀξύ ("sharp-tongued or sharp-witted old woman"); commenting on the interest shown in old women in Hellenistic art, like the drunken old woman by Myron of Thebes, he notes that "there is no surviving study of an old woman which does more than portray her as the representation of an almost sub-human species of animal life which is at best abject and pitiable, at worst contemptible and repellent."

63. Conacher 1967.230 cautions textual critics against excessive emendation in light of "the poet's obvious intent to pack as much as possible of the tradition into [the play]." An examination of the authenticity of the text is beyond the scope of this study. Mastronarde's 1988 Teubner edition, which I follow, retains the exodus to 1736 but deletes 1737 to the end (regarded by many as a later addition—cf. Wilamowitz 1903.593ff., Fraenkel 1963.117, Conacher 1967a.100–101, and Mastronarde 1980.19). For full discussion of the problem and the most successful defense of the basic integrity of the received text, see Mastronarde 1974 (contra Fraenkel 1963) and on the exodus in particular Conacher 1967a.

That the play's action is erratic and its meaning unclear does not mean that the material is disorganized: on the highly symmetrical arrangement of themes and episodes, see e.g., Ludwig 1954.130–35, Foley 1985.108, and Craik 1988.42–44.

64. The conflict between family and fatherland, self-interest and the needs of the polis, provides the basis of a number of important attempts at interpretation: see esp. Riemschneider 1940, de Romilly 1967, Rawson 1970, Foley 1985.114ff. and Burian and Swann 1981.

65. Zeitlin 1990.131. That *Phoen.* is in a sense as much about Thebes as a whole as any of its inhabitants is often recognized, although few would agree with Riemschneider 1940.29 that Thebes is the "true hero" of the play.

66. There appears to be a precedent for Jocasta's negotiation between her sons in the speech preserved in the Lille Stesichorus fragment (P. Lille 76a, b, c), although there is no indication that the speaker is elderly or that the address is made at the time the brothers are about to fight each other; for discussion, see Parsons 1977 and Burnett 1988. Euripides' *Oedipus* is dated on metrical grounds among his final plays (408–406 B.C.), certainly later than *Phoen.* On the relation between the plays, see Webster 1967.241–46. The mythical background of *Phoen.* is well presented in Craik 1988.35–40.

67. Grube 1941.354 and n.3, and 369–70, emphasizes the force of Oedipus' presence in the house and the references to him throughout the play, and he aptly suggests that for dramatic effect and prophetic power his appearance is something of a *deus ex machina*.

68. Cf. παρθένιον, 224; νεάνιδες, 302. In *Phoen.* Tiresias is untypically guided by his maiden daughter (cf. παρθένῳ χερί, 838), and even the maiden status of the Sphinx is emphasized (48, 806, 1023, 1042, 1730).

69. The scenes clearly mirror each other, with the *paidagōgos* leading Antigone in the first and her leading her father away in the latter; Kaimio 1988.13 n.12 fails to appreciate the connection.

70. On the play's relation to the *Seven*, see esp. Foley 1985.113ff.

71. Conacher 1967b argues that the alleged inconsistency between the burial motif and the exile motif in the exodus, a major stumbling block to accepting the end of the play up to 1736 as genuine, is reduced by directing our attention to Antigone's change of position: from outright defiance of Creon at 1643–57 to a series of pleas that she be allowed to bathe the corpse of Polyneices, bind his wounds, or simply embrace him (1666–71). Euripides allows Antigone to back down from her original resolve to bury Polyneices, setting the play at odds with Sophocles' *Antigone*, but compensates by her refusal to marry Haemon and voluntary exile with her father. This assumes the deletion of 1743–46, which is granted by almost all. Cf. Rawson 1970.122 and Foley 1985.130 and n.44.

72. That the Menoeceus episode is original with Euripides is accepted by most, although Vian 1963.206–15 argues for a tradition for the story by analogy with other Theban myths.

73. On the role of the chorus in the play, see the important study of Arthur 1977.

74. One can perhaps include the elderly nurses of *Hippolytus* and *Medea*, who in their uncommon devotion to their mistresses and their children are quasi-maternal figures.

75. Loraux 1987.15, 26; cf. 1269, 1282, 1349, 1458–59, 1483, 1552, 1635. Jocasta's motherhood assumes an archetypal quality in 676ff., where the chorus invokes a range of goddesses related to the founding of Thebes who as "suffering mothers" are kindred spirits to Jocasta: Io who is ancestress (προμάτορος) and mother of Ephaphus, Demeter who is mother of Persephone and identified with Earth herself, who produces the Spartoi only to lose them in fratricidal slaughter.

76. The idea is also represented linguistically. Until 81, ἐγώ appears only when Jocasta identifies herself in line 10 (and here as subject of a passive verb); she refers to herself elsewhere infrequently and only in oblique cases.

77. 306, 987, 1434, 1527, 1568, 1603.

78. Jocasta expresses similar vain hopes for the future at 1202 and 1212; cf. Polyneices' hopes to kill his brother at 634.

79. Foley 1985.115, 119.

80. Mastronarde 1979.30 notes that because of her slow entrance and partial vision, Jocasta does not see Polyneices until the ἰὼ τέκνον of 304.

81. Arnott 1989.57 observes that in the context of Greek scenic convention Jocasta's dance is neither unusual nor indecorous and underscores the different emotive values of lyric and iambic discourse. Kaimio 1988.39 n.30 notes the features Jocasta's song shares with typical recognition duets.

82. So too, Jocasta's opening allusion to the sun and to the foundation of Thebes locates the origin of the evil poetically rather than philosophically, and at 379ff. she says simply that "one of the gods" is responsible for their ills. Given her devotion to her family, it is not surprising that Jocasta finds the cause of her family's woes externally rather than in the character of the agents.

83. Od.11.275–76.

84. See above, n.38, Chap. 2. On the Oedipus myth as a negative paradigm for initiation, see Bremmer 1987a.

85. Conacher 1967.233 reads the play as "a series of paradoxical confrontations of the world of myth (in which the pattern of events is determined by some external and supernatural force) and the 'real' world of Euripidean drama, where events are usually presented as the result of human passions and human folly"; cf. Foley 1985.111ff. Recent critics have tended to emphasize the importance of human motives and choices to the play without recourse to divine or deterministic influences (e.g., Arthur 1975.39–42, Mastronarde 1974.284–86). Notwithstanding, the tensions between Polyneices and Eteocles originate in their response to Oedipus' curse (69ff.). Cf. Conacher 1967.238: "It was the sons' *fear* of the curse, not the curse itself, which induced their dangerous evasive action." Whether or not we regard the curse as having a "real" inherent power of its own or not, every character in the play speaks *as though* Oedipus' anger and curses (ἀραί, Ἐρινῦς, ἀλάστωρ) are to be taken seriously: cf. 254–55, 351, 474–75, 624, 765, 876–77, 1053–54, 1306, 1355, 1426, 1503–4, 1556–58, 1611.

86. 48–52, 806–11, 1019–50, 1688,1728–33 [1759–60].

87. See 327, 376, 763, 870, 1088, 1533–35.

88. While it is technically the death of Eteocles that frees Oedipus from his house arrest, neither Antigone nor Oedipus makes any reference to his confinement when he is summoned out at 1530ff.

89. Pearson 1909 *ad loc.*, following the scholiast, notes two possible meanings for στενάζων ἀρὰς τέκνοις (333–34): "groaning out curses on his children" or "lamenting the curses on his children." He prefers the latter possibility despite the strain it puts on the meaning of στένω and on the accompanying dative. The former reading, apart from underscoring the weakness and indecision of Oedipus, is also supported by the present tense in ἀρᾶται (67), which the context suggests is not historical (cf. ἔκρυψαν, 64; ζῶν δ' ἔστ' ἐν οἴκοις, 66). Although Polyneices speaks at 475 of the curses that "Oedipus once uttered against us (ἐφθέγξατ' . . . ποτε)," and Tiresias says at 875–76 that Oedipus "gasped out (ἐκ . . . ἔπνευσε) terrible curses on them," there is no need to assume that the cursing was restricted to occasions in the past.

90. On suicide in tragedy as "mainly a woman's death" and hanging as more disgraceful than the sword and "a woman's way of death," see Loraux 1987.7–30 *passim*. The relation between the destiny of Oedipus within and those without is beautiful-

ly anticipated in ἐπ᾽ αὐτόχειρά τε σφαγάν (332), which introduces the themes of sacrifical and self-slaughter later associated with the death of Menoeceus (σφαγέντα, 933; σφαγάς, 945; 1010; σφάξας, 1010; αὐτοσφαγῆ, 1316) and Oedipus' sons (αὐτόχειρ, 880; σφαγάς, 1431).

91. For images of light, white, and brightness in the *teichoskopia*, see 111, 119, 129, 146, 169, 172, 175–76, 183, 191. On the theme, see Podlecki 1962.357–62.

The scholiast observes at 88 how the situation reverses that in *Il.* 3, in which the younger Helen identifies the troops for the Trojan elders.

92. See e.g., Xen. *Oec.* 9.3–5; the scholiast *ad Alc.* 989 notes that Cretan boys were called σκότιοι, probably because they were kept in the women's quarters (cf. LSJ s.v. σκότιος). On the archaeological evidence for the seclusion of women, see Walker 1983; on the relation between female domesticity and their association with inner space and inner darkness, see Padel 1983.8–12.

93. Cf. 353, 1342, 1496, 1504, 1582.

94. βακτρεύμασι τυφλοῦ ποδός, 1539–40; παραβάκτροις . . . πόδα σὸν τυφλόπουν, 1548–49; γεραιὸν ἴχνος . . . βάκτρα, 1718–19); cf. Zeitlin 1990.155.

95. The theme is underscored by the similarities between Oedipus and Tiresias (on which see Podlecki 1962.361 n.12): their mutual blindness, old age, and difficulty walking—compare the "blind foot" of Tiresias (834; cf. 847) and Oedipus (1539–40, 1549, 1616; cf. 1699); the gold pins driven through Oedipus' feet when he was exposed (805; but see 26), the gold brooches with which he blinded himself (62), and the gold crown that Tiresias wears (856); Tiresias' entrance to Thebes from Athens guided by his maiden daughter and Oedipus' exit from Thebes to Athens guided by Antigone; Tiresias' Athenian connection (852–57) and Oedipus' final destination there (1705–7).

Zeitlin 1990.143 observes the significance of Tiresias' recent successful prophetic experience at Athens (851–57). As with Menoeceus in Thebes, the daughters of Erechtheus had to be sacrificed to procure Athens' successful campaign against Eumolpids. Such a "pure and disinterested civic act" could only be imported into Thebes from outside. For an opposing view see Vellacott 1975.198, who sees both instances of self-sacrifice as deceptive and ineffectual.

96. On the Freudian equation of blinding and castration, see Devereux 1973 as well as the caveat of Buxton 1980.25, 34–35.

97. Note the roots in βουλ in the scene: βουλεύματα (693), εὐβουλία (721, 746), βούλη (721), βουλεύου (735). Eteocles is called νεάζων at 713, and he and the younger Polyneices are both νεανίαι at 1243 and 1360.

98. Note the change in Creon's address, from the reverent πρεσβυτέρου (847) and πρέσβυ (896) to the more impatient γέρον (915; cf. γερασμίου, 923).

99. On Creon in *Medea*, see Falkner 1985.

100. On the antithesis between Creon's personal situation and the interests of the city, see Rawson 1970.118–21.

101. Foley 1985.121 and Craik 1988 *ad* 455 note that Jocasta's use of the Gorgon image is appropriate to the maternal tone of her lecture.

102. διαλλαγή and its cognates: 375 (Mastronarde deletes), 436, 443, 445, 468, 515, 701; cf. σύμβασις and its cognates: 71, 85, 587, 590.

103. φιλοτιμία: 532; cf. 567. τυραννίς, 506, 523, 524, 549; cf. 560. Ἰσότης: 536, 542; ἴσον: 538, 544, 547, and note Polyneices' and Eteocles' use of ἴσον at 487 and

501; it is significant that Eteocles has use for equality only as a military strategy (ἴσους ἴσοισι, 750).

104. τὸ πλέον, 539, 553; τὸ λίαν, 584; ἔρις, 81, 351, 1277, cf. 500, 798, 811, 1460, 1462, 1495 (bis); ἐχθρά, 540; cf. 374. On Solon as reconciler, see above Chap. 5 and corresponding note 52.

105. Cf. σοφός, 414, σοφόν, 453, σοφώτερον, 530; ἀμαθεῖς, 569, ἀμαθία, 584. The theme is picked up by Polyneices at 495 and Eteocles at 499.

106. Grube 1941.360. As Conacher 1967.238 notes, she "defeats both sons at their own game of words." We may contrast her speech with the more traditional and personal arguments that Aethra uses in her appeal to Theseus (*Supp.* 297–331) when she urges him to consider his religious obligations and the honor or shame his response will bring.

107. On Jocasta's view of language, see Foley 1985.122–23; for parallels and sources for her ideas, see Mastronarde 1986.202, 204–6 with notes 21 and 23.

108. Her maternal approach to political issues is anticipated in her remarks to Polyneices about the dangers of pursuing "a strange marriage in a strange house" (337ff.) and her questions about the nature of exile (387ff.), where she is interested primarily in the suffering of the exile.

109. On the culpabiity of both sons, see Ebener 1964.71–79 and de Romilly 1968.111–13; on the justice of Polyneices' claim, see Craik 1988 *ad* 154.

110. Although the questions at 376–78 may be rhetorical: see Mastronarde 1979. 121–24.

111. On the wall as a threshold between city and battlefield, see Arthur 1981. The *teichoskopia* identifies two landmarks on the Theban plain: the "tomb of the seven maidens of Niobe" (ἑπτὰ παρθένων τάφου Νιόβης, 159–60) by which Polyneices stands, where Niobe as a paradigm of maternal grief anticipates the bereavement of Jocasta; and the tomb of Zethus (μνῆμα τὸ Ζήθου, 145), which provides a precedent for the sibling rivalry of Polyneices and Eteocles (cf. also 606).

112. The scholiast *ad* 88 comments on the impropriety of Antigone's later exit.

113. μητήρ: 1429, 1436, 1439, 1443, 1444, 1452, 1455; τεκοῦσα: 1447; τέκνον: 1428, 1432, 1433.

In planning to bare her breast on the field of battle, Jocasta "outdoes" even Hecuba, the archetypal *mater dolorosa*, who thus supplicates Hector from the wall (*Il.* 22.79ff.).

114. The metaphor in παρασπίζουσα gains force from ὑπασπιστοῦ (1213), spoken by the messenger who is also shield-bearer to Eteocles; cf. ὑπασπίζων at *Heracl.* 216 of Iolaus' service to Heracles. Grube 1941.366 n.2 rightly insists on the full military force of the metaphor.

If 1430 is genuine (Mastronarde would delete), Jocasta's haste (προθυμία ποδός) recalls the earlier reference to her γεραίῳ ποδί (302–3) as well as Eteocles' dismissive περαίνει δ' οὐδὲν ἡ προθυμία (589); cf. the προθυμία of Creon at 902.

115. So Loraux 1987.9, 14–15, 26, 51–52.

116. Cf. the notion of equality in *OT* 408, 425, 1507.

117. Cf. Rabinowitz 1993.62–66. Within limits Menoeceus conforms to the pattern: like the παρθένος (and unlike Haemon) he is unmarried (ἤθεος), unacquainted with marriage (λέχος) and the marriage bed (εὐνῆς); like Polyxena in the *Hec.* he is a πῶλος or virgin colt and therefore suitable for sacrifice (945–47). Loraux 1987.35–36, 41–42 suggests that the need for a male victim reflects the super-masculine Theban

world of autochthonous "sown men," and that while Menoeceus dies with a blow of
the sword to the throat (1091–92) his death is—again like Jocasta's—more truly that
of a warrior, a self-sacrifice rather than a womanly suicide.

Jocasta herself sees her marriage as a cause of his death (1204–7).

118. Cf. Podlecki 1962.358, 361.

119. Cf. Vellacott 1975.172.

120. Mastronarde deletes 1637–38, but the sentiment is in keeping with Creon's
repeated attempts to return Antigone to her proper role at 1660 and 1662.

121. If 1737ff. of the exodus is genuine, the theme is carefully sustained: Antigone
leaves behind tears for her maiden friends and says she will wander ἀπαρθένευτα,
"unmaidenly" (1737–39); she refuses to heed her father's command to return to
friends her own age (1747); she says she is no longer fit to participate in the holy
thiasos in worship of Dionysus (1755–56).

122. On the theme in general, see Winnington-Ingram 1969.

123. For instance: in the servant's nervousness at the noisy approach of the chorus
(196–97), which recalls the hysterics of the chorus of the *Seven* (cf. Foley 1985.114);
in having Polyneices approach the chorus as a group of strangers to ask them where
they are from (277–79); in announcing the beginning and end of the *agon* almost formally (259, 441, 588); in calling attention to the excesses of tragic *rhesis* (592, 761).

124. Podlecki 1962.369. Foley 1985.119 refers to them as "almost a chorus by pro-
fession." References to Dionysus and choral dancing occur throughout the strophe of
the second stasimon (784–800) and also at 227–28, 235–36, 649–56, 1265, and
1751–57 (which Mastronarde deletes). Zeitlin 1990.142 calls Dionysus "the drama's
metaphorical point of reference."

125. The scholiast *ad* 202 remarks that the poet chose to compose his chorus of
foreigners rather than of Thebans to enable them openly to criticize Eteocles
(although in fact they do no such thing). As Arthur 1977 emphasizes, it is the chorus
that discovers and reveals the deeper patterns and profoundly repetitious nature of
the Theban cycle.

CHAPTER 7

1. See e.g., Webster 1967.246. Wilamowitz 1917 (1969).318 suggested that *Phoen.*
1703–7 (needlessly suspect by some editors) provided Sophocles the inspiration for a
tragedy about his own deme.

Text for Sophocles is cited from the Oxford edition of Lloyd-Jones and Wilson
(1990).

2. Cf. the chorus at 140–1, 150–51, Ismene at 327 (reading δύσμορφε after Büche-
ler), Theseus at 551–56, Creon at 745–47, Polyneices at 1255–63. On Oedipus' mask,
see Seale 1982.141 n.8.

3. Whitman 1958a.190; cf. Bowra 1944.310, Shields 1961.69, and Segal 1981.366.

4. Cf. Shields 1961.73, 121, Seale 1982.119, and *pace* Gellie 1972.159, who suggests oddly that the play does not involve a contrast between illusion and reality. On
the play as a process of revelation, cf. Burian 1974.408: "Sophocles does not bring
Oedipus to Colonus to die and be venerated as a hero, but to become a hero before our
eyes."

5. On the blindness of Oedipus, see esp. Shields 1961 (with helpful comparisons to

King Lear), Buxton 1980.25, and Seale 1982.113–43, who develops Antigone as "the primary visual symbol of his condition" (p.120); cf. also Kaimio 1988.14–16, 40, 85–86. On the themes of exile and supplication, see Gould 1973.90, Burton 1980. 272–73, Reinhardt 1979.195–97, and esp. Burian 1974. On the old age of Oedipus, esp. in its psychological implications, see van Nortwick 1989.

6. Knox 1964.145.

7. Cf. Mazon 1960.73: "La plainte la plus amère et la plus désespérée qu'un vieillard ait jamais poussée sur les tristesses de l'âge et l'approche de la mort."

8. Easterling 1967.1–2.

9. The latter is the approach that informs the interpretation of the play as a whole in Bowra 1944.307–55, who insists on the gradual and visible heroization of Oedipus before our eyes: "Without himself knowing it, he feels in himself the qualities of a hero, a *daimōn*, a being more powerful than men" (p.310). Linforth's 1951 polemic against this and similar readings (see esp. 119–29), despite its insight into the fundamentally human terms in which the hero is presented, goes too far in denying the presence and the importance of the religious elements of the play. A middle course is steered by Winnington-Ingram 1980.253–54, who while allowing that Oedipus "is superhuman from the start—larger than life," insists that "this terrible figure is drawn with some realistic human psychology." Similarly Kamerbeek 1984.19, who rightly remarks of the hero's behavior that until the miracles of the final scene, "[we] have to do with Oedipus the man. . . . On the whole these actions move on the human plane; their motives derive from human calculation."

10. Segal 1981.372.

11. Expressions of old age are applied to Oedipus at 20, 124, 143, 152, 200, 209, 238, 292, 305, 395, 744, 805, 961, 1008, 1146, 1209, 1237, 1256, 1259, 1513, 1691; on the old age of Creon and the chorus, see below and notes 34–40 and 84. Oedipus refers (with some contempt) to Polyneices and Eteocles as νεανίαι at 335, and to Antigone and Ismene as παρθένοι at 445,1606, 1646 (and implicitly at 343); cf. τηλικαῖσδε (1116) and τηλικοῦτος (751).

Jebb 1885 *ad* 1 suggests that Oedipus seems to be "about 20" years older here than in *OT*. But as Arnott 1989.147 notes, Antigone, whose marriageability is emphasized, seems to have aged at a slower rate: we must regard each play for its own particular time–scheme rather than look for detailed consistency between plays.

12. Clark used the phrase in a 1972 lecture entitled "The Artist Grows Old."

13. Reinhardt 1979.193.

14. Wilamowitz 1917 (1969).369–72,1923.358–61, Lesky 1965.129–30; cf. Perotta 1935.602, Mazon 1960.129 n.2, Byl 1975.134.

15. Robert 1915.1.469–80 suggested that Polyneices represented Iophon, to which Wilamowitz 1917 (1969).371 counters effectively; cf. Byl 1975.135.

16. Lipking 1981.69, 76–80.

17. See above chap. 6 and notes 4, 6.

18. Seidensticker 1972 provides an extensive if overly ambitious treatment of the play's formal and thematic relation with *OT*.

19. Socrates describes Cephalus as very old (μάλα πρεσβύτης, 328b) and as "on the threshold of old age" (328e, on Plato's apparent misunderstanding of which, see above chap. 1). On Sophocles' amorous nature, see Ath. 603e–604f; Ath. 510b–c objects that Sophocles was attributing to virtue what was in fact due to impotence

(τὴν ἀσθένειαν αὐτοῦ τὴν περὶ τὰς τῶν ἀφροδισίων ἀπολαύσεις). Ath. 69b–c implies that men naturally become impotent at age 60, even sooner if they eat lettuce (on the antaphrodisiac qualities of which, see Detienne 1977.67–71).

20. Plut. *Mor.*785a–b, perhaps failing to grasp the irony of the anecdote, suggests that the playwright appealed to the patriotism of the jury by reading to them from the first stasimon on the beauty of Colonus, and quotes 668–73. Other variants of the anecdote are cited by Jebb 1885.xl n.1

21. Jones 1967.219; cf. Van Nortwick 1989.14.

22. I am in basic agreement with the arrangement of the scene as discussed (with illustration) in Jebb 1885.xxxvii–xxxviii. Many have remarked on the strong sense of locale in the play and in the opening scenes in particular: see Gould 1973.90, Winnington-Ingram 1980.249 and 339–40, Segal 1981.364, Seale 1982.113, and Vidal-Naquet 1988.354–59. On matters of stagecraft, see especially Seale 1982.113–22 and Arnott 1962.35–36. Arnott rightly adds the qualification that the attention to the sacred ground on which Oedipus is located largely disappears after the opening scenes: when Creon and his men invade Oedipus' space and abduct his daughters, no mention is made by Oedipus or the chorus of their violation of sacred ground.

23. Cf. Segal 1981.364–69. It has been observed that the metaphor in κάμψειν (91) is from the last lap of a race.

24. On the Bronze Threshold see Jebb 1885 *ad* 57, who rightly relates the χαλκόπους ὁδός (57) with "the down-rushing threshold rooted in the earth with steps of bronze" (τὸν καταπάκτην ὁδὸν χαλκοῖς βάθροισι γῆθεν ἐρριζωμένον, 1590–91): "from this *spot*, the immediately adjacent *region* (including the grove) was known as the 'brazen threshold'."

On the importance of boundaries and thresholds in the play, see esp. Segal 1981.364ff. and Vidal-Naquet 1988.

25. Arnott 1962.42ff. and 99, who argues for presence of a stage altar located on a raised stage as a permanent feature of the fifth-century theater and suggests that Oedipus' seat may be no more than the altar itself.

On the symbolic value of Oedipus' trespass, see esp. Padel 1983.8–9: "The parallel between the unenterable place he penetrates at the beginning and the unapproachable, unseeable place which receives him at the end, suggests that other place which he forbiddenly and self-definingly entered earlier in his history, his mother's womb."

26. See Arnott 1989.83–84, who suggests that Oedipus is standing again by line 30. But surely here as elsewhere in the play he would ask for help in standing, and his vow that he shall "never leave this place" is more striking if he continues to lay claim to it by sitting there.

27. See above, chap. 1.

28. Burton 1980.288 points to a parallel passage in *Ant.* 586–93.

29. αὐτοπέτρου, which is Musgrave's emendation for the ἀντιπέτρου of the MSS., is accepted in editions of Jebb, Dawe, and Lloyd-Jones and Wilson.

30. Cf. Arnott 1962.35 (supported by Vidal-Naquet 1988.359) and Taplin 1977.441. Seale 1982.141 n.5 observes that such a location would be awkward given the length of time Oedipus is seated there and the number of characters with which he speaks.

31. Seale 1982.139.

32. Vidal-Naquet 1988.358, but retaining the ἀντιπέτρου of the MSS. At 494 n.95,

he calls the emendation unacceptable, claiming that "a hewn stone here stands in contrast to the unhewn stone on which Oedipus first sat down." But the point is more
simply that there would be no reason for a carved βῆμα in such a sacred area, one that
even the local inhabitants hasten past without stopping (128–33). Antigone's description of the area defines it completely in terms of its natural and inviolate character and
does not hint at the presence of any such landmark.

βῆμα occurs elsewhere in Sophocles only at El. 163 in the simple sense of "step."

33. On the importance of speech (λόγος) in the play, see esp. Segal 1981.392–99.

34. They are called φίλτατοι γέροντες at 724. They are elsewhere described as
"overseers of this land" (τῆσδ' ἔφοροι χώρας, 145), "well-born residents of this land"
(ἄνδρες χθονὸς τῆσδ' εὐγενεῖς οἰκήτορες, 728), "lords of the land" (γῆς ἄνακτες,
831), "guardians of this land" (ἄνδρες τῆσδε δημοῦχοι χθονός, 1348), and simply
"citizens" (ἄνδρες πολῖται, 1579).

35. Gardiner 1987.109–16.

36. Cf. Burton 1980.253, 264–65.

37. Burton 1980.295.

38. Pers., Ag., Heracl., HF, Supp., and Ant., and not including the chorus of elders
in the pro-satyric Alc.

39. On the relation between the content of the odes and age of the chorus, see Burton 1980.251–52 and 275ff.

40. On paradoxes of inaction, see above chap. 6 and corresponding n.24.

41. On the theme of social and political reintegration, see esp. Segal 1981.364ff.

42. Cf. Jebb 1885 ad 139: "advancing step by step, and asking at each step whether
he has come far enough," and Van Nortwick 1989.138: ". . . the chorus sounding like
a bomb squad defusing a dangerous device."

43. Cf. Seale 1982.122.

44. Knox 1964.151–52 speaks in regard to the rites of propitiation to be performed
for the Eumenides of "the hero's docility and eagerness to be instructed in matters of
religion," and contrasts this with "his growing assertiveness and intractability in his
relations with men." Winnington-Ingram 1980.266 n.49 (who cites the passage in
Knox) relates the age of Oedipus to his long experience and willingness to learn and
calls these "important questions," although he does not attempt to answer them.

45. Cf. Knox 1964.160; also Méautis 1957.165. Seale 1982.116–17 speaks of "the
revelation of Oedipus as a man of words . . . powerful in what he says rather than in
what he does," but restricts his consideration of this power to Oedipus' oracular role.

46. Euripides also makes use of elderly women as "wise counselors," who meet
with varying degrees of success: the nurse to Phaedra in Hipp., Aethra to Theseus in
Supp., Jocasta to Polyneices and Eteocles in Phoen. (see above chap. 6). He is also fond
of pairing male and female servants. In Hipp. the old man of the prologue and the
nurse provide examples of the wise counselor and evil counselor respectively; in Ion
the bad (though unwitting) counsel of the old man is pitted against the advice of the
kindly old Pythia. It is perhaps significant that Herodotus, who is deeply influenced
by tragedy and makes extensive use of wise counselors, shows no predilection for
casting the elderly in this role; cf. Lattimore 1939.

It is noteworthy that neither does Plato regard wisdom as a necessary by-product of
age or experience: the "philosopher-kings" of Republic are aged fifty and older, but
they rule not by virtue of their age but of their grueling education. Plato begins the

dialogue with a portrait of the complacent old Cephalus, who excuses himself from the deliberations precisely when they become difficult.

47. Shields 1961.73 observes of the hero that "it is not that he himself grows in wisdom and greatness, but rather that more and more of his wisdom and greatness are revealed to us." References to the knowledge and wisdom of old age appear in Sophocles fragments 260, 664 and 950 Radt (= Nauck^2 282, 603, 864).

48. Almost all modern editions, commentaries (Jebb, Pearson, Dawe, Lloyd-Jones, and Wilson), and translations adopt Musgrave's emendation ἔμπολιν at 637; cf. ἔμπολιν at 1156. I am intrigued by Vidal-Naquet 1988.343ff., who retains the ἔμπαλιν of the manuscripts and argues that Oedipus' status in Athens is best understood not as πολίτης but as πρόξενος and εὐεργέτης, relating this condition to the play's concern with boundaries and frontiers and with other expressions of Oedipus' liminal status: "Even when he becomes a hero of Athens, Oedipus remains a marginal figure." Yet for all its concern with thresholds, the play seems intent on bringing its themes to closure: politically with his passage into citizenship; domestically with his curses on Polyneices; and religiously with his transformation to *hêros*.

49. Segal 1981.364.

50. Knox 1964.145–46. Cf. στέρξον, 519; στέργω, 1094.

51. E.g., Burton 1980.287.

52. Cf. also Aeschylus *PB* 981. Kirkwood 1958.287 observes that Sophocles does not typically see suffering as part of a learning process.

53. On late learning in Greek drama, see Kamerbeek's commentary on *Ant. ad* 1270 (adding to his list *Alc.* 940). The reference to *Ant.* is particularly interesting in view of the final line (1353), in which the chorus observes that the retribution that comes from arrogant behavior γήρᾳ τὸ φρονεῖν ἐδίδαξαν, "teaches wisdom (even?) in old age." Creon has not elsewhere in the play been described specifically as old. The chorus may be using γῆρας here more loosely, and perhaps the weight of Creon's suffering can be said to have aged him beyond his years. Another possibility, though remote, is that this elderly chorus is speaking here of itself.

54. Cf. Van Nortwick 1989.139. On the psychological importance of reminiscence, see Butler 1963.

55. As Linforth 1951.107 observes, although the chorus nowhere speaks specifically of pollution, "their fear of it is implied in their conduct."

56. We are prepared for the idea in 107–8, where Oedipus says that Athens is "called most honored" (καλούμεναι . . . τιμωτάτη).

57. Slatkin 1986.

58. Slatkin 1986.217.

59. Burian 1974.411 and n.10.

60. Whitman 1958a.202–3 takes 229–30 as already referring to the murder of Laius and as rejecting the idea that it was a matter of retaliation. But that is unlikely since Oedipus has not yet made such a defense and this explanation would not have been part of the story attached to his ὄνομα that is generally circulated.

On the theme of reciprocity, helping friends and harming enemies in the play, see Hester 1977.24–32, Winnington-Ingram 1980.261ff., and esp. Blundell 1989.

61. The stranger describes the area as ἄθικτος (39). Oedipus describes his seat with ἀξέστου (19) and ἀσκέπαρνον (101) and asks the Eumenides not to be ἀγνώμονες (86) to him. In the parodos the chorus urge each other as they hunt for

Oedipus: προσδέρκου, προσφθέγγου, προσπεύθου (121–22). They describe the grove as ἄστιβες (126) and hold it in such reverence that they walk past ἀδέρκτως, ἀφώνως, ἀλόγως: "without looks, without speech, without words" (130–31), and it is in response to their song that Oedipus pleads with them *not* to regard him as ἄνομον (142). They urge Oedipus to hold in contempt whatever the city regards as ἄφιλον (186). They later describe the grove again with ἀφθέγκτῳ (157) and ἀβάτων (167), the Eumenides as ἀμαιμακετᾶν (127), and their rituals with ἄπυστα (489) and ἄστροφος (490). In the first stasimon, they speak of the beautiful ivy leaves (φυλλάδα) where the nightingales sing in a triplet as ἄβατον . . . ἀνήλιον ἀνήμενον ("pathless, sunless, windless," 675–77); of the "sleepless" (ἄυπνοι, 685) springs of the Cephisus and its pure (ἀκηράτῳ, 690) waters; and of the olive tree (φύτευμα, 701) as ἀχείρωτον (697). In the second antistrophe, the chorus distinguishes Athens again, for its horses, foals, and sea-power: it is εὔιππον, εὔπωλον, εὐθάλασσαν (711). In the *kommos* at 1447ff.: ἄφατος (1464), ἀφεγγές (1481); in the fourth stasimon ἀφανῆ (1556), ἀνικάτου (1568), and ἀδάματον (1572); and in the final *kommos* ἄσκοποι (1681), ἄκλαυτον (1708), ἀφανίσαι (1712). Cf. Whitman 1958a.277 n.38. The use of negatives and triplets is a feature of religious language; note the description of the ritual for the Eumenides: τρισσάς, 479; τρίς ἐννέα, 483.

62. Oedipus refers to the chorus as φίλοι again at 724; Antigone does likewise at 1677.

63. E.g., *Cho.* 84–105, *Or.* 95–97, *El.* 406. It is significant that in each case the rites of appeasement are directed to the Eumenides and that the issue of the *intent* of the author of the rites is never raised.

64. *Pace* Linforth 1951.81 n.8.

65. Cf. 891, 1169, 1631, and Antigone at 1103. Segal 1981.363 rightly speaks of "the division of the son-archetype into two figures, Polyneices and Theseus." The filial theme is implicit in Theseus' offer to take Oedipus to his home with him (639), where he will give him the care his sons have failed to provide.

66. The breakdown of relations between Thebes and Athens is perhaps suggested later with Creon's πικράς at 951 and Oedipus' πικρῶς at 990.

67. Freeman 1923.50 (cited in Kamerbeek 1984.4–5). Gouldner 1965.82 speaks usefully of the conflict between the shame culture or "action morality" as reflected in the public view of Oedipus' actions and the guilt culture that Oedipus represents.

68. Cf. Scodel 1984.117; like the monument to the friendship of Theseus and Pirithoos, which they pass on the way to his death, his gift to Athens will be eternal (1593–94). Burton 1980.275 notes the frequency of ἀεί in the first stasimon.

69. Cf. 1016–17, 1517. It is significant that Theseus begins his final speech δράσω (1773). So Winnington-Ingram 1980.266 n.49 and 273–74 observes that Theseus, "although he acts toward Oedipus with generous humanity . . . is not really involved in his tragedy, which he cannot understand."

70. Burton 1980.274; cf. Seale 1982.128–29. Winnington-Ingram 1980.251 notes the function of the ode in establishing a major pause in the action, concluding the second of the five movements into which he divides the play.

71. See Linforth 1951.156: "The effect of the poem is to recover the sympathy of the audience for Oedipus"; on the elderly chorus' natural sympathy for Oedipus see Gardiner 1987.114 and Kamerbeek 1984 *ad* 1239.

72. Although these are not identified, it seems safe to assume that love is to be understood as among the κούφας ἀφροσύνας.

73. Cf. Winnington-Ingram 1980.252 n.10.

74. Homer describes γῆρας formulaically as χαλεπόν, λυγρόν, στυγερόν, and ὀλοόν, to which Hesiod adds δειλόν and ὠμόν. Mimnermus speaks of old age as ἀργαλέον καὶ ἄμορφον . . . ἐχθρόν ὁμῶς καὶ ἄτιμον (5.7–8), and the Hymn to Aphrodite speaks of γῆρας ὁμοίοιον . . . νηλειές . . . οὐλόμενον, καματηρόν (244–246). See above, chaps. 1–3.

75. Euripides. πολιόν: Bacch. 258, Ion 700, Nauck² 362.2; πικρόν: Nauck² 282.11; πένθιμον: Alc. 622. Other adjectives applied more specifically to old age include ἄυπνον IA 4, βαρύ Alc. 672, δύσκολον Bacch.1251, and δυσπαλαίοιστον Supp.1108. On δυσώνυμον (Nauck² 575.1) and λυγρὸν φόνιόν τε (HF 649), see discussion below on Sophocles. λυγρόν: Aj. 506; λευκόν: Aj. 625.

76. For discussion and bibliography, see Hester 1977.29 and Appendix D.

77. Knox 1964.146–48 uses the figure of παράδειγμα of Oedipus in both plays: in OT Oedipus reveals the crucial differences between human and divine knowledge; in OC Oedipus as hēros is made equal to the gods.

78. ἐγὼ τὸ μὲν δὴ πανταχοῦ θρυλούμενον / κράτιστον εἶναι φημὶ μὴ φῦναι βροτῷ, Nauck² 285.1–2; cf. 980.1: τὸ μὴ γενέσθαι κρεῖσσον ἢ φῦναι βροτοῖς. For parallels, see Theog. 425–28, Certamen 78–9, Bacchyl. 5.160–62 (cf. Bowra 1944.353).

79. Webster 1967.31–32, 115 puts Oenomaus among Euripides' early plays (455–428 B.C.), so that its relation to Sophocles' own Oenomaus, produced in 414 B.C., cannot be determined. At Alc. 669–72 Admetus ridicules old men who complain about old age and long life but when death draws near do not find old age so oppressive.

80. Cf. Burton 1980.290–91.

81. Whitman 1958a.92, 213. Bowra 1944.314 , 351: "It [the third stasimon] is a human commentary on what has happened, and is therefore uncertain, indecisive, and incompletely informed. It judges the events by common standards, and to some extent shows their inadequacy." Cf. Hester 1977.25: "This chorus, like most of Sophocles', is not characterized by any knowledge or perception superior to that of the man in the street."

82. A view of religion to which the chorus reverts when they are frightened by the thunder; cf. 1482–84 and Jebb's note ad loc.

83. The old man at Trach. 1017–19 needs Hyllus' help to support Heracles' body.

84. Some translations read τηλικόσδε (732) in the sense of "despite my old age," but Creon's emphasis throughout on his age makes it more likely that he is casting himself in the role of city elder and ambassador.

85. The clumsy reference to Thebes as Oedipus' τροφός (760) is particularly ironic given the lack of care Oedipus receives in old age, for which Creon himself shares much of the blame.

86. Oedipus describes Creon in language commonly used to describe the sophists (e.g., their ability to speak on either side of an issue): 761–62, 774, 782, 806–7, 1000–1.

87. On the staging of this scene and the question of physical contact in it, see Arnott 1962.35, Kaimio 1988.76–77 and notes, Burton 1980.267, and Seale 1982. 130–31. Despite 856–57, neither the abduction of Antigone (which is likely executed

by Creon's attendants) nor Creon's threatened abduction of Oedipus require direct physical contact between Creon and the chorus; cf. Jebb 1885 *ad* 856 and his stage direction *ad* 875. Even apart from the issue of whether such action would be theatrically possible (i.e., the implications of a raised-stage theater for interaction between actors and chorus), the scenes are dramatically more effective without such contact: as Burton points out, "The pathos of the scene as well as its controlled excitement within the balanced pattern of strophic form are perhaps better served by the show than the reality of physical violence."

88. For echoes in language, cf. e.g., ἀμαυρῷ κώλῳ (182) and ἀμαυρῷ φωτί (1018); πικρά (615), πικράς (951) πικράς and πικρῶς (990); ἀνοσίου (281), ἀνοσίοις (281), and ἀνοσιώτατοι (946).

89. Cf. Seale 1982.125.

90. κράτος, σθένος and βία, 854, 874, 903, 916, 922, 935 [cf. 943]; cf. σθένει, 842.

91. Kirkwood 1958.152; cf. Bowra 1944.332, 335, Hester 1977.28, and esp. Blundell 1989.232–38. Segal 1981.378–80 observes that Creon (like Polyneices) interrupts Theseus' sacrifice and violates Oedipus' rights as suppliant.

92. On will as action in Sophocles, see Whitman 1958a.191. It may be significant that Prometheus is identified as one of the patron deities of the area (55–56).

93. Burton 1980.287 n.47 comments on the frequency with which irascible old men appear in comedy.

94. Oedipus turns to Antigone for advice at 170–72 and 216–17; she counsels Polyneices at 1414–46. Buxton 1982.134–45 observes that persuasion "characterizes the community to which Oedipus chooses to belong."

95. Winnington-Ingram 1980.257–58.

96. Hester 1977.30.

97. Easterling 1967.

98. On the theme of τροφή in relation to this scene, see Bowra 1944.327ff., Easterling 1967.3ff., 9, Winnington-Ingram 1980.276.

The theme is also prominent in *Ajax*. Tecmessa urges the hero to reverence (αἴδεσαι) both his father and mother whom he leaves in miserable old age (ἐν λυγρῷ γήρᾳ, 506–7). As he contemplates his death he takes care that Eurysaces, whom he commends to the care of his parents, shall become their γηροβοσκὸς εἰσαεί (570). Blundell 1989.76 notes that the theme of τροφή is implicit in 624–25, where the chorus imagines Ajax's mother: παλαιᾷ μὲν σύντροφος ἁμέρα, λευκῷ τε γήρᾳ.

99. Oedipus takes pains to present his arguments in the most traditional light. He says of the power of his curses (ἀράς, 1375) that

> they now have control of your supplication and this throne you want, if primeval Justice still sits together with the ancient laws of Zeus (ἡ παλαίφατος Δίκη ξύνεδρος Ζηνὸς ἀρχαίοις νόμοις).
>
> (1382)

The august language underscores the antiquity of the traditions that Oedipus upholds.

100. Polyneices' language suggests his concern with honor and dishonor: cf. 1304, 1409.

101. E.g., Kamerbeek 1984.6. The scholiast *ad* 375 finds the issue worthy of note.

On Polyneices as a sympathetic character, see Van Nortwick 1989.147 and n.19 with references.

102. Cf. Easterling 1967.7–10.

103. For other linkages between the themes of τιμή and τροφή, see e.g., Hesiod WD 185–89, Theog. 271–78, 821–22, and Eur. Alc. 658–65. Athenians would recall the legislation of Solon: ἐὰν τις μὴ τρέφῃ τοὺς γονέας ἄτιμος ἔστω (Diog. Laert. 1.55).

104. Winnington-Ingram 1980.258.

105. Lloyd-Jones and Wilson bracket 954–55.

106. Cf. Burton 1980.269–70 and Linforth 1951.108.

107. Winnington-Ingram 1980.253: "the greatest *coup de théâtre* in Sophocles." Seale 1982.137: "The dramatic reversal of the fixed visual impression declares the miracle."

108. Cf. Easterling 1967.12: "Oedipus' love for his daughters is shown in his reliance on them, his concern for their welfare, his joy at their safe return, particularly his generous gratitude for their labours (one needs love in order to be truly generous in one's gratitude) and such actions as his willingness to change his mind to please Antigone, an immense sacrifice for a man such as Oedipus."

109. Cf. Burton 1980.272.

110. Cf. Bowra 1944.317–18, *pace* Linforth 1951.95.

111. May 1986.51–61. It is significant that the last of the virtues that May lists, *hilaritas*, a lightness of spirit that affords a certain detachment on the human scene, is conspicuously absent in Oedipus, precluded by the indignities he has suffered and the attention he has had to give to his day to day survival.

112. Erikson 1959.98–99; cf. Slatkin 1986.219ff. on the "integrity" of Oedipus.

Glossary of Greek Terms

akmê: male prime of life, typically referring to maturity or "middle age"

anêr: "man" in general, occasionally implying a male in maturity who has married or otherwise established himself as head of an *oikos*

aretê: human virtue, or better, excellence, as understood within a given literary or social context

geraios, -a, -on: old

gêras: old age

gêrokomos: a male (typically a son) who cares for his parents in old age

gerôn: an old man

gêrotrophia: care of the aged

graia, graus: an old woman

gynê: woman or wife, usually one who has given birth

hebê: physical maturity and the period of young adulthood that follows

korê (kourê): a young woman who has achieved puberty

kouros: a young man who has achieved puberty

neos: a young man, usually between physical maturity and marriage

neotês: young manhood

oikos: the family or household, often in an extended sense

pais: a child, male or female, from birth to the onset of puberty

parthenos: a young woman who has not yet married (or, in some cases, given birth)

polis: the Greek "city-state"

presbys: old man, sometimes implying status or respect

threptêria: the care a son gives his aged parents to "repay" them for his nurture

References

Adkins, A.W. H. 1960. *Merit and Responsibility*. Oxford.

———. 1985. *Poetic Craft in the Early Greek Elegists*. Chicago.

Amundsen, B. W. and C. J. Diers. 1970. "The Age of Menopause in Classical Greece and Rome," *Human Biology* 42.79–86.

Arnott, P. 1962. *Greek Scenic Conventions in the Fifth Century B.C.* Oxford.

———. 1989. *Public and Performance in the Greek Theatre*. London and New York.

Arthur, M. 1973. "Early Greece: The Origins of the Western Attitude Toward Women," *Arethusa* 6.7–58.

———. 1975. "Euripides' *Phoenissae* and the Politics of Justice," Ph.D. diss., Yale University.

———. 1977. "The Curse of Civilization: The Choral Odes of the *Phoenissae*," *HSPh* 81.163–85.

———. 1981. "The Divided World of *Iliad* VI," in Foley 1981.19–44.

———. 1982. "Cultural Strategies in Hesiod's *Theogony*: Law, Family, Society," *Arethusa* 15.63–82.

Austin, N. 1966. "The Function of the Digressions in the *Iliad*," *GRBS* 7. 295–312.

———. 1975. *Archery at the Dark of the Moon*. Berkeley.

Avery, H. C. 1971. "Euripides' 'Heracleidai,'" *AJPh* 92. 539–65.

Baldry, H. C. 1952. "Who Invented the Golden Age?" *CQ* N.S. 2.83–92.

Barrett, D. S. 1981. "The Friendship of Achilles and Patroclus," *CB* 57.87–93.

Baxter, P. and U. Almagor, "Observations about Generations," in La Fontaine 1978.159–60.

Belmont, D. 1967. "Telemachus and Nausicaa: A Study of Youth," *CJ* 63.1–9.

Bergren, A. 1983. "Odyssean Temporality: Many (Re)Turns," in Rubino and Shelmerdine 1983.38–73.

Bertman, S. 1968. "Structural Symmetry at the End of the *Odyssey*," *GRBS* 9.115–23.

———, ed. 1976. *The Conflict of Generations in Ancient Greece and Rome*. Amsterdam.

———. 1989. "The Ashes and the Flame: Passion and Aging in Classical Poetry," in Falkner and de Luce 1989. 157–71.

Bettelheim, B. 1954. *Symbolic Wounds*, Glencoe, Ill.

Binstock, R. and E. Shanas, eds. 1985. *Handbook of Aging and the Social Sciences*. 2nd ed. New York.

Blundell, M. W. 1989. *Helping Friends and Harming Enemies: A Study in Sophocles and Greek Ethics*. Cambridge, England.

Boll, F. 1950. "Die Lebensalter," in *Kleine Schriften zur Sternkunde des Altertums*, ed. V. Stegemann. Leipzig 1950. 156–224 (= *Neue Jahrbücher* 1913, 31.89–146).

Boscherini, S. 1969. "Su di un 'errore' di Cicerone (*De senectute*, 54). Nota di semantica," *QUCC* 7. 36–41.

Bowra, C. M. 1938. *Early Greek Elegists*. Cambridge, Mass.

———. 1944. *Sophoclean Tragedy*. Oxford.

———. 1961. *Greek Lyric Poetry*. 2nd ed. Oxford.

Bremmer, J. N. 1987. "The Old Women of Ancient Greece," in *Sexual Asymmetry. Studies in Ancient Society*, eds. J. Blok and P. Mason. Amsterdam. 191–215.

———. 1987a. "Oedipus and the Greek Oedipus Complex," in *Interpretations of Greek Mythology*, ed. J. Bremmer. London. 41–59.

Brown, C. 1984. "Ruined by Lust: Anacreon, Fr. 44 Gentili (432 *PMG*)," *CQ* 34.37–42.

Buffière, F. 1980. *Eros adolescent. La pédérastie dan la Grèce antique*. Paris.

Burian, P. 1974. "Suppliant and Savior: *Oedipus at Colonus*," *Phoenix* 28.408–29.

———. 1977. "Euripides' *Heraclidae*: An Interpretation," *CPh* 72. 1–21.

Burian, P. and B. Swann. 1981. Introduction to *The Phoenician Women*. New York and Oxford. 3–17.

Burnett, A. P. 1976. "Tribe and City, Custom and Decree in *Children of Heracles*," *CPh* 71. 4–26.

———. 1979. "Desire and Memory: Sappho Frag. 94," *CPh* 74.16–27.

———. 1983. *Three Archaic Poets: Archilochus, Sappho, Alcaeus*. Cambridge, Mass.

———. 1988. "Jocasta in the West: The Lille Stesichorus," *ClAnt* 7.2.107–54.

Burton, R. W. B. 1980. *The Chorus in Sophocles' Tragedies*. Oxford.

Butler, R. 1963. "The Life Review: An Interpretation of Reminiscence in the Aged," *Psychiatry* 26.65–76.

Butler, R. and M. Lewis. 1976. *Sex After Sixty*. New York.

Buxton, R. G. A. 1980. "Blindness and Limits: Sophokles and the Logic of Myth," *JHS* 100.22–37.

———. 1982. *Persuasion in Greek Tragedy: A Study of Peitho*. Cambridge.

Byl. S. 1975. "Lamentations sur la vieillesse dans la tragédie grecque," in *Le monde grec. Hommages à C. Préaux*. Brussels. 130–39.

———. 1976. "Lamentions sur la vieillesse chez Homère et les poètes lyriques des VIIe et VIe siècles," *LEC* 44.234–44.

Calame, C. 1977. *Les choeurs de jeunes filles en Grece archaïque* .Vol. 1. Rome.

Cameron, A. and A. Kuhrt, eds. 1983. *Images of Women in Antiquity*. Detroit.

Cameron, H. D. 1971. *Studies on the* Seven Against Thebes *of Aeschylus*. The Hague.

Campbell, D. A. 1967. *Greek Lyric Poetry*. London and New York.

———. 1976. "The Language of the New Archilochus," *Arethusa* 9.151–57.

———. 1983. *The Golden Lyre. The Themes of the Greek Lyric Poets*. London.

Cantarella, E. 1987. *Pandora's Daughters*, tr. M. Fant. Baltimore and London (orig. publ. *L'ambiguo malanno*. Rome 1981).

Carson, A. 1990. "Putting Her in Her Place," in Halperin, Winkler, and Zeitlin 1990.135–69.

Chantraine, P. 1968–80. *Dictionnaire étymologique de la langue grecque*. Paris.

Chew, S. 1962. *The Pilgrimage of Life*. Yale.

Chudacoff, H. 1989. *How Old Age You?* Princeton.

Clark, M 1968. "The Anthropology of Aging: A New Area for Studies of Culture and Personality," in *Middle Age and Aging*, ed. Bernice Neugarten. Chicago. 433–43.

Clarke, H. W. 1967. *The Art of the Odyssey*. Englewood Cliffs, N.J.

Clarke, W. M. 1978. "Achilles and Patroclus in Love," *Hermes*. 106.381–96.

Claus, D. 1977. "Defining Moral Terms in *Works and Days* ," *TAPhA* 107.73–84.

Clay, J. Strauss. 1981–82. "Immortal and Ageless Forever," *CJ* 77.112–17.

———. 1983. *The Wrath of Athena*. Princeton.

———. 1989. *The Politics of Olympus*. Princeton.

Cole, T. 1992. *The Journey of Life*. Cambridge.

Cole, T. and S. Gadow, eds. 1986. *What Does It Mean to Grow Old?* Durham.

Conacher, D. J. 1967. *Euripidean Drama*. London and Toronto.

———. 1967a. "Themes in the Exodus of Euripides' *Phoenissae*," *Phoenix* 21. 92–101.

Cowgill, D. 1974. "Aging and Modernization: A Revision of the Theory," in *Late Life: Communities and Environmental Policy*, ed. J. F. Gubrium. Springfield, Ill.

Cowgill, D. and L. Holmes, eds. 1972. *Aging and Modernization*. New York.

Craik, E., ed. 1988. *Euripides. Phoenician Women*. Warminster, England.

Cropp, M. 1980. "*Herakleidai* 603–4, 630ff. and the Question of the Mutilation of the Text," *AJPh* 101. 283–86.

Cumming, E. and W. Henry. 1961. *Growing Old: The Process of Disengagement*. New York.

De Beauvoir, S. 1972. *The Coming of Age*, tr. Patrick O'Brien. New York.

Degani, E. 1974. "Il nuovo Archiloco," *A&R* 19.113–28.

Delebecque, E. 1951. *Euripide et la Guerre du Péloponnese*. Paris.

de Romilly, J. 1961. *L' évolution de pathétique d' Eschyle à Euripide*. Paris.

———. 1967. "*Phoenician Women* of Euripides: Topicality in Greek Tragedy," *Bucknell Review* 15.108–32, tr. D. Orrok (= "*Les Phéniciennes* d' Euripide, ou l'actualité dans la tragédie grecque," *Rev. Phil.* 39, 1965. 28–47).

———. 1968. *Time in Greek Tragedy*. Ithaca.

Detienne, M. 1963. *Crise agraire et attitude religeiuse chez Hésiode*, Collection "Latomus" 68.

———. 1977. *The Gardens of Adonis: Spices in Greek Mythology*, tr. J. Lloyd. Atlantic Highlands, N.J.

Devereux, G. 1955. "A Counteroedipal Episode in Homer's Iliad," *Bulletin of the Philadelphia Association for Psychoanalysis*. 4.90–97.

———. 1957. "Penelope's Character," *Psychoanalytic Quarterly*. 26.378–86.

———. 1973. "The Self-Blinding of Oidipous in Sophocles: *Oidipous Tyrannos*," *JHS* 93.36–49.

Di Benedetto, V. 1985. "Il tema vecchiaia e il fr. 58 di Saffo," *QUCC* n.s. 19 [48] 145–63.

Dickie, M. 1978. "Dike as a Moral Term in Homer and Hesiod," *CPh* 73. 91–101.

Donlan, W. 1971. "Homer's Agamemnon," *CW* 65.109–15.

———. 1979. "The Structure of Authority in the *Iliad*," *Arethusa* 12.51–70.

———. 1980. *The Aristocratic Ideal in Ancient Greece*. Lawrence.

Dornseiff, F. 1937. "Odysseus Letzte Fahrt," *Hermes* 72. 351–55.

Dover, K. J. 1964. "The Poetry of Archilochus," in *Entretiens sur l' antiquité classique 10: Archiloque*. Fondation Hardt. Geneva. 183–222.

———. 1972. *Aristophanic Comedy*. Berkeley.

———. 1973. "Classical Greek Attitudes to Sexual Behavior," *Arethusa* 6.59–75.

———. 1978. *Greek Homosexuality*. London.

DuBois, P. 1984. "Sappho and Helen," in Peradotto and Sullivan 1984.95–105.

———. 1988. *Sowing the Body*. Chicago.

Easterling, P. 1967. "Oedipus and Polyneices," *PCPhS* 13.1–13.

Ebener, D. 1964. "Die *Phönizierinnen* des Euripides als Spiegelbild geschichtliche Wirklichkeit," *Eirene* 2.71–79.

Eckert, C. W. 1963. "Initiatory Motifs in the Story of Telemachus," *CJ* 59.49–57.

Edwards, A. P. 1985. *Achilles in the* Odyssey. Königstein, Ger.

Edwards, M. 1987. *Homer. Poet of the* Iliad. Baltimore and London.

Ehrenberg, V. 1973. *From Solon to Socrates.* 2nd ed. London.

Eliade, M. 1958. *Birth and Rebirth,* tr. Willard Trask. New York.

Erbse, H. 1972. *Beiträge zum Verständis der* Odyssee. Berlin.

Erikson, E. 1959. *Psychological Issues.* New York.

Eyben, E. 1989. "Old Age in Greco-Roman Antiquity and Early Christianity: An Annotated Select Bibliography," in Falkner and de Luce 1989. 230–51.

Falkner, T. 1985. "Old Age in Euripides' *Medea,*" *CB* 61.76–78.

Falkner, T. and J. de Luce, eds. 1989. *Old Age in Greek and Latin Literature.* Albany.

Felson-Rubin, N. 1993. *Regarding Penelope.* Princeton.

Fenik, B. 1974. *Studies in the Odyssey.* Hermes Einzelschr. Vol. 30. Wiesbaden.

Fiedler, L. A. 1979. "Eros and Thanatos: Old Age in Love," in *Aging, Death, and the Completion of Being,* ed. David D. Van Tassel. Philadelphia. 235–54.

———. 1986. "More Images of Eros and Old Age: The Damnation of Faust and the Fountain of Youth," in *Memory and Desire. Aging-Literature-Psychoanalysis,* eds. K. Woodward and M. Schwartz. Bloomington.

Finley, J. H., Jr. 1978. *Homer's Odyssey.* Cambridge, Mass.

Finley, M. I. 1965. *The World of Odysseus.* New York.

——— 1981. "The Elderly in Classical Antiquity," *G&R* 28.156–71 (rept. in Falkner and de Luce 1989.1–20).

———. 1981a. *Economy and Society in Ancient Greece,* eds. B. Shaw and R. Saller. London.

Fitton, J. W. 1961. "The *Suppliant Women* and the *Herakleidai* of Euripides," *Hermes* 89. 430–61.

Foley, H. 1978. "'Reverse Similes' and Sex Roles in the *Odyssey,*" *Arethusa* 11. 7–26.

———, ed. 1981. *Reflections of Women in Antiquity.* New York.

———. 1985. *Ritual Irony.* Ithaca.

Fontenrose, J. 1974. "Work, Justice, and Hesiod's Five Ages," *CPh* 69. 2–16.

Forrest, W. G. 1975. "An Athenian Generation Gap?" *YClS* 24.37–52.

Fortes, M. 1984. "Age, Generation and Social Structure," in Kertzer and Keith 1984.99–122.

Foucault, M. 1978. *The History of Sexuality. Vol. 1: An Introduction*, tr. R. Hurley. New York (orig. publ. Paris, 1976).

———. 1980. *Power/Knowledge*. New York.

———. 1986. *The Use of Pleasure. The History of Sexuality. Vol. 2*, tr. R. Hurley. New York (orig. publ. Paris. 1984).

———. 1986a. *The Care of the Self. The History of Sexuality. Vol. 3*, tr. R. Hurley. New York (orig. publ. Paris. 1984).

Fraenkel, E. 1963. *Zu den Phoenissen des Euripides. Sitzungsberichte der Bayerischen Akademie der Wissenschaften*, Philosophisch-Historische Klasse. Heft 1. Munich.

Fränkel, H. 1973. *Early Greek Poetry and Philosophy*, tr. M. Hadas and J. Willis. New York.

Frazer, R. M. 1976. "The κλισμός" of Achilles, *Iliad* 24.596–98," *Phoenix* 30. 295–301.

Freeman, K. 1923. "The Dramatic Technique of the Oedipus Coloneus," *CR* 37.50–54.

Frisk, H. 1960–70. *Griechisches Etymologisches Wörterbuch*. Heidelberg.

Gagarin, M. 1973. "*Dike* in the *Works and Days*," *CPh* 68.81–94.

Gantz, T. 1983. "The Chorus of Aischylos' *Agamemnon*," *HSPh* 17.65–86.

Gardiner, C. 1987. *The Sophoclean Chorus: A Study of Character and Function*. Iowa City.

Garland, R. 1987. "Greek Geriatrics," *History Today* 37.12–18.

———. 1990. *The Greek Way of Life*. Ithaca.

Gellie, G. H. 1972. *Sophocles: A Reading*. Melbourne.

Gentili, B. 1973. "La ragazza di Lesbo," *QUCC* 16.124–28.

Gentili, B. 1973a. "Note Anacreontiche," *QUCC* 16.134–37.

———. 1988. *Poetry and Its Public in Ancient Greece*, tr. A. Cole. Baltimore (orig. publ. *Poesia e pubblico nella Grecia antica: da Omero al V secolo*, Rome 1985).

Gerber, D. E. 1970. *Euterpe*. Amsterdam.

———. 1975. "Mimnermus, Fragment 2.4–5," *GRBS* 16.263–68.

Giacomelli, A. 1980. "Aphrodite and After," *Phoenix*. 34.1–19.

———. 1980a. "The Justice of Aphrodite in Sappho Fr. 1," *TAPhA* 110.135–42.

Giangrande, G. 1968. "Sympotic Literature and Epigram," in *L' Epigramme Grecque, Entretiens sur l' antiquité classique*, 14.91–177. Geneva.

———. 1973. "Anacreon and the Lesbian Girl," *QUCC* 16.129–33.

Glotz, G. 1929. *The Greek City and Its Institutions*, tr. N. Mallinson. London.

Golden, M. 1990. *Children and Childhood in Classical Athens*. Baltimore.

Goldhill, S. 1986. *Reading Greek Tragedy*. Cambridge.

Gomme, A. W. 1972. *A Historical Commentary on Thucydides*. Vol. 2. Oxford.

Gordon, C., C. Gaitz and J. Scott. 1976. "Leisure and Lives: Personal Expressivity across the Life Span," in Binstock and Shanas 1976. 310–41.

Gould, J. 1973. "Hiketeia," *JHS* 94. 73–103.

———. "On Making Sense of Greek Religion," in *Greek Religion and Society*, eds. P. E. Easterling and J.V. Muir. Cambridge. 1–33.

Gouldner, A. 1965. *Enter Plato*. New York and London.

Griffin, J. 1980. *Homer on Life and Death*. Oxford.

Griffith, M. 1975. "Man and the Leaves: A Study of Mimnermus fr. 2," *California Studies in Classical Antiquity* 8. 73–88.

Grube, G. M. A. 1941. *The Drama of Euripides*. London.

Gulliver, P. 1963. *Social Control in an African Society*. Boston.

———. 1968. "Age Differentiation," in *International Encyclopedia of the Social Sciences*. Vol. 1. 157–62.

Gutenbrunner, S. 1950. "Eine nordeuropäische Stammesneckerei bei Homer?" *RhM* 93. 382–83.

Gutmann, D. 1976. "Alternatives to Disengagement: The Old Men of the Highland Druze," in *Time, Roles, and Self in Old Age*, ed. J. F. Gubrium. New York. 88–108.

———. 1977. "The Cross-Cultural Perspective: Notes Toward a Comparative Psychology of Aging," in *Handbook of the Psychology of Aging*, eds. J. Birren and K. Schaie. New York. 302–26.

———. 1987. *Reclaimed Powers*. New York.

Hagestad, G. and B. Neugarten. 1976. "Age and the Life Course," in Binstock and Shanas 1985. 36–58.

Hallett, J. P. 1979. "Sappho and Her Social Context: Sense and Sensuality," *Signs* 4. 447–64.

Halperin, D. 1990. *One Hundred Years of Homosexuality*. New York.

Halperin, D., J. Winkler and F. Zeitlin, eds. 1990. *Before Sexuality: The Construction of Erotic Experience in the Ancient Greek World*. Princeton.

Hammond, N. G. L. 1986. *A History of Greece to 322 B.C.* 3rd ed. Oxford.

Hanson, W. F. 1977. "Odysseus' Last Journey," *QUCC* 24. 27–48.

Harrison, J. 1912. *Themis*. Cambridge.

Havighurst, R. J. et al. 1968. "Disengagement and Patterns of Aging" in *Middle Age and Aging*, ed. B. Neugarten. Chicago. 161–72.

Haynes, M. S. 1962. "The Supposedly Golden Age for the Aged in Ancient Greece (A Study of Literary Concepts of Old Age)," *Gerontologist* 2. 93–98.

Henderson, J. 1975. *The Maculate Muse. Obscene Language in Attic Comedy.* New Haven.

———. 1976. "The Cologne Epode and the Conventions of Early Greek Erotic Poetry," *Arethusa* 9.2.159–79.

———. 1987. "Older Women in Attic Old Comedy," *TAPhA* 117.105–29.

Hester, D. A. 1977. "To Help One's Friends and Harm One's Enemies: A Study in the Oedipus at Colonus," *Antichthon* 11.22–41.

Holmes, L. D. 1976. "Trends in Anthropological Gerontology: From Simmons to the Seventies," *International Journal of Aging and Human Development* 7.3. 211–20.

———. 1983. *Other Cultures, Elder Years.* Wichita.

Houdijk, L. and P. Vanderbroeck. 1987. "Old Age and Sex in the Ancient Greek World," *WZRostock.* 36.57–61.

Hudson-Williams, T. 1926. *Early Greek Elegy.* Cardiff.

Hurwit, J. 1985. *The Art and Culture of Early Greece.* Ithaca.

Jaeger, W. 1945. *Paideia: The Ideals of Greek Culture,* tr. G. Highet. Vol. 1. New York.

Janko, R. 1981. " Ἀθάνατος καὶ ἀγήρως: The Genealogy of a Formula," *Mnemosyne* 34. 382–85.

Jebb, R. C. 1885. *Sophocles. The Plays and Fragments. Part II. The* Oedipus Coloneus. 2nd ed. Cambridge.

Jeffrey, L. H. 1976. *Archaic Greece.* New York.

Jenkins, R. 1982. *Three Classical Poets.* Cambridge, Mass.

Jocelyn, H. D. 1980. "A Greek Indecency and its Students: Laikazein," *PCPhS* 26.12–66.

Johnson, W. R. 1982. *The Idea of Lyric.* Berkeley.

Jones, J. 1967. *On Aristotle and Greek Tragedy.* London.

Kaimio, M. 1988. *Physical Contact in Greek Tragedy. A Study of Stage Conventions.* Annales Academiae Scientiarum Fennicae. Helsinki.

Kamerbeek, J. C. 1984. *The Plays of Sophocles. Part VII. The* Oedipus Coloneus. Leiden, Holland.

Katz, M. A. 1991. *Penelope's Renown.* Princeton.

Kertzer, D. and J. Keith, eds. 1986. *Age and Anthropological Theory.* Ithaca.

Keuls, E. 1985. *The Reign of the Phallus.* New York.

King, H. 1986. "Tithonus and the Tettix," *Arethusa* 19.15–35 (rept. in Falkner and de Luce 1989.68–89).

Kirk, G. S. 1962. *The Songs of Homer.* Cambridge.

———, tr. 1970. *The Bacchae.* Englewood Cliffs, N.J.

———. 1971. "Old Age and Maturity in Ancient Greece," *Eranos-Jb* 40.123–58.

———. 1974. *The Nature of Greek Myths*. Baltimore.

Kirkwood, G. 1958. *A Study of Sophoclean Drama*. Ithaca.

———. 1974. *Early Greek Monody*. Ithaca.

Kitto, H. D. F. 1939. *Greek Tragedy*. New York.

Knox, B. 1964. *The Heroic Temper: Studies in Sophoclean Tragedy*. Berkeley.

Krenkel, W. A. 1978. "Der Sexualtrieb: seine Bewertung in Griechland und Rom," *WZRostock* 27.178–79.

——— 1980. "Fellatio and Irrumatio," *WZRostock* 29.77–88.

Lacey, W. K. 1968. *The Family in Classical Greece*. Ithaca.

La Fontaine, J., ed. 1978. *Sex and Age as Principles of Social Organization*. New York.

Lanata, G. 1966. "Sul linguaggio amoroso di Saffo," *QUCC* 2.63–79.

Lattimore, R. 1939. "The Wise Advisor in Herodotus," *CPh* 34. 24–35.

Lefkowitz, M. 1974. "Critical Stereotypes and the Poetry of Sappho," *GRBS* 14.113–23.

———. 1976. "Fictions in Literary Biography: The New Poem and the Archilochus Legend," *Arethusa* 9.181–89.

———. 1981. *Lives of the Greek Poets*. Baltimore.

Lesky, A. 1963. *History of Greek Literature*, tr. J. Willis and C. de Heer. 2nd ed. New York.

———. 1965. *Greek Tragedy*, tr. H. Frankfort. London and New York.

———. 1977. "On the 'Heraclidae' of Euripides," *YClS* 25. 227–38.

LeVine, S. and R. A. LeVine. 1985. "Age, Gender, and the Demographic Transition: The Life Course in Agrarian Societies," in *Gender and the Life Course*, ed. A. S. Rossi. New York. 29–42.

Linforth, I. 1951. *Religion and Drama in Oedipus at Colonus*. University of California Publications in Classical Philology. 14.4 95–192.

———. 1952. "Notes on *Oedipus at Colonus*," in *Studies in Honour of Gilbert Norwood*. Toronto. 68–75.

Lipking, L. 1981. *The Life of the Poet: Beginning and Ending Poetic Careers*. Chicago.

Loraux, N. 1978. "Sur la race des femmes et quelques-unes de ses tribus," *Arethusa* 11. 43–88.

———. 1987. *Tragic Ways of Killing a Woman*. Cambridge, Mass. and London (orig. publ. *Façons tragiques de tuer une femme*, Paris, 1985).

Lord, A. B. 1960. *The Singer of Tales*. Cambridge, Mass.

Ludwig, W. 1954. *Sapheneia: Ein Beitrag zur Formkunst im Spätwerk des Euripides*. Tübingen.

McCartney, E. S. 1925. "Longevity and Rejuvenation in Greek and Roman Folklore," *PMASAL* 5.37–72.

MacCary, T. 1971. "Menander's Old Men," *TAPhA* 102.303–25.

———. 1982. *Childlike Achilles. Ontogeny and Phylogeny in the* Iliad. New York.

McEvilley, T. 1971. "Sappho, Fragment Ninety-Four," *Phoenix* 25.1–11.

Mackail, J. W. 1936. "The Epilogue of the *Odyssey*," in *Greek Poetry and Life. Essays Presented to Gilbert Murray*. Oxford.

McLean, J. H. 1954. "The *Heraclidae* of Euripides," *AJPh* 55. 197–224.

Macleod, C. W., ed. 1982. *Homer. Iliad XXIV*. Cambridge.

Marcovich, M. 1975. "A New Poem of Archilochus: P. Colon. inv. 7511," *GRBS* 16.5–14.

———. 1983. "Anacreon, 358 *PMG* (ap. Athen. XIII.599C)," *AJPh* 104.372–83 (rept. in *Studies in Greek Poetry*, M. Marcovich. Atlanta, 1991. 47–57).

Marquardt, P. 1982. "Hesiod's Ambiguous View of Women," *CPh* 77.283–91.

Marry, J. D. 1979. "Sappho and the Heroic Ideal: *erôtos aretê*," *Arethusa* 12. 71–92.

Martin, R. 1983. *Healing, Sacrifice and Battle. Amechania and Related Concepts in Early Greek Poetry*. Wiesbaden.

Mastronarde, D. J. 1974. "Studies in Euripides' *Phoinissai*," diss. Toronto.

———. 1979. *Contact and Discontinuity: Some Conventions of Speech and Action on the Greek Tragic Stage*. University of California Classical Studies. Vol. 21. Berkeley.

———. 1980. "P. Strasbourg WG 307 Re-examined (Eur. *Phoin.* 1499–1581, 1710–1736," *ZPE* 38.1–42.

———.1986. "The Optimistic Rationalist in Euripides: Theseus, Jocasta, Teiresias," in *Greek Tragedy and its Legacy. Essays presented to D. J. Conacher*, eds. M. Cropp, E. Fantham, and S. Scully. Calgary. 201–11.

Mastronarde, D. and J. Bremer. 1983. *The Textual Tradition of Euripides' Phoinissai*. University of California Studies in Classical Antiquity. Vol. 27. Berkeley.

Maxwell R. J. and P. Silverman. 1970. "Information and Esteem: Cultural Considerations in the Treatment of the Aged," in *In the Country of the Old* , ed. J. Hendricks. Farmingdale, N.Y. 33–44.

May, W. 1986. "The Virtues and Vices of the Elderly," in *Cole and Gadow* 1986.43–61.

Mazon, P. 1960. *Sophocle*. Vol. 3. Paris.

Méautis, G. 1957. *Sophocle. Essai sur le héros tragique*. Paris.

Merkelbach, R. 1957. "Sappho und ihr Kreis," *Philologus* 101.1–29.

Mette, H. J. 1982. "Von der Jugend," *Hermes* 110.257–68.

Minchin, E. 1986. "The Interpretation of a Theme in Oral Epic: *Iliad* 24.559–70," *G&R* 33. 11–19.

Minois, G. 1989. *A History of Old Age from Antiquity to the Renaissance*, tr. S. Tenison. Chicago (orig. publ. *Histoire de la vieillesse en occident de l'Antiquité à la Renaissance*, Paris, 1987).

Moulton, C. 1974. "The End of the *Odyssey*," *GRBS* 15. 153–79.

Murnaghan, S. 1987. *Disguise and Recognition in the* Odyssey. Princeton.

Murray, O. 1980. *Early Greece*. London.

Nagler, M. N. 1980. "*Entretiens avec Tirésias*," *CW* 74. 89–106.

Nagy, G. 1974. *Comparative Studies in Greek and Indic Meter*. Cambridge, Mass.

———. 1975. *The Best of the Achaeans*. Baltimore and London.

———. 1976. "Iambos: Typologies of Invective and Praise," *Arethusa* 9.2. 191–205.

———. 1979. *The Best of the Achaeans*. Baltimore and London.

Nash, L. 1978. "Concepts of Existence: Greek Origins of Generational Thought," *Daedalus* 107. 1–21.

Nilsson, M. 1950. *Mycenaean-Minoan Religion and its Survivals in Greek Religion*. Lund, Sweden.

Olender, M. 1990. "Aspects of Baubo: Ancient Texts and Contexts," in Halperin, Winkler and Zeitlin 1990. 83–113.

Onians, R. B. 1951. *The Origins of European Thought about the Body, the Mind, the Soul, the World, Time, and Fate*. Cambridge.

Ortner, S. 1974. "Is Female to Male as Nature is to Culture?", in *Woman, Culture, and Society*, eds. M. Rosaldo and L. Lamphere. Stanford. 67–87.

Östör, A. 1986. "Chronology, Category, and Ritual," in Kertzer and Keith 1986.281–304.

Otto, W. 1954. *The Homeric Gods*, tr. M. Hadas. New York (orig. publ. *Die Götter Griechenlands*, Bonn, 1929).

Padel, R. 1983. "Women: Model for Possession by Greek Daemons," in Cameron and Kuhrt 1983.3–19.

Parsons, P. 1977. "The Lille 'Stesichoros'," *ZPE* 26.7–36.

Page, D. L. 1955. *The Homeric Odyssey*. Oxford.

———. 1955a. *Sappho and Alcaeus*. Oxford.

———. 1964. "Archilochus and the Oral Tradition," in *Archiloque. Entretiens sur l'Antiquité Classique.* Fondation Hardt. Geneva. 117–79.

Parry, H. 1986. "The Homeric Hymn to Aphrodite: Erotic *Ananke*," *Phoenix.* 40. 253–64.

Patai, R. 1959. *Sex and Family in the Bible and the Middle East.* New York.

Patzer, H. 1982. *Die griechische Knabenliebe.* Sitzungsberichte der Wissenschlaftlichen Gesellschaft an der Johann Wolfgang Goethe-Universität Frankfurt am Main. Vol. 19.1. Wiesbaden.

Pearson, A. C. 1909. *Euripides. The Phoenissae.* Cambridge.

Pedrick, V. 1983. "The Paradigmatic Nature of Nestor's Speech in *Iliad* 11," *TAPhA* 113.55–68.

Peradotto, J. 1986. "Prophecy Degree Zero: Tiresias and the End of the *Odyssey*," in *Oralita: Cultura, Letteratura, Discorso.* Rome. 429–59.

———. 1990. *Man in the Middle Voice: Name and Narration in the* Odyssey. Princeton.

Peradotto, J. and J. Sullivan, eds. 1984. *Women in the Ancient World.* Albany.

Perotta, G. 1935. *Sofocle.* Milan.

Pickard-Cambridge, A. W. 1946. *The Theatre of Dionysus in Athens.* Oxford.

Podlecki, A. 1962. "Some Themes in Euripides' *Phoenissae*," *TAPhA* 93.355–73.

———. 1984. *The Early Greek Poets and Their Times.* Vancouver.

Pomeroy, S. 1975. *Goddess, Whores, Wives, and Slaves.* New York.

Powell, A. 1988. *Athens and Sparta.* Portland, Oreg.

Preisshofen, F. 1977. *Untersuchungen zur Darstellung des Greisenalters in der frühgriechischen Dichtung,* Hermes Einzelschr. Vol. 34. Wiesbaden.

Pucci, P. 1977. *Hesiod and the Language of Poetry.* Baltimore.

———. 1987. *Odysseus Polutropos. Intertextual Readings in the* Odyssey *and the* Iliad. Ithaca.

Querbach, C. A. 1976. "Conflicts between Young and Old in Homer's *Iliad*," in Bertman 1976. 55–64.

Querbach, C. W. 1985. "Hesiod's Myth of the Four Races," *CJ* 81.1–12.

Rabinowitz, N. S. 1993. *Anxiety Veiled. Euripides and the Traffic in Women.* Ithaca.

Rabinowitz, N. S. and A. Richlin, eds. 1993. *Feminist Theory and the Classics.* New York.

Ramnous, C. 1959. *La nuit et les enfants de la nuit dans la tradition grecque.* Paris.

Rankin, H. D. 1977. *Archilochus of Paros.* Park Ridge, N.J.

Rawson, E. 1970. "Family and Fatherland in Euripides' *Phoenissae*," *GRBS* 11.109–27.

Redfield, J. 1973. "The Making of the Odyssey" in *Parnassus Revisited*, ed. A.

C. Yu. Chicago. 141–54.

———. 1975. *Nature and Culture in the* Iliad. Chicago.

———. 1983. "The Economic Man," in Rubino and Shelmerdine 1983. 218–47.

Reik, T. 1960. *The Creation of Woman*. New York.

Reinhardt, K. 1979. *Sophocles*, tr. H. Harvey and D. Harvey, Oxford (orig. publ. *Sophokles*, 1933).

Reinhold, M. 1970. "The Generation Gap in Antiquity," *TAPhA* 117.347–65 (rept. in Bertman 1976.15–54).

Richardson, B. 1969. *Old Age Among the Ancient Greeks*. Baltimore (orig. publ. New York 1933).

Richlin, A. 1983. *The Garden of Priapus*. New Haven.

———. 1984. "Invective against Women in Roman Satire," *Arethusa* 17.67–80.

Riemschneider, W. 1940. *Held und Staat in Euripides'* Phoenissen. Berlin.

Robert, C. 1915. *Oidipus: Geschichte eine poetischen Stoffs im griechischen Altertum*. Berlin. 2 vols.

Roscher, W. H. 1906. "Die Hebdomadenlehre der griechischen Philosophen und Ärzte," *Abh. sächs. Gesellsch*. 24.6 .

Rose, P. W. 1975. "Class Ambivalence in the *Odyssey*," *Historia* 24.129–49.

Rosenmeyer, T. 1952. "The Wrath of Oedipus," *Phoenix* 6.92–112.

Rösler, W. 1980. *Dichter und Gruppe*. Munich.

Roussel, P. 1951. "Étude sur le principe d'ancienneté dans le monde hellénique du Ve siècle av. J.-C. a l' époque romaine," *Mémoires de l' Institut National de France, Académie des Inscriptions et Belles Lettres* 43.2.123–227.

Rubino, C. and C. Shelmerdine, eds. 1983. *Approaches to Homer*. Austin.

Russo, J. 1973–74. "Reading the Greek Lyric Poets (Monodists)," *Arion* N.S. 1.707–30.

———.1974. "The Inner Man in Archilochus and the *Odyssey*," *GRBS 15*. 139–52.

Schadewaldt, W. 1950. *Sappho: Welt und Dichtung: Dasein in der Liebe*. Potsdam.

———. 1960. "Lebenszeit und Greisenalter im frühen Griechentum," in *Hellas und Hesperien* 41–59 (= *Ant* 9,1933.282–302).

Schein, S. 1984. *The Mortal Hero*. Berkeley.

Schindler, J. 1975. "Zum Ablaut der neutralen s-Stämme des Indogermanischen," in *Akten der V. Fachtagung der Indogermanischen Gesellschaft*. Wiesbaden. 259–67.

Schmiel, R. 1974. "Youth and Age: Mimnermus 1 and 2," *RF* 102.283–89.

Schreckenburg, H. 1964. *Ananke. Untersuchungen zur Geschichte des Wortgebrauchs.* Munich.

Schwartz, G. S. 1975. "The *Kopros* Motif: Variations of a Theme in the *Odyssey*," *RSCI* 23. 177–95.

Scodel, R. 1982. "The Autobiography of Phoenix: *Iliad* 9.444–95," *AJPh* 103.128–36.

————. 1984. *Sophocles.* Boston.

Seale, D. 1982. *Vision and Stagecraft in Sophocles.* Chicago.

Sealey, R. 1976. *A History of the Greek City States ca. 700–338 B.C.* Berkeley.

Segal, C. 1971. "Nestor and the Honor of Achilles," *SMEA* 13.90–115.

————. 1973. "The Homeric Hymn to Aphrodite: A Structuralist Approach," *CW* 67.205–12.

————. 1981. *Tragedy and Civilization: An Interpretation of Sophocles.* Cambridge, Mass.

————. 1983. "*Kleos* and its Ironies in the *Odyssey*," *AC* 52. 22–47.

————. 1990. "Violence and the Other: Greek, Female and Barbarian in Euripides' *Hecuba*," *TAPhA* 120.109–31.

Seidensticker, B. 1972. "Beziehungen zwischen den beiden Oidipusdramen des Sophokles," *Hermes* 100. 255–74.

Sergent, B. 1986. *Homosexuality in Greek Myth*, tr. A. Goldhammer. New York (orig. publ. *L'homosexualité dans la mythologie grecque*, Paris, 1984).

Shey, H. J. 1976. "Tyrtaeus and the Art of Propaganda," *Arethusa* 9.5–28.

Shields, M. G. 1961. "Sight and Blindness Imagery in the *Oedipus at Colonus*," *Phoenix* 15.63–74.

Simmons, L. W. 1945. *The Role of the Aged in Primitive Society.* New Haven.

Sissa, G. 1990. "Maidenhood without Maidenhead: The Female Body in Ancient Greece," in Halperin, Winkler, and Zeitlin 1990. 339–64.

Skinner, M. B. "Woman and Language in Archaic Greece, or, Why is Sappho a Woman?", in Rabinowitz and Richlin 1993.125–44.

Slater, P. E. 1964. "Cross-Cultural Views of the Aged," in *New Thoughts on Old Age*, ed. R. Kastenbaum. New York. 229–35.

————. 1968. *The Glory of Hera.* Boston.

Slatkin, L. 1986. "*Oedipus at Colonus*: Exile and Integration," in *Greek Tragedy and Political Theory*, ed. J. Euben. Berkeley. 210–21.

Smith, P. 1980. "History and the Individual in Hesiod's Myth of the Five Races," *CW* 74.145–63.

————. 1981. *Nursling of Mortality. A Study of the Homeric Hymn to Aphrodite.* Frankfurt.

Snell, B. 1953. *The Discovery of the Mind in Early Greek Philosophy and Literature*, tr. T. Rosenmeyer. Cambridge, Mass. (orig. publ. *Die Entdeckung des Geistes*, Hamburg, 1948).

Snyder, J. 1989. *The Woman and the Lyre*. Carbondale, Ill.

Spelman, E. V. 1982. "Woman as Body: Ancient and Contemporary Views," *Feminist Studies* 8.109–31.

Spencer, P. 1965. *The Samburu. A Study of Gerontocracy in a Nomadic Tribe.* London.

Stahmer, H. M. 1978. "The Aged in Two Ancient Oral Cultures: The Ancient Hebrews and Homeric Greece," in *Aging and the Elderly. Humanistic Perspectives in Gerontology*, eds. S. Spicker, K. Woodward, and D. Van Tassel. Atlantic Highlands, N.J. 23–36.

Stanford, W. B. 1965. "The Ending of the Odyssey—An Ethical Approach," *Hermathena* 100.5–20.

———. 1968. *The Ulysses Theme*. Ann Arbor.

Stanley, K. 1976. "The Role of Aphrodite in Sappho Fragment 1," *GRBS* 17. 305–21.

Stanley-Porter, D. P. 1977. "Mute Actors in the Tragedies of Euripides," *BICS* 20.68–93.

Starr, C. 1982. "Economic and Social Conditions in the Greek World," in *Cambridge Ancient History*, eds. J. Boardman and N. Hammond. 2nd ed. Vol. 3. Part 3. Cambridge 1982. 417–41.

Steffen, V. 1955. "De Solonis elegia gratulatoria ad Mimnermum scripta," in *Quaestiones Lyricae*, 1. Poznan, Poland.

Stehle, E. 1990. "Sappho's Gaze: Fantasies of a Goddess and Young Man," *differences* 2.88–125.

Steinhagen, H. 1966. "Solons Lebensalter-Elegie (Fr. 19D). Eine Interpretation," *StudGen* 10 (1966) 599–606 (rept. in *Die Griechische Elegie*, ed G. Pfohl. Darmstadt. 1972. 263–81).

Stewart, A. F. 1986. "When Is a Kouros Not an Apollo? The Tenea 'Apollo' Revisited," in *Corinthiaca. Studies in Honor of D. A. Amyx*, ed. M. A. Del. Chiaro, Columbia. 54–70.

Stiebitz, F. 1926. "Zu Sappho 65 Diehl," *Philologische Wochenschrift,* nos. 45–46, cols. 1259–62.

Stigers, E. [Stehle]. 1979. "Romantic Sensuality, Poetic Sense: A Response to Hallett on Sappho," *Signs* 4.465–71.

———.1981. "Sappho's Private World," in Foley 1981.45–61 (orig. publ. in *Women's Studies* 1981 8.47–63).

Strauss, B. 1993. *Fathers and Sons in Athens*. Princeton.

Suder, W. 1991. *Geras. Old Age in Greco-Roman Antiquity. A Classified Bibliography*. Wroclaw, Poland.

Sussman, L. 1978. "Workers and Drones: Labor, Idleness and Gender Definition in Hesiod's Beehive," *Arethusa* 11. 27–41.

Szemerényi, O. 1964. *Syncope in Greek and Indo-European and the Nature of Indo-European Accent*. Naples.

Taplin, O. 1977. *The Stagecraft of Aeschylus: The Dramatic Use of Exits and Entrances in Greek Tragedy*. Oxford.

Taylor, H. and R. A. Brooks. 1981. Introduction to *The Children of Herakles*. Oxford. 3–26.

Thalmann, W. 1984. *Conventions of Form and Thought in Early Greek Poetry*. Baltimore.

Thornton, A. 1976. *People and Themes in Homer's* Odyssey. London and Dunedin.

Thury, E. M. 1989. "Euripides *Alcestis* and the Athenian Generation Gap," *Arethusa* 22.197–214.

Treu, M. 1956. *Von Homer zur Lyrik*. Munich.

———, ed. 1976. *Sappho*. 5th ed. Munich.

Turner, V. 1967. *The Forest of Symbols*. Ithaca.

Ussher, R. G., ed. 1973. *Aristophanes. Ecclesiazusae*. Oxford.

Van der Ben, N. 1986. "Hymn to Aphrodite 36–291: Notes on the pars epica of the Homeric Hymn to Aphrodite," *Mnemosyne* 39.1–41.

Van Eck, J. 1978. *The Homeric Hymn to Aphrodite*. Utrecht.

Van Hoof, A. J. L. 1983. "Oud-zijn in het oude Hellas," *TG* 14.141–48.

Van Nortwick, T. 1989. " 'Do Not Go Gently . . . ' *Oedipus at Colonus* and the Psychology of Aging," in Falkner and de Luce 1989. 132–56.

Vellacott, P. 1975. *Ironic Drama*. Cambridge.

Vernant, J.-P. 1965. "Le mythe hesiodique des races," in *Mythe et Pensee chez les Grecs*. Paris.19–47. (= "Hesiod's Myth of the Races: An Essay in Structural Analysis," in *Myth and Thought Among the Greeks*. London, 1983. 3–32.

Vian, F. 1963. *Les origens de Thèbes: Cadmos et les Spartes*. Paris.

Vidal-Naquet, P. 1986. *The Black Hunter. Forms of Thought and Forms of Society in the Greek World*. Baltimore (orig. publ. *Le Chasseur noir: formes de pensée et formes de société dans le monde grec*. Paris, 1981).

———. 1988. "Oedipus between Two Cities," in *Myth and Tragedy in Ancient Greece*, J.-P. Vernant and P. Vidal-Naquet, tr. J. Lloyd. New York. 329–59 [orig. publ. Paris, 1986].

Vilchez, M. 1983. "Sobre los periodos de la vida humana en la lirica arcaica y la tragedia griega," *Emerita* 51.63–95, 215–53.

Von Fritz, K. 1947. "Pandora, Prometheus, and the Myth of the Ages," *Rev. Rel.* 11.227–260.

Wade-Gery, H. T. 1952. *The Poet of the Iliad*. Cambridge.

Walcot, P. 1961. "The Composition of the Works and Days," *REG* 74.4–7.

———. 1966. *Hesiod and the Near East*. Cardiff, N.Y.

———. 1970. *Greek Peasants, Ancient and Modern*. New York.

Walker, B. 1985. *The Crone*. San Francisco.

Walker, S. 1983. "Women and Housing in Classical Greece: The Archaeological Evidence," in Cameron and Kuhrt 1983.81–91.

Weber, M. 1947. *The Theory of Social and Economic Organization*. New York.

Webster, T. B. L. 1967. *The Tragedies of Euripides*. London.

Wender, D. 1978. *The Last Scenes of the Odyssey*. Leiden.

West, M. L., ed. 1966. *Hesiod.* Theogony. Oxford.

———. 1971. "The Cosmology of Hippocrates' De Hebdomadibus," *CQ* 21. 365–88.

———. 1974. *Studies in Greek Elegy and Iambus*. Berlin and New York.

———. 1978. Hesiod. *Works and Days*. Oxford.

Whaton, G. E. 1981. *Sexuality and Aging. An Annotated Bibliography*. New York.

Whitman, C. H. 1958. *Homer and the Heroic Tradition*. New York.

———. 1958a. *Sophocles: A Study in Heroic Humanism*. Cambridge, Mass.

Wilamowitz-Moellendorf, U. von. 1895. *Euripides: Herakles*. 2nd ed. 3 vols. Berlin (rept. 1979–84, Darmstadt).

———. 1903. "Der Schluss der *Phönissen*," *Sitzungdberichte Akad. Berlin.* 587–600 (= *Kleine Schriften* VI, 344–59).

———. 1913. *Sappho und Simonides: Untersuchungen über griechische Lyriker*. Berlin.

———. 1917. "Oedipus auf Kolonos," in T. von Willamowitz- Moellendorf, *Die dramatische Technik des Sophokles*. Philol. Untersuch. Vol. 22. Berlin. (rept. 1969. 313–73).

———. 1923. *Griechische Tragödien*. Berlin.

Will, F. 1958. "Solon's Consciousness of Himself," *TAPhA* 89.301–11.

———. 1965–66. "Sappho and Poetic Motion," *CJ* 61.259–62.

Wills, G. 1963. "Agamemnon 1346–71, 1649–53," *HSCPh* 67.255–67.

Winkler, J. 1981. "Gardens of Nymphs: Public and Private in Sappho's Lyrics," in Foley 1981.63–89 (orig. publ. in *Women's Studies* 1981 8. 65–91).

———. 1990. *The Constraints of Desire. The Anthropology of Sex and Gender in*

Ancient Greece. New York.

———. 1990a. "The Ephebes' Song: Tragôdia and Polis," in Winkler and Zeitlin 1990.20–62.

Winkler, J. and F. Zeitlin, eds. 1990. *Nothing to Do with Dionysus?* Princeton.

Winnington-Ingram, R. P. 1969. "Euripides: Poiêtês Sophos," *Arethusa* 2. 127–42.

———. 1980. *Sophocles: An Interpretation.* Cambridge.

———. 1983. *Studies in Aeschylus.* Cambridge.

Woodbury, L. 1979. "Gold Hair and Grey, or the Game of Love. Anacreon Fr. 13.358.PMG, 13 Gentili," *TAPhA* 109.277–87.

Woodward, K. 1986. "Reminiscence and the Life Review: Prospects and Retrospects," in Cole and Gadow 1986.135–61.

Young, D. 1971. *Pindar Isthmian 7, Myth and Exempla.* Mnem. Suppl. 15. Leiden.

Zeitlin, F. 1980. "The Closet of Masks: Role-Playing and Myth-Making in the *Orestes* of Euripides," *Ramus* 9.55–71.

———. 1981. "Travesties of Gender and Genre in Aristophanes' *Thesmophoriazusae*," in Foley 1981.169–217.

———. 1990. "Thebes: Theater of Society and Self in Athenian Drama," in Winkler and Zeitlin 1990.130–67.

Zuntz, G. 1947. "Is the *Heraclidae* Mutilated?" *CQ* 41. 46–52.

———. 1955. *The Political Plays of Euripides.* Manchester, England.

Index